CW01151819

Flexible Systems Management

Series Editor

Sushil
Department of Management Studies
Indian Institute of Technology Delhi
New Delhi
India

Editorial Board

Gerhard Chroust, Institute for Telekooperation, Johannes Kepler University Linz, Austria
Julia Connell, University of Newcastle, Newcastle, NSW, Australia
Stuart Evans, Integrated Innovation Institute, Carnegie Mellon University, USA
Takao Fujiwara, Toyohashi University of Technology, Toyohashi, Aichi, Japan
Mike C. Jackson OBE, University of Hull, UK
Rashmi Jain, Montclair State University, Montclair, NJ, USA
Ramaraj Palanisamy, St. Francis Xavier University, Antigonish, NS, Canada
Edward A. Stohr, Stevens Institute of Technology, NJ, USA

The main objective of this series on Flexible Systems Management is to provide a rich collection of research as well as practice based contributions, from different contexts, that can serve as reference material in this upcoming area. Some of these books will be published in association with 'Global Institute of Flexible Systems Management'.

It will help in cross-fertilizing ideas from different perspectives of flexibility so as to consolidate and enrich the paradigm of flexible systems management. The audience for the volumes under this series includes researchers, management students/teachers, and practitioners interested in exploring various facets of flexibility research and practice.

The series features five types of books:

- *Post conference volumes* containing peer reviewed high quality research papers around a theme and clustered in sub-themes that can act as good reference material.
- *Contributed thematic volumes* based on invited papers from leading professionals, from academia as well practicing world, containing state of the art on an emerging theme.
- *Research monographs* based on research work making a comprehensive contribution to the body of knowledge.
- *Books based on novel frameworks and methodologies* covering new developments that are well tested and ready for wider application in research as well as practice.
- *Business practices and case-based* books documenting flexibility practices, strategies and systems in real life organizations.

More information about this series at http://www.springer.com/series/10780

Julia Connell · Renu Agarwal
Sushil · Sanjay Dhir
Editors

Global Value Chains, Flexibility and Sustainability

Springer

Editors
Julia Connell
University of Newcastle
Newcastle, NSW
Australia

Renu Agarwal
University of Technology Sydney
Sydney, NSW
Australia

Sushil
Department of Management Studies
Indian Institute of Technology Delhi
New Delhi
India

Sanjay Dhir
Department of Management Studies
Indian Institute of Technology Delhi
New Delhi
India

ISSN 2199-8493 ISSN 2199-8507 (electronic)
Flexible Systems Management
ISBN 978-981-10-8928-2 ISBN 978-981-10-8929-9 (eBook)
https://doi.org/10.1007/978-981-10-8929-9

Library of Congress Control Number: 2018935882

© Springer Nature Singapore Pte Ltd. 2018
This work is subject to copyright. All rights are reserved by the Publisher, whether the whole or part of the material is concerned, specifically the rights of translation, reprinting, reuse of illustrations, recitation, broadcasting, reproduction on microfilms or in any other physical way, and transmission or information storage and retrieval, electronic adaptation, computer software, or by similar or dissimilar methodology now known or hereafter developed.
The use of general descriptive names, registered names, trademarks, service marks, etc. in this publication does not imply, even in the absence of a specific statement, that such names are exempt from the relevant protective laws and regulations and therefore free for general use.
The publisher, the authors and the editors are safe to assume that the advice and information in this book are believed to be true and accurate at the date of publication. Neither the publisher nor the authors or the editors give a warranty, express or implied, with respect to the material contained herein or for any errors or omissions that may have been made. The publisher remains neutral with regard to jurisdictional claims in published maps and institutional affiliations.

Printed on acid-free paper

This Springer imprint is published by the registered company Springer Nature Singapore Pte Ltd. part of Springer Nature
The registered company address is: 152 Beach Road, #21-01/04 Gateway East, Singapore 189721, Singapore

Preface

Global economies are increasingly being structured through global value chains (GVCs) which account for increased international trade, global GDP, and employment (Gereffi and Stark 2016, p. 6). As Kaplinsky and Morris (2016, p. 2) point out, value chain analysis goes beyond just the firm-specific analysis that is the focus of much of the innovation literature, concentrating on inter-linkages, which allows for scrutiny of the dynamic flows between economic, organizational, and other activities. The evolution of GVCs across diverse sectors has a number of implications which have resulted in a growing literature on the topic. The implications include GVC governance, corporate social responsibility, job creation, and flexibility. The nature of GVCs means that they also have multiple relationships with small and medium-sized enterprises (SMEs) that may be associated with industrial clusters. Clusters have been defined as '…geographic concentrations of interconnected companies, specialized suppliers, service providers, firms in related industries, and associated institutions (e.g., universities, standards agencies, trade associations) in a particular field that compete but also cooperate' (Porter 2000, p. 15). Cortright (2006) identifies four key areas that characterize clusters: industrial connections—buyer–supplier relationships and the value chain, geographic extent, cluster life cycles, and inter-firm relationships. Flexibility is an important factor in relation to all of the four areas, as firms and the related GVCs need to be agile and responsive as discussed in several chapters in this book.

The chapters in this book are selected from papers presented at the GLOGIFT 16 (Sixteenth Global Conference on Flexible Systems Management) held at the UTS Business School, University of Technology Sydney, Australia, during December 4–6, 2016. Nearly 100 research papers were presented at the conference by academicians as well as practitioners from various countries. The participating authors were from various parts of India, the USA, Singapore, Australia, Hungary, Latvia, and Japan. The objective of the conference was to provide a knowledge-sharing platform for the dissemination of both academic and practical findings emerging from empirical studies, qualitative modeling, case studies, new concepts, and state-of-the-art studies. The selected papers presented at the conference were subsequently reviewed and then organized in the form of an edited volume. This volume is intended to serve as valuable reference material in the area of global value chains, flexibility, and sustainability.

The selected chapters cover a variety of issues concerning the theme of Global Value Chains, Flexibility, and Sustainability and are organized into the following three parts:

I   Global Value Chains
II Strategy and Flexibility
III Sustainability

Part I on the topic of Global Value Chains incorporates seven chapters. Chapter 1 is by Sushil and is titled the *Valuation of Flexibility Initiatives Along the Value Chain*. As the chapter is conceptual/exploratory, the flexibility initiatives outlined here are based on the relevant literature and insights from practice. Sushil points out that value chains comprise value-adding activities which may contribute to customer value both directly and indirectly, and he identifies various types of flexibility concerning both types. The chapter discusses the valuation of selected flexibility initiatives along the value chain with case examples. The chapter also includes a proposal for types of modeling that can be conducted for the valuation and comparison of flexibility initiatives using the interpretive ranking process (IRP). Chapter 2 in this part, *Exploiting Locational Resources in a World of Global Value Chains: Strategic Considerations for Clustered Firms and Cluster Managers*, is by Rhode, Royer, and Burgess. The aim of the chapter is to bring together a strategic firm perspective with cluster management activities. In order to do this, the authors analyze the locational resources of cluster firms that may be embedded in global value chains. They maintain that, through global value chains, while regions can be vulnerable to exclusion and job loss, they also have opportunities to develop value-adding and job-generation activities that can be integrated into global value chains. The authors bring together the findings of cluster research from a resource-oriented perspective, thus contributing to a better understanding of how firms can exploit the resources that they have access to locally. In addition, the process assists cluster managers toward upgrading those locational resources and/or embedding them in global value chains. Chapter 3 in this part also focuses *on* the topic of clusters. Written by Shrotriya and Dhir, *MSME Competitiveness for the Global Value Chain—A TRIZ-Based Approach* —moves the focus to India. The chapter's focus is the micro, small, and medium enterprise (MSME) sector in India. The authors claim that MSMEs can play a crucial role in employment, globalization, and in relation to global value chains (GVCs) owing to their entrepreneurial- and innovation-driven growth. In such a dynamically changing environment, it is important to develop an effective growth and consolidation plan through structured research. Thus, the authors propose that TRIZ can fill such a gap as it is an analytical approach for innovative problem-solving which has been applied in a variety of spheres related to management and technology. TRIZ is an abbreviation which stands for 'Theoria Resheneyva Isobretatelshehuh Zadach' in Russian relating to a 'Theory of Inventive Problem Solving.' This chapter focuses on deriving the factors and solutions which are significant for strengthening the MSME electronic goods clusters in India, although the authors also suggest that this approach can be tailored to focus on other sectors. Chapter 4 in this part, *Do Mergers Destroy Value in India?*, is by Rani, Yadav, and Jain. The chapter deals with the announcement of 150 mergers in India during the period 2013 to 2016. Specifically, it examines the short-term abnormal returns that were made through absorption using event study methodology. The results indicate the presence of high event-induced variance in abnormal returns. Chapter 5 in this part is authored by Sobel-Read and MacKenzie. Titled *Law and the Operation of Global Value Chains: Challenges at the Intersection of Systematisation and Flexibility*, it concerns how GVC integration processes can have potentially unforeseen consequences on the ability of firms to enter into flexible relationships. The authors purport that economic, operational, and social factors are steadily causing supply chains—in the form of global value chains—to become more systemically integrated. However, flexibility and chain integration are said to be mutually exclusive, with tensions existing between them. Two particular aspects identified in relation to these tensions are control and liability which are explored in this chapter, as well as the factors that are driving this shift toward greater liability and the key practical consequences of these actions. Chapter 6 in this part, *Technology Transfer and Innovation in Global International Joint Ventures—Emerging Markets' Perspective*, is by Parameswar and Dhir. The chapter explores the effect of two important factors, i.e., the type of international joint ventures (IJVs) and the interdependence between the parent firms on learning, technology transfer, and innovation by emerging market firms abroad. It uses case study methodology and finds that learning, technology transfer, and innovation are facilitated in global IJVs. Chapter 7 in this part is authored by Betaraya, Nasim, and Mukhopadhyay titled *Modelling Subsidiary Innovation Factors for Semiconductor Design Industry in India*. The chapter utilizes total interpretive structural modeling (TISM) to develop hierarchical structures of macro factors for R&D subsidiary innovation in the Indian semiconductor design subsidiaries so as to better understand the interplay of these factors.

Part II of the book on Strategy and Flexibility comprises seven chapters. Chapter 8 *Innovative Inventory Management for Flexible Adaptation* authored by Fekete and Hartványi focuses on the structural and functional differentiating properties of a material sub-network which oscillates between plastic and rigid modes. Based on old viable networks that are well known for their adaptability and robustness, the authors propose an innovative inventory management solution for creating symmetrical weak–weak links and nested plasticity and degeneracy in the organization's material sub-network. As most supply chains are predominantly rigid, this chapter details the methods of determining different inventory management modes and inventory elements corresponding to the behavioral archetypes of the nodes in the network, thus provisioning the missing adaptive nested plasticity for connectedness in disruptive settings. Chapter 9 *Flexible Benchmarking Approach of Talent Management: A Case Study of MIDHANI* is authored by Likhi, Sabita, and Rao. This chapter highlights the flexible approach of talent management in one such Indian company, a Defense Public Sector Enterprise. Further, the chapter attempts to detail the various HR initiatives and schemes of the organization, so as to benchmark itself in the turbulent global era, following the case study method. The elements of integrated talent management as identified by the company are workforce planning, attracting talent, recruitment, compensation, performance management scheme, leadership development/ professional development, employee engagement, employee retention, reward and recognition program, and succession planning. Chapter 10 titled *Strategy Alignment of Critical Continuity Forces w.r.t. Technology Strategy and Business Strategy and Their Hierarchical Relationship Using TISM* is authored by Kedia and Sushil. This chapter presents four critical continuity forces each w.r.t. technology strategy and business strategy which are found to be essential for a dynamic and turbulent business environment. Organizations are known to adopt a flexible technology strategy and business strategy, but maintaining their alignment can be a challenge for leaders. The literature suggests that continuity forces hold back an organization from change by creating inertia in the organization. In Chap. 10, critical continuity forces w.r.t. technology strategy and business strategy are analyzed using an articulated mental model referred to as total interpretive structural modeling (TISM), with the core competency being the most dependent force among all the critical continuity forces. Kume and Fujiwara in Chap. 11 titled *Manufacturing Flexibility Under Uncertain Demand by a Real Options Approach* propose a decision-making method for the optimal investment in soft drink plant expansion by addressing the uncertainty of potential demand. The authors examine two methods based on option theory. The first is the Bermudan call options to flexibly coordinate the number of part-time workers to allow for increases in recruitment in summer and simultaneously a decrease in winter, while the second method is the American call option. This option is used to expand equipment capacity to meet not only summer demand, but also long-term upside demand even at a high sunk cost. A comparison of these options through a Monte Carlo simulation provides insights into how the dividend-like effects of seasonal demand variation on the exercise of American call options exist. It also shows some signaling threshold demand levels can be a trigger criterion for flexible investment decision-making if enough lead times are given. Chapter 12 *Resistance to Integrate Information Systems in Healthcare Service: A Study on Developing Country* is authored by Umme and Chowdhury. The authors claim that although information systems are vital for meeting the service expectations of customers and stakeholders, the integration of information systems in health services is inhibited. This inhibition they argue is due to numerous 'resistance' factors that need to be addressed to ensure a quality healthcare service. Focusing on the healthcare sector in Bangladesh, they relate the resistance factors to two domains: (i) factors contributing to resistance to health information systems (HIS) in developing country contexts and (ii) strategies to mitigate the resistance. To address these gaps, the chapter proposes a methodology using an analytic hierarchy process (AHP) and an integrated quality function deployment (QFD) approach. Although the chapter uses the Bangladesh healthcare sector as a case study, the authors propose that the findings and implications have significance for the healthcare services of other developing countries. The next chapter (Chap. 13) *Towards an Effective Agricultural e-Trading System in India* authored by Suri analyzes the electronic National Agriculture Market (e-NAM) and AGMARKNET project. It identifies situation-, actor-, and process-related gaps in AGMARKNET for its improvement and integration with e-NAM. Chapter 14, the final chapter in this part, is entitled the *Impact of Behavioral Flexibility on Flexible HR System and Organizational Role Stress* and is authored by Jaiswal. In this chapter, behavioral flexibility is manifested in the different actions that employees use to handle non-routine actions as well as in the HR systems of an organization. This chapter has attempted to establish a link between the three constructs—organizational role stress, employees' behavioral flexibility in the workplace, and flexible HR systems. A questionnaire with standard scales was used as an instrument for data collection from management employees of various sectors, the regression results were inferred to hypotheses testing, and all hypotheses were accepted. It is intended that this chapter will thus help both employees and organizations by enabling firms to have more efficient HR systems and consider behavioral components in relation to employee recruitment.

Part III of the book, Sustainability, comprises seven chapters. Chapter 15 *Organizational Sustainability—Why the Need for Green HRM?* is authored by Kirsch and Connell. This chapter is intended to examine the impact of change on the implementation of sustainability programs and presents the survey-based study of a large Asia-Pacific-based professional services company. It emphasizes that if senior management introduces sustainability initiatives without any attempt to embed them within company practice/client relationships, reward systems, and more, they are likely to fail. As a result, it is suggested that a circular economy needs to be accompanied by 'Green HRM' policies and practices. Chapter 16 *Sustainability in Conformity Assessment: Flexibility of Technical Harmonization* is authored by Liepiņa, Lapiņa, and Mazais. This chapter focuses on the assessment of historic technical harmonization approaches in line with the development of manufacturing and technologies, changes in management strategies, and development of global value chains (GVCs) where different stages of the production process are located across different countries. The authors have proposed a new technical harmonization approach, which encompasses all elements essential for product quality assurance and conformity assessment to facilitate product global supply and distribution across GVCs. The development of this new methodological approach would facilitate the work of manufacturers and stakeholders and would promote sustainable development of entrepreneurship. Further, there is a high potential for further improvement of technical harmonization approach and sustainability of conformity assessment that would facilitate global trade participation in GVCs. In Chap. 17, titled *Evaluation of Market Surveillance Implementation and Sustainability*, Mjakuškina and Lapiņa analyze approaches to market surveillance through different product groups, in order to evaluate the differences between the sectors and countries. They describe how intermediate inputs are an important part of world trade, particularly as they are increasingly being sourced through imports rather than domestic production and are a key component of the establishment of global value chains. The nature of internal markets when sourcing inputs, combined with the effects of the global supply chain, makes it an essential ingredient—especially one that requires changes in the approach to market surveillance. For example, the authors find that different countries have been developing their own standardization arrangements and are starting to produce more products that only conform to their own safety standards rather than global standards. Chapter 18, *A Glimpse of Sustainable Electronics Manufacturing for India: A Study Using PEST-SWOT Analysis*, is authored by Singh, Kumar, Gupta, and Madaan. The authors point out that high-technology manufacturing industries require the best of technical solutions which are chiefly driven by the government policies enacted. The electronics manufacturing industry (EMI) in India is crucial to the country's economy, and this chapter interrogates the government factors influencing its growth. Although 'Make in India' initiatives and recently announced policies have provided some impetus, weak labor laws and difficult exit policies are obstructing sustainable growth. Cheap manufacturing in foreign and WTO treaties mellow the opportunities offered. Consequently, connected clusters are proposed by the authors so as to gain substantial advantages in terms of coordination and input. To map the growth of the sector, a set of indicators are chosen to serve as standards, and a conceptual framework was developed to assist sustainable growth. Chapter 19 *Selection of Sustainable Suppliers* is authored by Kumar and Singh. A sustainable supply chain demands sustainable supplier selection (SSS), and this chapter serves to add to the existing literature on this topic. The environmental dimension was prioritized over the other two, which were social and economic dimensions. After reviewing the criteria derived from the relevant literature, broad criteria are considered by the authors. The study illustrated the method of analysis using a case on auto component suppliers. It concludes by ranking the sustainability of suppliers on certain measures such as cost, quality, flexibility, services, market share, and green performance. Green performance has been measured in relation to factors concerning green process and product design, the selection of green raw materials, carbon emissions, energy consumptions, etc. The integrated tool used has been proposed to be of benefit to managers in purposes other than supplier selection, such as project selection, facility location, the hiring of people, the selection of sources of energy, and the study has scope to include more factors. Chapter 20 *Flexible Waste Management Practices in Service Sector: A Case Study* is authored by Singh and Sushil. Hotels consume a large amount of durable and non-durable goods as part of their catering and hospitality services, but there is no generic model of waste management identified in the literature for the hotel industry. This chapter studied a five-star hotel chain as a case study. It divided hotel waste into three categories—energy waste, effluent discharge, and solid waste. In order to calculate its environmental impact and provide a waste management model for the service sector, specifically, it presents a basic hierarchy of waste management. A cross-interaction matrix is developed that demonstrates an effect on situational elements. Government directive is found to be the main dominating actor in waste management situations. The framework has served to improve waste management policy in the hotel industry. Chapter 21, the last chapter in this part, *Shifts Between Technology Push and Market Pull Strategies for Sustainable Development in Manufacturing Industries* is authored by Sethi, Ahuja, and Singla. Prevalent research is available on technology push (TP) and market pull (MP) or demand pull (DP). While earlier studies emphasized MP to shape technology development, this chapter has focused on the shifting focus of the literature to TP orientation. A tabular representation represents prior work conducted in TP and MP domains, and six primary objective dimensions of sustainable development are also identified. The chapter concludes by developing certain questions for TP-DP practitioners. It is proposed to evaluate the multiple responses to these queries by a flexible system methodology, and ultimately, to develop a management process which can balance both TP and MP strategies.

In summary, the various chapters in this book illustrate the concept of flexibility in the context of global value chains. As many of the authors point out, in an environment of greater global competition, advancing technological change and increasing customer expectations, flexibility provides a mechanism that can help to cope with uncertainty, as it can facilitate fast and adaptable responses (Zhang et al. 2010). Such responses are considered in detail in the chapters included here. In the first part of the book 'Global Value Chains,' various authors discuss how to improve the efficiency and effectiveness of global value chains through various types of analysis. Some focus on cluster management, mergers and joint ventures, and in one case, the legal aspects of control and liability concerning the integration of value chains. The second part includes chapters concerning 'Strategy and Flexibility.' Strategies concern topics such as inventory management, talent management, strategic alignment, decision-making, behavioral change, and HR systems. The third and final part of the volume concerns the topic of 'Sustainability.' Here, the chapters focus on various initiatives intended to promote sustainability across respective value chains bearing in mind the concept of flexibility.

Given the range of topics, contexts, and methods used to analyze the integration of flexibility across global value chains, it is expected that this volume will be a useful addition to the literature on the topic as well as a practical resource for practitioners. In general, it is anticipated that this edited volume on Global Value Chains, Flexibility, and Sustainability will provide a useful resource for a variety of audiences such as management students and researchers, practicing business managers, consultants, and professional institutions.

Finally, we would like to thank all of the authors and reviewers who helped to bring this volume to fruition. In particular, we would like to thank Rejani Raghu who so effectively communicated with the authors and reviewers as well as helped to format the final manuscript.

Newcastle, Australia	Julia Connell
Sydney, Australia	Renu Agarwal
New Delhi, India	Sushil
New Delhi, India	Sanjay Dhir

References

Cortright, J. (2006). *Making sense of clusters: regional competitiveness and economic development*. Washington, DC: Brookings Institution Metropolitan Policy Program.

Gereffi, G., & Fernandez-Stark, K. (2016). *Global value chain analysis: a primer* (2nd ed.), Duke Center on Globalization, Governance and Competitiveness at the Social Science Research Institute.

Kaplinsky, R., & Morris, M. (2016). Handbook for value chain research. https://www.ids.ac.uk/ids/global/pdfs/VchNov01.pdf. Accessed 02 December 2017.

Porter, M. E. (2000). Location, competition, and economic development: local clusters in a global economy. *Economic Development Quarterly*, *14*(1), 15–34.

Zhang, Q., Vonderembse, M., Lim, J. (2010). Value chain flexibility: a dichotomy of competence and capability. *International Journal of Production Research*, *40*(3), 561–583.

Contents

Part I Global Value Chains

1 **Valuation of Flexibility Initiatives Along the Value Chain** 3
   Sushil

2 **Exploiting Locational Resources in a World of Global Value Chains: Strategic Considerations for Clustered Firms and Cluster Managers** 15
   Stephan Rohde, Susanne Royer and John Burgess

3 **MSME Competitiveness for the Global Value Chain—A TRIZ-Based Approach** 33
   Shishir Shrotriya and Sanjay Dhir

4 **Do Mergers Destroy Value in India?** 47
   Neelam Rani, Surendra S. Yadav and P. K. Jain

5 **Law and the Operation of Global Value Chains: Challenges at the Intersection of Systematisation and Flexibility** 63
   Kevin Sobel-Read and Madeleine MacKenzie

6 **Technology Transfer and Innovation in Global International Joint Ventures—Emerging Markets' Perspective** 77
   Nakul Parameswar and Sanjay Dhir

7 **Modelling Subsidiary Innovation Factors for Semiconductor Design Industry in India** 89
   Dixit Manjunatha Betaraya, Saboohi Nasim and Joy Mukhopadhyay

Part II Strategy and Flexibility

8 **Innovative Inventory Management for Flexible Adaptation** 119
   István Fekete and Tamás Hartványi

9	**Flexible Benchmarking Approach of Talent Management: A Case Study of MIDHANI** .... D. K. Likhi, C. Sabita and Akanksha Rao	133
10	**Strategy Alignment of Critical Continuity Forces w.r.t. Technology Strategy and Business Strategy and Their Hierarchical Relationship Using TISM** .... Prakash Kumar Kedia and Sushil	145
11	**Manufacturing Flexibility Under Uncertain Demand by a Real Options Approach** .... Katsunori Kume and Takao Fujiwara	161
12	**Resistance to Integrate Information Systems in Healthcare Service: A Study on Developing Country** .... Nusrat Jusy Umme and Md. Maruf Hossan Chowdhury	173
13	**Towards an Effective Agricultural e-Trading System in India** .... P. K. Suri	187
14	**Impact of Behavioral Flexibility on Flexible HR System and Organizational Role Stress** .... Priyanka Jaiswal	205

Part III Sustainability

15	**Organizational Sustainability—Why the Need for Green HRM?** .... Christina Kirsch and Julia Connell	223
16	**Sustainability in Conformity Assessment: Flexibility of Technical Harmonization** .... Raimonda Liepiņa, Inga Lapiņa and Jānis Mazais	241
17	**Evaluation of Market Surveillance Implementation and Sustainability** .... Svetlana Mjakuškina and Inga Lapiņa	257
18	**A Glimpse of Sustainable Electronics Manufacturing for India: A Study Using PEST-SWOT Analysis** .... Manoj Kumar Singh, Harish Kumar, M. P. Gupta and J. Madaan	271
19	**Selection of Sustainable Suppliers** .... Pravin Kumar and Rajesh Kumar Singh	283

20	**Flexible Waste Management Practices in Service Sector: A Case Study**	301
	Aarti Singh and Sushil	
21	**Shifts Between Technology Push and Market Pull Strategies for Sustainable Development in Manufacturing Industries**	319
	A. P. S. Sethi, I. P. S. Ahuja and Anuj Singla	
Index		333

Editors and Contributors

About the Editors

Julia Connell is an Adjunct Professor at Curtin University, Visiting Professor at the Graduate School of Business, and Research Development Advisor at Hasanuddin University, Indonesia. Prior to joining Curtin University, she was the Dean of Graduate Studies at the Australian Catholic University. Before that, she served as the Association Dean Postgraduate/Director of the Graduate School of Business, University of Technology, Sydney. She has also held a number of other roles such as associate dean international, and director of research at other universities, and was a visiting/invited professor at various universities in the UK, France, and Dubai. She has published over 80 refereed journal articles and co-edited five books, many on employment-related issues, change, and people development. Research concerning industrial clusters, economic development, and knowledge sharing led to her involvement in this conference. She has also consulted for a number of organizations such as the Australian Workplace and Productivity Agency, the NSW Police, local government Energy Australia, and QBE.

Renu Agarwal is an Associate Professor, Operations and Supply Chain Management in the Management Discipline Group within the UTS Business School, Sydney, Australia. As Director of Supply Chain Management programs, she provides leadership in service value networks, supply chain management, service innovation and dynamic capability building, management practices, and innovation and productivity. She has been instrumental in securing funding and managing both federal and state government grants on management practices for Australia and New Zealand in collaboration with LSE, McKinsey, and Stanford. More recently, she has been instrumental in the development of the Australian Management Capability Survey in collaboration with Stanford University and funded by DIIS, and launched by the Australian Bureau of Statistics to 15000 Australian businesses to assess the impact of sustainable supply chain management, digital business and innovation management practices on innovation and productivity. She is also the Research

Director, Future of Innovation and Innovative Systems at the Centre for Business and Social Innovation, UTS Business. She has published in several top-tier journals, including *Decision Sciences*, *International Journal of Production Economics*, *International Journal of Production Research*, *International Journal of Operations and Production Management*, and is the Editor of 'The Handbook of Service Innovation' published by Springer. Currently, she is the Editor of the upcoming 'Routledge Companion to Global Value Chains: Reinterpreting and Reimagining Mega Trends in the World Economy' and Guest Editor of the special issue of the *Global Journal of Flexible Systems Management* (Springer) titled 'The Future of Manufacturing Global Value Chains, Smart Specialization and Flexibility'.

Sushil is Abdulaziz Alsagar Chair Professor (professor of strategic, flexible systems, and technology management) and Chair of the Strategic Management Group at the Department of Management Studies, Indian Institute of Technology (IIT) Delhi. He has served as a Visiting Professor and delivered seminars in numerous leading universities, including Kyoto University; University of Minnesota; Stevens Institute of Technology, NJ; University of Lethbridge; and Université Paris 1 Panthéon-Sorbonne. He is an active researcher and has supervised more than 60 doctoral dissertations. He has written 20 books in the areas of flexibility, strategy, systems thinking, and technology management and published over 300 papers in various refereed journals and conferences. He has pioneered the area of 'flexible systems management' and made original contributions to the field of knowledge in the form of interpretive approaches in management. He is the Founder–Editor-in-Chief of the *Global Journal of Flexible Systems Management* and serves on the editorial boards of leading international journals. He is the founder–president of the professional body, *Global Institute of Flexible Systems Management*. He has acted as a consultant to both governmental and industrial organizations and has served as an independent director on the boards of RINL and HSCC.

Sanjay Dhir is an Assistant Professor of Strategic Management at the Department of Management Studies, IIT Delhi. He is also the Coordinator for the Executive MBA (Technology Management) at DMS, IIT Delhi, and Director, GIFT School of Strategic Alliances Management. He is a Fellow (Ph.D.) of the Indian Institute of Management (IIM), Lucknow. He worked at Mahindra and Mahindra Ltd (Automotive), R&D Department, Nasik, for 3 years. He has published several research papers in leading international journals, including case studies at Richard Ivey School of Business, Western Ontario, jointly distributed by Ivey, and Harvard Business School. His research papers have been presented and published as conference proceedings at several prestigious academic conferences such as Academy of Management (AoM), Academy of International Business (AIB), Strategic Management Society (SMS), Southern Management Association (SMA), International Simulation Conference of India (ISCI, IIT Mumbai), and Strategic Management Forum (SMF, IIM Lucknow). His major areas of interest are strategic management, joint ventures, innovation management, management of change and transformation, implementation strategy, and international strategy. He is also a Coordinator of the stakeholders' engagement cell at IIT Delhi, and Associate Editor of the *Global Journal of Flexible Systems Management* (Springer). He is also the Editor of the e-journal *Global Journal of Business Excellence* managed by the GIFT society, which aims to create and enhance business excellence practices in Asia and the Pacific.

Contributors

I. P. S. Ahuja Department of Mechanical Engineering, Punjabi University, Patiala, Punjab, India

Dixit Manjunatha Betaraya Faculty of Management Studies and Research, Aligarh Muslim University, Aligarh, India; Intel Technology India Pvt. Ltd., Bangalore, India

John Burgess School of Management, Curtin University, Perth, Australia

Md. Maruf Hossan Chowdhury Management Discipline Group, UTS Business School, Ultimo, NSW, Australia

István Fekete ICG Integrated Consulting Group Kft., Budapest, Hungary

Takao Fujiwara Institute of Liberal Arts and Sciences, Toyohashi University of Technology, Tempaku, Toyohashi, Aichi, Japan

M. P. Gupta Department of Management Studies, Indian Institute of Technology Delhi, New Delhi, India

Tamás Hartványi Széchenyi István University, Győr, Hungary

P. K. Jain Department of Management Studies, Indian Institute of Technology Delhi, New Delhi, India

Priyanka Jaiswal FORE School of Management, New Delhi, India

Prakash Kumar Kedia Department of Management Studies, Indian Institute of Technology Delhi, New Delhi, India

Christina Kirsch E2Q Consulting Sydney, Sydney, NSW, Australia

Harish Kumar Department of Management Studies, Indian Institute of Technology Delhi, New Delhi, India

Pravin Kumar Department of Mechanical Engineering, Delhi Technological University, Delhi, India

Katsunori Kume Department of Electrical and Electronic Information Engineering, Toyohashi University of Technology, Tempaku, Toyohashi, Aichi, Japan

Inga Lapiņa Department of Quality Technologies, Institute for Quality Engineering, Faculty of Engineering Economics and Management, Riga Technical University, Riga, Latvia

Raimonda Liepiņa Department of Quality Technologies, Institute for Quality Engineering, Faculty of Engineering Economics and Management, Riga Technical University, Riga, Latvia

D. K. Likhi Mishra Dhatu Nigam Limited, Hyderabad, India

Madeleine MacKenzie University of Newcastle, Newcastle, Australia

J. Madaan Department of Management Studies, Indian Institute of Technology Delhi, New Delhi, India

Jānis Mazais Department of Quality Technologies, Institute for Quality Engineering, Faculty of Engineering Economics and Management, Riga Technical University, Riga, Latvia

Svetlana Mjakuškina Department of Quality Technologies, Institute for Quality Engineering, Faculty of Engineering Economics and Management, Riga Technical University, Riga, Latvia; Products and Services Surveillance Department, Consumer Rights Protection Centre, Riga, Latvia

Joy Mukhopadhyay ThinkCorp Consultancy Services, Bangalore, India

Saboohi Nasim Faculty of Management Studies and Research, Aligarh Muslim University, Aligarh, India

Nakul Parameswar Department of Management Studies, Indian Institute of Technology Delhi, New Delhi, India

Neelam Rani Indian Institute of Management Shillong, Shillong, India

Akanksha Rao Mishra Dhatu Nigam Limited, Hyderabad, India

Stephan Rohde International Institute of Management and Economic Education, Europa-Universität Flensburg, Flensburg, Germany

Susanne Royer International Institute of Management and Economic Education, Europa-Universität Flensburg, Flensburg, Germany

C. Sabita Mishra Dhatu Nigam Limited, Hyderabad, India

A. P. S. Sethi Department of Mechanical Engineering, Baba Banda Singh Bahadur Engineering College, Fatehgarh Sahib, Punjab, India

Shishir Shrotriya Department of Management Studies, Indian Institute of Technology Delhi, New Delhi, India

Aarti Singh Department of Management Studies, Indian Institute of Technology Delhi, New Delhi, India

Manoj Kumar Singh Department of Management Studies, Indian Institute of Technology Delhi, New Delhi, India

Rajesh Kumar Singh Operations Management Area, Management Development Institute (MDI), Gurgaon, Haryana, India

Anuj Singla Department of Mechanical Engineering, Punjabi University, Patiala, Punjab, India

Kevin Sobel-Read University of Newcastle, Newcastle, Australia

P. K. Suri Delhi School of Management, Delhi Technological University, New Delhi, India; NIC, Govt. of India, New Delhi, India

Nusrat Jusy Umme School of Information Systems, Curtin Business School, Perth, Australia

Surendra S. Yadav Department of Management Studies, Indian Institute of Technology Delhi, New Delhi, India

Part I
Global Value Chains

Chapter 1
Valuation of Flexibility Initiatives Along the Value Chain

Sushil

Abstract Value chains comprise of value-adding activities which may contribute to the customer value both directly and indirectly. This chapter first identifies the flexibility initiatives concerning the activities associated with direct as well as indirect value chains. It identifies various types of flexibilities along the value chain, such as, inbound logistics flexibility, operations flexibility, outbound logistics flexibility, marketing and sales flexibility, after sales service flexibility, procurement flexibility, human resource flexibility, and technology flexibility. It is conjectured that the flexibility initiatives will add more value as we go downstream the value chain, i.e., toward the customer. The chapter discusses the valuation of select flexibility initiatives along the value chain with case examples. The chapter is exploratory in nature, and the identification of flexibility initiatives is based on literature as well as insights from practice. It then proposes the types of modeling that can be carried out for the valuation of flexibility initiatives and comparison of the same using Interpretive Ranking Process (IRP).

Keywords Flexibility initiatives · Interpretive ranking process
Valuation · Value chain

1.1 Introduction

Value chains comprise a series of activities that add value to the product or service delivered to the customer. Some of the activities add value directly and thus comprise the direct value chain such as inbound logistics, operations, outbound logistics, marketing and sales, and after sales service. Certain other activities add value in an indirect manner and are treated in the indirect value chain. These include firm infrastructure, human resource management, technology development, and

---

Sushil (✉)
Department of Management Studies, Indian Institute of Technology Delhi,
Vishwakarma Bhawan, Shaheed Jeet Singh Marg, New Delhi 110016, India
e-mail: sushil@dms.iitd.ac.in; profsushil@gmail.com

procurement (Porter 1985, 1991). Each process or activity along the value chain adds value either directly or indirectly. Value chain analysis has evolved in multiple ways, linking strategy formulation on one hand to operational and supply chain issues on the other. Hergert and Morris (1989) identified concerns about using accounting data for value chain analysis. They identified the difficulties that are both inherent and avoidable. The concept of value has also been examined from a relationship marketing perspective by Ravald and Gronroos (1996) relating value added to customer needs and profitability. With growing uncertainty, the concept of value chain flexibility has gained prominence. Zhang et al. (2002) tried to relate it with environmental uncertainty and competitive advantage. The relationship of manufacturing postponement and centralized distribution with performance is analyzed by Nair (2005), in which he observed the mediating role of value chain flexibility. Soon and Udin (2011) investigated the flexible value chain in terms of business drivers and response effects in the context of supply chain management. Thus, flexibility in value chains is being analyzed by both researchers and practitioners. However, different types of flexibility initiatives may be undertaken in these value-adding activities.

It is envisaged that these flexibility initiatives would further add value along the activities in the value chain. It is conjectured that, in the direct value chain, the value creation by flexibility initiatives would be higher as we go downstream the value chain, i.e., toward the customer. It is proposed to use Interpretive Ranking Process (IRP) to validate this proposition. If by using IRP the ranking of select flexibility initiatives in after sales service and marketing and sales are higher than flexibility in operations and inbound supply chains, this proposition would hold well. In any case, such an interpretive ranking would help in prioritizing flexibility initiatives in different components of the value chain.

The chapter provides a brief review of flexibility valuation to help understand valuation models and plans. It then identifies select flexibility initiatives along the direct as well as indirect value chain. Finally, it provides an outline of IRP modeling for multi-criteria flexibility valuation. This is in terms of select flexibility initiatives to be ranked and the criteria to be applied in terms of benefits and costs associated with these flexibility initiatives. The chapter is exploratory in nature and needs to be supported further by different types of modeling to prove (or disprove) the research proposition.

1.2 Flexibility Valuation: A Brief Review

The valuation of flexibility of different types is an upcoming research area. This chapter gives a brief review of past studies in terms of the valuation of flexibility of different types. The valuation of flexibility of different types has been studied in the past in a limited manner. At an early stage, the impact of decision flexibility was assessed on the value of information by Merkhofer (1977). Mason (1984) took the context of volatile markets for valuing financial flexibility. The study of the valuation of flexible production systems is reported by Triantis and Hodder (1990) and that of manufacturing flexibility valuation by Gupta (1993). Allen and Pantzalis (1996) have examined the breadth of multinational corporations in terms of the valuation of operating flexibility, whereas Huchzermeier and Cohen (1996) dealt with it in relation to exchange rate risk. Schober and Gebauer (2009) derived the valuation of flexibility regarding the modification and upgradation of information systems, whereas the intangible benefits in enterprise resource planning have been valued by Murphy and Simon (2002). The valuation of product-mix flexibility was conducted by Bengtsson and Olhger (2002), and flexibility in project selection has been evaluated by Kulatilaka (1993). Taking the context of economic crisis, Lee and Makhija (2009) have researched the valuation of flexibility in international investments. Cortazar et al. (2008) have studied the valuation of multidimensional real options. The valuation of real options has been the most common approach utilized in majority of the studies mentioned above. From this brief review on the valuation of flexibility, it can be observed that research in this area needs further development. In particular, there are very few studies reported on multi-criteria ranking for the valuation of flexibility initiatives.

The valuation of flexibility requires a generic model. Sushil (2015a, 2018a) has provided a basic model to analyze flexibility value by assessing the benefits generated by the fulfillment of needs in terms of different flexibility initiatives on one hand and the costs incurred for capacity building for implementing these initiatives on the other. A multi-criteria valuation of select flexibility initiatives by using IRP (Sushil 2009) is reported by Sushil (2017b). This is integrated with Total Interpretive Structural Modeling (TISM) (Sushil 2012, 2016, 2017c) for deriving the weight of criteria. It further proposes a big data framework to be used in integrated TISM–IRP for evidence-based ranking. A similar methodology may be used for ranking flexibility initiatives along the direct value chain to examine the research proposition. The valuation of flexibility in the context of value chains is a gap in the research literature and thus explored in this chapter as an initial step to fill this research gap.

1.3 Flexibility Initiatives Along Direct Value Chain

In each of the activities of the direct value chain, select flexibility initiatives have been identified and discussed in terms of the practices being followed by organizations. As per the activities in the direct value chain, it discusses five different types of flexibility, i.e., inbound logistics flexibility, operations flexibility, outbound logistics or distribution flexibility, marketing and sales flexibility, and after sales service flexibility as shown in Fig. 1.1.

Infrastructure Flexibility			— Cloud computing — Big data analytics capabilities			
Human Resource Flexibility			— Flexi-time/Flexi-place — Flexible compensation			
Technology Development Flexibility			— Cross-functional teams — Involvement of lead customers			
Procurement Flexibility			— Outsourcing procurement			Benefit of Flexibility less Cost of Flexibility = Value added
Inbound Logistics Flexibility Variable capacity of supply chain	**Operations Flexibility** Variable manufacturing capacity	**Outbound Logistics Flexibility** Direct marketing through e-commerce Order tracking	**Marketing and Sales Flexibility** Dynamic pricing Product upgradation and switching	**After Sales Service Flexibility** Customized services		

Flexibility Initiatives along Indirect Value Chain ↑↓

Flexibility Initiatives along Direct Value Chain ↑↓ →→→→→

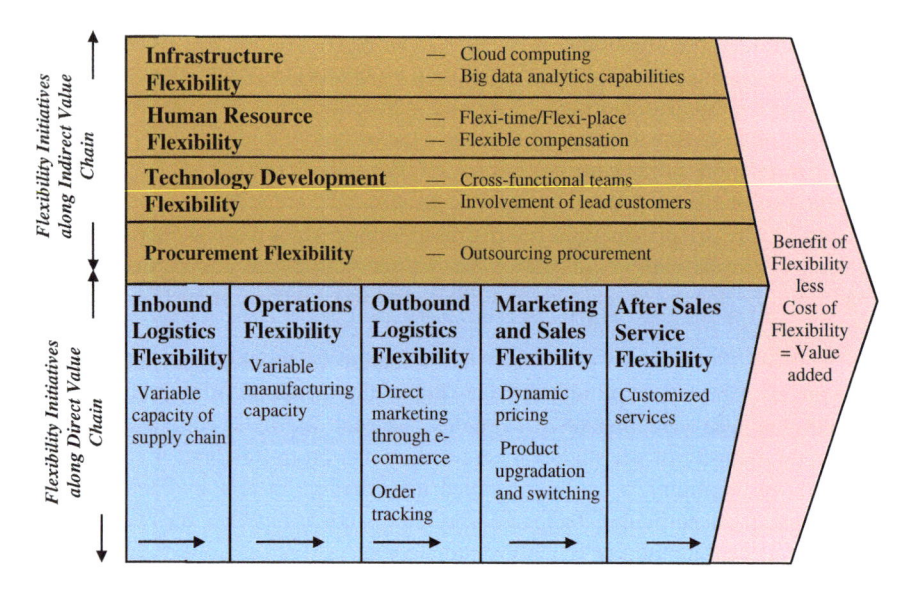

Fig. 1.1 Different types of flexibilities along the direct and indirect value chain

1.3.1 Inbound Logistics Flexibility

Inbound logistics concerns the beginning of the direct value chain. Any reduction in cost and improvement of quality of inbound logistics has a direct bearing on the value created for the customer. Both cost and quality considerations have been well covered in literature on inbound logistics and supply chain management. Another dimension that creates value is "flexibility" by making it more responsive to the changing requirements. Supply chain flexibility has gained the attention of both researchers and practitioners over the past decade. It has been dealt with in terms of its constructs and their relationships. With the business becoming more network-based, the issue of supply chain flexibility is gaining prominence. The performance of various flexibility configurations in the supply chain has been analyzed by Garavelli (2003). Various dimensions of supply chain flexibility and its valuation are investigated by Singh and Acharya (2013), Kumar et al. (2013), Mangla et al. (2015), and Shibin et al. (2016).

An important flexibility initiative on this front would be:

– "Variable capacity of supply chain"

The demand variability both in terms of volume and change in composition of parts requires variable capacity in the whole supply chain. This may be originated by changing customer requirements, market fluctuations, competition, design changes, and changes in government policies and regulations. For example, at a point in time when fuel prices were high, the Indian customer demanded a diesel version of vehicles. Currently, the downward spiral of fuel prices and governmental restrictions due to pollution considerations has put a blockade on demand for diesel vehicles. This has a direct bearing on the capacity requirement of inbound logistics. The whole chain of vendors for the manufacturers of diesel cars (such as Toyota, Honda, and Volkswagen) would thus need to vary their capacity upwards or downward so that they can support the variable capacity of these manufacturers of diesel vehicles.

1.3.2 Operations Flexibility

As discussed in the previous section, the variability in demand of diesel vehicles requires flexibility in manufacturing operations also. This points toward a flexibility initiative on this front as:

- "Variable manufacturing capacity'

The area of flexibility in manufacturing operations has been researched and practiced widely. Some important types of flexibility that create value in manufacturing operations are volume flexibility, routing flexibility, machine flexibility, design-change flexibility, labor flexibility, and so on (Sushil 2015b). A number of reviews on manufacturing flexibility can be seen in literature on the topic such as Sethi and Sethi (1990), Beach et al. (2000), Sharma and Sushil (2002), and Mishra et al. (2014) that provide various types of flexibilities and its relationship with environmental uncertainty, business strategies, and innovation. Honda practiced manufacturing flexibility in terms of replacing jigs and fixtures by robots so as to reduce the setup time for shifting from one model to the other.

1.3.3 Outbound Logistics Flexibility

The outbound logistics or distribution system requires flexibility in terms of a variety of mechanisms to meet the requirements of different customers. Traditionally, the distribution system comprising the distributors, wholesalers, and retailers has been used to provide the "push based" system. In the customer-centric market, a market pull system is desirable. Electronic and mobile platforms offered a lot of flexibility both to the manufacturers and customers in outbound logistics. The Dell's direct marketing model is a classic example of reaching customers with customized products with logistics flexibility of order tracking. Similar models with many innovations have evolved in e-tailing market place. This adds value to the customer in terms of getting the products/services as per their needs and at a lower cost. Thus, important flexibility initiatives in case of outbound logistics or distribution flexibility are:

- "Direct marketing through e-commerce
- Order tracking"

1.3.4 Marketing and Sales Flexibility

Flexibility in marketing and sales activities are prevalent in practice, although on the research front this requires building frameworks, models, and measures. Wasuja et al. (2012) provided a total interpretive structural model of cognitive bias in sales persons. The implications of marketing flexibility in case situations have been highlighted by Shalender and Singh (2015). Shalender et al. (2017) tested a marketing flexibility scale for automobile companies. Some significant factors of customer experience have been hierarchically structured by Sharma et al. (2016).

The main types of flexibilities linked with marketing and sales activities are product flexibility, pricing flexibility, and promotion flexibility. Important flexibility initiatives in this area are:

- "Dynamic pricing
- Product upgradation and switching"

Honda resorted to dynamic pricing in the Indian context to cut down prices significantly in order to regain reducing market share. Maruti Suzuki has constantly upgraded its products and spreaded it to a wide range of customer segments. It has extended its brand from "economy" to "economy with style".

1.3.5 After Sales Service Flexibility

After sales service is the last activity in the direct value chain and adds value to the customer by making the products and services more usable. Generally, these services are outsourced. For example, for mobile services, complaint handling is conducted through call centers. In the case of automobiles, the service stations are usually managed by third parties. An important flexibility initiative in this activity is to provide

- "Customized services"

The requirements for different customers are different, thus needing the services to be offered in a customized manner for higher value addition. Information and communication technology plays a vital role in providing after sales service flexibility. Most of the e-tailors such as Amazon and Flipkart provide a variety of schemes, e.g., return of goods purchased, multiple payment options, order cancellation or change, etc.

1.4 Flexibility Initiatives Along Indirect Value Chain

The indirect value chain also adds a lot of value, which may not be directly visible to the customer. The flexibility in these activities is also expected to add value. Important flexibilities in indirect value chains are infrastructure flexibility, human resource flexibility, technology development flexibility, and procurement flexibility as shown in Fig. 1.1.

1.4.1 Infrastructure Flexibility

The basic firm infrastructure adds value by streamlining other activities. The most vital infrastructure in today's context is the IT infrastructure. Select common initiatives to generate flexible infrastructure are:

- "Cloud computing
- Big data analytics capabilities"

Cloud computing reduces IT infrastructure cost and enhances the value-added options for meeting changing computing requirements. The basic infrastructure that builds big data analytics capabilities may impact organizational performance. This has been examined by Gunasekaran et al. (2017) in the context of supply chain and organizational performance. The alignment of business analytics capability and business strategy has been empirically tested by Akter et al. (2016).

1.4.2 Human Resource Flexibility

The flexibility in the human resource management function is contributing in a significant manner for value addition and organizational performance. Srivastava (2016) provided a panorama of flexible HR practices. Yadav et al. (2016) developed a hierarchical model of different work place flexibility elements such as time flexibility, pay and benefits flexibility, place of work flexibility, learning flexibility, performance appraisal flexibility, and career planning flexibility. Issues linked with telecommuting and co-working have been deliberated by Raffaele and Connell (2016). Afrianty et al. (2016) have taken the context of Indonesia to study the impact of work–life balance policies.

The most common flexibility initiatives are:

- "Flexi-time/Flexi-place
- Flexible compensation"

Flexi-time/Flexi-place coupled with working from home and telecommuting is emerging as a common practice, particularly in service organizations. Consulting companies like McKinsey, BCG, and KPMG are using it as a common practice that helps in work–life balance and supporting diversity by improving involvement of female employees catering to their diverse home commitments as well. This is also supported by flexible leave structures. Flexible compensation adds value by enhancing the motivation level of employees. However, at the same time, these flexible HR practices enhance coordination requirements.

1.4.3 Technology Development Flexibility

Flexibility in technology development and related activities enhances innovation and thereby development of higher value-added products and services. Select flexibility initiatives that add value and influence innovation are:

– "Cross-functional teams
– Involvement of lead customers"

Cross-functional teams generate innovative products seeking ideas from various quarters. This has been practiced by many companies such as 3M, Ford, Apple, and so on. Involvement of lead customers in technology and product development helps in incorporating customer needs into new products and thereby adding value through this activity. The lead customers have been involved by Mahindra in developing new car models in India. Compaq invited lead customers to give feedback on what they found better in competitors' products, which was then used to make the design of PCs more customer friendly.

1.4.4 Procurement Flexibility

Every firm has to procure various items and services for their support systems. Reduction in the cost of procurement directly reduces the overheads, but flexibility in procurement adds value in multiple ways, including cost. Procurement flexibility enhances options and readjustments as per changing organizational requirements. Many times, this can be achieved through outsourcing or centralizing the procurement functions coupled with the use of e-platforms. Some important support areas are security, health and insurance services, the procurement of office equipment, maintenance and upkeep, etc. A typical flexibility initiative in this regard is:

– "Outsourcing procurement"

Vendor selection for outsourcing is crucial to generate desired flexibility in this function. Ware et al. (2014) and Kaur et al. (2016) provided a flexible framework for integrated supplier selection using various multi-criteria ranking methods.

1.5 Multi-criteria Valuation Using IRP

The Interpretive Ranking Process (IRP) (Sushil 2009. 2017a) has two sets of variables: one concerns ranking variables, i.e., flexibility initiatives, and the other reference variables, i.e., value addition criteria (adding value by enhancing benefits and/or reducing costs). It develops a cross-interaction matrix of flexibility initiatives versus value addition criteria and interprets the relationships. Then, it uses a pair-wise comparison of the dominance of one initiative over the other for all criteria and finally generates a dominance matrix. The flexibility initiatives with higher net dominance are ranked higher and this can be used in selecting preferred value-adding flexibility initiatives to be implemented. This process has been refined to generate weights by using Total Interpretive Structural Modeling (TISM) (Sushil 2012), the details of which can be seen in Sushil (2017b) for multi-criteria ranking of flexibility initiatives. The use of IRP is delimited here to the basic design in terms of flexibility initiatives and the value addition criteria, which are summarized in Table 1.1.

These flexibility initiatives and value addition criteria are only illustrative in nature and give the basic design of the decision problem that acts as input to the IRP. The rest of the steps of IRP are not demonstrated here, which are developed further by expert involvement (Sushil 2018b). The final ranks obtained are indicated in Table 1.2 as per the analysis given in Sushil (2018b). As the flexibility initiatives such as "customized service, product upgradation, direct marketing, and dynamic pricing" are ranked higher than "variable manufacturing and supply chain capacity", the research proposition is supported by multi-criteria valuation. In a similar manner, the ranking of flexibility initiatives in the indirect value chain activities can also be carried out.

Table 1.1 Ranking and reference variables for IRP

S. No.	Code	Variable
Ranking variables (flexibility initiatives)		
1.	F1	Variable capacity of supply chain
2.	F2	Variable manufacturing capacity
3.	F3	Direct marketing through e-commerce
4.	F4	Order tracking
5.	F5	Dynamic pricing
6.	F6	Product upgradation and switching
7.	F7	Customized services
Reference variables (value addition criteria)		
1.	V1	Low inventory
2.	V2	Higher revenue
3.	V3	Meeting individual customer requirements
4.	V4	Responsiveness to changing needs
5.	V5	Supply chain costs
6.	V6	Technology cost
7.	V7	Training cost

Table 1.2 Ranks of flexibility initiatives by efficient IRP (Sushil 2018b)

Rank	Flexibility initiatives
I	F6—Product upgradation and switching
II	F7—Customized services
III	F3—Direct marketing through e-commerce
IV	F5—Dynamic pricing
V	F2—Variable manufacturing capacity
VI	F4—Order tracking
VII	F1—Variable capacity of supply chain

1.6 Conclusion

This chapter addresses the need for flexibility in different value chain activities and identified select flexibility initiatives for both direct and indirect value chain activities. This also emphasized the valuation of these flexibility initiatives in terms of value addition criteria (benefits as well as costs). Higher benefits increase the value addition, whereas this can also be achieved by a reduction in costs. In the case of costs incurred for implementing flexibility initiatives, these would reduce the value addition. Thus, it needs to evaluate different flexibility initiatives with reference to multiple value addition criteria; both the benefits derived and the costs to be incurred. It proposes use of the IRP for this kind of valuation in an interpretive manner. However, this may also be done by other multi-criteria ranking methods such as AHP, ANP, and so on and the results may be compared with IRP. It is advocated that interpretive methods such as the IRP (may be integrated with TISM) and would be more useful as the value addition criteria are both tangible and intangible in nature and the measurement scales would also vary. As pointed out earlier, this chapter is based on conceptual design; therefore, the basic design of IRP-based ranking problems require further investigation in case situations to examine the research propositions in real-life settings.

References

Afrianty, T. W., Issa, T., & Burgess, J. (2016). Indonesian work life balance policies and their impact on employees in the higher education sector. In: C. J. Sushil & J. Burgess (Eds.), *Flexible work organizations: The challenges of capacity building in Asia* (pp. 119–133). New Delhi: Flexible Systems Management, Springer.

Akter, S., Wamba, S. F., Gunasekaran, A., Dubey, R., & Childe, S. J. (2016). How to improve firm performance using big data analytics capability and business strategy alignment? *International Journal of Production Economics, 182*, 113–131.

Allen, L., & Pantzalis, C. (1996). Valuation of the operating flexibility of multinational corporations. *Journal of International Business Studies, 27*(4), 633–653.

Beach, R., Muhlemann, A. P., Price, D. H. R., Paterson, A., & Sharp, J. A. (2000). A review of manufacturing flexibility. *European Journal of Operational Research, 122*(1), 41–57.

Bengtsson, J., & Olhager, J. (2002). Valuation of product-mix flexibility using real options. *International Journal of Production Economics, 78*(1), 13–28.

Cortazar, G., Gravet, M., & Urzua, J. (2008). The valuation of multidimensional American real options using the LSM simulation method. *Computers & Operations Research, 35*(1), 113–129.

Garavelli, A. C. (2003). Flexibility configurations for the supply chain management. *International Journal of Production Economics, 85*(1), 141–153.

Gunasekaran, A., Papadopoulos, T., Dubey, R., Wamba, S. F., Childe, S. J., Hazen, B., et al. (2017). Big data and predictive analytics for supply chain and organizational performance. *Journal of Business Research, 70*(1), 308–317.

Gupta, D. (1993). On measurement and valuation of manufacturing flexibility. *International Journal of Production Research, 31*(12), 2947–2958.

Hergert, M., & Morris, D. (1989). Accounting data for value chain analysis. *Strategic Management Journal, 10*(2), 175–188.

Huchzermeier, A., & Cohen, M. A. (1996). Valuing operational flexibility under exchange rate risk. *Operations Research, 44*(1), 100–113.

Kaur, H., Singh, S. P., & Glardon, R. (2016). An integer linear program for integrated supplier selection: A sustainable flexible framework. *Global Journal of Flexible Systems Management, 17*(2), 113–134.

Kulatilaka, N. (1993). The value of flexibility: The case of a dual—Fuel industrial steam boiler. *Financial Management, 22*(3), 271–280.

Kumar, R., Singh, R. K., & Shankar, R. (2013). Study on coordination issues for flexibility in supply chain of SMEs: A case study. *Global Journal of Flexible Systems Management, 14*(2), 81–92.

Lee, S.-H., & Makhija, M. (2009). Flexibility in internationalization: Is it valuable during an economic crisis? *Strategic Management Journal, 30*(5), 537–555.

Mangla, S. K., Kumar, P., & Barua, M. K. (2015). Flexible decision modeling for evaluating the risks in green supply chain using fuzzy AHP and IRP methodologies. *Global Journal of Flexible Systems Management, 16*(1), 19–35.

Mason, S. P. (1984). Valuing financial flexibility, NBER Working Paper, Cambridge, MA.

Merkhofer, M. W. (1977). The value of information given decision flexibility. *Management Science, 23*(7), 716–727.

Mishra, R., Pundir, A. K., & Ganapathy, L. (2014). Manufacturing flexibility research: A review of literature and agenda for future research. *Global Journal of Flexible Systems Management, 15*(2), 101–112.

Murphy, K. E., & Simon, S. J. (2002). Intangible benefits valuation in ERP projects. *Information Systems Journal, 12*(4), 301–320.

Nair, A. (2005). Linking manufacturing postponement, centralized distribution and value chain flexibility with performance. *International Journal of Production Research, 43*(3), 447–463.

Porter, M. E. (1985). *Competitive advantage: Creating and sustaining superior performance*. New York: The Free Press.

Porter, M. E. (1991). Towards a dynamic theory of strategy. *Strategic Management Journal, 12*(S2), 95–117.

Raffaele, C., & Connell, J. (2016). Telecommuting and co-working communities: What are the implications for individual and organizational flexibility? In C. J. Sushil, & J. Burgess (Eds.), *Flexible work organizations: The challenges of capacity building in Asia* (pp. 21–35). New Delhi: Flexible Systems Management, Springer.

Ravald, A., & Gronroos, C. (1996). The value concept and relationship marketing. *European Journal of Marketing, 30*(2), 19–30.

Schober, F., & Gebauer, J. (2009). How much to spend on flexibility? Determining the value of information system flexibility. In *Proceedings of the Fifteenth Americas Conference on Information Systems*, San Francisco, California, August 6th-9th, 2009.

Sethi, A. K., & Sethi, S. P. (1990). Flexibility in manufacturing: A survey. *International Journal of Flexible Manufacturing Systems, 2*(4), 289–328.

Shalender, K., & Singh, N. (2015). Marketing flexibility: Significance and implications for automobile industry. *Global Journal of Flexible Systems Management, 16*(3), 251–262.

Shalender, K., Singh, N., & Sushil. (2017). AUTOFLEX: Marketing flexibility scale for automobile companies. *Journal of Strategic Marketing, 25*(1), 65–74.

Sharma, O. P., & Sushil. (2002). Issues in managing manufacturing flexibility: A review. *Global Journal of Flexible Systems Management, 3*(2&3), 11–29.

Sharma, M., Tiwari, P., & Chaubey, D. S. (2016). Summarizing factors of customer experience and building a structural model using total interpretive structural modelling technology. *Global Business Review*, 0972150916630825.

Shibin, K. T., Gunasekaran, A., Papadopoulos, T., Dubey, R., Singh, M., & Wamba, S. F. (2016). Enablers and barriers of flexible green supply chain management: A total interpretive structural modeling approach. *Global Journal of Flexible Systems Management, 17*(2), 171–188.

Singh, R. K., & Acharya, P. (2013). Supply chain flexibility: A framework of research dimensions. *Global Journal of Flexible Systems Management, 14*(3), 157–166.

Soon, Q. H., & Udin, Z. M. (2011). Supply chain management from the perspective of value chain flexibility: An exploratory study. *Journal of Manufacturing Technology Management, 22*(4), 506–526.

Srivastava, P. (2016). Flexible HR to cater to VUCA times. *Global Journal of Flexible Systems Management, 17*(1), 105–108.

Sushil. (2009). Interpretive ranking process. *Global Journal of Flexible Systems Management, 10*(4), 1–10.

Sushil. (2012). Interpreting the interpretive structural model. *Global Journal of Flexible Systems Management, 13*(2), 87–106.

Sushil. (2015a). Valuation of flexibility. *Global Journal of Flexible Systems Management, 16*(3), 219–220.

Sushil. (2015b). Diverse shades of flexibility and agility in business. In Sushil & G. Chroust (Eds.), *Systemic flexibility and business agility* (pp. 3–19). New Delhi: Flexible Systems Management, Springer.

Sushil. (2016). How to check correctness of total interpretive structural models? *Annals of Operations Research.* https://doi.org/10.1007/s10479-016-2312-3.

Sushil. (2017a). Efficient interpretive ranking process incorporating implicit and transitive dominance relationships. *Annals of Operations Research.* https://doi.org/10.1007/s10479-017-2608-y.

Sushil. (2017b). Multi-criteria valuation of flexibility initiatives using integrated TISM—IRP with a big data framework. *Production Planning & Control, 28*(11–12), 999–1010.

Sushil. (2017c). Modified ISM/TISM process with simultaneous transitivity checks for reducing direct pair comparisons. *Global Journal of Flexible Systems Management, 18*(4), 331–351.

Sushil. (2018a). Valuation of flexibility initiatives: A conceptual framework. In Sushil, T. P. Singh, & A. J. Kulkarni (Eds.), *Flexibility in resource management.* Singapore: Flexible Systems Management, Springer Nature.

Sushil. (2018b). Interpretive multi-criteria valuation of flexibility initiatives on direct value chain, *Benchmarking: An International Journal,* Accepted.

Triantis, A. J., & Hodder, J. E. (1990). Valuing flexibility as a complex option. *Journal of Finance, 45*(2), 549–565.

Ware, N. R., Singh, S. P., & Banwet, D. K. (2014). Modeling flexible supplier selection framework. *Global Journal of Flexible Systems Management, 15*(3), 261–274.

Wasuja, S., Sagar, M., & Sushil. (2012). Cognitive bias in salespersons in specialty drug selling of pharmaceutical industry. *International Journal of Pharmaceutical and Healthcare Marketing, 6*(4), 310–335.

Yadav, M., Rangnekar, S., & Bamel, U. (2016). Workplace flexibility dimensions as enablers of organizational citizenship behavior. *Global Journal of Flexible Systems Management, 17*(1), 41–56.

Zhang, Q., Vonderembse, M. A., & Lim, J. S. (2002). Value chain flexibility: A dichotomy of competence and capability. *International Journal of Production Research, 40*(3), 561–583.

Chapter 2
Exploiting Locational Resources in a World of Global Value Chains: Strategic Considerations for Clustered Firms and Cluster Managers

Stephan Rohde, Susanne Royer and John Burgess

Abstract The focus of this research is locational resources in overlapping value-adding webs of firms who at the same time may be embedded in global value chains. Through global value chains, regions are both vulnerable to exclusion and hence job loss. However, they also have opportunities to develop value-adding and job generation activities that are integrated into global value chains. The purpose of this chapter is to bring together a strategic firm perspective with cluster management activities. The rationale behind our conceptualisation of locational resources is to enable cluster managers to reduce the complexity of analysing location factors. This gives them criteria to assess the value of resources for cluster firms and shows avenues for sustaining and upgrading them, and placing them within the opportunities offered beyond the region. To achieve this, we bring together the findings of cluster research from a resource-oriented perspective. We contribute to a better understanding of how firms can exploit the resources that they have access to locally and suggest how cluster managers can shape these locational resources.

Keywords Cluster management · Global value chains · Local resources
Value-adding web

An earlier version of this chapter has been presented at the 16th TCI Annual Global Conference in Kolding/Denmark, 2013. The slides are available at the following link: https://www.slideshare.net/TCINetwork/tci2013-4-septacademicsusanne-royer.

S. Rohde · S. Royer (✉)
International Institute of Management and Economic Education,
Europa-Universität Flensburg, 24937 Flensburg, Germany
e-mail: royer@uni-flensburg.de

S. Rohde
e-mail: stephan.rohde@uni-flensburg.de

J. Burgess
School of Management, Curtin University, Perth, Australia
e-mail: John.burgess@rmit.edu.au

© Springer Nature Singapore Pte Ltd. 2018
J. Connell et al. (eds.), *Global Value Chains, Flexibility and Sustainability*,
Flexible Systems Management, https://doi.org/10.1007/978-981-10-8929-9_2

2.1 Introduction: Local Clusters and Global Value Chains

Cooperation has emerged as a crucial factor supporting competitive advantages in many contexts (Dyer and Singh 1998; Gulati 1999; Lavie 2006, 2007). Access to valuable shared (as well as non-shared) resources is regarded as highly relevant in terms of generating competitive advantage (Lavie 2006). Worldwide value chains (Gereffi et al. 2005) or strategic alliances (Burgers et al. 1993; Hoang and Rothaermel 2016) are also the focus of research as well as the contributions of regional clusters (Porter 2000; Tallman et al. 2004; Bell et al. 2009). Regarding business models of companies '[m]uch of the literature still underemphasizes [...] boundary-spanning aspects and centers on [...] firm-level characteristics' (Amit and Zott 2015: 346). When we want to understand the competitive potential of different business models today, we should therefore take into account more than firm internal resources: value is created in regional and global networks.

Research also suggests a link between both of these topic areas. For example, Arregle et al. (2013) investigate the influence of the institutional environment of different (countries and) regions on the degree of internationalisation of Japanese multinational enterprises (MNEs). They suggest a '"semi-globalized" institutional perspective and test it by examining how MNEs implement their strategic approach to country institutional environments at the region level' (Arregle et al. 2013: 924). It thus becomes obvious that regional characteristics matter regarding firm strategy. Cammet (2006: 3) sees a 'coexistence of, and inter-linkages between, global value chains and localised growth pools'.

The relevance of regional specificities is a point of reference from which to investigate clusters. Porter (2000: 15) defines clusters as 'geographic concentrations of interconnected companies, specialized suppliers, service providers, firms in related industries, and associated institutions (e.g. universities, standards agencies, trade associations) in a particular field that compete but also cooperate'. Clusters can be differentiated between 'organic' and 'developed' clusters, respectively, between 'bottom-up' and 'top-down' initiatives. While the former cluster types are privately organised and financed by the members involved, the latter ones are financed with public money (Fromhold-Eisebith and Eisebith 2005; Jungwirth and Müller 2010, 2014). Clusters can thus be regarded as possible contexts for the value creation of firms in regions. Understanding how such regional contexts affect the value creation of firms is the point of reference for this chapter.

The single-firm perspective is the starting point of our conceptualisation of value creation possibilities in this context (for our perspective see Brown et al. 2007). A single firm in our conceptualisation would be embedded in a network of other actors as well as a certain institutional context in the location where it operates. In addition, there would be usually further links with other actors from other regions and countries (with different institutional contexts also included). Taking the perspective of a single-firm as a focal player in such a constellation reduces the complexity. In this chapter, we concentrate on the value-adding potential of locational resources for certain actors (see also Royer and Burgess 2013 for this focus).

For this purpose, we define locational resources based on Wernerfelt's (1984: 172) definition of firm resources as 'anything which could be thought of as a strength or weakness' of a given location.

The chapter links strategic thinking from a firm perspective into cluster management activities and, as such, represents an attempt to address a deficit in the cluster literature (Pitelis 2012: 1360). It is suggested that cluster managers are more effective when they are able to identify the valuable locational resources of the cluster firms, which through policy action can be nurtured, sustained and upgraded. The first research question is therefore:

> *How can locational resources be systematised and conceptualised in order to better understand their value creation potential for single firms embedded in regional clusters as relevant parts of global value chains?*

When public policy aims to create value through cluster development, there should be an understanding of how clusters can contribute to the value creation of established firms and new ventures. Here, we strive for the development of a framework for cluster managers (often paid for by public policy) to identify valuable cluster resources that support value creation and competitive advantage. We also consider how to foster and develop cluster resources. Therefore, our second research question is:

> *Which points of reference for cluster managers result from the developed systematisation and conceptualisation of locational resources in terms of ways to develop and upgrade them?*

The remainder of this chapter is structured as follows. To answer the first question, we build on the resource-oriented cluster literature, which is outlined in the following section with a focus on the elements to later integrate into our conceptualisation. In the third section, we build on Jungwirth et al.'s (2011) conceptualisation of public, private and club goods in the cluster context. These goods are a point of reference for us that link the performance of a cluster manager to the value creation of the cluster firms. Thus, it may be of help in answering the second research question posited. It follows an investigation of the cluster management role that links to the resource-oriented perspective outlined previously. Several propositions are developed that reflect the relationships between cluster manager activities with different degrees of exclusivity for companies located in the cluster. The chapter ends with conclusions in the fourth section.

2.2 Clusters from a Resource-Oriented Perspective

Researchers have started to investigate clusters from a resource-oriented perspective (De Oliveira Wilk and Fensterseifer 2003; Tallman et al. 2004; Hervás-Oliver and Albors-Garrigós 2007; Fensterseifer 2009; Brown et al. 2010b, 2013; Festing et al. 2012; Steffen 2012; Fensterseifer and Rastoin 2013; Leick 2013; Gretzinger and

Royer 2014). Building on a resource-oriented understanding of value creation in clusters, we investigate locational resources in overlapping value-adding webs of firms. The focus is on the regional context of a cluster, i.e. the location and the embedded resources.

2.2.1 Clusters as Value-Adding Webs

To give answers to the posited questions, this chapter conceptualises how cluster managers may support cluster development in their respective location from a resource-oriented perspective. We are specifically interested in locational (or contextual) resources. Further, we want to understand the value creation of firms in the context of local resources that are fostered by cluster managers. Therefore, we need a conceptualisation of (shared) local resources as such but also the tangible and intangible contributions of cluster managers. We define clusters in a way that is compatible with this focus using Brown et al. (2007, 2008, 2010b) definition of clusters as our starting point. Brown et al.'s define clusters as overlapping value-adding webs in terms of a

> series of linkages between single firms in a certain surrounding. Understanding clusters as value adding webs takes the connectivity of individual firms on different levels in a cluster into account. Value is added by horizontal, vertical and lateral actors. (Brown et al. 2008: 159)

Following this conceptualisation, a cluster possesses

> a certain number of value adding webs around single firms which overlap each other and are 'constituted by a connection of horizontal, vertical and lateral value adding activities contributed by different actors in proximity to one another which all act in relation to a specific industry sector. The actors have relationships characterised by interdependencies of different strength and quality that define the boundaries'. (Brown et al. 2007: 20, 2010b: 15)

Brown et al. (2010b) differentiate between resources at the firm, network and context level. Every actor has resources at the firm level that may be more or less valuable in terms of leading to firm-specific strategic competitive advantage. While cluster actors may realise Ricardian and Schumpeterian rents at the firm level (Peteraf 1993; Teece et al. 1997), relational rents (Dyer and Singh 1998) may accrue from shared resources at the network level. In this chapter we are, however, mainly interested in investigating which kind of rents are to be generated on the locational level.

At the locational level, we refer to contextual rents (Brown et al. 2010b) defining them as being 'created by the actors of a value adding web due to valuable contextual resources such as advantageous locational conditions or beneficial legal factors' (Brown et al. 2007: 26). According to Brown et al. (2010b), locational resources are subdivided into three categories: regional, industry-specific and institutional resources. Regional resources include local natural resources, for example, the climate and raw materials. Industry-specific resources are certain market characteristics. An example is an innovation-based competition.

Institutional resources include formal and informal rules of competition (North 1991). Formal institutions are laws and regulations. Informal institutions are aspects such as values, norms and cultural habits.

2.2.2 Valuable Locational Resources in Clusters

Our point of reference is the pool of resources that is often embedded in a cluster (Enright 1999). Such resources have a particular value for the participants and for the cluster as a whole (Dahl and Pedersen 2003). A pool of qualified human resources (Hervás-Oliver and Albors-Garrigós 2007) in a certain location has high value for individual firms and for the cluster. This is especially important around location decisions as it can determine access to qualified employees, information networks and specialist knowledge providers (Mitchell et al. 2014). It becomes even more important as new firms seek to establish themselves in locations that offer a portfolio of physical, human, social and intellectual resources. Large cities have clear advantages as they offer living conditions, infrastructure and specialist support services that new firms and entrepreneurs are likely to find attractive in terms of location decisions (Florida 2012).

The resource-oriented cluster literature investigates the impact of resources at different levels of the cluster and cluster performance (Tallman et al. 2004; Hervás-Oliver and Albors-Garrigós 2007; Brown et al. 2010b; Festing et al. 2012; Steffen 2012). In this chapter, we are interested in relations that are linked and embedded in the regional context and may not be moved away from the region easily. Concurrently, access to these locational resources may be not automatically possible for all players located in the region but can be exclusive for cluster members.

The conceptualisation of clusters as value-adding webs sketched in Sect. 2.2.1 differentiates between three resource categories, i.e. firm, relational and locational resources (Brown et al. 2010b). However, the latter two resource categories have certain interfaces. The broad definition of locational resources (based on Wernerfelt's (1984) definition of firm resources) includes—or does not explicitly exclude—local inter-organisational relations. This rationale can be deepened by taking a closer look at locational resources. Institutional resources as a sub-category of locational resources offer potential overlaps towards the relational level, because institutional characteristics are highly relevant for the formal and informal relations of actors in clusters (Brown et al. 2007).

According to Brown et al. (2010b) locational resources are, in principle, available for every company in a cluster. This can, however, be further developed by integrating a more differentiated view of locational resources. Fensterseifer and Rastoin (2013) differentiate between systemic and restricted-access resources in clusters. Systemic resources can be accessed by all companies located in a certain cluster, as, for example, is the case for the local pool of labour. However, to access restricted-access resources of a cluster, the companies have to fulfil certain preconditions. An example for a restricted-access resource is specialised cluster-specific knowledge where located companies must have a certain level of prior knowledge to be able to utilise it (Fensterseifer 2009; Fensterseifer and Rastoin 2013). Mechanisms and processes of knowledge transmission and sharing, and improving the absorptive capacity of small and medium-sized enterprises (SMEs) within a cluster can contribute to individual and cluster-based value-adding activities (Mitchell et al. 2010).

A sound knowledge of (potentially) value creating resources on the locational level about how to develop such resources thus appears to be beneficial for public policy makers to come to a better understanding of 'valuable resources from the geographic or industrial context' (Brown et al. 2010b: 35). The industrial context here refers to the specificities of competition in a certain region. Porter (2000: 20–21), in his so-called diamond model, suggests the context for firm strategy and rivalry, demand conditions and related and supporting industries are relevant factors regarding the competitive advantages of certain sectors in particular locations. Examples of valuable resources include high rivalry in a local cluster or extensive and internationally linked supply chains that drive the productivity growth and innovation capacities of the cluster firms.

However, a general problem facing clusters is one of the size and growth, attracting research and training institutions, attracting horizontal actors and developing potential synergies. This requires not only proximity but also some threshold size to a cluster. A further problem is that of the bundling and access to cluster resources; in many cases, these may not be widely available for a variety of reasons and can be difficult for small and new firms to access (Collins et al. 2013). SMEs are not only hampered by inadequate resources but they also often lack absorptive capacity—the ability to access, translate and absorb knowledge and expertise that may otherwise be available to large corporations (Mitchell et al. 2010). These factors represent a challenge for cluster development and an important focus for cluster managers (Giuliani 2005).

2.3 Conceptualising Locational Resources

The cluster in our perspective consists of horizontal, vertical and lateral actors that interact with each other in a certain fashion in a particular location. This understanding is in line with Kapoor and Lee's suggestion that '[f]irms are embedded in a business ecosystem of interdependent activities carried out by their customers, complementors and suppliers' (Kapoor and Lee 2013: 276). What we further take into account are lateral actors who act as cluster supporters and facilitators. We would put not only cluster managers under this category but also universities, other research institutions, private experts and consultants, and public authorities in their role as providers of infrastructure. We seek to highlight the perspective of one of these lateral actors in this chapter, namely, the perspective of the cluster manager as a facilitator of a cluster and the locational resources.

Locational factors are one relevant part of Dunning's OLI paradigm (Dunning 2000) which may be used to provide an understanding of relevant resources in the particular location of a cluster (Brown et al. 2007). They may be structured into regional resources (e.g. climate), competitive resources (e.g. a high degree of competition on the basis of innovation in a certain region) and institutional resources (e.g. social, cultural or legal specificities). Based on Brown et al. (2007), we suggest that contextual rents may accrue from such locational resources. After a first evaluation of the beneficial potential of a locational resource, an assessment of the possibilities to exclusively keep it to the cluster follows (see Brown et al. 2010b: 28 who adapt the resource characteristics from Collis and Montgomery 2005: 37–39, 42–44 to the cluster context). It is not, however, a simple task to identify the locational resources in a certain cluster on a level of aggregation that supports further analysis. This is a well-known problem when analysing resources at the firm level (Collis and Montgomery 2005). It is therefore critical in the context of a certain cluster to not only conduct a first estimation of value creating resources, but also to break them down into useful units of analysis. Just highlighting a valuable cultural context is, for example, not sufficient to assist understanding value creation at the locational level. However, when considering the history of interaction with each other in communities in relation to work and life-related activities, and thereby institutionalised structures of communication and exchange in a certain region, may provide a relevant point of reference towards developing an understanding of the contribution towards value creation on the single-firm level.

Taking locational resources into account for resource profiles means that a list of regional, competition-related and institutional resources is created. Regarding these resources, it also has to be assessed as to whether it makes it possible for cluster firms to exploit external opportunities to neutralise external threats and how exclusive the access to the resources is for the cluster firms (Festing et al. 2012: 266).

Table 2.1 illustrates how locational resources may be assessed regarding their value creation potential in a cluster. In order to achieve a more differentiated understanding of how far cluster firms are able to appropriate potential contextual rents, the locational resources are systematised according to their accessibility.

The identification and assessment of the value creation potential of locational resources for companies offer a systematic understanding of locational factors to cluster managers. In general, cluster management activities 'are expected to stimulate the positive externalities due to which the cluster is initiated' (Jungwirth et al. 2011: 266). However, companies can be excluded to different degrees from cluster management activities (Jungwirth et al. 2011).

This research further develops this to identify points of intervention for cluster managers. Our starting point with regard to this is Jungwirth et al.'s (2011) differentiation between public, private and club goods in the cluster context as illustrated in Table 2.2. It is assumed that the degree of excludability affects the possibilities to tailor cluster management activities to the needs of the cluster firms. The better the possibilities to exclude firms which are not cluster members but

Table 2.1 Value creation potential of locational resources

| Systematisation of locational resources | Value? Does a resource enable cluster actors to exploit external opportunities or neutralise external threats? | Rare? Is a resource currently controlled by only a small number of competing locations? | Assessment if resources have potential to generate locational advantage | Accessibility of locational resources from a firm perspective |||
				Ubiquities All companies can utilise the locational resources	Systemic resources Only firms located in the cluster can utilise the locational resources	Restricted-access resources Only firms located in the cluster and fulfilling certain preconditions can utilise the locational resources
Regional resources Type of area Natural resources (e.g. minerals or a particular climate) Others	+/−/∼	+/−	$\sqrt{}(\sqrt{})$	+/−	+/−	+/−
Industry-related resources Rivalry between horizontal cluster actors Entry barriers to the cluster Bargaining power of vertical cluster actors (suppliers and buyers) Bargaining power of	+/− ∼	+/−	$\sqrt{}(\sqrt{})$	+/−	+/−	+/−

(continued)

Table 2.1 (continued)

Systematisation of locational resources	Value? Does a resource enable cluster actors to exploit external opportunities or neutralise external threats?	Rare? Is a resource currently controlled by only a small number of competing locations?	Assessment if resources have potential to generate locational advantage	Accessibility of locational resources from a firm perspective		
				Ubiquities All companies can utilise the locational resources	*Systemic resources* Only firms located in the cluster can utilise the locational resources	*Restricted-access resources* Only firms located in the cluster and fulfilling certain preconditions can utilise the locational resources
external suppliers and buyers Threat of substitutes	+/−/~	+/−	√/(√)			
Institutional resources Social specificities Cultural specificities Legal specificities				+/−	+/−	+/−

Source First four rows from Brown et al. (2010b: 28) (VRIO elements adapted from Barney and Hesterly 2010: 70 and 84), rows 5–7 adapted from Rohde (2016) (systemic and restricted-access resources adapted from Fensterseifer and Rastoin 2013: 272)
+ YES; − NO; ~ neutral; √: further investigation; (√): no further investigation of resources

located in the same area from profiting from cluster management activities, the better the cluster management can customise their activities to the members.

The differentiation of cluster management activities into public, club and private goods is integrated into the resource-oriented conceptualisation of locational resources of clusters since it allows an explicit investigation of how cluster management can contribute to the competitiveness of companies in clusters (see Table 2.3). Based on the systematisation of cluster management activities and the locational resources, potential levels of intervention can be conceptualised and highlight how cluster management may be able to develop and upgrade the locational resources of clusters.

Table 2.2 Different types of goods provided by clusters

Type of cluster management activity	Example	Excludability	Specialisation potential from a firm perspective
Public goods	'Pursuing public relations and regional marketing' (Jungwirth et al. 2011: 268)	'Exclusion from the positive effects of public relations and regional marketing, which can be for example a positive reputation of the cluster and subsequent higher sales opportunities, is affecting all actors in the region and no individual can be excluded from these effects'. (Jungwirth et al. 2011: 268)	Low
Club goods	'Providing qualification measures for employees' (Jungwirth et al. 2011: 270)	'[…] the degree of excludability depends on the form the measure takes place. Non-members can be excluded from taking place in physical settings, but some e-learning possibilities might be accessible for everybody. However, as the probability of the first case is much higher than the second one, excludability can be affirmed'. (Jungwirth et al. 2011: 270)	Medium
Private goods	'Other services like personnel procurement' (Jungwirth et al. 2011: 268)	'An exclusion of the good for non-members is feasible'. (Jungwirth et al. 2011: 268)	High

Source First three rows adapted from Jungwirth et al. (2011: 268–270)

Table 2.3 Levels of intervention for cluster management activities and locational resources

Type of cluster management activity: Development of ...	Type of influenced locational resources
Public goods	Systemic resources
Club goods	Restricted-access resources (type 1 = available for all (paying) cluster members)
Private goods	Restricted-access resources (type 2 = available only for certain cluster members)

Source First row adapted from Jungwirth et al. (2011: 268) and second row adapted from Fensterseifer and Rastoin (2013: 272) (modified by the authors)

On the one hand, cluster managers can upgrade the systemic resources of a cluster by providing public goods, because they are accessible for companies located in the cluster. Marketing activities to foster the reputation of a certain region or cluster is one example for the provision of a public good. On the other hand, a cluster management can contribute to restricted-access resources of a cluster by offering club goods and private goods to companies in the cluster. Club goods represent an intermediate form of cluster management activities because they can influence restricted-access resources. This is due to the sense that the companies have to be cluster members in order to have access. However, for the member companies, these provided goods influence resources and can have a systemic character, because they are available for all (paying) members. We call these restricted-access resources that have a systemic character for cluster members as 'restricted-access resources (type 1)'. From a theoretical stance, this is a matter of definition. However, as club goods are limited to those companies that are members of the club, club goods can influence restricted-access resources. The provision of club goods by cluster managers could improve the social capital of the member firms in the cluster. Such social capital may support cluster development and growth (Mitchell et al. 2014).

An example of a private good is access to cooperation support provided by the cluster manager to impart specific knowledge and to develop communications and cooperation between particular firms to strengthen bonding capital within the cluster. Such support also offers bridging capital as specialist gatekeepers can link the respective cluster members to the outside world (Mitchell et al. 2014). Access to these services and activities is exclusive to the respective receiving member firms of the cluster. We call these restrictive-access resources 'restricted-access resources (type 2)'.

Following this rationale, it can be assumed that an increasing degree of excludability of a provided good by the cluster manager can contribute to the value creation of the located firms. This is because the provided services and influenced locational resources are more tailored to the respective firms. From these perspectives, a number of propositions may be derived to further conceptualise locational resources in order to understand their value creation potential for single firms embedded in regional clusters.

Proposition 1: *The more a company uses public goods provided by a cluster manager, the greater the contextual rents the company may gain due to valuable systemic resources in the location.*

Proposition 2: *The more a company uses club goods provided by a cluster manager, the greater the contextual rents the company may gain due to valuable restricted-access resources (type 1) in the location.*

Proposition 3: *The more a company uses private goods provided by a cluster manager, the greater the contextual rents the company may gain due to valuable restricted-access resources (type 2) in the location.*

These propositions assume a positive relationship between the cluster management activities, in terms of provided goods and the value creation of the (potentially) receiving firms in the cluster. Thus, the goods provided by the cluster management are the independent variables and the value creation effects for the companies are the dependent variables in this process.

Identifying and developing the types of locational resources means that cluster managers may be in a better position to foster and upgrade these resources. Locational resources in the form of systemic resources are a potential asset and driver of contextual rents for all players in a certain location, whether they are cluster members or not. This also implies that non-cluster members may 'free-ride' on the engagement of cluster members reducing the incentives to foster such goods by private actors. Restricted-access resources with systemic characteristics for cluster members do not hold this issue. Restricted-access resources are a valuable incentive for cluster members due to them being potential sources of contextual rents. Restricted-access resources in the classical form of exclusive private goods may be better developed in cluster contexts as well due to better connections across firm boundaries and therefore being a valuable locational resource for single-cluster members.

With regard to locational resources, 'public policy consideration is placed on developing and sustaining the overall environment to derive valuable resources […]' (Brown et al. 2010b: 35). It is further suggested to differentiate between 'different kinds of incentives [that] may be used to implement policy such as funding, favourable tax treatment or financing opportunities' (Brown et al. 2010b: 30). For example, a pool of qualified labour, or the entrepreneurial activity in a cluster, may be very relevant to locational resources in terms of our resource-oriented perspective that can be improved by the different activities of lateral actors in the various categories of systemic resources. Entrepreneurial activity in a cluster as a valuable locational resource may be fostered by activities of lateral actors, such as universities (often financed by the public).

Another valuable resource with the potential for contextual rent generation may lie in a business environment that provides supporting infrastructure to cluster members. This is in terms of restricted-access resources (type 1) creating incentives for firms to become cluster members and contribute to cluster development. In this context, social capital may provide both a bridge to the outside world for the cluster members and a bond that provides identity and generates information sharing

(Mitchell et al. 2014). We are specifically interested in the type of intervention between locational resources and cluster management activities in this context. Of special interest are systemic resources as well as restricted-access resources with a systemic character for cluster members. This leads us to a final proposition:

Proposition 4: *Systemic resources in a certain location are more a matter of public funding, while restricted-access resources (type 2) are a matter of private initiative. Restricted-access resources (type 1) may be a matter of private as well as public funding.*

For cluster managers, the focus is on identifying the conditions that contribute to the competitive advantage of the cluster and provide an inducement for individual firms to join the cluster (e.g. Brown et al. 2010a; Jungwirth et al. 2011). There are also conditions that cluster managers can identify and develop that support the development of social capital and the transfer of knowledge within the cluster. These link the cluster to the outside world, developing bridging and bonding capital within the cluster (Mitchell et al. 2014). Cluster managers can identify, but not change, locational and industry features; however, they can consciously develop institutional resources to develop social capital and increase the absorptive capacity of all firms, especially SMEs (Giuliani 2007).

2.4 Conclusion

This chapter has brought together the findings of previous conceptual and case study research to illustrate the analytical framework that we have developed. It highlights the competitive advantages offered to single (and new) firms from cluster participation. We extracted relevant analytical avenues in order to come to a better understanding of different types of locational resources for value creation of firms and the influence cluster managers may have on sustaining and fostering such resources.

The concept of clusters as overlapping value-adding webs by Brown et al. (2007, 2008, 2010b) highlights the importance of cluster relevant resources at the firm level, the relational level and the contextual level. The firm level is quite well researched, as documented in the literature of the resource-based view of the firm (Barney 1991). The relational view has also become a more central perspective in the field of corporate strategy (Dyer and Singh 1998; Lavie 2006).

Contributions of a resource-oriented perspective in understanding the locational decisions of firms can be found in Dunning (2000). Applying this perspective to the location of a regional cluster represents a new approach (as taken by Brown et al. 2010b or Festing et al. 2012). It still was (and to a certain extent is) the case that locational resources and their contribution to value creation, on the one hand, and the possibilities of lateral actors to sustain and upgrade such resources, on the other hand, are relevant topics in a world where clusters constitute a dominant public policy in many countries. Specifically, we saw it as a deficit that location advantages are often understood as something that are accessible for all actors in that location. Thus, we saw the need to come to a more detailed specification of locational resources. From the perspective of the single firm, it appeared especially relevant to come to a better understanding regarding the possibilities of a more exclusive access to location advantages.

To address this deficit in the cluster literature, we took Jungwirth et al. (2011) differentiation of public, club and private goods in a cluster context as a point of reference and linked it to our understanding of potentially valuable locational resources (building on Brown et al. 2007). In that context, we added to the resource-based perspective on clusters Fensterseifer and Rastoin's (2013) differentiation of locational resources into systemic and restricted-access resources. Bringing all these elements together results in ideas as to how locational resources can be systematised and conceptualised, particularly in a way that facilitates the understanding of how these may contribute to competitive advantage in the form of what we call contextual rents for single firms. Four propositions are derived that give points of reference to firms and cluster managers regarding the development and upgrade of different types of locational resources in a cluster context.

Cluster management and cluster development can be an important factor in sustaining a cluster and in facilitating the development of new businesses within clusters. This requires not only knowledge of the cluster context and its resources, but a framework for resource sharing and access. There also remains the quality of cluster management and this relates to resources, effectiveness and leadership (Sydow et al. 2011).

By highlighting different types of locational resources, their role regarding value creation and the appropriation of firms embedded into global value chains becomes clearer. Further, it makes it possible to decide who should contribute the most to the funding of cluster management—the public, the firms or both.

Local clusters with underlying locational resources often form only one pillar of the resource profile of cluster members, the other pillar lies in the global resources which firms have access to via their global value chains. Analysing locational resources without taking this understanding into account may result in insufficient understanding of local value creation potential. Therefore, it is useful for cluster managers when identifying and developing valuable local resources to take into account that cluster members are not only a part of the local network but are usually also integrated into global value chains.

In summary, this article offers a conceptual framework for the analysis of local value creation potential for clustered firms and cluster managers. In addition, points of intervention can be identified for cluster managers to upgrade the locational resources and/or embed them in global value chains. However, this chapter is limited to strategic considerations. An empirical application of the developed framework and testing the derived propositions is beyond the scope of this chapter. Thus, further research is required to generate empirical findings regarding the value creation potential of locational resources for clustered firms and their complementary as well as competitive roles in a world of global value chains.

References

Amit, R., & Zott, C. (2015). Crafting business architecture: The antecedents of business model design. *Strategic Entrepreneurship Journal, 9*(4), 331–350.

Arregle, J.-L., Miller, T. L., Hitt, M. A., & Beamish, P. W. (2013). Do regions matter? An integrated institutional and semiglobalization perspective on the internationalization of MNEs. *Strategic Management Journal, 34*(8), 910–934.

Barney, J. B. (1991). Firm resources and sustained competitive advantage. *Journal of Management, 17*(1), 99–120.

Barney, J. B., & Hesterly, W. S. (2010). *Strategic management and competitive advantage—concepts and cases* (3rd ed.). Boston: Prentice Hall.

Bell, S. J., Tracey, P., & Heide, J. B. (2009). The organization of regional clusters. *Academy of Management Review, 34*(4), 623–642.

Brown, K., Burgess, J., Festing, M., Keast, R., Royer, S., Steffen, C., et al. (2010a). Public policies to enhance cluster development. In C. Jayachandran, M. Thorpe, R. Subramanian, & V. Nagadevara (Eds.), *Business clusters: Partnering for strategic advantage* (pp. 260–280). New Delhi, India: Routledge/Taylor and Francis.

Brown, K., Burgess, J., Festing, M., & Royer, S. (2013). Resources and competitive advantage in clusters. In M. Festing & S. Royer (Eds.), *Schriftenreihe: Internationale personal und strategieforschung* (Vol. 13). Munich: Rainer Hampp Verlag.

Brown, K., Burgess, J., Festing, M., Royer, S., Steffen, C., & Waterhouse, J. (2007). The value adding web—A multi-level framework of competitive advantage realisation in firm-clusters. ESCP-EAP Working Paper No. 27, ESCP-EAP European School of Management, Berlin.

Brown, K., Burgess, J., Festing, M., Royer, S., Steffen, C., & Waterhouse, J. (2008). Single firms and competitive advantage in clusters—Context analysis identifying the embeddedness of a winery in the hunter valley'. In M. Festing & S. Royer (Eds.), *Current issues in international human resource management and strategy research* (pp. 157–177). Munich: Rainer Hampp Verlag.

Brown, K., Burgess, J., Festing, M., Royer, S., Steffen, C., Waterhouse, J., et al. (2010b). Conceptualising clusters as overlapping value adding webs. In K. Brown, J. Burgess, M. Festing, & S. Royer (Eds.), *Value adding webs and clusters—Concepts and cases* (pp. 11–42). Munich: Rainer Hampp Verlag.

Burgers, W. P., Hill, C. W. L., & Kim, W. C. (1993). A theory of global strategic alliances—The case of the global auto industry. *Strategic Management Journal, 14*(6), 419–432.

Cammet, M. (2006). Development and the changing dynamics of global production: Global value chains and local clusters in apparel manufacturing. *Competition & Change, 10*(1), 23–48.

Collins, D., Bray, M., & Burgess, J. (2013). Responding to global warming mitigation policies: The hunter valley construction and engineering cluster. In K. Brown, J. Burgess, M. Festing, & S. Royer (Eds.), *Resources and competitive advantage in clusters* (pp. 113–131). Munich: Rainer Hampp Verlag.

Collis, D. J., & Montgomery, C. A. (2005). *Corporate strategy: A resource-based approach* (2nd ed.). Boston: McGraw-Hill/Irwin.

Dahl, M.S., & Pedersen, C. Ø. R. (2003). Knowledge flows through informal contacts in industrial clusters: Myths or realities? DRUID Working Paper No 03-01. ISBN 87-7873-132-1.

De Oliveira Wilk, E., & Fensterseifer, J. E. (2003). Use of resource-based view in industrial cluster strategic analysis. *International Journal of Operations & Production Management, 23*(9), 995–1009.

Dunning, J. H. (2000). The eclectic paradigm as an envelope for economic and business theories of MNE activity. *International Business Review, 9*(2), 163–190.

Dyer, J. H., & Singh, H. (1998). The relational view: Cooperative strategy and sources of interorganizational competitive advantage. *Academy of Management Review, 23*(4), 660–679.

Enright, M. J. (1999) Regional clusters and firm strategy. In A. D. Chandler, P. Hagström, & Ö. Sölvell (Eds.), *The dynamic firm—The role of technology, strategy, organization, and regions* (pp. 315–342). Oxford.
Fensterseifer, J. E. (2009) Strategic resources and sustainability of competitive advantages in industrial clusters: Towards a general analytical framework. In *EnANPAD 2009*, São Paulo. Available online: http://www.anpad.org.br/admin/pdf/ESO2196.pdf. Last access 11-09-2016.
Fensterseifer, J. E., & Rastoin, J.-L. (2013). Cluster resources and competitive advantage: A typology of potentially strategic wine cluster resources. *International Journal of Wine Business Research, 25*(4), 267–284.
Festing, M., Royer, S., & Steffen, C. (2012). Unternehmenscluster Schaffen Wettbewerbsvorteile: Eine Analyse Des Uhrenclusters in Glashütte. *Zeitschrift Führung + Organisation (ZfO), 81*(4), 264–272.
Florida, R. (2012). *The rise of the creative class* (10th ed.). New York: Basic Books.
Fromhold-Eisebith, M., & Eisebith, G. (2005). How to institutionalize innovative clusters? Comparing explicit top-down and implicit bottom-up approaches. *Research Policy, 34*(8), 1250–1268.
Gereffi, G., Humphrey, J., & Sturgeon, T. (2005). The governance of global value chains. *Review of International Political Economy, 12*(1), 78–104.
Giuliani, E. (2005). Cluster absorptive capacity why do some clusters forge ahead and others lag behind? *European Urban and Regional Studies, 12*(3), 269–288.
Giuliani, E. (2007). The selective nature of knowledge networks in clusters: Evidence from the wine industry. *Journal of Economic Geography, 7*(2), 139–168.
Gretzinger, S., & Royer, S. (2014). Relational resources in value adding webs: The case of a Southern Danish firm cluster. *European Management Journal, 32*(1), 117–131.
Gulati, R. (1999). Network location and learning: The influence of network resources and firm capabilities on alliance formation. *Strategic Management Journal, 20*(5), 397–420.
Hervás-Oliver, J. L., & Albors-Garrigós, J. (2007). Do cluster capabilities matter? An empirical application of the resource-based view in clusters. *Entrepreneurship & Regional Development, 19*(2), 113–136.
Hoang, H., & Rothaermel, F. T. (2016). How to manage alliances strategically—why do so many strategy alliances underperform and what can companies do about it? *MIT Sloan Management Review, 58*(1), 69–76.
Jungwirth, C., Grundgreif, D., & Müller, E. F. (2011). How to turn public networks into private clubs? The challenge of being a cluster manager. *International Journal of Entrepreneurial Venturing, 3*(3), 262–280.
Jungwirth, C., & Müller, E. F. (2010) The sustainability of clusters—consequences of different governance regimes of top-down and bottom-up cluster initiatives. *Frontiers of Entrepreneurship Research, 30*(14), Article 4.
Jungwirth, C., & Müller, E. F. (2014). Comparing top-down and bottom-up cluster initiatives from a principal-agent perspective: What we can learn for designing governance regimes. *Schmalenbach Business Review, 66*(3), 357–381.
Kapoor, R., & Lee, J. M. (2013). Coordinating and competing in ecosystems: How organizational forms shape new technology investments. *Strategic Management Journal, 34*(3), 274–296.
Lavie, D. (2006). The competitive advantage of interconnected firms: An extension of the resource-based view. *Academy of Management Review, 31*(3), 638–658.
Lavie, D. (2007). Alliance portfolios and firm performance: A study of value creation and appropriation in the U.S. software industry. *Strategic Management Journal, 28*(12), 1187–1212.
Leick, B. (2013). Balancing firm and network-based resources to gain competitive advantage: A case study of an artisanal musical instruments cluster in Germany. *Management Review, 24*(2), 77–95.
Mitchell, R., Boyle, B., Burgess, J., & McNeill, K. (2014). You can't make a good wine without a few beers: Gatekeepers and knowledge flow in industrial districts. *Journal of Business Research, 67*(10), 2198–2206.

Mitchell, R., Waterhouse, J., McNeill, K., & Burgess, J. (2010). Proximity and knowledge sharing in clustered firms. In K. Brown, J. Burgess, M. Festing, & S. Royer (Eds.), *Value adding webs and clusters: Concepts and cases* (pp. 62–78). Munich: Rainer Hampp Verlag.

North, D. C. (1991). Institutions. *The Journal of Economic Perspectives, 5*(1), 97–112.

Peteraf, M. A. (1993). The cornerstones of competitive advantage: A resource-based view. *Strategic Management Journal, 14*(3), 179–191.

Pitelis, C. (2012). Clusters, entrepreneurial ecosystem co-creation, and appropriability: A conceptual framework. *Industrial and Corporate Change, 21*(6), 1359–1388.

Porter, M. E. (2000). Location, competition, and economic development: Local clusters in a global economy. *Economic Development Quarterly, 14*(1), 15–34.

Rohde, S. (2016). A resource-based view of cross-border clusters: Conceptualizing locational resources. In I. Bernhard (Ed.), *Geography, open innovation, diversity and entrepreneurship* (pp. 551–560). Trollhättan: University West.

Royer, S., & Burgess, J. (2013) *Towards a better understanding of value creation in clustered firms—A resource-oriented perspective with the focus on locational resources and the role of lateral cluster actors*. Paper presented at the 16th TCI Annual Global Conference, Kolding/Denmark, 2013.

Steffen, C. (2012) How firms profit from acting in networked environments: Realising competitive advantages in business clusters. A resource-oriented case study analysis of the german and swiss watch industry. In M. Festing & S. Royer (Eds.), *Schriftenreihe: Internationale Personal- und Strategieforschung, Band 11*. Munich: Rainer Hampp Verlag.

Sydow, J., Lerch, F., Huxham, C., & Hibbert, P. (2011). A silent cry for leadership: Organizing for leading (in) clusters. *Leadership Quarterly, 22*(2), 328–343.

Tallman, S., Jenkins, M., Henry, N., & Pinch, S. (2004). Knowledge, clusters and competitive advantage. *Academy of Management Review, 29*(2), 258–271.

Teece, D. J., Pisano, G., & Shuen, A. (1997). Dynamic capabilities and strategic management. *Strategic Management Journal, 18*(7), 509–533.

Wernerfelt, B. (1984). A resource-based view of the firm. *Strategic Management Journal, 5*(2), 171–180.

Chapter 3
MSME Competitiveness for the Global Value Chain—A TRIZ-Based Approach

Shishir Shrotriya and Sanjay Dhir

> *It's easy to see and hard to foresee.*
> —Benjamin Franklin

Abstract The Micro, Small and Medium Enterprises (MSME) sector is one of the most vibrant sectors of growing economies like India. The MSMEs can play a crucial role in employment, globalization, and can be very effective in the Global Value Chain (GVC) owing to their entrepreneurial and innovation driven growth. India's MSME sector has been facing stiff competition from large industry houses and global players. In this dynamically changing environment, it is important to work out and implement an effective growth and consolidation plan, through structured research. TRIZ is the Russian acronym for the "Theory of Inventive Problem Solving" is an analytical approach for innovative problem solving which has been applied in a variety of spheres related to management and technology. This chapter focuses on deriving the factors and solutions which are significant for strengthening the MSME clusters in India through a TRIZ-based approach. The authors have chosen to apply the TRIZ methodology in the context of the Electronic Goods sector in India. This can be suitably tailored to focus toward other sectors following the approach suggested by the authors of this chapter.

Keywords Global value chains · India · MSME

3.1 Introduction

Indian MSMEs account for around 40% of our workforce and contribute 8% to our GDP with 40% share of exports. The Indian MSME sector is second largest globally with 1.3 million plus numbers, just second to China. Owing to the growing

---

S. Shrotriya (✉) · S. Dhir
Department of Management Studies, Indian Institute of Technology Delhi,
Vishwakarma Bhawan, Shaheed Jeet Singh Marg, New Delhi 110016, India
e-mail: shishir_sh@rediffmail.com

S. Dhir
e-mail: sanjaydhir.iitd@gmail.com

© Springer Nature Singapore Pte Ltd. 2018
J. Connell et al. (eds.), *Global Value Chains, Flexibility and Sustainability*,
Flexible Systems Management, https://doi.org/10.1007/978-981-10-8929-9_3

significance of MSMEs for the economy, there is a renewed thrust on MSME development in India through government policies and schemes to bring together the various stakeholders in the context of our economic growth. The main mechanisms through which MSMEs contribute to equitable development are employment and income generation in the formal and informal sectors, through the human capital endowment of the poor, provision of basic goods and services and through the enhanced creation of public revenue. Thus, MSME sector development has the potential of overcoming the menace of unemployment and leads a push to equitable social growth.

Due to the impact of globalization, domestic reforms and the continuous alignment of policies on the small-scale industry sector are necessary (Subrahmanya 2004). For sustaining the growth of the MSME sector, there is need for simplifying legal and regulatory frameworks, good governance, adequate, and easy to get to finance and suitable infrastructure (Rathod 2007). Accordingly, the Micro, Small and Medium Enterprises Development (MSMED) Act was notified in 2006, which defines investment ceilings of the sector and addresses policy issues affecting MSMEs. This Act aims to consolidate the development of MSMEs by enhancing their competitiveness in the dynamically changing markets. It also provisions the legal framework for recognition of both manufacturing and services enterprises and a consultative statutory mechanism with advisory functions at the national and state level to help the variety of stakeholders from the MSME sector.

The Government of India has emphasized the strategies for marketing, skill development, technology, infrastructure creation, and credit availability for the MSME sector as outlined in the MSME strategic action plan (2015).

In this chapter, we look at the strategies for MSMEs to be competitive in the Global Value Chains (GVCs) through TRIZ-based methodology. TRIZ in Russian stands for "Theoria Resheneyva Isobretatelshehuh Zadach", meaning the "Theory of Inventive Problem Solving", propounded in 1940 by Genrich S. Altshuller, in the former USSR (Cavalluncci 2017).

3.2 Literature Review

Bridging the gap through various policy, programs, and other initiatives has the potential of making India the global hub of MSME. MSME development can act as an instrument emphasizing the enhancement of the industry competiveness, enhanced productivity, efficiency and contribution toward the various sectors of the economies in the agriculture, manufacturing, and services domains (Subrahmanya et al. 2010).

The technological innovations, undertaken by MSMEs in diverse sectors, become a significant contributor to their success (Hoffman et al. 1998). That said, the capacity and innovative capability of MSMEs can significantly vary based on the sector, resources, size, focus, and the operating business environment (Burrone and Jaiya 2005). However, manufacturing sector innovations could be governed by an extremely complex process driven by a variety of factors (Becheikh et al. 2006).

Entrepreneurship and innovation are the key factors of MSME growth, coupled, and competitiveness (Ussman et al. 2001). The current global scenario is difficult for small-scale industries, owing to increasing internal and external competitions (Naik 2002). The vibrancy and dynamic aspects of the MSME sector are largely unrealized under the era of deregulation and de-reservation (Mathew 2004). In order to sustain social growth, it is significant that, at the strategy level, there is a mechanism by which MSME enterprises become a means of public security (Mathew 2004). To achieve growth, and to ensure the buildup of global industrial hubs, productivity, and quality, besides many other factors are the most prominent and inevitable needs.

Special programs to facilitate extended support for the MSME sector are required to be driven continuously for growth opportunities. An efficient MSME ecosystem is essential for transforming the holistic growth of industry in India (Subrahmanya et al. 2010).

3.2.1 Gaps and Challenges for Indian MSMEs

All the policies pursued by the Government of India (GOI) have been directed toward a diversified economy with a dynamic MSME sector, rendering widespread employment opportunities to attract new labor strength and offer stimulating career opportunities since the inception of MSME act in 2006.

The National Policy on Electronics 2012 also highlighted various issues such as inflexible and archaic labor laws, tax structure, gaps in infrastructure, supply chain and logistics, limited focus on Research and Development (R&D), inadequate funding, and most importantly low value addition

3.3 Methodology

The theory of inventive problem solving TRIZ provides 40 principles for problem solving while helping to remove contradictions. The model for basic TRIZ tool usage flow is as follows (Fig. 3.1):

The summary of each step while identifying inventive principles and their application for optimum solutions is described in (Table 3.1).

TRIZ has been widely used by innovators worldwide since the conceptualization of this innovative methodology. Some of world's best organizations like General Electric, Intel, Samsung, Motorola, Airbus, and more are using TRIZ (Gadd 2011). It shows the potential of TRIZ for innovation that connects science, technology, and management.

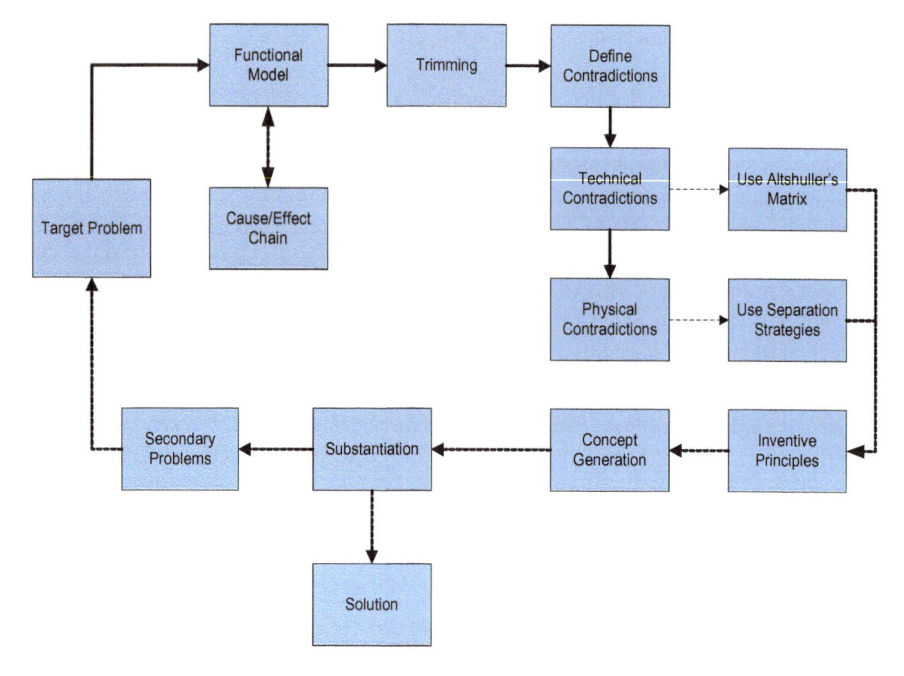

Fig. 3.1 General basic TRIZ tool usage flow (adapted from Savransky 2000; Gadd 2011)

3.3.1 Problem Statement Development Flowchart Through TRIZ Methodology

TRIZ proposes better solutions if the problem is clearly defined in a problem statement. However, the initial problem statement undergoes a problem refinement process through which the specific problem is converted into general problems with clearly outlined contradictions (Fig. 3.2).

Step 1: Target Problem

This chapter illustrates the process of deriving the factors and solutions which are significant for strengthening the India MSME clusters in India, through a TRIZ-based approach. We have chosen to apply the TRIZ methodology in the context of consumer electronics products in India, which can be suitably tailored to focus toward other sector following the approach suggested by the authors in this chapter. Despite the progress in electronics systems design and manufacturing, over the last few decades in India, a large part of the demand of consumer electronics is still fulfilled by imports. Indian MSMEs engaged in this sector are not able to meet the domestic demands of electronics goods. Table 3.2 enumerated the objectives and challenges for MSMEs as outlined in the strategic action plan of the Ministry in 2015.

Table 3.1 Summary of significant steps of TRIZ flow

S. No.	Step	Description
1	Target problem	It includes the problem definition and problem statement
2	Problem modeling	Functional model of problem statement can be modeled by functional analysis or cause and effect analysis
3	Trimming	It is an analytical tool for removing certain components from one system and redistributing their useful functions among remaining systems
4	Technical contradiction	If improvement of one parameter of a system leads to worsening of another parameter, then it is a situation of technical contradiction. It is expressed by If…, Then…, But…statement
5	Physical contradictions	When two opposite requirements are placed upon a single physical parameter of an object, these requirements occur due to conflicting requirements of technical contradiction. It is expressed by Want…For…And…For statement
6	Altshuller's matrix	It is a matrix that identifies the set of principles (out of Altshuller's 40 principles) and may be used to solve the contradictions between two parameters
7	Separation strategies	It is used for solution of physical contradictions by using physical contradiction solution algorithm to identify the applicable 40 principles. Other methodologies are satisfaction and bypass to solve the physical contradictions
8	Application of inventive principles	To identify applicable inventive principles for solving technical and physical contradictions using Altshuller's contradiction matrix and physical contradiction solution algorithms, respectively
9	Substantiation	Practical proof of concept that was envisaged while applying inventive principles. It may lead to another problem that may be overcome by the same process and find a solution till secondary problem is achieved of insignificant nature
10	Solutions	After application of inventive principles, we may have optimum solution

Step 2: Functional Modeling

The Indian Micro, Small and Medium Enterprises Development (MSMED) Act 2006 defines the coverage and investment ceiling of 25 lakhs (manufacturing) and 10 lakhs (services), 5 crore (manufacturing), 2 crore (services), 10 crore (manufacturing), and 5 crore (services) for the micro, small, and medium enterprises, respectively. The Act defines medium enterprises for the first time and provides a framework to integrate the three tiers of these enterprises, namely, micro, small, and medium. In the Indian context, MSME clusters for the electronics systems distribute as geographical concentrations of enterprises, especially Small and Medium Enterprises (SME), faced with somewhat similar challenges as discussed earlier.

Fig. 3.2 Problem refinement process (adapted from Savransky 2000)

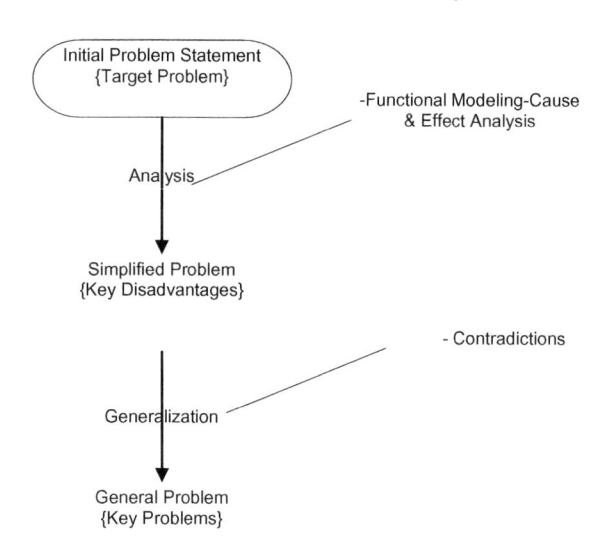

```
Initial Problem Statement
    {Target Problem}
           |                    - Functional Modeling-Cause
        Analysis                  & Effect Analysis
           ↓
    Simplified Problem
    {Key Disadvantages}
           |                    - Contradictions
       Generalization
           ↓
    General Problem
     {Key Problems}
```

Table 3.2 Objectives and challenges for MSMEs sector in the consumer electronics sector

Objectives	Challenges
Competitiveness in the global market	Lack of technology
Global markets access	Limited capital and knowledge
Safeguarding intellectual property	Inadequate innovation and patenting processes
Improve consumption of domestic products	Low quality and low production capacity
Improve quality	Constraints of technology and modernization
Improve gross value add	Nonavailability of high tech machinery and trained manpower
Self-reliance	Inadequate investments and R&D focus
India to become a manufacturing hub	High cost of carrying inventory and high freight owing to import of components and products

The MSMED (Amendment) Bill, 2015 focusses to enhance the existing limit for investment in plant and machinery taking into account the price index and cost of inputs consistent with the emerging role of the MSMEs in various global value chains. It includes medium enterprises apart from small enterprises to enable to avail the benefits and become competitive. It also empowers the government to revise the existing limits for investment, considering the inflation and dynamic market situation.

Similarly, the National Policy on Electronics, 2012 focusses on the electronics as "meta resource" which forms the significant parts of machine and equipment imported and aims to transform India into global hub in Electronics system design and manufacturing. The policy promotes indigenous manufacturing and domestic capabilities in terms of strategic electronics and create MSME ecosystem which can compete with global quality and harness its strategic use. The policy also outlines to adopt best e-waste management practice and to become global leader in Electronics Manufacturing Services (EMS).

The Government of India realizes that if the current trend of demand and domestic supply of electronic goods continues, then import of electronics would far exceed the import of oil by 2020. Accordingly, the government has identified challenges in infrastructure gap, tax structure, supply chain logistics, labour laws, R&D focus, funding and value addition.

3.3.2 Contradiction Modeling

We can use comparative approach for identifying the parameters of MSME ecosystem by comparing with original engineering parameters. The abstraction and generalization study leading to contextual mapping of MSME ecosystem parameters with original Engineering parameters of the Altshuller's TRIZ matrix (Altshuller 1999) is the key step for problem solving using TRIZ methodology. This has been worked out in consultation with TRIZ and MSME domain experts, as follows (Table 3.3):

Table 3.3 Parameters of MSME ecosystem corresponding to engineering parameters

Engineering parameter	Corresponding electronics sector MSME parameters	Engineering parameter	Corresponding electronics sector MSME parameters
1. Weight of moving object	1. Weight of MSME ecosystem	24. *Loss of information*	18. *Loss of information*
2. Weight of stationary object			
3. Length of moving object	2. Vertical integration in MSME sector	25. *Loss of time*	19. *Loss of time*
4. Length of stationary object			
5. Area of moving object	3. Horizontal Integration of MSME ecosystem	26. *Quality of substance/ matter*	20. *Quality of electronics products design creation*
6. Area of stationary object			
7. Volume of moving object	4. Volume of MSME ecosystem	27. *Reliability*	21. *Quality and reliability of MSME ecosystem*
8. Volume of stationary object			
9. Speed	5. Rate of conversion of idea (concept) into a product	28. *Measurement accuracy*	22. *Ecosystem accuracy*
10. Force (intensity)	6. Demand of electronics products and services	29. *Manufacturing precision*	23. *Manufacturing accuracy*

(continued)

Table 3.3 (continued)

Engineering parameter	Corresponding electronics sector MSME parameters	Engineering parameter	Corresponding electronics sector MSME parameters
11. Stress or pressure	7. Environmental pressure on MSMEs	30. *Harmful effects to object*	24. *Harmful effects to ecosystem*
12. Shape	8. Shape of ecosystem through global value chain (cyclic)	31. *Harmful effects from object*	25. *Harmful effects from ecosystem*
13. Stability of the object\s composition	9. Coordination	32. *Ease of manufacture*	26. *Ease of manufacture*
14. Strength	10. Entrepreneurship	33. *Ease of operations*	27. *Ease of running the ecosystem*
15. Duration of action of moving object	11. Time duration for implementation of envisaged goals and programs	34. *Ease of repair*	28. *Ease of corrective actions to ecosystem*
16. Duration of action by stationary object			
17. Temperature	12. General infrastructure	35. *Adaptability or versatility*	29. *Strategic flexibility*
18. Illumination intensity	13. Transparency		
19. Use of energy by moving object	14. Investment	36. Device complexity	30. Complexity of MSME ecosystem
20. Use of energy by stationary object			
21. Power	15. Investment per unit time	37. *Extent of automation*	31. Difficulty in detecting ecosystem faults and their impact
22. Loss of energy	16. Loss of investment	38. Extent of automation	32. Extent of ICT
23. Loss of substance	17. Loss of electronics products	39. Productivity	33. Gross value add of the ecosystem

3.4 Grand Challenge

The grand challenge is to boost the contribution of domestic electronics sector MSME companies in the Global Value Chain, to remain competitive across global markets, global products and global investors.

3.4.1 Direct Solution to the Grand Challenge

A direct solution to the problem would be to promote and take up collaboration and tie-up with global players for domestic production through schemes like "Make in India". Further, if domestic products cannot be made competitive, imports can be made prohibitive by the government. However, these direct solutions are plagued with challenges and their real impact on MSME sector growth needs to be examined in details.

3.4.2 Problems with Direct Solution

Global player's collaboration will not lead to self-reliance for Indian companies, as the design, development, and manufacturing knowledge which cannot be easily captured in collaborations. Further, problems associated with the nonavailability of raw material, manufacturing infrastructure, and associated costs may not bring in the desired results for the MSME sector, so we need to seek inventive solution and work on various types of contradiction removal.

3.4.3 TRIZ Solution

If the quality of domestic manufactured electronics products is improved to be on par with international standards, then MSMEs can become competitive in the global markets. For this strict quality, standards and norms are to be followed by the respective sectors.

3.4.3.1 Parameters Need to Be Improved—Quality and Reliability

The TRIZ contradiction matrix is formulated based on Altshuller's original matrix that any improvement in one parameter often worsens the other parameters. For example, the improvement in quality and reliability of a product often leads to increased costs. It means that there are contradictions while improving one parameter. It may be noted that effect of a parameter may be positive or negative. The increment in positive parameters is meant to improve some parameters, and similarly reduction in a negative parameter is also meant to improve certain other parameters. TRIZ methodology allows us to undertake contradiction removal between the improving and worsening parameters with the help of inventive principles given in the contradiction matrix, contextually tailored to solve the contradiction between these two parameters taken and analyzed from the TRIZ matrix.

Now, we need to improve the quality and reliability of the Indian MSME Electronics products. As seen from the contradiction matrix, this is observed to have contradictions with worsening parameters like speed, implementation time, loss of investment, and loss of electronics products. For instance, if strict international quality norms are enforced, the quality and reliability will improve but compliance to the standards and setting up of required infrastructure can bring delays to the production. On application of the relevant inventive principles prescribed by TRIZ, we see that the principle of "Fail fast; Learn Fast" is applied to mature the products through concepts like accelerated testing. Similarly, in order to obviate the worsening parameters leading to increases in implementation time due to quality enforcement, the TRIZ principle of "Taking Out" suggests external testing labs to save time and also undertaking lean manufacturing by eliminating non-value-add services. Likewise, the problem of "Loss of products" could be circumvented through the concept of "Preliminary Action" wherein quality teams can be involved during the design cycle and design teams are well trained on the desired quality aspects. The other harmful effects from the MSME ecosystem leading to high costs due to enforcement of quality norms can be solved through the principles of "Parameter Change" where the flexible teams can be utilized for design as well quality and concepts of virtual prototyping are resorted to, in order to reduce costs.

3.5 Discussion

The challenges of "Strengthening the Indian MSME Clusters for GVC Challenges" were modeled in "TRIZ", which is the (Russian) acronym for the "Theory of Inventive Problem Solving", developed by G. S. Altshuller and his colleagues in the former U.S.S.R (1940). TRIZ is being applied to a variety of problem solving cases both in Engineering and Management fields (Hua et al. 2006). The chapter signifies application of TRIZ approach to arrive at the possible solutions by first developing the TRIZ matrix in the context of the problem and then applying the various inventive principles outlined in the TRIZ methodology to the context of this targeted problem. The structured analysis focuses on deriving the factors and solutions which are feasible after removing the contradictions for strengthening the Indian MSME industry and be effective in the Global Value Chain (GVC).

The present MSME ecosystem structure needs more robustness in functioning. It is suggested that it is now time to think beyond the normal solution to problems; we need to think in an innovative manner for functioning of MSMEs. The challenges faced by the MSME ecosystem necessitate better demand–supply coordination, quality and reliability, self-regulation and flexibility in manufacturing, etc.

The electronics goods and services generated by Indian MSMEs are lacking in quality and reliability and therefore cannot compete with imported electronics coming to India. Other major factor relates to the high cost of domestic manufacturing which prevents the competitiveness of the Indian MSMEs. This chapter analyze that if the quality of electronics products and services improve to the level of global standards and become cost competitive, it will enhance the self-sufficiency in electronic systems and components.

We have taken the 33 parameters for functioning of MSME ecosystem working within the global value chains. The consumption of electronics components and systems is increasing day by day, and electronics chips and processors are inevitable part of any system designing. When we work toward improving the quality of electronics products generated by the MSME ecosystem in India, we observe contradictions with other parameters. When one parameter is improving and another parameter is worsening, then it is referred as engineering or technical contradiction in TRIZ. The TRIZ contradiction matrix (Altshuller 1999) provides the solution to remove the technical contradiction in form of 40 inventive principles. For example, while improving quality, we find contradictions with the implementation time. The contradiction matrix provides the set of four inventive solutions <21, 35, 11, 28>. The first solution as suggested by contradiction matrix should be exploited first. If the first solution is not able to achieve the desired result then second, third, or fourth solution should be applied as standby solutions and these could be utilized when desired result is not effective by using the first inventive principle.

3.6 TRIZ Solutions

The TRIZ analysis for improvement of quality and reliability of products generated by MSME ecosystem finds that for improvement of the quality of products, stringent quality checks should be carried out at very fast rate. The inventive principle «skipping» relates to 'Fail fast; Learn fast' methodology, which could help to achieve maturity of any technology at an early stage. A mature product or a technology would automatically lead to lesser failure rate during quality checks. So, this principle states that drive out the fear from fast and bulk volume of failure. The quality products will also boost the export of electronics along with fulfillment of domestic demand.

The findings of TRIZ analysis through inventive solutions emphasize on utilization of independent quality audit team. It would save time of production agency and would bring the transparency in total quality checks. Further, independent quality audit team should be tasked with root cause analysis for failure along with fault findings. It means that task of fault findings and root cause finds should be carried out concurrently, which would definitely improve the quality of products.

The analysis also suggests that pre-quality checks should be carried out and necessary changes should be done before offering to external and independent quality audit team. The external audit agency may be involved during design and manufacturing phases of product development for controlled quality environment. Further, design and manufacturing teams should be completely aware about the quality and reliability aspects, and quality and reliability training should be imparted to design and manufacturing team. The TRIZ analysis also emphasized upon Flexible Manufacturing cell, Strategic quality planning, Early supplier Involvement (ESI) and decrease setup time to enhance the quality of products.

3.7 Conclusion

There are number of sectors of economy which further have number of industries from large scale to MSME. Every sector depends on inputs like raw materials, finance, processes, technology know-how, etc. to function and sustain. Indian electronics sector heavily depends on external sources for such inputs. This is because there is a technological gap between indigenous products and imported goods. The chapter has outlined how some of the challenges for strengthening the MSME are identified and solutions can be modeled and investigated through an objective analysis using TRIZ. These solutions are in specific for policy makers and practitioners. The academicians can utilize the TRIZ modeling in the context of chosen field to undertake creative problem solving applicable to that context.

Some of the key implications derived from TRIZ analysis are as follows:

- Improving quality and reliability of electronics products would enhance the competiveness of Indian MSMEs.
- Attain self-sufficiency in strategic electronics components and systems in the field of defence, nuclear, space, and internal security.
- Enhance the cooperation with WTO and other countries so that Indian products have ample opportunity to access to global markets; due to low quality, the Indian-made products have failed to gain access to global markets.
- Precommitment between all stakeholders before launching a MSME developmental project, i.e., inter-ministry/departments/state government discussion and commitment for full cooperation during the project with clearly defined roles and responsibilities.
- Improve coordination by changing the communication mode between stakeholders from conventional communication system, i.e., one–one or one–multiple to cloud-based distributed platform. These platforms need to be supported by academia–industry–government interface consultation and design and development clinics.
- Policy makers and coordinating agencies need to consider improvement in implementation time by decentralized monitoring and outcome oriented analysis at grass-root levels, like district and cluster level, and then all these cluster-level monitoring agencies should be monitored by national-level monitoring agency.
- Governmental agencies and other partners need to work out at developing entrepreneurship and upgrade skills, so that the sector can become a mass job provider and cater to a hub for global companies for manufacturing.
- Organizational flexibility can only cope with changing socioeconomic scenario. Therefore, design of various MSME developmental programs should be made collaborative and flexible to include and impact all stakeholders in the system.
- Entrepreneurship is the key driver for whole ecosystem as it provides adaptability to dynamic and turbulent economic environment. It has the potential to integrate MSME with the innovation and skill ecosystems. If both these ecosystems are integrated, India would become global manufacturing and skills hub of the Indian and global economy.

The chapter depicts the inventive principle approach for the challenges that MSME sector growth is facing in India. The TRIZ is a well-proven innovative methodology to provide the best solution for a problem. As, it was invented for innovative solution of engineering challenges, however, over the period of time it is being utilized across the wide spectrum of subjects, i.e., social, political and management, etc. The major challenges of MSME ecosystem are identified through problem refinement process as suggested by TRIZ, as only clear understanding of underlying contradictions can lead to practical solutions. We have mapped the engineering parameters with MSME ecosystem's parameter based on literature review and functional analysis with the help of domain experts. Then we identified contradictions between improving parameter and worsening parameters, by mapping these parameters to the contradiction matrix (Altshuller 1999). The present study has a few limitations as it does not lead to an ideal solution. However, all solutions are within well-proven framework of TRIZ methodology. Further, all solutions provided by TRIZ are indicative in nature and not an exclusive solution. The actual implication of solutions is to be tested only at the time of implementation and analyzed with respect to the cost incurred in harmful and useful effects. The parameter mapped in the TRIZ solution for the MSME sector can be extended to other sectors by researchers for applying this problem-solving approach to other fields of application.

References

Altshuller, G. (1999). *The innovation algorithm: TRIZ, systematic innovation and technical creativity* (pp. 268–271). Technical Innovation Center.

Becheikh, N., Landry, R., & Amara, N. (2006). Lessons from innovation empirical studies in the manufacturing sector: A systematic review of the literature from 1993–2003. *Technovation, 26* (5/6), 644–664.

Burrone, E., & Jaiya, G. S. (2005). *Intellectual property (IP) rights and innovation in small and medium-sized enterprises.* Geneva: World Intellectual Property Organization.

Cavalluncci, D. (Ed.). (2017). *TRIZ—The theory of inventive problem solving: Current research and trends in French academic institutions.* New York: Springer.

Gadd, K. (2011). *TRIZ for engineers: Enabling inventive problem solving.* Chichester: Wiley.

Hoffman, K., Parejo, M., Bessant, J., & Perren, L. (1998). Small firms R&D, technology and innovation in the UK: A literature review. *Technovation, 18*(1), 39–55.

Hua, Z., Yang, J., Coulibaly, S., & Zhang, B. (2006). Integration TRIZ with problem-solving tools: A literature review from 1995 to 2006. *International Journal of Business Innovation and Research (IJBIR), 1*(1–2), 111–128.

Mathew, M. (2004). Small industry and globalization. *Economic and Political Weekly, XXXIX*(20), 1999–2000.

MSMED Act. (2006). Micro Small and Medium Enterprise Development Act.

Naik SD. (2002). *Small scale industries: Preparing for WTO challenges*, The Hindu Business Line.

National Electronics Policy-2012 (NEP-2012).

MSME strategic action plan. (2015). (Online access http://msme.gov.in/sites/default/files/MSME-Strategic-Action-Plan.pdf).

Rathod, C. B. (2007). Contribution of Indian small scale entrepreneurs to economic growth in India: Opportunities and challenges in global economy. *Prabandh—Journal of Management and Research, 23*(June), 1–12.

Savransky, S. D. (2000). *Engineering of creativity: Introduction to TRIZ methodology of inventive problem solving*. Boca Raton, Fla: CRC Press.

Subrahmanya, M. H. B. (2004). Small industry and globalization: Implications, performance and prospects. *Economic and Political Weekly, 39*(18), 1826–1834.

Subrahmanya, M. H. B., Mathirajan, M., & Krishnaswamy, K. N. (2010). Importance of technological innovation for SME growth: Evidence from India. Working paper, World Institute for Development Economics Research, No. 2010, 03, ISBN 978-92-9230-238-2.

Ussman, A. M., Almeida, A., Ferreira, A. J., Franco, M., & Mendes, L. (2001). SMEs and innovation: Perceived barriers and behavioural patterns. *The International Journal of Entrepreneurship and Innovation, 2*(2), 111–118.

Chapter 4
Do Mergers Destroy Value in India?

Neelam Rani, Surendra S. Yadav and P. K. Jain

Abstract The present chapter delves into 'how market reacts to the corporate merger deals in India?'. The present work focuses on mergers concluded through absorptions only. The period of study is from 2003 to 2016. The empirical findings based on 150 cases of mergers in India are analysed. We find that shareholders of Indian acquiring companies adopting mergers through absorption experience negative abnormal returns over event window of 41 days (−20, +20). However, high event-induced variance is also observed in abnormal returns. The present study suggests that such high variances in abnormal returns can be explained by the effects of announcement period of mergers completed through absorption.

Keywords Abnormal returns · Amalgamation · Consolidation
Cumulative abnormal return · Event study · Merger through absorption
Short-run performance

4.1 Introduction

Corporate restructuring practices such as mergers, acquisitions, spin-offs, consolidation, etc. have become very popular in the global corporate landscape. A company may decide to gradually grow overtime through internal expansion or by external expansion. This expansion can be done by acquiring new assets, by replacing dispensable equipments/assets or by enlarging the product portfolio.

N. Rani (✉)
Indian Institute of Management Shillong, Shillong, India
e-mail: nr@iimshillong.ac.in

S. S. Yadav · P. K. Jain
Department of Management Studies, Indian Institute of Technology Delhi,
Hauz Khas, New Delhi, India
e-mail: ssyadav@dms.iitd.ac.in

P. K. Jain
e-mail: pkjain@dms.iitd.ac.in

However, in external expansion specifically, a firm buys existing businesses to grow at a faster rate through corporate combinations. These combinations have emerged as prominent aspects of corporate restructuring. Mergers, acquisitions and takeovers are various forms of corporate combinations. These practices play a significant role in the external growth of corporates domestically and internationally. Many leading companies across the globe have adopted these strategies of expansion growth. They have been gaining attention because of the globalisation of businesses, enhanced competition due to shrinkage of trade barriers and free movement of capital across countries. Intense competition has prompted Indian companies to restructure their business operations by the means of acquisition and takeovers owing to increasing exposure to competition in domestic markets as well as overseas markets. Mergers and acquisitions scale up and consolidate production and marketing operations. These are the strategic steps initiated to maximise company's prospects. These practices are prevalent in a vast array of diverse fields such as pharmaceuticals, telecommunications, IT and chemical and business process outsourcing as well as in traditional industries. These strategic policies are formulated to enhance market share and enlarge the existing customer base by entering into new ventures and coming up with new product segments.

A merger is a transaction involving unification of two or more entities into single entity. Mergers can be done via absorption or amalgamation. Mergers via absorption involves a process of combining two or more firms, wherein the resulting firm contains the identity of acquiring firm only. An amalgamation/consolidation on the other hand is the process of combining two or more firms into a new firm, wherein all the existing firms are dissolved. In business terminology, the acquired/absorbed firm is known as the target firm and the firm aiming to acquire is known as the acquiring firm.

The present chapter investigates the abnormal returns (short term in nature) to acquiring firm's shareholders upon the announcement of merger through absorption.

The chapter is organised into six sections including the current section. Section 4.2 reviews the extant literature on returns of mergers while also explaining the objectives of the present work. Section 4.3 briefs the process of merger specifically in Indian context. Data sources, methodology and scope of study have been outlined in Sect. 4.4. The major findings are contained in Sect. 4.5. Conclusions and implications for policy have been delineated in Sect. 4.6.

4.2 Literature Survey

Mergers and acquisitions as a generic topic embody vast body of literature. The empirical research has widely investigated the basic question of profitability. Extant literature has used many research approaches to investigate the mergers' profitability and improved efficiency post-mergers. In a recent study, Zola and Meier (2008) reviewed 88 empirical studies that were conducted during the period 1970–2006.

They identified two approaches used in the studies to evaluate the impact of M&A on shareholders' value. They observed that 36 (41%) of these studies employed methodology of event study to analyse the returns in the event window. The other noted approach used by the empirical studies is long-term accounting measures to investigate post-merger performance. Zola and Meier (2008) noticed that 28% studies have used this approach to analyse the synergies of mergers and acquisitions.

The *first approach* is based on *event study methodology* which is the most common approach used in past studies. Event study methodology is based on calculating excess returns to stockholders in the period surrounding the announcement of a deal. The methodology is based on postulation that stock markets are forward-looking and stock prices are simply the discounted value of expected future cash flows to shareholders (Rani et al. 2016). Positive abnormal returns represent value creation for shareholders which could possibly be attributed to improved efficiency, enhanced market power, tax benefits (DePamphilis 2011). Franks and Harris (1989), Cakici et al. (1996), Eckbo and Thorburn (2000), Fuller et al. (2002), Goergen and Renneboog (2004), Moeller et al. (2005), Martynova and Renneboog (2006), Petmezas (2009) find positive abnormal returns, whereas Eckbo (1983), Byrd and Hickman (1992), Datta and Puia (1995), Biswas et al. (1997), Walker (2000) discover negative, and Servaes (1994), Biswas et al. (1997), Mulherin and Boone (2000), Andrade et al. (2001) observe no significant results.

Researches in recent years have reported that excess returns to the acquirer stockholders are influenced by firm-level characteristics such as type of acquirers (public/private, listed/non-listed), form of payment (cash/stock/earn-outs), relative size of acquirer and target.

The analysis of *accounting information* from accounting statements is the *other approach* used widely. This approach analyses how financial performance of acquirers change before and after acquisitions by comparing the reported financial results. The focus of these studies is to analyse the accounting information covering profitability such as EPS, net income, return on equity or assets; also leverage and liquidity Mueller (1980, 1986), Ravenscraft and Scherer (1989), Healy et al. (1992), Cosh et al. (1998), Parrino and Harris (1999), Ghosh and Jain (2000), Yeh and Hoshino (2000), Ghosh (2001), Pawaskar (2001), Gugler et al. (2003), Rahman and Limmack (2004), Ramakrishnan (2008), Rani et al. (2015a).

Bruner (2005) identified factors which determine the success or failure of a merger. He argued that the acquirer is typically governed by the synergies to be realised in the deal. The prime synergies expected by acquirer are cost savings, financial synergies and revenue enhancements. These benefits tend to assume different degrees of measurements from investors' point of view, with several studies showing cost savings discounted the least and the others such as tax-related, new markets, low cost of capital, etc. somewhat more. He noted that 'The popular view is that M&A is a loser's game'.

Grubb and Lamb (2000) investigate the success rate of M&A. They found that only about 20% of all mergers achieve the expected synergies. Majority of mergers typically destroy shareholder wealth. They concluded that mergers fail to create any real financial returns to shareholders.

Kale and Singh (2005), Kumar and Bansal (2008), Selvam et al. (2009), Kumar (2009), Rani et al. (2012) Leepsa and Mishra (2012), Rani et al. (2013, 2015b) have analysed the performance of Indian mergers and observe mixed results.

However, to our best possible understanding, existing research has not investigated the impact of mergers (specially through absorptions) on the shareholders wealth in short run in Indian context. The empirical research in India has not examined the performance of mergers and acquisitions separately. The aim of this chapter is to investigate the impact of mergers only on shareholders wealth in short run. This chapter aims to plug this block by empirically analysing the market response to a sample of Indian mergers through absorption only.

The unique contribution of this work is evaluating mergers in India, as the institutional context in which firms operate in India differs significantly from the environment in advanced economies such as USA and Japan. Khanna and Palepu (2000) termed this difference in institutional environment as 'institutional voids'. They opined as India is an emerging economy with institutional voids. This void is referred to missing market institutions and presence of family business groups, which have implications for Indian acquirers absorbing businesses. Thus, it is interesting to investigate how market reacts to merger deals in India. The objective of the chapter is to examine the abnormal return for the sample of the acquiring firms when target firm is completely absorbed with the operations of the acquiring firm.

4.3 The Process of Merger in Indian Context

As per the Indian regulations, *Merger through consolidation and Merger through absorption* are the two forms of mergers and amalgamations. A merger is a transaction where one firm combines with the other or more businesses into one business for deriving expected benefits/synergies. The term 'amalgamation' is used for merger in Indian regulations. As per Section 21(A) of Income Tax Act 1961, 'amalgamation is the merger of one or more companies with another or the merger of two or more companies to form a new company, in such a way that all assets and liabilities of the amalgamating companies become assets and liabilities of the amalgamated company and shareholders not less than nine-tenths in value of the shares in the amalgamating company or companies become shareholders of the amalgamated company'.

The legal procedures for mergers in India involve the following steps. The various steps of the process are described in Fig. 4.1.

The focus of the present chapter is on acquiring companies opting for mergers through absorption only. The short-term return on the first public announcement of mergers is examined in this chapter.

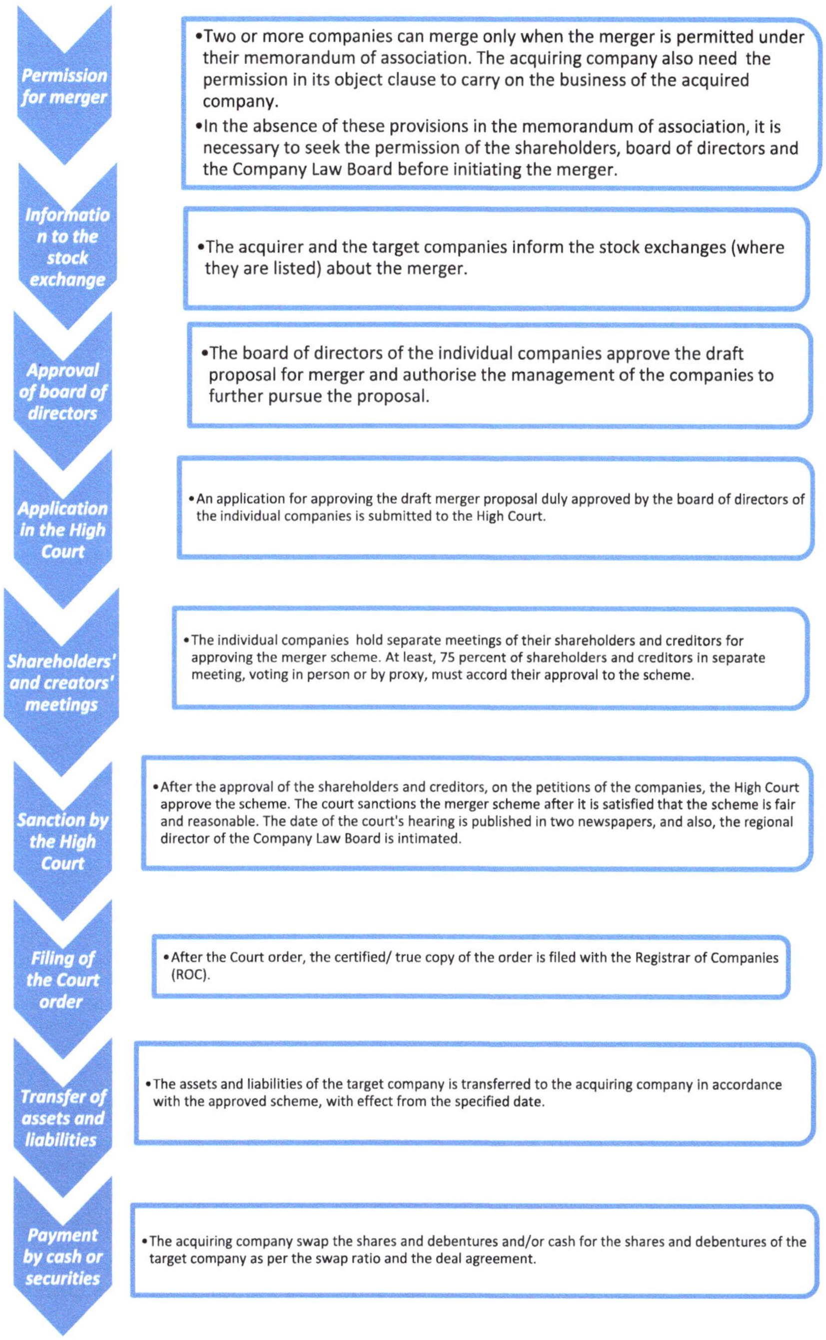

4 Do Mergers Destroy Value in India? 51

Permission for merger
- Two or more companies can merge only when the merger is permitted under their memorandum of association. The acquiring company also need the permission in its object clause to carry on the business of the acquired company.
- In the absence of these provisions in the memorandum of association, it is necessary to seek the permission of the shareholders, board of directors and the Company Law Board before initiating the merger.

Information to the stock exchange
- The acquirer and the target companies inform the stock exchanges (where they are listed) about the merger.

Approval of board of directors
- The board of directors of the individual companies approve the draft proposal for merger and authorise the management of the companies to further pursue the proposal.

Application in the High Court
- An application for approving the draft merger proposal duly approved by the board of directors of the individual companies is submitted to the High Court.

Shareholders' and creators' meetings
- The individual companies hold separate meetings of their shareholders and creditors for approving the merger scheme. At least, 75 percent of shareholders and creditors in separate meeting, voting in person or by proxy, must accord their approval to the scheme.

Sanction by the High Court
- After the approval of the shareholders and creditors, on the petitions of the companies, the High Court approve the scheme. The court sanctions the merger scheme after it is satisfied that the scheme is fair and reasonable. The date of the court's hearing is published in two newspapers, and also, the regional director of the Company Law Board is intimated.

Filing of the Court order
- After the Court order, the certified/ true copy of the order is filed with the Registrar of Companies (ROC).

Transfer of assets and liabilities
- The assets and liabilities of the target company is transferred to the acquiring company in accordance with the approved scheme, with effect from the specified date.

Payment by cash or securities
- The acquiring company swap the shares and debentures and/or cash for the shares and debentures of the target company as per the swap ratio and the deal agreement.

Fig. 4.1 Step-wise legal procedures for mergers in India

There are two crucial terms related to the process of mergers: appointed and effective date. The appointed date signifies the date of absorption/amalgamation. This refers to the date on which the acquirer company absorbs the assets and liabilities of the target company as per agreement. The effective date connotes the completion of all the necessary formalities of the merger.

4.4 Data Sources, Methodology and Scope of Study

Table 4.1 shows the year-wise distribution (2003–2016) of the mergers announced by the listed companies between 1 January 2003 and 31 March 2016. There were 2,473 cases of mergers announced during 1 January 2003 to 31 March 2016, as reported by Centre for Monitoring Indian Economy (CMIE) database Prowess. There are instances of multiple mergers initiated by the same company in a single announcement. Year-wise distribution shows that 1570 companies announced merger deals. But there are companies which made multiple announcements across years. Finally, 1087 companies made 2505 announcements. Out of 2505 announcements of mergers during the period 1 January 2003 to 31 March 2016 available on CMIE database, 142 negotiations were called off or proposal dropped/denial of news. The deals were further checked for mergers through absorption. Mergers through consolidation and amalgamation were not considered. Announcement dates and dates of High Court approval of mergers of the complete transactions are based on information from CMIE database Prowess and have been manually verified from the online archives of Bombay Stock Exchange (BSE). After checking for the confounding activities, 150 companies were left in the sample.

Table 4.2 shows the year-wise distribution (2003–2016) of the number of M&As undergone by the sample companies and the number of announcements of mergers studied between 1 January 2003 and 31 March 2016. Year-wise distribution shows that 425 companies completed deals and the numbers of announcements investigated in the sample of event study. The firms that underwent any significant event such as announcements of dividends or ex-dates on any kind of dividend (stock or cash), bonus shares, within a timeframe of 20 days prior and after the announcement of deal, were excluded from the sample to avoid any possible data contamination or the confounding effect.

The main objective of the present chapter is to investigate the short-term abnormal returns of merger through absorption. The study focuses on the acquiring firm's shareholders. To examine the short-term stock price reaction due to merger announcement, event study methodology has been used.

The first day of the release of information about the event (here, announcement of merger) is termed as the announcement date and we name it as day '0'. Other days are expressed according to the announcement date. Here, the announcement day is defined as the day when the stock exchange receives information about the

4 Do Mergers Destroy Value in India?

Table 4.1 Frequency of announcements of mergers

Year	No. of acquirer companies	No. of target companies
2003	85	147
2004	93	146
2005	137	234
2006	173	284
2007	144	244
2008	118	172
2009	117	199
2010	142	252
2011	142	209
2012	119	160
2013	120	159
2014	83	145
2015	82	122
2016	15	32
Total	1570	2505

Source CMIE prowess

Table 4.2 Distribution of sample, year-wise (2003–2016)

Year	No. of mergers completed	No. of announcements studied
2003	15	9
2004	20	15
2005	18	21
2006	39	31
2007	59	28
2008	28	26
2009	15	4
2010	9	5
2011	18	2
2012	22	1
2013	51	2
2014	48	4
2015	70	1
2016	13	1
Total	425	150

Source CMIE prowess

board approval of the merger and acquisition deal. The dates have been manually verified from the online archives of corporate announcements of stock exchange

The period prior to the occurrence of the event is defined as the estimation period. The estimation window and event window should not overlap, as it ensures that the event-related returns do not influence the estimators of the normal return model. For the study, 255 (−280, −26)-day estimation window has been considered. The event periods are the days before and after the date of the announcement of mergers. The cumulative abnormal returns over alternate windows is also taken into consideration to account for early share price reactions. The study reports average abnormal returns, median abnormal returns, cumulative average abnormal returns and the precision-weighted cumulative average abnormal return (Cowan 1992; Rani et al. 2016). For further insights, one parametric t-test (Brown and Warner 1980) and one non-parametric generalised sign test (Cowan 1992) have been conducted (Rani[1] et al. (2013)). Tables 4.3 and 4.4 report the results.

4.5 Empirical Results and Findings

The results of the event study are summarised in this section. The relevant data contained in Table 4.3 reports the median abnormal returns (MARs), average abnormal returns (AARs), corresponding t-statistic values and GSign Test, the number of the positive and negative ARs, and CAARs for each day in the event window. In addition, Figs. 4.1 and 4.2 present a graphical representation of the value of average abnormal return (AAR) and cumulative average abnormal return (CAAR) corresponding to each day of the event window. AAR, MAR and CAAR proportion of positive and negative average abnormal return along with the t-statistics and of statistical significance for average abnormal return are contained in this table.

Table 4.3 indicates that the pattern of negative AARs starts from 20 days before the announcement day during the pre-announcement window, and the returns are positive for 8 days while they are negative for 12 days. Out of these eight positive AAR values, two values are significant. The negative returns do not show any significance on either of the eight days. The AAR on the announcement day (0) is less than 1% (0.86%); this is maximum and significant (at 5% level). In fact, it has been noted that on the announcement (day 0), 82 out of the total 150 companies observed positive ARs. The positive and significant AARs on the announcement (day 0) indicate that the announcements of mergers are viewed positively by the investors, although the negative reaction post-announcement day indicates that the investors experience abnormal return of negative 5% (−4.70%).

Furthermore, cumulative returns over various size event windows are also calculated to determine the crucial period for investment. Average abnormal returns on the announcement day and cumulative average abnormal returns (CAARs) and the precision-weighted cumulative average abnormal return (PWCAAR) for varying event windows have been analysed. Results are tabulated in Table 4.4.

---

[1]Refer Rani et al. (2013) for detailed discussion of the test.

4 Do Mergers Destroy Value in India?

Table 4.3 Abnormal returns and test statistics on and around merger announcements

Day	Abnormal return Average (%)	Cumulative average (%)	Median (%)	Positive: negative	t-statistic	G sign Z statistic
−20	−0.71	−0.71	−0.55	50:100	−2.083[a]	−2.625[b]
−19	−0.07	−0.79	−0.41	66:84	−0.219	−0.32
−18	−0.24	−1.03	−0.60	60:90	−0.71	−0.947
−17	0.54	−0.49	−0.17	69:81	1.574	0.407
−16	−0.52	−1.02	−0.53	56:91	−1.533	−1.900
−15	0.22	−0.79	−0.08	70:76	0.65	0.495
−14	−0.07	−0.86	−0.43	64:83	−0.198	−0.576
−13	−0.13	−0.99	−0.16	66:78	−0.38	−0.017
−12	−0.27	−1.26	−0.22	67:78	−0.785	0.073
−11	−0.20	−1.46	−0.26	68:76	−0.599	0.317
−10	−0.39	−1.85	−0.51	58:86	−1.131	−1.355
−9	−0.15	−2.01	−0.20	68:79	−0.452	0.086
−8	−0.54	−2.55	−0.40	62:82	−1.593	−0.686
−7	0.56	−1.99	0.04	75:72	1.645	1.245
−6	0.10	−1.89	−0.51	64:81	0.293	−0.427
−5	0.62	−1.26	0.36	81:63	1.828	2.491[a]
−4	−0.39	−1.65	−0.41	63:81	−1.141	−0.519
−3	0.30	−1.36	−0.09	71:73	0.867	0.819
−2	0.83	−0.53	−0.02	72:73	2.414[a]	0.906
−1	0.31	−0.22	−0.21	70:76	0.908	0.495
0	0.86	0.64	0.76	82:68	2.510[a]	2.832[b]
1	−0.40	0.24	−0.83	60:86	−1.167	−1.166
2	−0.14	0.10	−0.33	66:81	−0.398	−0.245
3	−0.84	−0.73	−0.67	55:91	−2.449[a]	−1.996[a]
4	−0.46	−1.19	−0.45	61:84	−1.344	−0.927
5	−0.07	−1.26	−0.92	59:86	−0.203	−1.26
6	−0.80	−2.06	−0.99	56:91	−2.328[a]	−1.900
7	−0.12	−2.18	−0.60	60:86	−0.354	−1.166
8	−0.59	−2.77	−0.65	56:89	−1.715	−1.760
9	0.28	−2.48	0.00	73:73	0.83	0.993
10	−0.31	−2.80	−0.73	55:89	−0.914	−1.857
11	−0.43	−3.23	−0.55	64:80	−1.259	−0.351
12	−0.48	−3.71	−0.67	56:90	−1.411	−1.830
13	−0.17	−3.88	−0.35	64:82	−0.507	−0.502
14	0.15	−3.73	−0.27	65:80	0.446	−0.26
15	0.12	−3.61	−0.30	65:84	0.349	−0.558
16	−0.37	−3.98	−0.29	64:82	−1.093	−0.502
17	0.31	−3.67	−0.11	70:75	0.915	0.573

(continued)

Table 4.3 (continued)

Day	Abnormal return			Positive: negative	t-statistic	G sign Z statistic
	Average (%)	Cumulative average (%)	Median (%)			
18	−0.33	−4.00	−0.45	59:87	−0.973	−1.332
19	−0.06	−4.06	−0.31	67:81	−0.171	−0.155
20	−0.63	−4.70	−0.49	58:87	−1.853	−1.427

[a,b]Denote significance at 5 and 1%, respectively
Source Authors' calculations

Table 4.4 Cumulative average abnormal returns (CAARs) for merger announcements across various event windows

Event window	Average abnormal return			Positive: negative	t-statistic	G sign Z statistic
	Cumulative (%)	Precision-weighted (%)	Median (%)			
(0, 0)	0.86	0.78	0.76	82:68	2.510[a]	2.832[b]
(−20, −2)	−0.50	−9.20	−1.44	68:82	−0.336	−0.065
(−15, −2)	0.48	−4.60	−0.33	73:77	0.378	0.757
(−10, −2)	0.92	−2.88	−0.01	74:76	0.894	0.921
(−5, −2)	1.33	−3.05	−0.55	68:86	1.939	0.01
(−5, 0)	2.44	−4.15	1.17	85:65	2.912[b]	2.730[b]
(−1, 0)	1.14	−1.36	0.56	85:65	2.352[a]	2.900[b]
(0, +1)	0.43	−2.50	0.09	74:76	0.895	1.079
(0, +5)	−1.04	−6.89	−1.62	57:92	−1.245	−1.874
(+2, +5)	−1.48	−4.81	−1.96	53:95	−2.163[a]	−2.464[a]
(+2, +10)	−2.97	−15.19	−4.31	46:103	−2.894[b]	−3.682[b]
(+2, +15)	−3.76	−22.66	−5.61	44:105	−2.938[b]	−4.011[b]
(+2, +20)	−4.82	−29.57	−5.66	44:105	−3.235[b]	−4.011[b]
(−1, +1)	0.74	−3.79	0.40	76:74	1.243	1.33
(−2, +2)	1.40	−4.73	0.87	82:67	1.831	2.236[a]
(−5, +5)	0.58	−10.48	−1.10	69:80	0.51	0.099
(−10, +10)	−1.32	−19.19	−3.61	66:83	−0.843	−0.394
(−20, +20)	−4.59	−37.90	−3.73	65:85	−2.097[a]	−0.723

[a,b]Denote significance at 5 and 1%, respectively
Source Authors' calculations

The calculation of CARs also helps in assessing the net magnitude of the overall returns. The results presented in Table 4.4 indicate that CAAR begin to appear positive from the third day prior to the announcement day; observe a positive pattern only till the announcement day of the event window. The CAAR value of twentieth day in the pre-event window starts from negative 0.71% and reaches to a peak of almost 0.86% on the announcement day and settles at negative 4.57% on the last day of the event window.

It is worth noting that the precision-weighted cumulative average abnormal return is negative for all the windows except the day of announcement although the cumulative abnormal returns for the event window (−5, 0) are positive and significant, and the PWCAAR is negative. It indicates the presence of high event-induced variance. It is also evident from the relevant data presented in Table 4.5. There is a difference of up to the extent of 31% in the standard deviation of abnormal returns during various event windows and standard deviation of returns in estimation window of 255 days.

The graphs presented in Figs. 4.2 and 4.3 also corroborate the findings. It is evident from the graph of CAAR (Fig. 4.3) that CAAR declines drastically after the event.

Table 4.5 Event-induced variance of abnormal returns

Standard deviation of returns during estimation window	
(−280, −26)	0.04
Standard deviation of abnormal returns during event window	
(0, 0)	0.04
(−20, −2)	0.22
(−15, −2)	0.17
(−10, −2)	0.14
(−5, −2)	0.09
(−5, 0)	0.11
(−1, 0)	0.06
(0, +1)	0.07
(0, +5)	0.12
(+2, +5)	0.09
(+2, +10)	0.15
(+2, +15)	0.19
(+2, +20)	0.22
(−1, +1)	0.09
(−2, +2)	0.11
(−5, +5)	0.17
(−10, +10)	0.26
(−20, +20)	0.35

Source Authors' calculations

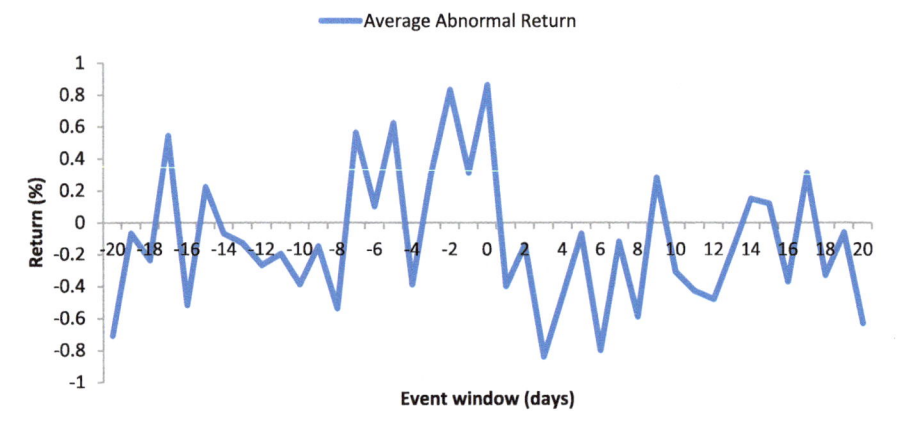

Fig. 4.2 Average abnormal returns around announcement, (−20, +20) days event window

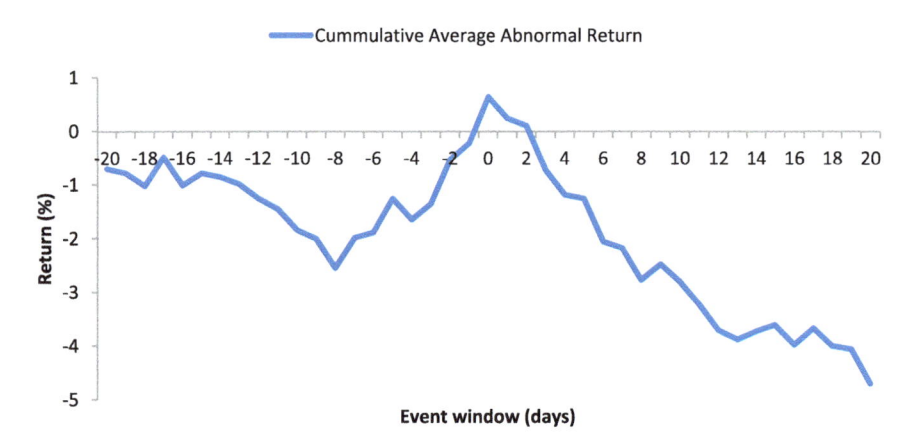

Fig. 4.3 Cumulative average abnormal returns around announcement, (−20, +20) days event window

4.6 Conclusion

Merger is a strategy used by firms to increase their profitability by realising synergies, scaling up their operations and expanding their portfolios. A merger is thus a tool where two or more firms enter into a legal contract to combine their operations into a single firm. Mergers can be executed through absorption or through amalgamation/consolidation. In a merger through absorption, the acquirer is the surviving company which retains the identity and transfers all the assets and liabilities of the merged companies. An amalgamation is a process where two or more firms combine to form a new one. In amalgamation, all the existing firms are dissolved as compared to absorption where the acquiring firm retains the identity. Thus, in merger/absorption terminology, the firm that has been acquired/absorbed is known as the target firm and the firm that acquires is known as the acquiring firm. A fundamental characteristic of merger (either through absorption or consolidation) is that the acquiring company (existing or new) takes over the ownership of other companies and combines their operations with its own operations. A fundamental characteristic of merger (either through absorption or consolidation) is that the acquiring company (existing or new) obtains the right to ownership of all the existing entities.

The present chapter analyses the short-term performance of the announcement of mergers through absorption during the period 2003–2016. Empirical findings suggest mixed results. However, the abnormal returns are positive on announcement. We find that shareholders of Indian acquiring companies experience negative abnormal returns over event window of 41 days (−20, +20) while opting for mergers through absorption. Mergers are used as a tool for reviving sick or potentially sick firms. Perhaps that is one of the reasons for this mixed reaction. However, the results suggest occurrence of high event-induced variance in abnormal return. The present study reports a high event-induced variance in the average abnormal return due to the announcement of mergers through absorption.

Mergers represent an effective mechanism to transfer the resources to the entity where they are most needed by releasing and removing the resources where they are underperforming. The empirical evidence presented in this chapter suggests that the manager should clearly state the synergies expected from the transaction at all the steps involved to complete the transaction.

The present study's scope is limited to the evaluation of the performance of acquiring firms only on the first public announcement of the merger. However, the understanding of step-wise performance can be taken up separately. Because the completion of merger in India is a complex legal process consisting of various steps as described in Sect. 4.3, also, a study on the dynamic process of merger leading to ultimate absorption will further deepen the understanding of mergers. Does market respond differently to the announcements of completion of various steps is another query which needs further attention.

References

Andrade, G., Mitchell, M., & Stafford, E. (2001). New evidence and perspectives on mergers. *Journal of Economic Perspectives, 15*(2), 103–120.

Biswas, R., Fraser, D. R., & Mahajan, A. (1997). The international market for corporate control: Evidence from acquisitions of financial firms. *Global Finance Journal, 8*(1), 33–54.

Brown, S. J., & Warner, J. B. (1980). Measuring security price performance. *Journal of Financial Economics, 8*(3), 205–258.

Bruner, R. F. (2005). *Deals from hell: M&A lessons that rise above the ashes.* New York: John Wiley & Sons.

Byrd, J. W., & Hickman, K. A. (1992). Do outside directors monitor managers? *Journal of Financial Economics, 32*(2), 195–221.

Cakici, N., Hessel, C., & Tandom, K. (1996). Foreign acquisitions in the United States: Effect on shareholder wealth of foreign acquiring firms. *Journal of Banking and Finance, 20*(2), 307–329.

Cosh, A., Hughes, A., Lee, K., & Singh, A. (1998). Takeovers, institutional investment and the persistence of profits. In I. Begg & B. Henry (Eds.), *Applied Economics and Public Policy* (pp. 107–144). Department of Applied Economics Occasional Paper No. 63, Cambridge University Press, Cambridge. Available at: www.cbr.cam.ac.uk/pdf/wp030.pdf.

Cowan, A. R. (1992). Nonparametric event study tests. *Review of Quantitative Finance and Accounting, 2*(4), 343–358.

Datta, D. K., & Puia, G. (1995). Cross-border acquisitions: An examination of the influence of relatedness and cultural fit on shareholder value creation in US acquiring firms. *Management International Review, 35*(4), 337–359.

DePamphilis, D. (2011). *Mergers, acquisitions, and other restructuring activities*. London: Academic Press.

Eckbo, B. E. (1983). Horizontal mergers, collusion, and stockholder wealth. *Journal of Financial Economics, 11*(1), 241–273.

Eckbo, B. E., & Thorburn, K. S. (2000). Gains to bidder firms revisited: Domestic and foreign acquisitions in Canada. *Journal of Financial and Quantitative Analysis, 35*(1), 1–25.

Franks, J. R., & Harris, R. S. (1989). Shareholder wealth effects of corporate takeovers: The U.K. experience 1955–1985. *Journal of Financial Economics, 23*(2), 225–249.

Fuller, K., Netter, J., & Stegmoller, M. (2002). What do returns to acquiring firms tell us? Evidence from firms that make many acquisitions. *Journal of Finance, 57*(4), 1763–1793.

Ghosh, A. (2001). Does operating performance really improve following corporate acquisition? *Journal of Corporate Finance, 7*(2), 151–178.

Ghosh, A., & Jain, P. C. (2000). Financial leverage changes associated with corporate mergers. *Journal of Corporate Finance, 6*(4), 377–402.

Goergen, M., & Renneboog, L. (2004). Shareholder wealth effects of European domestic and cross-border takeover bids. *European Financial Management, 10*(1), 9–45.

Grubb, T., & Lamb, R. (2000). *Capitalize on merger chaos* (pp. 9–14). New York: Free Press.

Gugler, K., Mueller, D. C., Yurtoglu, B., & Zulehner, C. (2003). The effects of mergers: An international comparison. *International Journal of Industrial Organization, 21*(5), 625–653.

Healy, P. M., Palepu, K. G., & Ruback, R. S. (1992). Does corporate performance improve after mergers? *Journal of Financial Economics, 31*(2), 135–175.

Kale, P., & Singh, H. (2005). Acquisitions and alliances: Indian companies and value creation. *TMTC Journal of Management, 3*(January), 13–18.

Khanna, T., & Palepu, K. (2000). Is group affiliation profitable in emerging markets? An analysis of diversified Indian business groups. *The Journal of Finance, 55*(2), 867–891.

Kumar, R. (2009). Post merger corporate performance an Indian perspective. *Management Research Review, 32*(2), 145–157.

Kumar, S., & Bansal, L. K. (2008). The impact of mergers and acquisitions on corporate performance in India. *Management Decision, 46*(10), 1531–1543.

Leepsa, N. M., & Mishra, C. S. (2012). Post merger financial performance: A study with reference to select manufacturing companies in India. *International Research Journal of Finance and Economics, 83*(83), 6–17.

Martynova, M., & Renneboog, L. (2006) Mergers and acquisitions in Europe. ECGI—Finance Working Paper No. 114/2006; Center Discussion Paper Series No. 2006–06. Available at SSRN: http://ssrn.com/abstract=880379.

Moeller, S. B., Schlingemann, F. P., & Stulz, R. M. (2005). Wealth destruction on a massive scale? *A Study of Acquiring-Firm Returns in the Recent Merger Wave, Journal of Finance, 60*(2), 757–782.

Mueller, D. (1980). *The determinants and effects of mergers: An international comparison*. Gunn and Hain, Cambridge, MA: Oelgeschlager.

Mueller, D. C. (1986). *Profits in the long run*. Cambridge, New York: Cambridge University Press.

Mulherin, J. H., & Boone, A. L. (2000). Comparing acquisitions and divestitures. *Journal of Corporate Finance, 6*(2), 117–139.

Parrino, J. D., & Harris, R. S. (1999). Takeovers management and replacements, and post-acquisition operating performance: Some evidence from 1980s. *Journal of Applied Corporate Finance, 11*(4), 88–97.

Pawaskar, V. (2001). Effect of mergers on corporate performance in India. *Vikalpa, 26*(1), 19–32.

Petmezas, D. (2009). What drives acquisitions? Market valuations and bidder performance. *Journal of Multinational Financial Management, 19*(1), 54–74.

Rahman, R. A., & Limmack, R. J. (2004). Corporate acquisitions and the operating performance of malaysian companies. *Journal of Business Finance and Accounting, 31*(3/4), 359–400.

Ramakrishnan, K. (2008). Long-term post-merger performance of firms in India. *Vikalpa, 33*(2), 47–63.

Rani, N., Yadav, S. S., & Jain, P. K. (2012). Impact of mergers and acquisitions on returns to shareholders of acquiring firms: Indian economy in perspective. *Journal of Financial Management and Analysis, 25*(1), 1–26.

Rani, N., Yadav, S. S., & Jain, P. K. (2013). The impact of domestic acquisitions on acquirer shareholders' wealth in India. *Global Journal of Flexible Management System, 13*(4), 179–193.

Rani, N., Yadav, S. S., & Jain, P. K. (2015a). Financial performance analysis of mergers and acquisitions: Evidence from India. *International Journal of Commerce and Management, 25*(4), 402–423.

Rani, N., Yadav, S. S., & Jain, P. K. (2015b) Innovative mode of financing and abnormal returns to shareholders of indian acquiring firms. In Sushil & G. Chroust (Eds.), *Systemic Flexibility and Business Agility, Flexible Systems Management* (pp. 367–383). New Delhi: Springer.

Rani, N., Yadav, Surendra S., & Jain, P. K. (2016). *Mergers and acquisitions: A study of financial performance*. Motives and Corporate Governance: Springer Verlag.

Ravenscraft, D. J., & Scherer, F. M. (1989). The profitability of mergers. *International Journal of Industrial Organization, 7*(1), 101–116.

Selvam, M., Babu, M., Indumathi, G., & Ebenezer, B. (2009). Impact of mergers on the corporate performance of acquirer and target companies in India. *Journal of Accounting and Auditing, 5*(11), 55–64.

Servaes, H. (1994). Do takeover targets overinvest? *Review of Financial Studies, 7*(2), 253.

Walker, M. M. (2000). Corporate takeovers, strategic objectives, and acquiring-firm shareholder wealth. *Financial Management, 29*(1), 53.

Yeh, T. M., & Hoshino, Y. (2000). The effects of mergers and acquisitions on Taiwanese corporations. *Review of Pacific Basin Financial Markets and Policies, 3*(2), 183–199.

Zola, M., & Meier, D. (2008). What is M&A performance? *Academy of Management Perspectives, 22*(3), 55–77.

Chapter 5
Law and the Operation of Global Value Chains: Challenges at the Intersection of Systematisation and Flexibility

Kevin Sobel-Read and Madeleine MacKenzie

Abstract Flexibility makes it possible for firms to be nimble, responsive and resilient. At the same time, a range of economic, operational and social factors are steadily causing supply chains—in the form of global value chains—to become more systemically integrated. Flexibility and chain integration, however, are in many ways mutually exclusive. This chapter explores some of the results of this tension. In particular, the chapter shows how the chain integration processes in play today are having potentially unforeseen consequences on the ability of firms to enter into flexible relationships. Historically, through the use of contract relationships rather than vertical integration, firms were simultaneously able to increase flexibility and limit potential liability caused by their suppliers. But because of ongoing global value chain integration, this protection from liability is currently eroding: lead firms are becoming liable for the conduct of suppliers, even when they enter into arm's-length contract relationships with those suppliers. The result is that even as the law of contracts continues to permit flexibility in chain operation, the law more broadly is coming to infuse that operational flexibility with liability for conduct by other actors in the chain—actors who are connected by contract alone, or even by strings of contracts. The chapter further discusses the factors that are driving this shift towards greater liability as well as some of the key practical consequences.

Keywords Flexibility · Global value chains · Law · Legal liability Systemic integration

K. Sobel-Read (✉) · M. MacKenzie
University of Newcastle, Newcastle, Australia
e-mail: kevin.sobel-read@newcastle.edu.au

5.1 Introduction

In the operation of supply chains, there is an inescapable tension between flexibility and chain integration. That is, in today's landscape, two phenomena are taking place simultaneously. On the one hand, many firms are seeking increased flexibility in their relationships with suppliers in order to more nimbly adapt to, among other things, market fluctuations. On the other hand, for many reasons which will be discussed below, supply chains—in the form of global value chains—are becoming more systemically integrated.

In this tension between flexibility and chain integration, two particular aspects emerge as central: control and liability. These concepts have been integral to supply chain operation for decades. And perhaps precisely because of this solid historical foundation, it might appear that the roles of both control and liability in supply chain operation are stable and static.

Today, however, there is a nascent shift in the ways that control and liability impact supply chains. In order to explore this shift, this chapter situates global value chains within the current state of the law. Through a conceptual analysis—and with some assistance from anthropology—it becomes evident that the intersection of law and global value chains is a dynamic one. In this dynamic scenario, the role of control over a supply chain, as well as the potential for liability within it, is changing: the relationship between control and liability is not what it once was. In this chapter, we provide some suggestions as to the consequences of these changes on supply chain operation.

In performing this analysis, we interrogate what the law contributes in regard to these developments. It is interesting to note that the law tends to receive very little attention in the scholarship on global value chains. Part of our purpose is to illustrate why the law deserves greater attention in these regards.

5.2 Background

5.2.1 Flexibility

In the current marketplace, it is difficult for firms to create a sustainable competitive advantage by depending only on their own strengths. 'Fine slicing' of the supply chain allows firms to specialise in a particular function and together take advantage of their different capabilities to provide a more competitive consumer offering. The fragmentation of supply chains has allowed firms to reduce costs, increase organisational agility, unlock previously unattainable resources and reach customers in different markets.

The process of globalisation has created novel opportunities for this fragmentation of production (Amador and Cabral 2016). Liberalisation of international trade has provided the legal and economic environment for firms to operate across jurisdictions and a reduction in transaction costs has generated further incentive. Firms are now able to take better advantage of the differences between their operating environments. For example, wage laws in one location may make it more affordable to complete repetitive, labour-intensive tasks in that location, while research and development may be better completed in a location with a highly educated population and favourable innovation policies. The increasing interconnectedness of the global economy, arising from technological progress, has further enabled this process.

While flexibility analysis was once confined to the internal capabilities of manufacturing firms, there is now a burgeoning area of academic literature concerning the flexibility of supply chains as a system of production (Singh and Acharya 2014). Within this field, flexibility has been interpreted in a variety of different ways and there is no general agreement as to its definition (Kumar et al. 2006). In general terms, at least, it may be described as the ability to change or react with little penalty in time, effort, cost or performance (Upton 1994). It similarly concerns the ability of the supply chain to respond to fluctuations occurring within their surrounding environment, including consumer preferences, customer attributes, legal or political changes, economic factors and technological advancements.

The concept of 'flexibility' therefore speaks to several aspects of supply chain operation. Sethi and Sethi (1990), for instance, have identified fifty different types of flexibility along functional lines. More contemporary literature tends to focus on twenty-two different types, grouped under the umbrellas of upstream exterior flexibility, interior flexibility and downstream exterior flexibility (Tiwari et al. 2015). Upstream exterior flexibility largely depends on the activities of suppliers and relationship management procedures. It includes sourcing, demand management, information systems and coordination flexibility. Interior flexibility refers to the ability of each individual enterprise to respond to changing circumstances. It includes manufacturing, product, machine, labour, routing, volume, process, operation, new product development, postponement and material handling flexibilities. Downstream exterior flexibility largely depends on the logistics or post-production capabilities of the supply chain. It includes trans-shipment, logistics, delivery, access and response to market flexibility.

Lee (2004), by contrast, focuses on three overlapping conceptual categories of flexibility: adaptability, alignment and agility. The adaptability of the supply chain describes the ability of the chain's design to adjust in response to structural shifts in consumer markets. This might include modifying the chain composition, the product offered or the technology used. The alignment of the supply chain refers to the nature of the relationships between the firms and the extent to which one firm may govern the others. Supply chain agility concerns the ability of the supply chain to respond to temporary shocks in demand or supply.

Across these many definitional approaches, the primary driver of flexibility is uncertainty. Nevertheless, uncertainty may manifest itself in a variety of different ways, each of which affects a different aspect of flexibility (Tiwari et al. 2015). For example, uncertainties in consumer demand for a particular product are likely to encourage flexibility at the downstream end of the supply chain, involving logistics and distribution, or the development of the supply chain in a way that rarely involves a transfer of risk between firms. On the other hand, uncertainty in the supply of resources from upstream suppliers is likely to encourage flexibility at the upper end of the chain, or the creation of an inventory buffer (Tachizawa and Thomsen 2007).

Either way, flexibility in a supply chain environment must, necessarily, be primarily concerned with the relationship *between* firms in the supply chain; this distinguishes it from single enterprise flexibility (Xiao 2015). The risk that production will not occur on time, that bottlenecks will occur or that other unforeseen supply issues will arise can often be traced back to a lack of discipline within a supply chain and imperfect information among firms (Linawati 2017). Flexible supply chains are those that are able to respond—across firms—without changing their entire design (Singh and Acharya 2014).

The ability to respond, flexibly, invokes efficiency concerns. Indeed, some scholars have suggested that flexibility also leads to reduced efficiency and increased costs (Linawati 2017), particularly where the supply chain involves small-scale firms that may struggle to focus on flexibility, costs and efficiency simultaneously (Ebben and Johnson 2005). However, recent value chain analysis would suggest that this is not the case more generally. Although there may be a point where cost and efficiency losses exceed the benefits of additional fragmentation, the point at which this occurs is becoming increasingly distant as transaction costs decrease (Gereffi and Lee 2012). In economic terms, therefore, a firm must increase flexibility to the point where its marginal benefits are equal to marginal costs.

To test these outcomes, recent scholars have sought to model supply chain flexibility in a conceptual, empirical and mathematical sense (Tiwari et al. 2015). Broadly speaking, this body of research confirms that the flexibility coefficient of a supply chain is primarily a function of time and cost. That is to say, each link in the chain may adjust to meet changes in their surrounding environment in a relatively short time at a higher cost, or a longer period of time at a lower cost (Xiao 2015). Successful supply chains will look to find ways to minimise the pay-off. In this respect, both empirical studies and mathematical models have been used to demonstrate a significant positive correlation between knowledge and information sharing and cost in respect of supply chain flexibility (Gavirneni et al. 1999; Blome et al. 2014).

The research also highlights the importance of 'dynamic matching' along the chain. While each firm will invariably attract a different flexibility coefficient—arising from the inputs they are working with and their internal capabilities—the flexibility of the chain as a whole depends on minimising the variance between adjacent firms (Xiao 2015). This leads to obvious incentive problems. Each firm, rationally acting in its own self-interest, may seek to achieve a different flexibility coefficient. As a result, there may be large variations in flexibility along the chain. This highlights the impact of governance on supply chain performance (Tiwari et al. 2015).

5.2.2 Global Value Chains

In excess of two-thirds of all transnational trade is now conducted by multinational corporations (Cattaneo et al. 2013), and half of that trade takes place between corporate subsidiaries (Altenburg 2006; Sikkaa and Willmott 2010). For a range of reasons that have been discussed elsewhere (Sobel-Read 2014), what were once strings of corporate *supply* chains have developed into what a group of scholars have come to term global *value* chains (Kaplinsky 2004; Gereffi et al. 2005; Humphrey and Schmitz 2008). That is, it was previously the case that large corporations—in some instances individually and in others through one-to-one supplier relationships—created, manufactured and sold a given product (Gereffi and Fernandez-Stark 2011). Today, however, the research, design, production and retail of most products are performed through coordinated chain components that now stretch systemically across complex networks of firms; in other words, through global value chains (Cattaneo et al. 2013).

The insights gained from global value chain analysis, along with the models it has generated, have been adopted by the World Trade Organisation, the World Bank and the Organisation for Economic Cooperation and Development (OECD, WTO and World Bank Group 2014; Gereffi 2014). Most importantly, these insights show that global supply chains have become more systemic, connecting powerful lead companies in developed countries not only with a multitude of intermediaries but also with labourers and farmworkers in disparate locations around the world (Kaplinsky 2004). As one example, Cafaggi et al. provide an in-depth analysis of coffee-bean growers in Brazil. Therefore, reasons ranging from efficiency to reputation, Italian roaster Illy has begun to directly coordinate local growers in regard to activities as diverse as 'technological transfer, quality management and control, and packing and transportation' (Cafaggi et al. 2012). This newly systemic trend is common across global value chains, even if the scope varies across industries.

We might say that, unlike the separate link-to-link nature of global *supply* chains, global *value* chains are marked by a *fusion* of the links: in form and function, global value chains are increasingly integrated processes.

In the literature, there are four factors that are driving this process of chain integration. First, there is efficiency. Multinational businesses are becoming more aware of the inefficiencies of fragmentation. These range from the transaction costs of maintaining so many suppliers to the managerial difficulties of coordinating them. In a global value chain world, profit is the product of the full range of activity pursued by the chain. In following, by minimising inefficiencies across the chain, a lead firm can maximise that profit (Kaplinsky 2004). This minimisation of inefficiencies requires increased coordination by the lead firm, a consequence of which is greater integration.

Second, 'differentiation' is becoming an increasingly central strategy in the marketing and sale of products. In short, because global competition is limiting firms' ability to compete on price alone, many multinational corporations are turning to strategies of differentiation, which often entail claims regarding the source, quality or composition of a good or product. Relatedly, firms have become increasingly cognisant of the significant value to be derived through differentiation in the form of more targeted market research and segmentation. In this way, the adaptation of product and service offerings to meet changing patterns of consumption has become an important source of value creation. Cavusoglu and Raghunathan (2007) use the example of Frito-Lay, who have increased the number of potato chip varieties they offer from 10 to 78. In 2010, UK customers were able to purchase a Volkswagen Polo in 52.6 billion different configurations (Felipe Scavarda et al. 2010). Both the ability to make and sustain claims about differentiation, as well as the agility necessary to meet these diverse and changing customer demands (Gligor 2014), require coordination across the chain, and therefore greater integration.

Third, control by lead firms over the entire supply chain is becoming ever more necessary in order to limit risks to the firms' reputation—and thus risks to sales and profits—stemming from high-profile disclosures of poor labour conditions at, or environmental harms caused by, suppliers (Conley and Williams 2005; Lin 2009). Nike is one of the now-classic examples here. This growing public awareness of social and environmental issues has led consumer-facing firms to self-impose conduct and quality standards on their product offerings, across their chains (Gereffi and Lee 2012). The result, again, is greater chain integration.

And fourth, mounting pressures on quality control throughout the chain are likewise driving lead firms to more stringently coordinate their supply chains. These pressures have many sources, including the changing requirements of public regulation (for instance, stricter food safety laws) and emerging demands to satisfy third-party standards (such as fair trade certification). The consequence, yet again, is further chain integration.

5.2.3 Law

Law is important in regard to global supply chains for three key reasons. First, law imposes restraints on ways that commerce can take place. This role—as a restraint—is arguably how law is often seen by business actors: as a *barrier* to avoid or to overcome.

The law imposes these restraints in different ways. On the one hand, the government laws of any implicated countries, together with international law, provide the boundaries of the 'playing field' on which any international commerce takes place. On the other hand, the law sets the possible parameters of each individual transaction, including the relationships between the parties. This is largely done by means of the laws that govern contracts and those that regulate corporate–subsidiary relationships. Hence, in regard to what a firm must do in order to be compliant with a contract, and what the circumstances are that justify deviation from that performance, it is the law that will provide the answer. The law likewise imposes limitations on interfirm relationships, just as it does on leadership actions.

As such, the level of control that a parent firm holds over a subsidiary, as well as the circumstances under which shareholders can sue corporate directors for poor business decisions, are all prescribed by the law. Consequently, the role of law as a barrier is certainly true—in part, at least. But the reality is that the law plays a much larger role in commerce than this aspect alone.

So second, in a broader sense, the law also creates the infrastructure for international commerce to be possible in the first place. This is because in order to permit transnational commerce, each country's laws are set up so as to interface with the laws of other countries, that is to say, to allow that commerce to take place across the jurisdictions. In other words, the law actually *creates* connections, especially international ones. This could be compared with an analogy concerning compatible nozzles on different-sized hoses.

Law, therefore, is the procedural mechanism that allows nation states to do business with other nation states. Indeed, the countries of the world differ from each other, sometimes in stark contrast from one another in the values that they hold and in the ways that they function. Still, by historical convention—and as facilitated by and driven by global commerce—each country is constructed on a particular model of modern statehood. As such, each has an identifiable government, a head of state, a police department, a customs office, an immigration office, a flag, etc. In other words, in order for a nation to be a state, it must adhere to at least a minimum set of rules—it must look like what it has come to be agreed that a 'state' should look like.

Crucial here is the fact that each nation state must operate by laws that allow it to interface with other nation states. These laws—including customs and immigration laws, not to mention contract laws and judicial enforcement mechanisms—'translate each set of domestic laws into a global lingua franca' (Sobel-Read 2016). In this way, global commerce becomes possible: each transaction, from the simple purchase of a good to be shipped from an international location, to direct foreign investment and the ownership of subsidiaries, becomes possible through the interface of two (or more) legal systems.

And third, in a narrower sense but of equal importance, law creates the means for links between the firms in a supply chain. This occurs in two different ways: via the contracts that link arm's-length transactions or relationships, and via the rules that bind vertically integrated firms. These two different kinds of relationships are organised by, and subject to, two completely separate bodies of law, that is to say, two completely different sets of rules:

$$\text{contracts} \rightarrow \text{contract law}$$
$$\text{vertical integration} \rightarrow \text{corporate/company law}$$

Global value chains are, of course, characterised by multiple firms—whether a few, a hundred or a thousand. Therefore, the links *between* the firms must be of central significance because it is the links that hold the chain together; here, law is the glue of the links.

5.2.4 Anthropology

Anthropology is relevant here because the law does not occur in a vacuum. Instead, law is driven by both reason and perception. That is to say, policy decisions are made based on what we think the world looks like—and should look like—at any given moment.

Anthropology teaches us that all people, all groups, grow up firmly believing that the way they do things is 'normal' (Douglas 2002). And most believe that because their way of doing things is 'normal' it is also therefore 'better' and therefore '*right*'.

But for at least two simple reasons, anthropologists have shown that there is no real 'normal' or 'right way'. First, every group on the planet currently does things differently as compared to how they used to do things in the past (see Wolf 1997). So we know that the concepts of 'normal' and 'right' are not static but instead must always be changing. Second, every group on the planet does many—and sometimes most—things differently from each other (see Geertz 2000). So no one group has a monopoly on the concepts of what is 'normal' or 'right'.

'Normal' and 'right', therefore, are just snapshots of what a given group believes at any particular time. However, those perceptions and understandings are also dynamic and subject to change, whether driven by internal forces or external ones.

This applies equally to the laws that currently structure global commerce. In other words, even though we are at a moment where a certain kind of regulation of chain activity might seem 'normal' or even 'right', we know that this legal infrastructure is dynamic and not only can but will change.

In regard to this dynamism, keep in mind that the regulation of commerce in general, and of supply chains in particular, has *always* been changing and developing. Indeed, corporations, for instance, have not even always had the right to sue and be sued.

5.3 Discussion

5.3.1 The Changing Relationship of Control and Liability

Against that background, we turn now to issues of flexibility and chain integration, and likewise of control and liability. As we have seen, there are two means for firms to link in a supply chain: by arm's-length relationships and through vertical integration. There are, further, two bodies of law that match up to those two means, namely contract law for arm's-length relationships and company/corporate law for vertical integration.

Historically, firms typically managed flexibility and control in their supply chains by turning to arm's-length contract relationships when they wanted flexibility, and to vertical integration when they wanted control. At the same time, the likelihood (or lack thereof) that a given firm would be *liable* for the actions of other firms in the chain mapped effectively onto this flexibility/integration paradigm.

That is to say, control and liability went largely hand-in-hand. So the more control a given firm had over the actions of a supplier firm, the more likely it was that the lead firm would be liable for actions taken by those other firms. In this way, where firms were vertically integrated, the lead firm usually had a great deal of control and was relatively likely to be liable; and where firms engaged in arm's-length relationships by contract, the lead firm tended to have little control and a very low likelihood of liability for any action by the supplier. In sum, as things stood:

$$\text{vertical integration} = \text{control} + \text{liability}$$
$$\text{contract} = \text{flexibility} + \text{freedom from liability}$$

This relationship held true through much of the 1900s and into the current century. However, we are now in a new era. Because of transformations in the way that global business operates, because of changes in the law and because of perceptions about global value chains, an evolving paradigm shift is occurring. Most significantly, considerable control is now also occurring across contracts. This shift opens up new possibilities for firms but as a result it simultaneously creates new risks for liability.

As noted, flexibility is important for operating businesses and supply chains, based on the need to adapt to market fluctuations and so forth. Concurrently, there is also, as discussed previously, growing inertia pushing towards chain integration. So firms, especially lead firms, are for many reasons frequently seeking an *increase* in flexibility in their relationships with suppliers, but at the same time are being forced to push for greater integration across the chain.

The result is that these integration processes are having potentially unforeseen consequences that may forever change firms' ability to enter into flexible relationships. This is because, for several reasons, lead firms are becoming liable for the conduct of suppliers, *even when* they enter into arm's-length contract relationships with those suppliers.

This shift towards greater liability is driven by two things: changes in perceptions and changes in the law. First (and here we see the contribution from anthropology), as the general public and policy-makers come to see supply chains as integrated entities, the more the policy choices and rules about those supply chains will come to reflect that integration by imposing rules on entire chains, even when only connected by contracts.

These changing perceptions, in turn, are coming from both the outside (exogenous factors) and the inside (endogenous factors). In regard to the outside, the Nike example referred to above is illustrative. In the 1990s, publicity emerged showing that Nike products were being manufactured through using what was referred to as 'slave labour'. Even though Nike did not in fact have a legal relationship with those factories, it immediately became clear that in the eyes of the public, Nike and its suppliers should be considered together, relationally binding one to the other. From the inside perspective, one frequently sees in firms' own documents, including government filings and websites, the reference to the firm itself, together with its supply chain, as 'we' and 'us'.

Second, in line with these changes in perception, law is increasingly positioning itself so as to be able to impose liability on firms for conduct by other actors in the chain—actors who are connected by contract alone, or even by strings of contracts. This process is occurring in multiple areas of law.

5.3.2 New Models of Control and Liability: Examples of the Insertion of Law into Supply Chain Operation

What we see, therefore, is that the framework and the seeds already exist for liability across a chain, even though liability is not *yet* required in many instances. But as the general public and policy-makers alike continue to see entire global value chains as integrated entities, we may soon be at the tipping point such that these existing frameworks are revised to impose actual liability.

Here are several examples.

Violations of due diligence: The United Nations Guiding Principles on Business and Human Rights demonstrate ever more thorough attention on processes of due diligence, along with heightening expectations of corporate compliance. Though not legally enforceable, the Principles create a global benchmark, representing a softer type of market-based regulation (Backer 2016). That is, the Principles create a reputational risk for businesses that do not adhere, in terms of their relationships with regulators as well as with consumers, at a time when ethical consumerism is increasing. Completion of the due diligence requirements may also, in some jurisdictions, create a legal safe harbour for companies that are subject to legal proceedings (McGregor and Smit 2017). At any rate, these Principles demonstrate an incremental shift towards the imposition of liability.

Anti-trafficking statutes: The California Transparency in Supply Chains Act of 2010, S. 657, 2009–2010 Sess. (Cal. 2010), imposes reporting requirements on companies regarding their 'efforts to eradicate slavery and human trafficking from its direct supply chain for tangible goods offered for sale' (Sec. 3(a)(1)). It should be noted, however, that the requirement is not triggered until a company has over $100 million in annual worldwide gross receipts. Nevertheless, we see that although it is only a reporting requirement, it still sows the seeds for the actual imposition of liability.

Traceability statutes: These statutes require that a lead firm must be able to trace foodstuffs that they sell through each of its suppliers back to the farmer. They exist for purposes of being able to localise and contain contamination and other agricultural health hazards that might occur (Rowan 2002; Kumar, Heustis and Graham 2015). Such legislation exists in the EU and the US and elsewhere (see, for example, Articles 14, 16, 18 and 19 of the General Food Law Regulation

(EC) 178/2002 and Food Safety Modernization Act 2011 s 204(d)(2)). Like the UN Guiding Principles and the California Transparency in Supply Chains Act, these statutes do not necessarily impose liability on the lead firm because of its control per se; but again, potential is there for such actual imposition. Requiring a lead firm to maintain knowledge of their supply chain is a significant increase in responsibility. It is not too difficult to imagine the legislature taking the next step and penalising the whole supply chain where it is determined, for example, that imported foodstuffs have originated from an infected area.

Judicial case law: A final example involves corporate subsidiaries rather than contract relationships, but supports the same conclusions. The issue here is under what circumstances a lead firm can be found to be *negligent* for the unlawful conduct of its subsidiaries. Historically, this risk of liability was almost nil. That said, a recent Canadian case shows that changing perceptions by judges are leading to expanding scopes of liability. In *Choc v. Hudbay Minerals Inc.* (2013 ONSC 1414 (Can.)), a judge refused to dismiss an action that was filed against a Canadian parent company. The plaintiffs, who were a group of Indigenous Mayan Q'eqchi' from Guatemala, claimed that the parent company should have done more to protect employees from gang rape, murder and other atrocities occurring at the hands of security personnel working for a *subsidiary* of the parent. To be clear, the judge did not decide that the parent *had* committed a wrong and was liable, but the judge was willing to at least hear evidence on the subject—which is a fairly significant development in the state of the law.

5.3.3 *Consequences of These Shifts/Looking Forward*

What is most important here is not the examples themselves but rather the shifts that they represent. Indeed, the potential implications of increasing liability across a given chain are significant. It is worth highlighting that these implications are relevant across a range of operational concerns. As both an overarching and a foundational matter, the shifts outlined here disrupt traditional understandings of when a firm should vertically integrate a supplier and when the firm should enter into a contractual relationship with that supplier.

Indeed, as noted, there is, from many fronts, increasing pressure on firms—especially lead firms—to maintain flexibility in the operation of their supply chains. Law, as we have seen, provides the structure for the links between the firms in a chain; and from a legal perspective, this flexibility is best achieved through contractual relationships with suppliers.

Further, it was once the case that contractual relationships offered protection from liability. But now this protection is eroding as the law also imposes restraints on supply chain operation. So even as the law of contractual relationships permits flexibility in *operation*, the law more broadly is coming to infuse that operational flexibility with *liability*.

There are two consequences to be noted here, one conceptual and the other practical. First, conceptually, it was previously the case, as noted above, that decisions about vertical integration were based on the following balance:

$$\text{vertical integration} = \text{control} + \text{liability}$$
$$\text{contract} = \text{flexibility} + \text{freedom from liability}$$

But now, the calculation is beginning to look like this:

$$\text{vertical integration} = \text{control}$$
$$\text{contract} = \text{flexibility}$$

In other words, previously the choice of supplier relationship was weighted in favour of a contract, because the contract offered two positives (flexibility + freedom from liability) whereas vertical integration provided only one (control). But now, the playing field has been levelled. The calculation of which relationship to engage in must necessarily be pursued by means of other factors.

Second, and in following, these changing dynamics have very real and practical consequences on firms. For instance, these added risks of liability raise the costs of oversight of the chain, including specifically the costs of monitoring and ensuring compliance across each link. And more fundamentally, these changes—and indeed, the continuing uncertainty within which they are evolving—entail *risk*, and therefore cost, when weighing the integration/flexibility decision.

5.4 Conclusion

The next step here is empirical investigation. Until then, currently changing perceptions *about* global value chains are driving revisions to the laws that affect the operation of those chains. With these legal revisions and their practical consequences, prior understandings about the relationships within supply chains need to be replaced with novel calculations as outlined in this chapter.

References

Altenburg, T. (2006). Introduction to the special issue: Shaping value chains for development. *European Journal of Developmental Research, 18*(4), 493.

Amador, J., & Cabral, S. (2016). Global value chains: A survey of drivers and measures. *Journal of Economic Surveys, 30*(2), 278–301.

Backer, L. C. (2016). Shaping a global law for business enterprises: Framing principles and the promise of a comprehensive treaty on business and human rights. *North Carolina Journal Of International Law & Commercial Regulation, 42*(2), 417–504.

Blome, C., Schoenherr, T., & Eckstein, D. (2014). The impact of knowledge transfer and complexity on supply chain flexibility: A knowledge-based view. *International Journal of Production Economics, 147,* 307–316.

Cafaggi, F., Joppert Swensson, L. F., Macedo Junior, R. P., Gross, C. P., Almeida, L. G. D., & Ribeiro, T. A. (2012). *Accessing the global value chain in a changing institutional environment: Comparing aeronautics and coffee.* Inter-American Development Bank, www.iadb.org/intal/intalcdi/PE/2013/11680.pdf.

Cattaneo, O., Gereffi, G., Miroudot, S., & Taglioni, D. (2013) *Joining, upgrading and being competitive in global value chains: A strategic framework.* World Bank Policy Research Working Paper No. 6406, 4, www-wds.worldbank.org/external/default/WDSContentServer/IW3P/IB/2013/04/09/000158349_20130409182129/Rendered/PDF/wps6406.pdf.

Cavusoglu, H., & Raghunathan, S. (2007). Efficiency of vulnerability disclosure mechanisms to disseminate vulnerability knowledge. *IEEE Transactions on Software Engineering, 33*(3), 171–185.

Conley, J., & Williams, C. (2005). Engage, embed, and embellish: Theory versus practice in the corporate social responsibility movement. *Journal of Corporation Law, 31*(1), 1–38.

Douglas, M. (2002 [1966]). *Purity and Danger: An analysis of concepts of pollution and taboo.* London: Routledge Classics.

Ebben, J. J., & Johnson, A. C. (2005). Efficiency, flexibility, or both? Evidence linking strategy to performance in small firms. *Strategic Management Journal, 26*(13), 1249–1259.

Felipe Scavarda, L., Reichhart, A., Hamacher, S., & Holweg, M. (2010). Managing product variety in emerging markets. *International Journal of Operations & Production Management, 30*(2), 205–224.

Food Safety Modernization Act 2011 (USA).

Gavirneni, S., Kapuscinski, R., & Tayur, S. (1999). Value of information in capacitated supply chains. *Management Science, 45*(1), 16–24.

Geertz, C. (2000). *Deep play: Notes on the Balinese cockfight.* In C. Geertz (Ed.), The interpretation of cultures (2nd Edn.). New York: Basic Books.

General Food Law Regulation (EC) 178/2002.

Gereffi, G. (2014). A global value chain perspective on industrial policy and development in emerging markets. *Duke Journal of Comparative and International Law, 24*(3), 433–458.

Gereffi, G., & Fernandez-Stark, K. (2011). *Global value chain analysis: A primer.* Duke University Centre on Globalization, Governance & Competitiveness, 8. www.cggc.duke.edu/pdfs/2011-05-31_GVC_analysis_a_primer.pdf.

Gereffi, G., Humphrey, J., & Sturgeon, T. (2005). The governance of global value chains. *Review of International Political Economy, 12*(1), 92–94.

Gereffi, G., & Lee, J. (2012). Why the world suddenly cares about global supply chains. *Journal of Supply Chain Management, 48*(3), 24–32.

Gligor, D. M. (2014). A cross-disciplinary examination of firm orientations' performance outcomes: The role of supply chain flexibility. *Journal of Business Logistics, 35*(4), 281–298.

Humphrey, J., & Schmitz, H. (2008). Inter-firm relationships in global value chains: Trends in chain governance and their policy implications. *International Journal of Technological Learning, Innovation and Development, 1*(3), 270.

Kaplinsky, K. (2004). Spreading the gains from globalization: What can be learned from value-chain analysis? *Problems of Economic Transition, 47*(2), 74.

Kumar, V., Fantazy, K. A., Kumar, U., & Boyle, T. A. (2006). Implementation and management framework for supply chain flexibility. *Journal of Enterprise Information Management, 19*(3), 303–319.

Kumar, S., Heustis, D., & Graham, J. M. (2015). The future of traceability within the US food industry supply chain: A business case. *International Journal of Productivity and Performance Management, 64*(1), 129–146.

Lee, H. L. (2004). The triple-a supply chain. *Harvard Business Review, 82*(10), 102–113.

Lin, L. (2009). Legal transplants through private contracting: codes of vendor conduct in global supply chains as an example. *American Journal of Comparative Law, 57*(3), 719.

Linawati, N. (2017). Supply chain flexibility: Drivers and enablers—A literature review. *International Journal of Organizational Innovation, 9*(4), 116–132.

McGregor, A., & Smit, J. (2017). Human rights due diligence in corporate global supply chains. *Governance Directions, 69*(1), 16–21.

OECD, WTO, and World Bank Group. (2014). *Global value chains: Challenges, opportunities, and implications for policy* (pp. 12–20). http://www.oecd.org/tad/gvc_report_g20_july_2014.pdf.

Rowan, C. (2002). Traceability: Integration is key. *Food Engineering & Ingredients, 27*(1), 14.

Sethi, A. K., & Sethi, S. P. (1990). Flexibility in manufacturing: A survey. *International Journal of Flexible Manufacturing Systems, 2*(4), 289–328.

Sikkaa, P., & Willmott, H. (2010). The dark side of transfer pricing: Its role in tax avoidance and wealth retentiveness. *Critical Perspectives on Accounting, 21*(4), 345.

Singh, R. K., & Acharya, P. (2014). Identification and evaluation of supply chain flexibilities in Indian FMCG sector using DEMATEL. *Global Journal of Flexible Systems Management, 15*(2), 91–100.

Sobel-Read, K. (2014). Global value chains: A framework for analysis. *Transnational Legal Theory, 5*(3), 364–407.

Sobel-Read, K. (2016). A new model of sovereignty in the contemporary era of integrated global commerce: What anthropology contributes to the shortcomings of legal scholarship. *Vanderbilt Journal of Transnational Law, 49,* 1073.

Tachizawa, E. M., & Thomsen, C. G. (2007). Drivers and sources of supply flexibility: An exploratory study. *International Journal of Operations & Production Management, 27*(10), 1115–1136.

Tiwari, A. K., Tiwari, A., & Samuel, C. (2015). Supply chain flexibility: A comprehensive review. *Management Research Review, 38*(7), 767–792.

Upton, D. M. (1994). The management of manufacturing flexibility. *California Management Review, 36*(2), 72–89.

Wolf, E. R. (1997). *Europe and the people without history*. Berkeley, CA: University of California Press.

Xiao, Y. (2015). Flexibility measure analysis of supply chain. *International Journal of Production Research, 53*(1), 3161–3174.

Chapter 6
Technology Transfer and Innovation in Global International Joint Ventures—Emerging Markets' Perspective

Nakul Parameswar and Sanjay Dhir

Abstract International Joint Ventures (IJVs) formed by firms in emerging markets have been extensively examined to provide an avenue for learning, technology transfer and innovation. Outward Foreign Direct Investment (OFDI) from emerging markets to other nations has been increasing in the last few decades. Wholly owned subsidiaries and global IJVs are two prominent forms of OFDI from emerging markets. There is a need to examine global IJVs ability to facilitate learning, technology transfer and innovation in emerging market firms. This study attempts to explore the effect of two important factors: type of IJVs and interdependence between parent firms on learning, technology transfer and innovation from global IJVs formed by emerging market firms abroad. Case study methodology has been used to examine the propositions. The study finds that learning, technology transfer and innovation are facilitated in global IJVs irrespective of the type of IJVs or interdependence between parent firms.

Keywords Emerging markets · Global IJVs · Innovation · International joint ventures · Learning · Outward foreign direct investment · Technology transfer

6.1 Introduction

International Joint Ventures (IJVs) as an area of research in strategic management domain came into prominence after proliferation of IJVs between Japanese and US firms to take advantage of economies of scale in the 1970s. IJVs are considered as a popular mechanism to enter new and emerging markets by firms across the globe

---

N. Parameswar (✉) · S. Dhir
Department of Management Studies, Indian Institute of Technology Delhi,
Vishwakarma Bhawan, Shaheed Jeet Singh Marg, New Delhi 110016, India
e-mail: nakuliitd@yahoo.in

S. Dhir
e-mail: sanjaydhir.iitd@gmail.com

© Springer Nature Singapore Pte Ltd. 2018
J. Connell et al. (eds.), *Global Value Chains, Flexibility and Sustainability*,
Flexible Systems Management, https://doi.org/10.1007/978-981-10-8929-9_6

(Beamish 1994; Luo et al. 2001; Meschi and Riccio 2008; Dhir and Sushil 2016, 2017). Gradually, the wave of IJVs spread across the world as firms recognized the advantages offered by it. IJVs allow firms to leverage their partners' resources, know-how, market reputation, market relations as well as share risks (Hamel et al. 1989; Doz and Hamel 1998; Barringer and Harrison 2000; Culpan 2008). Classical strategic management perspectives of transaction cost economics (Williamson 1975), resource dependence (Pfeffer and Salancik 1978; Barney 1991; Eisenhardt and Martin 2000), strategic choice, stakeholder theory, organizational learning (Hamel 1991; Doz and Hamel 1998; Khanna et al. 1998; Fang and Zou 2010) and institutional theory (DiMaggio and Powell 1983) have been widely used to justify the formation of IJVs.

Literature is concentrated on multiple dimensions of Outward Foreign Direct Investment (OFDI), from emerging markets to other nations (Buckley et al. 2007; Yiu et al. 2007; Yamakawa et al. 2008; Xia et al. 2014; Sarma 2016). OFDI consists of investment through IJVs as platform investment and investment as wholly owned subsidiaries (WOS) established independently in the target country. The major reasons identified for OFDI are industry-related factors such as intense competition, learning opportunities and high risk in home country (Yiu et al. 2007; Yamakawa et al. 2008; Luo et al. 2009; Wang et al. 2012), institutional factors such as availability of credit, regulatory regime and firm legitimacy in the market (Stoian 2013; He et al. 2015) and resource-based factors such as overcoming resource deficiency, leveraging patents and cost of capital (Tan and Meyer 2010; Lu et al. 2011; Ramasamy et al. 2012).

In the recent past, there has been a surge in OFDI in the form of IJVs by emerging market firms abroad (Globerman and Shapiro 2008; Sushil 2017a). These IJVs are a means for emerging market firms to increase their global reach. Emerging market governments are facilitating local firms to go global (WIR 2006, 2008). OFDI from India has been increasing in the last few years (Pradhan 2008; Saikia 2012). Literature acknowledges that IJVs facilitate technology transfer through investment by developed nation firms in emerging markets (Wang and Blomstrom 1992; Young and Lan 1997; De La Potterie and Lichtenberg 2001; Park 2011) and as a medium that enables innovation (Harrigan 1988; Kogut and Singh 1988; Zhou and Li 2008; Idris and Tey 2011; Dhir and Mital 2012, 2013a; Sun and Lee 2013; Ma et al. 2015; Park et al. 2015). However, literature examining technology transfer and innovation facilitated through IJVs by emerging market firms abroad is scant.

This study attempts to examine technology transfer and innovation facilitated by foreign investment in the form of IJVs formed by Indian firms abroad from 2010 to 2015. The subsequent section shall undertake to develop propositions based on extant IJVs literature. Next, research methodology and analysis shall be presented. Finally, in conclusion, implications and future research shall be discussed.

6.2 Literature Review and Proposition Development

IJVs in general have been recognized as a medium for technology transfer. Majority of studies in extant literature has examined technology transfer to firms through IJVs formed in emerging markets. The two important factors that influence technology transfer through foreign investments are the cost of technology transfer to the transferor firm and the technology adoption cost for the technology accepting firm (Wang and Blomstrom 1992; Saggi 2002; Sinani and Meyer 2004). For the developing countries, substantial opportunities exist for increased technology transfer which could be catalyzed through conducive policy changes (Young and Lan 1997; Luo et al. 2009; Park et al. 2015). Furthermore, it has been observed that relational capital (Dhanaraj et al. 2004), cultural distance (Simonin 1999; Leyland 2006) and IJVs size (Dhanaraj et al. 2004; Dhir and Mital 2013b; Park et al. 2015) yield substantial influence on the transfer of explicit and implicit knowledge between parents firms in IJVs. In IJVs by firms from emerging markets abroad, these factors would yield a substantially similar influence. Moreover, there exists a need to look at the influence of type of IJVs determined by purpose of IJVs and type of interdependence on technology transfer between parent firms in IJVs formed by firms from emerging markets in other countries. Extant literature has identified four types of IJVs based on its key purpose—resource seeking, market seeking, capital seeking and strategic asset seeking (Dunning 2000; Luo and Park 2001; Makino et al. 2002, 2007). Resource seeking, market seeking and capital seeking IJVs are intended to obtain resources, and access to new markets and funds, which cannot be readily internalized by parent firms. However, strategic asset seeking IJVs are intended to learn and internalize partner technology and skills (Hamel 1991; Makino et al. 2007) which could be internalized. From the context of IJVs by emerging market firms abroad, there exists a need to examine which type of IJVs facilitates higher magnitude of technology transfer. Therefore, there is a need to examine the scope of technology transfer in strategic asset seeking IJVs vis-à-vis resource, market and capital seeking IJVs.

Proposition 1a: Strategic asset seeking IJVs facilitate technology transfer.
Proposition 1b: Resource seeking IJVs facilitate technology transfer.
Proposition 1c: Market seeking IJVs facilitate technology transfer.
Proposition 1d: Capital seeking IJVs facilitate technology transfer.

IJVs are a means to collaborate between firms that leads to formation of interdependence between firms and their partners (Harrigan 1986; Hillman et al. 2009; Kale and Singh 2009; Iriyama et al. 2014; Meier et al. 2016). Partner interdependence has an influence on opportunism and trust (Gill and Butler 1996; Inkpen and Currall 2004; Madhok 2006; Talay and Akdeniz 2014), partner control (Kumar and Seth 1998; Yan and Gray 2001; Todeva and Knoke 2005) and IJVs performance (Yan and Gray 1994; Park and Russo 1996; Luo and Park 2004; Kemp and Ghauri 2008). Further, interdependence evolves during the IJVs through inter-partner learning, internalization of partner skills and technology (Hamel 1991; Kale et al.

2000). Interdependence in IJVs is classified into three types: pooled, sequential and reciprocal (Thompson 1967; Gill and Butler 1996; Madhok et al. 2015). Pooled interdependence is the case wherein both firms pool resources to create mutual benefits. Sequential interdependence is seen when one partner's objective is met by the IJVs whereas the second partner's objective is met by IJVs mediated through the first partner. Generally, this sequential interdependence is observed in IJVs where a parent firm is a minority partner. Reciprocal interdependence is observed when there is mutual dependence between partners. There exists a need to examine the influence of interdependence between firms in IJVs formed by emerging market firm abroad on technology transfer and innovation.

Proposition 2a: Pooled interdependence facilitates technology transfer to emerging market firm through IJVs formed by emerging market firm in developed nations.

Proposition 2b: Sequential interdependence facilitates technology transfer to emerging market firm through IJVs formed by emerging market firm in developed nations.

Proposition 2c: Reciprocal interdependence facilitates technology transfer to emerging market firm through IJVs formed by emerging market firm in developed nations.

6.3 Research Methodology

This study on IJVs formed by Indian firms in developed nations considers the period from 2010 to 2015. Data on OFDI in the form of IJVs for the period from 2010 to 2015 was obtained from Reserve Bank of India web page on overseas investment. A total of $9413.12 million has been invested in the form of IJVs by Indian firms abroad during 2010 to 2015. Table 6.1 provides the sector-wise categorization, and Table 6.2 provides categorization of overseas investment in the form of IJVs from India to G8 nations and non-G8 nations during 2010–2015.

Table 6.1 Sector-wise categorization of Indian overseas investment as IJVs during 2010–2015 (in USD million)

Sector	Total
Agriculture and mining	3987.245
Community, social and personal services	253.7898
Construction	222.8141
Electricity, gas and water	101.9943
Financial, insurance and business services	1099.0459
Manufacturing	2468.631
Miscellaneous	18.5355
Transport, storage and communication services	285.7056
Wholesale, retail trade, restaurants and hotels	975.3601
Grand total	9413.1213

Source Reserve Bank of India data on overseas investment, 2016

Table 6.2 Destination of Indian overseas investment from 2010 to 2015

Year	G8 nation	Non-G8 nation	Grand total
2010–2011	370.3772	1564.2916	1934.6688
2011–2012	998.485	561.1972	1559.6822
2012–2013	310.9559	568.4836	879.4395
2013–2014	354.1758	3955.5494	4309.7252
2014–2015	351.4486	378.157	729.6056
Grand total	2385.4425	7027.6788	9413.1213

Source Reserve Bank of India data on overseas investment, 2016

The propositions shall be validated using case study methodology (Momaya et al. 2017; Kundi and Sharma 2015). Three IJVs from the manufacturing sector in Australia, Tunisia and Russia have been extensively studied using data from their annual reports, parent firm annual reports, industry reports, regulators report and other published data sources.

6.4 Analysis

Case 1: Norwest Energy EP413: Norwest Energy project EP413 is a JV between Norwest Energy (27.94%), Australia Worldwide Exploration Ltd. (44.25%) and Bharat Petro Resources (27.80%) India. The JV was set up to explore petroleum resources in northern Perth Basin in Australia. The Indian partner Bharat PetroResources is the wholly owned subsidiary of Bharat Petroleum and was incorporated in 2006 to embark on exploration of oil fields across the world and secure crude supply to its parent firm. Norwest Energy is an active oil exploration firm in the United Kingdom and Australia, and Australia Worldwide Exploration Ltd. undertakes active exploration projects in Australia, Indonesia and New Zealand.

From the perspective of Bharat PetroResources, this project is a resource seeking IJV considering the supply of oil and gas to its parent firm from the Perth Basin. Further, it is a strategic asset seeking IJV considering that Indian firm's partner with global oil exploration firms to learn and internalize their skills and technology. This project has sequential interdependence as both Norwest and Australia Worldwide Exploration Ltd. have the responsibility of undertaking primary functions of exploration and production.

Through this project, Bharat PetroResources which is relatively a new firm in oil exploration and production field is attempting to understand and internalize the latest technologies used by Norwest and Australia Worldwide Exploration Ltd. The prime aim of internalizing latest technology is to minimize the cost of oil and gas exploration in the long term. Moreover, this project allows the Indian firm to observe and understand the field rehabilitation processes adopted to mitigate environmental degradation in the oil well's vicinity. Knowledge of latest technology and rehabilitation processes is important in the oil and gas industry, and these IJVs shall facilitate Bharat PetroResources, a relatively new firm as compared to other two partners, to learn, internalize and further apply them subsequently in the future.

Case 2: Tunisian India Fertilizers (TIFERT): TIFERT is an IJV between two Indian fertilizer and chemical firms, Gujarat State Fertilizers and Chemical Ltd. (GSFC) and Coromandel International Ltd. along with two Tunisian companies, Compagnie des Phosphates de GAFSA (CPG) and Groupe Chimique Tunisien (GCT). Each Indian firm has 15% ownership contribution whereas each Tunisian firm has 35% ownership. Tunisia is one of the leading phosphate producers in the world, and phosphoric acid, a product of phosphate, is an important raw material for fertilizer manufacturing. The international market has limited availability of phosphoric acid and the supply is erratic leading to high price fluctuation. This IJV provides raw material security to the Indian firms as the whole production of phosphoric acid from the Skhira plant is supplied to Indian firms.

TIFERT is primarily a resource seeking IJV for the Indian firms. However, this IJV provides Indian firms an avenue to observe operations of phosphate mining and its conversion into phosphate derivatives. TIFERT is a sequential IJV as Indian firms are utilizing phosphoric acid as a raw material in their processes. Further, this IJV could also be termed as reciprocal in nature as constitution of this venture was facilitated by an agreement of assured purchase of phosphate derivatives by Indian firms.

TIFERT could be termed as a platform investment by the Indian firms to understand phosphoric acid production as both these firms are in the process of backward integrating in the fertilizer industry. These firms are aspiring to be end to end players in the fertilizer and chemical industry; this IJV shall provide multiple learning opportunities for both the firms which may be useful in the long time horizon. Further, continuous and uninterrupted supply of raw material from TIFERT has facilitated GSFC and Coromondel International Ltd. to keep up to the price ceiling on fertilizers in India as well as roll out new products in the Indian market.

Case 3: Aurospharma Company: Aurospharma is an IJV between Aurobindo Pharma Ltd., India and OJSC DIOD, Russia. Both the firms have 50% stake in the IJV. Aurospharma aims to construct a manufacturing plant to roll out Non-Penicillin and Non-Cephalosporin Rx generics and other over-the-counter (OTC) drugs in Russia.

Aurospharma is a capital seeking and market seeking IJV from the Indian perspective as it provides Aurobindo Pharma Ltd. access to the Russian market at a relatively low investment as compared to its independent establishment. Aurospharma is in the nature of pooled interdependence wherein both Aurobindo Pharma Ltd. and DIOD are contributing their resources for mutual benefits. Further, Aurospharma complies with the conditions of 'Strategy for Development of the Russian Pharmaceutical Industry for 2020' approved by Russian Ministry of Industry and Trade and allows public health care in Russia to reduce dependence on import of drugs. Aurobindo Pharma Ltd. is aided on its international expansion strategy and leverage DIOD in easy localization of production process as well as growth in Russia.

Aurospharma allows Aurobindo Pharma an avenue to diversify into healthcare goods from being a manufacturer of generic drugs. Close interaction with DIOD during the process of the plant setup and manufacturing has allowed Aurobindo Pharma to gain insights on cutting-edge technological development in generic drug manufacturing. Further, new product development in Aurobindo Pharma has been aided by Aurospharma.

6.5 Conclusion

Table 6.3 provides a snapshot of the cases and their support for respective propositions. The case analysis supports the propositions constructed from extant IJVs literature. From the analysis, it is evident that irrespective of the type of IJV and the type of interdependence between IJV's partners, international venturing in the form of global IJVs by emerging market firms provides an avenue for learning, technology transfer and subsequently innovation. Moreover, the experience gained by emerging market firms through international venturing in the form of global IJVs facilitates better learning considering the challenges experienced in the host country.

The type of IJVs is determined based on the core purpose of IJVs formation; however, learning and technology transfer may not be limited only to strategic asset seeking IJVs. Similarly, the type of interdependence depicts the process flow within the IJVs, which may not determine the magnitude of learning and technology transfer. Global IJVs not only provide learning opportunity in core business area but also provide experiential learning opportunity which is not limited to any area. Repatriation of learning and technology transfer to the home country (i.e. emerging markets) shall lead to operational and strategic improvement in parent firms leading to increased competitive advantage and customer satisfaction.

For the academicians, this study opens up a new area of research within OFDI domain. Literature is scant on drivers, antecedents and factors that influence

Table 6.3 Snapshot of case and proposition validity

Case	Type of IJV	Type of interdependence	Technology transfer and innovation facilitated? (Yes/No)	Proposition supported
Norwest energy EP413	Resource seeking Strategic asset seeking	Sequential	Yes	1a 1b 2b
Tunisian India fertilizers (TIFERT)	Resource seeking	Sequential Reciprocal	Yes	1b 2a 2c
Aurospharma company	Capital seeking Market seeking	Pooled	Yes	1c 1d 2a

formation of global IJVs by emerging market firms in other countries as well as the outcome of such IJVs. For the practitioners, this study conceptualizes and relates to the type of IJVs and interdependence between partners on technology transfer and innovation. For the policymakers, this study would allow conceptualizing new policy facilitating global IJVs from emerging markets in pursuit of technology transfer and learning. Further, with the inception of the 'Make in India' initiative, transfer of modern technology from foreign nations could be facilitated through OFDI.

This study uses case study methodology to empirically validate the propositions. Future research could be undertaken to build hypotheses from propositions and statistically test the same or model a hierarchy for using TISM modelling (Sushil 2017b). Two major aspects of IJVs, IJV type and interdependence between partners, are examined for their influence on learning, technology transfer and innovation in global IJVs. However, there could be multiple other factors that may have an impact on global IJVs. Future research could be undertaken to explore, identify and examine their role in technology transfer and innovation in global IJVs.

References

Barney, J. (1991). Firm resources and sustained competitive advantage. *Journal of Management, 17*(1), 99–120.

Barringer, B. R., & Harrison, J. S. (2000). Walking a tightrope: Creating value through interorganizational relationships. *Journal of Management, 26*(3), 367–403.

Beamish, P. W. (1994). Joint ventures in LDCs: Partner selection and performance. *Management International Review, International Management: Highlights in Finance—Accounting, 34* (International Management: Highlights in Finance—Accounting—Issues: 30 Years of MIR), 60–74.

Buckley, P. J., Clegg, L. J., Cross, A. R., Liu, X., Voss, H., & Zheng, P. (2007). The determinants of Chinese outward foreign direct investment. *Journal of International Business Studies, 38*(4), 499–518.

Culpan, R. (2008). The role of strategic alliances in gaining sustainable competitive advantage for firms. *Management Revue, 19*(1/2), 94–105.

De La Potterie, B. V. P., & Lichtenberg, F. (2001). Does foreign direct investment transfer technology across borders? *Review of Economics and Statistics, 83*(3), 490–497.

Dhanaraj, C., Lyles, M. A., Steensma, H. K., & Tihanyi, L. (2004). Managing tacit and explicit knowledge transfer in IJVs: The role of relational embeddedness and the impact on performance. *Journal of International Business Studies, 35*(5), 428–442.

Dhir, S., & Mital, A. (2012). Decision-making for mergers and acquisitions: The role of agency issues and behavioral biases. *Strategic Change, 21*(1–2), 59–69.

Dhir, S., & Mital, A. (2013a). Value creation on bilateral cross-border joint ventures: Evidence from India. *Strategic Change, 22*(5–6), 307–326.

Dhir, S., & Mital, A. (2013b). Asymmetric motives in Indian bilateral cross-border joint ventures with G7 nations: Impact of relative partner characteristics and initial conditions. *International Journal of Strategic Business Alliances, 3*(1), 69–92.

Dhir, S., & Sushil. (2016). Global competitiveness of informal economy organizations. In Sushil, J. Connel & J. Burgess (Eds.), *Flexible work organizations: The challenges of capacity building in Asia, flexible systems management* (pp. 209–224). New Delhi: Springer.

Dhir, S., & Sushil. (2017). Flexibility in modification and termination of cross-border joint ventures. *Global Journal of Flexible Systems Management, 18*(2), 139–151.

DiMaggio, P. J., & Powell, W. W. (1983). The iron cage revisited: Institutional isomorphism and collective rationality in organizational fields. *American Sociological Review, 48*(2), 147–160.

Doz, Y. L., & Hamel, G. (1998). *The alliance advantage: The art of creating value through partnership*. London: Harvard Business Press.

Dunning, J. H. (2000). The eclectic paradigm as an envelope for economic and business theories of MNE activity. *International Business Review, 9*(2), 163–190.

Eisenhardt, K. M., & Martin, J. A. (2000). Dynamic capabilities: What are they? *Strategic Management Journal, 21*(10/11, Special Issue: The Evolution of Firm Capabilities), 1105–1121.

Fang, E., & Zou, S. (2010). The effects of absorptive and joint learning on the instability of international joint ventures in emerging economies. *Journal of International Business Studies, 41*(5, Part Special Issue: Conflict, Security, and Political Risk: International Business in Challenging Times), 906–924.

Gill, J., & Butler, R. (1996). Cycles of trust and distrust in joint-ventures. *European Management Journal, 14*(1), 81–89.

Globerman, S., & Shapiro, D. (2008). Outward FDI and the economic performance of emerging markets. In *The rise of transnational corporations from emerging markets: Threat or opportunity* (pp. 229–271). Cheltenham: Edward Elgar.

Hamel, G. (1991). Competition for competence and inter-partner learning within international strategic alliances. *Strategic Management Journal, 12*(S1), 83–103.

Hamel, G., Doz, Y. L., & Prahalad, C. K. (1989). Collaborate with your competitors and win. *Harvard Business Review, 67*(1), 133–139.

Harrigan, K. R. (1986). *Managing for joint venture success*. Lexington Books.

Harrigan, K. R. (1988). Joint ventures and competitive strategy. *Strategic Management Journal, 9*(2), 141–158.

He, C., Xie, X., & Zhu, S. (2015). Going global: Understanding China's outward foreign direct investment from motivational and institutional perspectives. *Post-Communist Economies, 27*(4), 448–471.

Hillman, A. J., Withers, M. C., & Collins, B. J. (2009). Resource dependence theory: A review. *Journal of Management, 35*(6), 1404–1427.

Idris, A., & Tey, L. S. (2011). Exploring the motives and determinants of innovation performance of malaysian offshore international joint ventures. *Management Decision, 49*(10), 1623–1641.

Inkpen, A. C., & Currall, S. C. (2004). Transferring, translating, and transforming: An integrative framework for managing. *Organization science, 15*(5), 586–599.

Iriyama, A., Shi, W. S., & Prescott, J. E. (2014). Frequency and directional reversal of equity ownership change in international joint ventures. *Asia Pacific Journal of Management, 31*(1), 215–243.

Kale, P., & Singh, H. (2009). Managing strategic alliances: What do we know now, and where do we go from here? *The Academy of Management Perspectives, 23*(3), 45–62.

Kale, P., Singh, H., Perlmutter, H. (2000). Learning and protection of proprietary assets in alliances: Building relational capital. *Strategic Management Journal, 21*(3, Special Issue: Strategic Networks), 217–237.

Kemp, R. G. M., & Ghauri, P. N. (2008). Interdependency in joint ventures: The relationship between dependence asymmetry and performance. *Journal on Chain and Network Science, 1*(2), 101–110.

Khanna, T., Gulati, R., & Nohria, N. (1998). The dynamics of learning alliances: Competition, cooperation, and relative scope. *Strategic Management Journal, 19*(3), 193–210.

Kogut, B., & Singh, H. (1988). The effect of national culture on the choice of entry mode. *Journal of International Business Studies, 19*(3), 411–432.

Kumar, S., & Seth, A. (1998). The design of coordination and control mechanisms for managing joint venture-parent relationships. *Strategic Management Journal, 19*(6), 579–599.

Kundi, M., & Sharma, S. (2015). Efficiency analysis and flexibility: A case study of cement firms in India. *Global Journal of Flexible Systems Management, 16*(3), 221–234.

Leyland, L. M. (2006). The role of culture on knowledge transfer: The case of the multinational corporation. *The Learning Organization, 13*(3), 257–275.

Lu, J., Liu, X., & Wang, H. (2011). Motives for outward FDI of Chinese private firms: Firm resources, industry dynamics, and government policies. *Management and Organization Review, 7*(2), 223–248.

Luo, Y., & Park, S. H. (2001). Strategic alignment and performance of market-seeking MNCs in China. *Strategic Management Journal, 22*(2), 141–155.

Luo, Y., & Park, S. H. (2004). Multiparty cooperation and performance in international equity joint ventures. *Journal of International Business Studies, 35*(2), 142–160.

Luo, Y., Shenkar, O., & Nyaw, M. (2001). A dual parent perspective on control and performance in international joint ventures: Lessons from a developing economy. *Journal of International Business Studies, 32*(1), 41–58.

Luo, Y., Xue, Q., & Han, B. (2009). How emerging market governments promote outward FDI: experience from China. *Journal of World Business, 45*(1), 68–79.

Ma, Z., Yu, M., Gao, C., Zhou, J., & Yang, Z. (2015). Institutional constraints of product innovation in China: Evidence from international joint ventures. *Journal of Business Research, 68*(5), 949–956.

Madhok, A. (2006). How much does ownership really matter? Equity and trust relations in joint venture relationships. *Journal of International Business Studies, 37*(1), 4–11.

Madhok, A., Keyhani, M., & Bossink, B. (2015). Understanding alliance evolution and termination: Adjustment costs and the economics of resource value. *Strategic Organization, 13*(2), 91–116.

Makino, S., Chan, C. M., Isobe, T., & Beamish, P. W. (2007). Intended and unintended termination of international joint ventures. *Strategic Management Journal, 28*(11), 1113–1132.

Makino, S., Lau, C., & Yeh, R. (2002). Asset-exploitation versus asset-seeking: Implications for location choice of foreign direct investment from newly industrialized economies. *Journal of International Business Studies, 33*(3), 403–421.

Meier, M., Lütkewitte, M., Mellewigt, T., & Decker, C. (2016). How managers can build trust in strategic alliances: A meta-analysis on the central trust-building mechanisms. *Journal of Business Economics, 86*(3), 229–257.

Meschi, P.-X., & Riccio, E. L. (2008). Country risk national cultural differences between partners and survival of international joint ventures in Brazil. *International Business Review, 17*(3), 250–266.

Momaya, K. S., Bhat, S., & Lalwani, L. (2017). Institutional growth and industrial competitiveness: Exploring the role of strategic flexibility taking the case of select institutes in India. *Global Journal of Flexible Systems Management, 18*(2), 111–122.

Park, C., Vertinsky, I., & Becerra, M. (2015). Transfers of tacit vs. explicit knowledge and performance in international joint ventures: The role of age. *International Business Review, 24*(1), 89–101.

Park, S. H., & Russo, M. V. (1996). When competition eclipses cooperation: An event history analysis of joint venture failure. *Management Science, 42*(6), 875–890.

Park, B. Il. (2011). Knowledge transfer capacity of multinational enterprises and technology acquisition in international joint ventures. *International Business Review, 20*(1), 75–87.

Pfeffer, J., & Salancik, G. R. (1978). *The external control of organizations: A resource dependence perspective*. New York: Harper and Row.

Pradhan, J. P. (2008). The evolution of indian outward foreign direct investment: Changing trends and patterns. *International Journal of Technology and Globalisation, 4*(1), 70–86.

Ramasamy, B., Yeung, M., & Laforet, S. (2012). China's outward foreign direct investment: Location choice and firm ownership. *Journal of World Business, 47*(1), 17–25.

Saggi, K. (2002). Trade foreign direct investment, and international technology transfer: A survey. *The World Bank Research Observer, 17*(2), 191–235.

Saikia, D. (2012). India's outward foreign direct investment. *International Business Management, 6*(1), 55–59.

Sarma, C. (2016). Offshore financial centers and India's outward FDI determinants. *World Journal of Social Sciences, 6*(1), 188–199.

Simonin, B. L. (1999). Ambiguity and the process of knowledge transfer in strategic alliances. *Strategic Management Journal, 20*(7), 595–623.

Sinani, E., & Meyer, K. E. (2004). Spillovers of technology transfer from FDI: The case of Estonia. *Journal of Comparative Economics, 32*(3), 445–466.

Stoian, C. (2013). Extending dunning's investment development path: The role of home country institutional determinants in explaining outward foreign direct investment. *International Business Review, 22*(3), 615–637.

Sun, S. L., & Lee, R. P. (2013). Enhancing innovation through international joint venture portfolios: From the emerging firm perspective. *Journal of International Marketing, 21*(3), 1–21.

Sushil. (2017a). Multi-criteria valuation of flexibility initiatives using integrated TISM—IRP with a big data framework. *Production Planning and Control, 28*(11–12), 999–1010.

Sushil. (2017b). Modified ISM/TISM process with simultaneous transitivity checks for reducing direct pair comparisons. *Global Journal of Flexible Systems Management, 18*(4), 331–351.

Talay, M. B., & Akdeniz, M. B. (2014). In time we trust? The effects of duration on the dynamics of trust-building processes in inter-organizational relationships. *Strategic Management Review, 8*(1), 77–90.

Tan, D. C., & Meyer, K. E. (2010). Business groups' outward FDI: A managerial resources perspective. *Journal of International Management, 16*(2), 154–164.

Thompson, J. D. (1967). *Organizations in action: Social science bases of administrative theory*. New York: McGraw Hill.

Todeva, E., & Knoke, D. (2005). Strategic alliances and models of collaboration. *Management Decision, 43*(1), 1–22.

Wang, C., Hong, J., Kafouros, M., & Boateng, A. (2012). What drives outward FDI of Chinese firms? *Testing the Explanatory Power of Three Theoretical Frameworks, International Business Review, 21*(3), 425–438.

Wang, J.-Y., & Blomstrom, M. (1992). Foreign investment and technology transfer: A simple model. *European Economic Review, 36*(1), 137–155.

Williamson, O. E. (1975). *Markets and hierarchies: Analysis of antitrust implications*. New York: Free Press.

WIR. (2006). *FDI from developing and transition economies: Implications for development*. New York, Geneva.

WIR. (2008). *Transnational corporations and infrastructure challenge*. New York, Geneva.

Xia, J., Ma, X., Lu, J. W., & Yiu, D. W. (2014). Outward foreign direct investment by emerging market firms: A resource dependence logic. *Strategic Management Journal, 35*(9), 1343–1363.

Yamakawa, Y., Peng, M. W., & Deeds, D. L. (2008). What drives new ventures to internationalize from emerging to developed economies? *Entrepreneurship: Theory and Practice, 32*(1), 59–82.

Yan, A., & Gray, B. (1994). Bargaining power management control, and performance in United States–China joint ventures: A comparative case study. *Academy of Management Journal, 37*(6), 1478–1517.

Yan, A., & Gray, B. (2001). Negotiating control and achieving performance in international joint ventures: A conceptual model. *Journal of International Management, 7*(4), 295–315.

Yiu, D. W., Lau, C., & Bruton, G. D. (2007). International venturing by emerging economy firms: The effects of firm capabilities, home country networks, and corporate entrepreneurship. *Journal of International Business Studies, 38*(4), 519–540.

Young, S., & Lan, P. (1997). Technology transfer to China through foreign direct investment. *Regional Studies, 31*(7), 669–679.

Zhou, C., & Li, J. (2008). Product innovation in emerging market-based international joint ventures: An organizational ecology perspective. *Journal of International Business Studies, 39*(7), 1114–1132.

Chapter 7
Modelling Subsidiary Innovation Factors for Semiconductor Design Industry in India

Dixit Manjunatha Betaraya, Saboohi Nasim and Joy Mukhopadhyay

Abstract In the past two decades, globalization of innovation has accelerated. Subsidiaries of multinational enterprises are playing a very important role in the globalized innovation value chain. Foreign Direct Investment (FDI) flow to developing countries like India and China has increased substantially in the past 5 years. In light of this, the study of subsidiaries and their contribution to global innovation in these economies is very important and relevant. This chapter illustrates the use of a qualitative approach known as Total Interpretive Structural Modelling (TISM) to model the macro factors responsible for R&D Subsidiary Innovation (SI) in the Indian semiconductor design subsidiaries and structure them to better understand the interplay of these factors. Implications for practitioners and researchers are highlighted. Understanding the factors that impact R&D subsidiary innovation in India is helpful in understanding the role of subsidiaries from developing economies in the innovation value chain.

Keywords Innovation · Multinational enterprise · Semiconductor Subsidiaries · TISM

D. M. Betaraya (✉) · S. Nasim
Faculty of Management Studies and Research, Aligarh Muslim University, Aligarh, India
e-mail: dixit.m.betaraya@gmail.com

S. Nasim
e-mail: saboohinasim@gmail.com

D. M. Betaraya
Intel Technology India Pvt. Ltd., Bangalore, India

J. Mukhopadhyay
ThinkCorp Consultancy Services, 836, 1st Cross, 3rd Main, Kengeri Satellite Town, Bangalore 560060, India
e-mail: joymukh@yahoo.com

© Springer Nature Singapore Pte Ltd. 2018
J. Connell et al. (eds.), *Global Value Chains, Flexibility and Sustainability*, Flexible Systems Management, https://doi.org/10.1007/978-981-10-8929-9_7

7.1 Introduction

While globalization of innovation has lagged behind production, the past two decades has witnessed a significant increase in the sourcing of technology and innovation from different parts of the world. Globalization of innovation has been accelerated in the recent years due to advances in transportation and Information and Communication Technologies (ICT) (Dunning and Lundan 2009). Multinational enterprises (MNE) have played a significant role in the globalization of innovation by setting up subsidiaries across the globe.

Recent research in the field of international business and strategic management indicates that subsidiaries of MNEs play a critical role in the innovative activities of the MNE firm (Ghoshal and Bartlett 1988; Frost 2001; Moore 2001; Frost et al. 2002; Almeida and Phene 2004; Mahnke et al. 2005; Zhao and Luo 2005; Mu et al. 2007). This is because subsidiaries are able to link the internal MNE network with the local host country environment in which they are embedded to create new technologies which lead to innovation (Mu et al. 2007; Dunning and Lundan 2009). The role of subsidiaries from emerging economies is attracting interest amongst researchers due to increased FDI to these economies. Foreign direct investment (FDI) inflows to emerging economies like China and India has seen an aggregate increase from 24% before 2008 to 32% in 2013 while in the same time period, FDI inflows to developed economies like US and EU has been cut nearly by half, from 56% to 30% (UNCTAD 2014).

In recent times, innovation has been reorganized significantly. Innovation activities which used to be concentrated at the headquarters of the MNEs have been decentralized. There are two levels of decentralization that have occurred. The first level is within the MNE, where subsidiaries have started playing a key role in the innovative activities utilizing the strong intra-firm networks. The second level is outside the MNE, where innovative activities are carried out by local firms or institutions (Lema et al. 2015). This chapter focuses on the first level of innovation decentralization where subsidiaries from emerging markets are growing up the innovation value chain.

Semiconductor industry is highly knowledge-based as evidenced by the patenting activity and is dominated by MNE (Phene and Almeida 2008). There has been a tremendous increase in the number of semiconductor design subsidiaries in India (Krishna et al. 2012). Therefore, Indian semiconductor design industry is an appropriate setting for a global innovation value chain study. This chapter examines various factors that are responsible for subsidiary innovation (SI) in the semiconductor design subsidiaries located in India which is an emerging economy. Preliminary set of factors identified through an extensive literature review are grouped into three constructs: Local Environment (LE), Subsidiary Traits (ST) and Headquarter Strategy (HS). Since innovation is highly context-specific (Wolfe 1994), these factors are validated by experts in the semiconductor design industry in India.

Individual micro-variables and their relationship to subsidiary innovation is an area that has been well studied by earlier researchers. However, the interaction of the micro-variables amongst themselves has been under-explored. This chapter attempts to fill that gap by exploring the interaction amongst the subsidiary innovation factors in the Indian semiconductor industry. To study the interaction between the micro-variables, this chapter proposes to use qualitative technique known as Total Interpretive Structural Modelling (TISM). The relevance of the subsidiary innovation framework and the relationship amongst the various SI factors are confirmed, laying the groundwork for a larger empirical and case study research.

7.2 Semiconductor Design Industry in India

Semiconductor industry has changed the way we live life today. It is a key driver of growth not only for a few electronic appliances but of the entire electronics value chain. It serves the data processing, consumer electronics, automotive, communications and industrial markets. According to a report by Ernst and Young (2011), globally, the revenue from semiconductor industry was US$226 billion in the year 2009. The industry has two important phases: design and manufacturing. The design phase is research and innovation intensive while the manufacturing phase is capital intensive (Brown et al. 2005).

In the early days of semiconductor design, it was mandatory to collocate the design and manufacturing facility. The ability to separate the location of semiconductor design and manufacturing activities in the 1990s allowed multinational companies to locate fabless design houses in countries where engineering talent was abundantly available. Texas Instruments was the first company to set up a semiconductor design house in Bangalore, India in the year 1985 (Keller and Pauly 2009). Since then, there has been a rapid increase in the number of MNEs setting up design centres in India. By the end of 2010, amongst the top 20 US semiconductor companies, only two had not established design centres in India. This emphasizes the importance of India as a global semiconductor design hub.

As compared to China, India has been found to house advanced design capabilities. The comparison was based on the number of design leads as well as the number and size of specialized design teams (Fuller 2014). Fuller (2014) also found that India produces more utility patents with lead Indian inventors as compared to China. Most of the patents filed from India came from MNEs. Thus, subsidiaries of semiconductor design MNEs located in India have played a significant role in innovation.

7.3 Literature Review: Identification of Factors

Based on an exhaustive literature search which covered 64 papers covering subsidiaries located across the globe, 15 SI factors have been identified. The literature search results included papers from the year 1977 to year 2015 and covered journals of international repute. Table 7.1 lists the SI factors studied by various researchers.

The 15 SI factors have been classified into three macro variables, namely, Local Environment (LE), Subsidiary Traits (ST) and HQ Strategy (HS). Ability to source knowledge and resources from the local host environment provides a unique Country-Specific Advantage (CSA) to the subsidiary in technological innovation (Mu et al. 2007; Phene and Almeida 2008). In addition, subsidiaries need to have certain traits to convert the generic CSA into value that can be harnessed to generate innovation (Zaheer and Nachum 2011). MNE HQ sets the goal, makes sure that there is adequate information flow between the various subunits, takes decisions on resources and ensures that SI is diffused to the rest of the organization (Egelhoff 2010). Thus, the strategy adopted by the HQ towards subsidiary plays a critical role in SI.

Keeping the focus on local environment, subsidiary traits and the HQ strategy constructs, we modify the existing conceptual model of subsidiary initiative (Birkinshaw 1999) for subsidiary innovation is shown in Fig. 7.1.

Table 7.1 Subsidiary innovation factors studied by earlier researchers

No.	Factors of LE	Definition	Authors
1	Local embeddedness	Network with local external entities like universities, R&D labs, suppliers, customers, outsourcing partners, etc.	Almeida (1996), Zahra et al. (2000), Håkanson and Nobel (2001), Frost et al. (2002), Andersson et al. (2002, 2007), Almeida and Phene (2004), Mu et al. (2007), McDonald et al. (2008), Phene and Almeida (2008), Damijan et al. (2010), Figueiredo and Brito (2011), Meyer et al. (2011), Batsakis (2012), Collinson and Wang (2012), Ciabuschi et al. (2014)
2	Local market	Local market environment includes market size and local competition	Zahra et al. (2000), Damijan et al. (2010), Karna et al. (2013), Kim (2013), Miravitlles et al. (2013)

(continued)

Table 7.1 (continued)

No.	Factors of LE	Definition	Authors
3	Local resources	Availability of qualified technical personnel in the host country	Birkinshaw et al. (1998), Molero and Garcia (2008), Demirbag and Glaister (2010), Ke and Lai (2011), Kim (2013), Li et al. (2013), Miravitlles et al. (2013)

No.	Factors of ST	Definition	Authors
1	Slack	Slack is the pool of resources in an organization that is in excess of the minimum necessary to produce a given level of organizational output	Damanpour (1987), Ghoshal and Bartlett (1988), Nohria and Gulati (1996, 1997), Geiger and Cashen (2002), Herold et al. (2006), Zhong (2010)
2	Leadership	Subsidiary leadership is defined as the tangible actions taken by the subsidiary management and the existence of a clear vision	Birkinshaw et al. (1998), Elenkov and Manev (2009), Denti and Hemlin (2012)
3	Self-determination	Self-determination is the freedom to make one's own choice	Mudambi et al. (2007)
4	Teamwork	Teamwork is the cooperative networking and communication between or within subsidiaries or different units of an MNC	Mudambi et al. (2007)
5	Knowledge dynamic capability	Ability to source, combine/integrate and regenerate new knowledge from various sources is defined as knowledge dynamic capability	Minbaeva et al. (2003), Mahnke et al. (2005), Phene and Almeida (2008), Chang et al. (2012), Michailova and Zhan (2015)
6	Credibility	Subsidiary credibility is the track record of the ability to deliver at or above the expectations of the headquarters	Birkinshaw (1999), Ambos et al. (2010)
7	Communication	Communication within the subsidiary, with other subsidiaries and with headquarters	Ghoshal and Bartlett (1988), Ghoshal et al. (1994), Nobel and Birkinshaw (1998), Birkinshaw (1999), Noorderhaven and Harzing (2009)

No.	Factors of HS	Definition	Authors
1	R&D investment	Financial investment on R&D projects	Mishra and Gobeli (1998), Miravitlles et al. (2013)

(continued)

Table 7.1 (continued)

No.	Factors of HS	Definition	Authors
2	Autonomy	Subsidiary autonomy is defined as the ability to make local decisions by the subsidiary management	Ghoshal and Bartlett (1988), Ghoshal and Nohria (1989), Birkinshaw and Morrison (1995), Birkinshaw (1999), Birkinshaw et al. (1998), Nobel and Birkinshaw (1998), Boehe (2008), McDonald et al. (2008), Pogrebnyakov and Kristensen (2011), Collinson and Wang (2012)
3	Subsidiary mandate	Subsidiary mandate or charter set by the HQ defines the role, objectives and operation scope of the subsidiary	Roth and Morrison (1992), Birkinshaw and Morrison (1995), Birkinshaw (1996), Birkinshaw and Hood (1997, 1998), Moore (2001), Cantwell and Mudambi (2005), Boehe (2008), Mudambi (2011)
4	HQ involvement	Time, money and attention of executives and senior managers at HQ to the functioning of the subsidiaries	Johanson and Vahlne (1977), Bouquet et al. (2009), Ciabuschi et al. (2011), Ciabuschi et al. (2012a, b)
5	Expat resources	Expatriates are managers or senior technical staff who work outside their native country	Edström and Galbraith (1977), Downes and Thomas (2000), Harzing (2001a, b), Minbaeva et al. (2003), Björkman et al. (2004), Elenkov and Manev (2009), Fang et al. (2010), Chang et al. (2012)

7.3.1 Preliminary Verification of Factors by Experts

Multiple studies focused on determinants or factors of technological innovation have shown inconsistent results. The reasons attributed to this inconsistency include nature, definition and measurement of innovation, measurements of the determination of innovation, effect of different stages of innovation process on innovation rate, kinds of firms used as sample and the geographical context of the empirical survey (Souitaris 2003). Hence, it is recommended to validate the factors of SI for the specific country and industry context.

In light of the fact that innovation is context-specific, an idea engineering exercise was conducted to validate the factors identified through literature review by eliciting response from experts comprising senior managers and senior technical contributors with greater than 15 years of experience in the field of semiconductor

7 Modelling Subsidiary Innovation Factors … 95

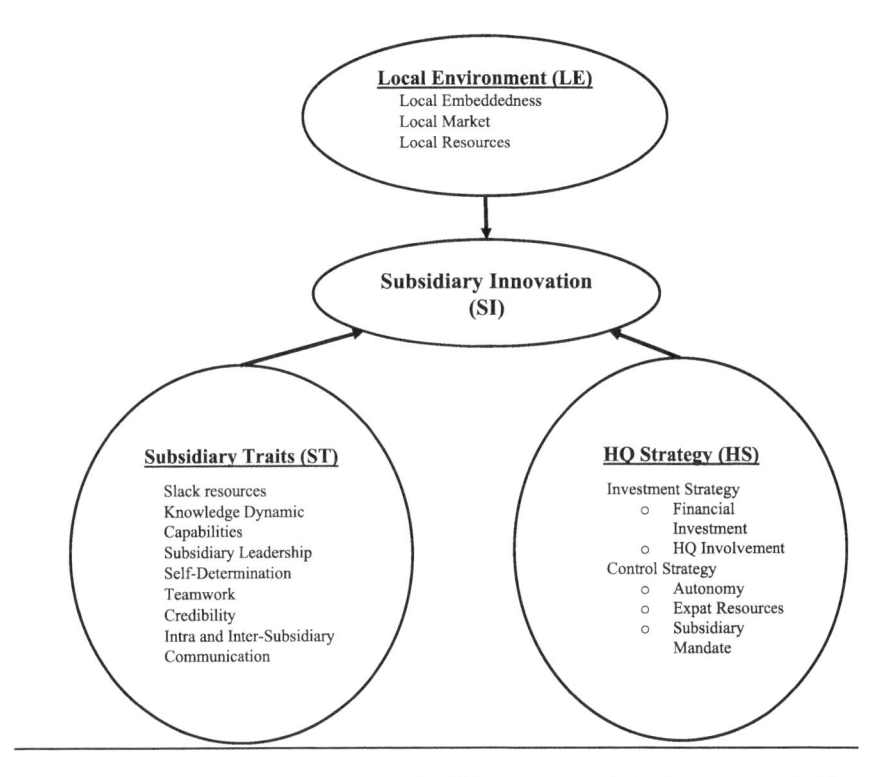

Fig. 7.1 Local environment, subsidiary traits, HQ strategy and its impact on subsidiary innovation

design industry from multiple subsidiaries located in India. The results obtained from the expert opinion survey indicate that barring two HS factors, remaining were found to be statistically significant (Betaraya et al. 2018). While the two HS factors, namely, HQ involvement and expatriate resources have been found to be statistically insignificant, given their p-value being close to 0.05 and the authors own experience in this field, we have decided to retain them for modelling purpose.

7.4 Modelling (TISM) of Local Environment, Subsidiary Traits and Headquarter Strategy Factors

The results of expert survey indicate a consensus amongst experts about the various SI factors. However, the interplay amongst these factors is quite complex to analyse. This requires analysis of the interactions of the various factors with the three macro factors to bring better clarity. Identifying the relationships amongst the various factors can be of great value to researchers and practitioners in the area of subsidiary innovation.

7.4.1 Introduction to Total Interpretive Structural Modelling (TISM)

Interpretive Structural Model (ISM) is a qualitative technique used in the preliminary stage of problem-solving to help make sense of complex relations. By systematically applying the graph theory repetitively, ISM allows the interpretation of embedded objects in the structural model (Nasim 2011). However, ISM has the limitation in terms of its inability to interpret in what way factor A influences factor B.

The limitation of interpretation in ISM is addressed by TISM using the interpretive matrix tool (Sushil 2005, 2012). In this approach, the causal thinking of experts is captured explicitly in the matrix while collecting data. TISM as a modelling technique has been used by a number of researchers in diverse management topics. This includes, modelling of continuity and change factors in E-Government (Nasim 2011; Nasim and Sushil 2014), Indian private higher technical education (Prasad and Suri 2011), factors affecting construction labour productivity (Sandbhor and Botre 2014), strategic performance management of Indian telecom service providers (Yadav and Sushil 2014), enablers of a flexible control system for industry (Jayalakshmi and Pramod 2015), agile performance in health care (Patri and Suresh 2017), etc.

This chapter attempts to apply TISM to the LE, ST and HS factors responsible for SI. One of the risks of TISM is that experts' views may not be consistent and hence not transitive. To address this risk, we consider the majority view (using opinion of two out of three) (Nasim 2011).

7.4.2 TISM Methodology

TISM methodology is used to delineate the hierarchical relationship amongst the factors of the three meta-constructs, namely, LE, ST and HS affecting SI in the semiconductor design subsidiaries located in India. To identify the contextual relation and the logic behind the indicated relations, experts' opinion in elicited.

Table 7.2 Steps to build TISM

Step No.	Purpose	Explanation
1	Identify and define elements	Identify and define the elements whose relations are to be modelled
2	Define contextual relationship	State the contextual relation between the elements
3	Interpretation of relation	Seek clarification from the experts on the interpretation/logic behind the expressed relation
4	Interpretive logic of pairwise comparison	The ith element is compared individually to all the elements from $(i + 1)$th to the nth element. For each link if the answer is Yes, an explanation is to be provided by the experts

(continued)

Table 7.2 (continued)

Step No.	Purpose	Explanation
5	Reachability matrix and transitivity check	Translate interpretive knowledge base to the form of reachability matrix. Replace 'Yes' by '1' and 'No' by '0'
6	Level partition on reachability matrix	Determine antecedent and reachability set for all the elements. If reachability set is the same as the intersection of antecedent and reachability set, then that element belongs to that level. Remove the element/s and iterate till all levels are determined
7	Develop digraph	Arrange the elements graphically in levels and draw directed links as per the reachability matrix
8	Interaction matrix	Translate the digraph to matrix form with relevant cells having the interpretation from the knowledge base
9	Total interpretive structural model	Replace nodes in digraph by the element definition. Interpretation of the relation is placed next to the links

The model developed is subject to assessment from a different set of experts to enhance its validity.

A nine-step process is followed to develop the TISM. The details of each of the steps are illustrated by earlier researchers (Nasim 2011; Prasad and Suri 2011; Sushil 2012, 2016, 2017) and illustrated in Table 7.2. Appendix 1 shows the reachability matrix for LE, ST and HS factors. Appendix 2 indicates the results of various steps of iterations for the LE, ST and HS factors to level partition the reachability matrix. Appendix 3 depicts the digraphs for the macro factors of SI.

7.5 Modelling the Subsidiary Innovation Factors in the Semiconductor Design Subsidiaries in India

Based on the nine-step process, three total interpretive structural models (TISM-ST, TISM-HS and TISM-LE) have been developed to model the relationship between the micro-variables of subsidiary traits, headquarter strategy and local environment. Each of these models is discussed separately below.

7.5.1 *Modelling Subsidiary Trait (ST) Factors*

The final TISM of the micro-variables related to subsidiary traits is presented in Fig. 7.2, and the relations identified are discussed. The final model is developed by building the reachability matrix (Appendix 1), partitioning the reachability matrix (Appendix 2), creating a digraph depicting the relationship between the nodes (Appendix 3) and the direct interaction matrix (Appendix 4) explaining the reasons behind the relations as indicated by experts.

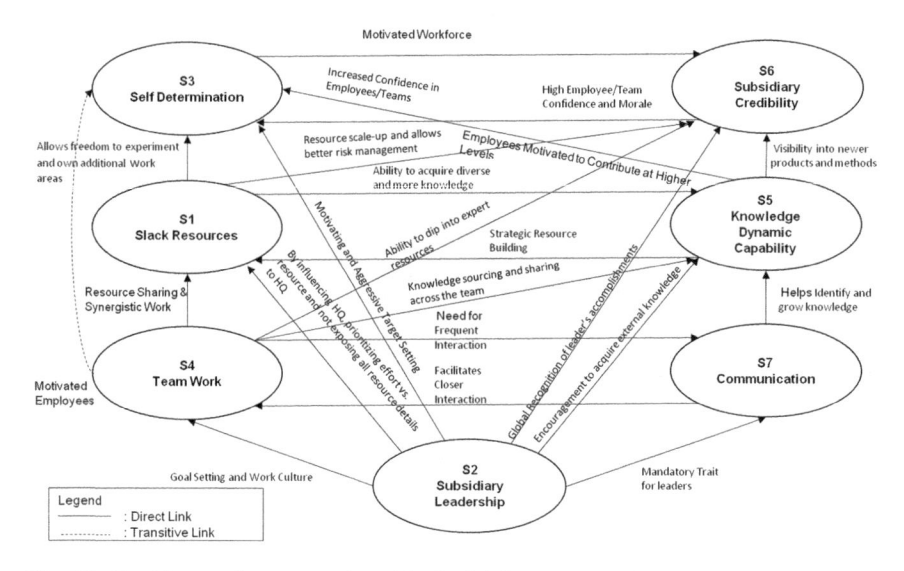

Fig. 7.2 Total interpretive structural model of subsidiary trait (ST) factors

Based on inputs from experts, the seven ST micro-variables are partitioned into four levels. Subsidiary leadership emerged as the basic ST factor in the semiconductor design subsidiary domain leading to teamwork and communication within the subsidiary, which in turn, enhances the availability of slack resources and dynamic knowledge capability of the subsidiary, which in turn, drives subsidiary self-determination and credibility. Motivation, communication, goal and culture setting, encouraging employees to learn and acquire new knowledge and influencing the headquarters are some of the reasons that make subsidiary leadership as the primary driving factor amongst the ST factors.

In addition to direct links, there is also a significant transitive link between teamwork and self-determination. Teamwork leads to intrinsic motivation amongst the team members (Mudambi et al. 2007) which influences self-determination of the team.

7.5.2 Modelling Headquarter Strategy (HS) Factors

The structural model (TISM-HS) developed based on experts' opinion on headquarter strategy micro-variables is shown in Fig. 7.3. The working details of this model development can be referred to in Appendices 1 to 4.

Based on expert opinion, the five headquarter strategy micro-variables are partitioned into three levels. R&D Investment and HQ Involvement have emerged as the basic HS factors that drive expatriate resourcing, which, in turn, drives subsidiary mandate and autonomy. Higher R&D investment implies that higher stakes for the MNE are involved and hence increases HQ involvement. Higher R&D investment goes into projects which are global in nature which implies wider

7 Modelling Subsidiary Innovation Factors ...

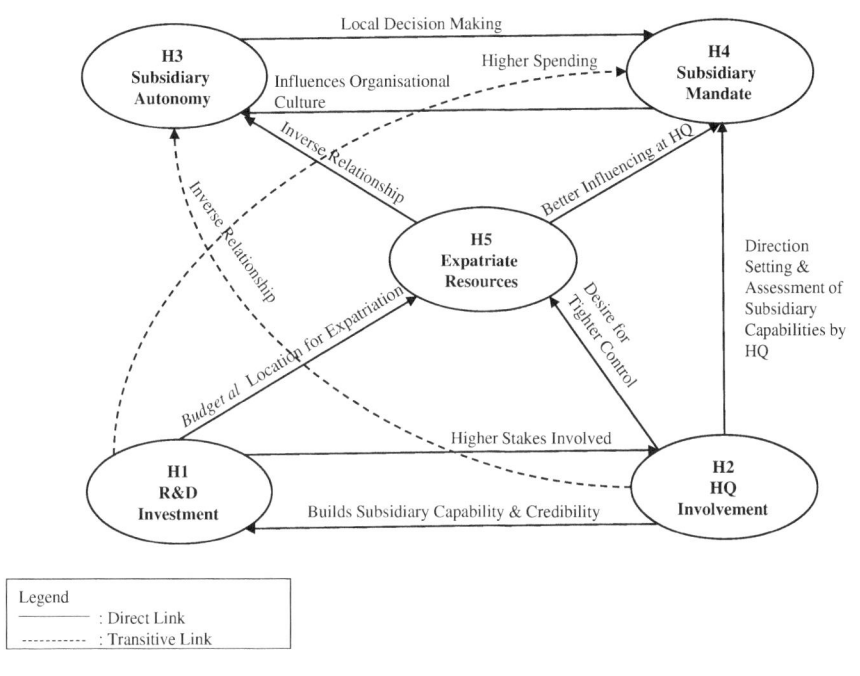

Fig. 7.3 Total interpretive structural model of HQ strategy (HS) factors

subsidiary mandate. Increased investment allows budgeting for expatriate resources along with increased control which implies higher HQ involvement.

Having higher autonomy allows local decision-making which can broaden the subsidiary mandate, while having a broader mandate results in a culture which encourages independent behaviour. Thus, autonomy and subsidiary mandate are interrelated. As seen from the figure, HQ involvement drives subsidiary mandate while R&D investment and HQ involvement are interrelated.

7.5.3 Modelling Local Environment (LE) Factors

Given that there are only three LE factors, it is not surprising to see that they are all at the same level. TISM for LE factors is shown in Fig. 7.4.

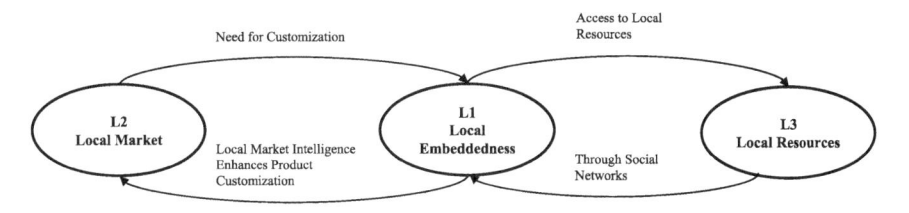

Fig. 7.4 Total interpretive structural model of local environment (LE) factors

There is a bidirectional relationship of local embeddedness with local market and local resources. However, as per experts, there is no direct or significant transitive relationship between local market and local resources. This could be because semiconductor industry has globalized innovation process which does not face localization pressure (Phene and Almeida 2008).

7.6 Model Assessment and Synthesis

Developing a model to establish relationship between variables is quite challenging. TISM as compared to ISM is more demanding in terms of time due to soliciting expert inputs on all the relationships amongst the variables. For example, the TISM-ST model, which has seven variables, has 42 links that need inputs from experts. Availability of time from experts to volunteer for this activity is very difficult and thus limits the number of expert inputs to the model. Thus, for initial development of the model, the response from three experts was collected. This can lead to lower quality of the model which is a major limitation of this approach.

However, once the model is built, the number of significant relationship amongst the variables expressed by the initial experts comes down significantly. For example, the number of significant relationships after the model development for TISM-ST came down from 42 to 23. It is also easier to find greater number of experts to assess the pictorial representation of relationships. Thus, a post facto assessment of the model by a separate panel of three experts was carried out to address the quality limitation.

The acceptability of the model was established using a 5-point Likert scale ranging from 1 (Strongly Disagree) to 5 (Strongly Agree) to gauge the extent of agreement/disagreement for each link in the model. Each model link was accepted if the average score of the experts for that relationship was greater than three, and the entire model was accepted if the average of all the links exceeded the score of three. This methodology is consistent with the approach taken by earlier researchers (Nasim 2011).

7.6.1 Synthesis of TISM Assessment

Based on experts' feedback as summarized in Appendix 5, all the three TISM models are accepted with average scores of 3.90 for TISM-ST, 3.67 for TISM-HS and 3.58 for TISM-LE. As evident from the scores, experts have expressed greater agreement with the model that depicts the subsidiary traits as compared to the headquarter strategy and local environment models.

Analysis of the individual links of the three models (Appendix 5) indicates that there is a greater agreement of the ST and LE factors as compared to the headquarter strategy factors as the least scores for ST and LE are 3.33 and that of HS is

3.0. Experts do not agree that there is a strong relationship between R&D investment and subsidiary mandate as well as the inverse relationship between HQ involvement and subsidiary autonomy. Given that the scores are 3 for both these links, which is borderline, these links are retained in the final model.

To summarize, the results of expert assessment of the model further inject confidence about the relevance and significance of the proposed factors of ST, HS and LE in the semiconductor design subsidiaries in India.

7.7 Implications for Researchers and Practitioners

The identification and modelling of the ST, HS and LE factors undertaken by this study serve as key inputs to researchers as well as practitioners. Using TISM to model key research constructs helps provide clarity to researchers in their research domain.

Implications for subsidiary and headquarter managers in the semiconductor design industry from this study can be summarized as follows:

- The TISM-ST model in relation to the subsidiary traits factors identifies that subsidiary leadership is the single most critical factor which influences the characteristics of the subsidiary and shapes its contribution to the multinational corporation. Thus, having a strong leader who has a clear vision and decision-making capability is very critical for the subsidiary.
- From the TISM-HS model, active involvement from HQ managers and substantial R&D investment is deemed to be very important.
- The TISM-LE model highlights that embedding within the local environment not only impacts the ability to attract good quality resources but also allows the subsidiary to customize products for the local market.

Implications for researchers from this study include a methodical approach to conduct an exploratory study, where variables are identified through a literature review followed by context confirmation of these variables by expert survey and developing a hierarchical model using TISM. Researchers can further validate these models by conducting a broad and large empirical study.

One of the key limitations of the study is comparatively fewer respondents and the use of qualitative research methodology. This shortcoming can be overcome by conducting a questionnaire-based survey and preparing case studies about semiconductor design subsidiaries located in India. This study makes a small contribution towards increasing the subsidiary innovation knowledge base.

7.8 Conclusion

Understanding the factors that impact the innovation and performance of subsidiaries is very critical for the MNE from a global innovation value chain perspective. While many past studies have focused on individual or a set of factors and their impact on subsidiary innovation, there has been little research done to understand the interplay amongst the factors. This chapter validates the subsidiary innovation factors in the Indian semiconductor design subsidiary context, classifies the factors in to three macro constructs, namely, subsidiary traits, headquarter strategy and local environment, and builds three hierarchical models to depict the interaction of factors amongst themselves using a qualitative technique known as TISM.

The three models are verified to enhance their validity. Based on expert validation, all the models are accepted. It is expected that the methodology used to develop these models as well as the models themselves will be of use to researchers and practitioners interested in the study of subsidiary innovation in the emerging economy context.

Appendix 1: Reachability Matrices

Reachability Matrix for ST Factors

	S1	S2	S3	S4	S5	S6	S7
S1	1	0	1	0	1	1	0
S2	1	1	1	1	1	1	1
S3	0	0	1	0	0	1	0
S4	1	0	1	1	1	1	1
S5	1	1	1	0	1	1	0
S6	0	0	1	0	0	1	0
S7	0	0	0	1	1	0	1

Reachability Matrix for HS Factors

	H1	H2	H3	H4	H5
H1	1	1	0	1	1
H2	1	1	1	1	1
H3	0	0	1	1	0
H4	0	0	1	1	0
H5	0	0	0	1	1

7 Modelling Subsidiary Innovation Factors ...

Reachability Matrix for LE Factors

	L1	L2	L3
L1	1	1	1
L2	1	1	1
L3	1	1	1

Appendix 2: Partitioning the Reachability Matrix into Different Levels

ST Factors

Variable	Reachability set	Antecedent set	Intersection set	Level
RM level partitioning—iteration 1				
S1	1,3,5,6	1,2,4,5,6	1,5,6	
S2	1,2,3,4,5,6,7	2,3,5,6	2,3,5,6	
S3	**3,6**	**1,2,3,4,5,6**	**3,6**	**1**
S4	1,3,4,5,6,7	2,3,4,7	3,4,7	
S5	1,2,3,5,6	1,2,3,4,5,7	1,3,5	
S6	**3,6**	**1,2,3,4,5,6**	**3,6**	**1**
S7	4,5,7	2,4,7	4,7	
RM level partitioning—iteration 2				
S1	**1,5**	**1,2,4,5**	**1,5**	**2**
S2	1,2,4,5,7	2,5	2,5	
S4	1,4,5,7	2,4,7	4,7	
S5	**1,5**	**1,2,4,5,7**	**1,5**	**2**
S7	4,5,7	2,4,7	4,7	
RM level partitioning—iteration 3				
S2	2,4,7	2	2	4
S4	**4,7**	**2,4,7**	**4,7**	**3**
S7	**4,7**	**2,4,7**	**4,7**	**3**
Summary of iteration steps				
S3	3,6	1,2,3,4,5,6	3,6	1
S6	3,6	1,2,3,4,5,6	3,6	1
S1	1,5	1,2,4,5	1,5	2
S5	1,5	1,2,4,5,7	1,5	2
S4	4,7	2,4,7	4,7	3
S7	4,7	2,4,7	4,7	3
S2	2	2	2	4

For HS Factors

Variable	Reachability set	Antecedent set	Intersection set	Level
RM level partitioning—iteration 1				
H1	1,2,4,5	1,2	1,2	
H2	1,2,3,4,5	1,2,3,4	1,2,3,4	
H3	**3,4**	**2,3,4**	**3,4**	**1**
H4	**3,4**	**1,2,3,4,5**	**3,4**	**1**
H5	4,5	1,2,5	5	
RM level partitioning—iteration 2				
H1	1,2,5	1,2	1,2	
H2	1,2,5	1,2	1,2	
H5	**5**	**5**	**5**	**2**
RM level partitioning—iteration 3				
H1	**1,2**	**1,2**	**1,2**	**3**
H2	**1,2**	**1,2**	**1,2**	**3**
RM level partitioning—iteration 1–3				
H3	3,4	2,3,4	3,4	1
H4	3,4	1,2,3,4,5	3,4	1
H5	5	5	5	2
H1	1,2	1,2	1,2	3
H2	1,2	1,2	1,2	3

For LE Factors

Variable	Reachability set	Antecedent set	Intersection set	Level
RM level partitioning—iteration 1				
L1	**1,2,3**	**1,2,3**	**1,2,3**	**1**
L2	**1,2,3**	**1,2,3**	**1,2,3**	**1**
L3	**1,3,3**	**1,2,3**	**1,2,3**	**1**

Appendix 3: Initial Digraphs

For ST Factors

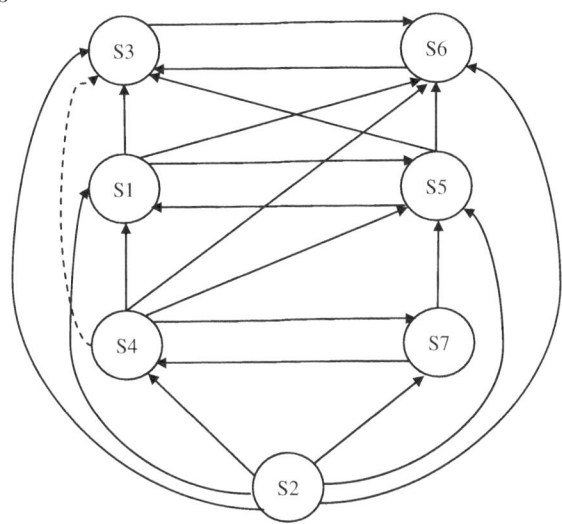

For HS Factors

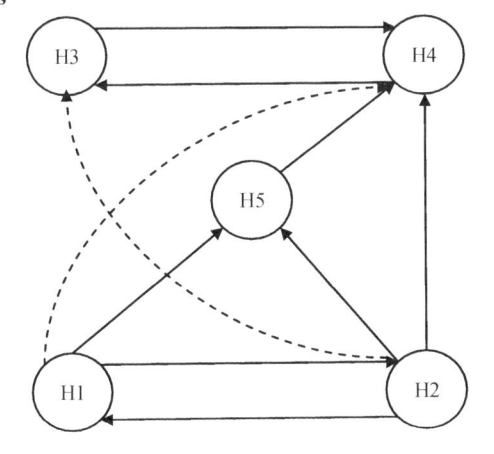

For LE Factors

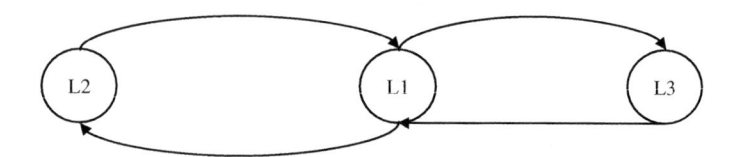

Appendix 4: Direct Interaction Matrices

For ST Factors

	S1	S2	S3	S4	S5	S6	S7
S1			Allows freedom to experiment and own additional work areas		Ability to acquire diverse and more knowledge	Because of resource scale-up and allows better risk management	
S2	By influencing HQ, prioritizing effort versus resource and not exposing all resource details to HQ		By motivating and setting aggressive targets	By goal setting and work culture	Due to encouragement to acquire external knowledge	Global recognition of leader's accomplishments	Mandatory trait for leaders
S3						Motivated workforce	
S4	Resource sharing and synergistic work		Motivated employees		Knowledge sourcing and sharing across the team	Ability to dip into expert resources	Need for frequent interaction
S5	Strategic resource building		Employees motivated to contribute at higher levels			Visibility into newer products and methods	

(continued)

7 Modelling Subsidiary Innovation Factors …

(continued)

	S1	S2	S3	S4	S5	S6	S7
S6			High employee/team confidence and morale				
S7				Facilitate closer interaction	Helps identify and grow knowledge		

For HS Factors

	H1	H2	H3	H4	H5
H1		Higher stakes involved		Higher spending	Budget allocation for expatriation
H2	Builds subsidiary capability and credibility		Inverse relationship	Direction setting and assessment of subsidiary capabilities	Desire for tighter control
H3				Local decision-making	
H4			Influences organizational culture		
H5				Better influencing at HQ	

For LE Factors

	L1	L2	L3
L1		Local market intelligence enhances product customization	Access to local resources
L2	Encouraging and forcing customization		
L3	Through social networks		

Appendix 5: Model Assessment by Experts

TISM-ST Model Assessment

S. No.	Variables linked	Reason quoted by previous experts	E1	E2	E3	Link average score	Model average score
1	Slack resources impacts/affects self-determination	Allows freedom to experiment and own additional areas	3	4	4	3.67	3.90 Accept the model
2	Slack resources impacts/affects knowledge dynamic capability	Ability to acquire diverse and more knowledge	3	4	4	3.67	
3	Slack resources impacts/affects subsidiary credibility	Because of resource scale-up and allows better risk management	4	4	2	3.33	
4	Subsidiary leadership impacts/affects slack resources	By influencing HQ, prioritizing effort versus resources and not exposing all resource details to HQ	4	4	3	3.67	
5	Subsidiary leadership impacts/affects self-determination	By motivating and setting aggressive targets	5	3	5	4.33	
6	Subsidiary leadership impacts/affects teamwork	By goal setting and work culture	5	4	4	4.33	
7	Subsidiary leadership impacts knowledge dynamic capability	Due to encouragement to acquire external knowledge	5	4	4	4.33	
8	Subsidiary leadership impacts/affects subsidiary credibility	Global recognition of leader's accomplishment	5	3	5	4.33	
9	Subsidiary leadership impacts/affects communication	Mandatory trait for leaders	5	4	5	4.67	
10	Self-determination impacts/affects subsidiary credibility	Motivated work force	4	4	3	3.67	

(continued)

7 Modelling Subsidiary Innovation Factors …

(continued)

S. No.	Variables linked	Reason quoted by previous experts	E1	E2	E3	Link average score	Model average score
11	Teamwork impacts/affects slack resources	Resource sharing and synergistic work	5	4	3	4.00	
12	Teamwork impacts/affects self-determination	Motivated employees	4	4	4	4.00	
13	Teamwork impacts/affects knowledge dynamic capability	Knowledge sourcing and sharing across the team	4	4	4	4.00	
14	Teamwork impacts/affects subsidiary credibility	Ability to dip into expert resources	4	4	5	4.33	
15	Teamwork impacts/affects communication	Need for frequent interaction	3	4	4	3.67	
16	Knowledge dynamic capability impacts/affects slack resources	Strategic resource building	4	3	3	3.33	
17	Knowledge dynamic capability impacts/affects self-determination	Employees motivated to contribute at higher levels	4	4	3	3.67	
18	Knowledge dynamic capability impacts/affects subsidiary credibility	Visibility into newer products and methods	4	4	4	4.00	
19	Subsidiary credibility impacts/affects self-determination	High employee/team confidence and morale	4	4	3	3.67	
20	Communication impacts/affects teamwork	Facilitates closer interaction	4	4	5	4.33	
21	Communication impacts/affects knowledge dynamic capability	Helps identify and grow knowledge	2	4	4	3.33	

TISM-HS Model Assessment

S. No.	Variables linked	Reason quoted by previous experts	E1	E2	E3	Link average score	model average score
1	R&D investment impacts/affects HQ involvement	Higher stakes involved	4	3	4	3.67	3.67 Accept the model
2	R&D investment impacts/affects subsidiary mandate	Higher spending	3	3	3	3.00*	
3	R&D investment impacts/affects expatriate resources	Budget allocation for expatriation	4	4	3	3.67	
4	HQ involvement impacts/affects R&D investment	Builds subsidiary capability and credibility	3	4	5	4.00	
5	HQ involvement impacts/affects subsidiary autonomy	Inversely related	4	3	2	3.00*	
6	HQ involvement impacts/affects subsidiary mandate	Direction setting and assessment of subsidiary capabilities by HQ	4	3	4	3.67	
7	HQ involvement impacts/affects expatriate resources	Desire for tighter control	4	4	4	4.00	
8	Subsidiary autonomy impacts/affects subsidiary mandate	Local decision-making	5	4	4	4.33	
9	Subsidiary mandate impacts/affects subsidiary autonomy	Organizational culture	4	4	4	4.00	
10	Expatriate resources impacts/affects subsidiary mandate	Better influencing at HQ	4	4	2	3.33	

TISM-LE Model Assessment

S. No.	Variables linked	Reason quoted by previous experts	E1	E2	E3	Link average score	Model average score
1	Local embeddedness impacts/affects local market	Local market intelligence enhances product customization	4	3	4	3.67	3.58 Accept the model
2	Local embeddedness impacts/affects local resources	Access to local resources	3	3	4	3.33	
3	Local market impacts/affects local embeddedness	Need for customization	4	3	4	3.67	
4	Local resources impacts/affects local embeddedness	Through social networks	4	3	4	3.67	

References

Almeida, P. (1996). Knowledge sourcing by foreign multinationals: Patent citation analysis in the U.S. semiconductor industry. *Strategic Management Journal, 17*(S2), 155–165. https://doi.org/10.1002/smj.4250171113.

Almeida, P., & Phene, A. (2004). Subsidiaries and knowledge creation: The influence of the MNC and host country on innovation. *Strategic Management Journal, 25*(8/9), 847.

Ambos, T. C., Andersson, U., & Birkinshaw, J. (2010). What are the consequences of initiative-taking in multinational subsidiaries? *Journal of International Business Studies, 41*(7), 1099–1118.

Andersson, U., Forsgren, M., & Holm, U. (2002). The strategic impact of external networks: Subsidiary performance and competence development in the multinational corporation. *Strategic Management Journal, 23*(11), 979–996.

Andersson, U., Forsgren, M., & Holm, U. (2007). Balancing subsidiary influence in the federative MNC: A business network view. *Journal of International Business Studies, 38*(5), 802–818.

Batsakis, G. (2012). R&D subsidiaries' innovative performance "revisited": A multilevel approach. In *Presented at the DRUID Conference, Copenhagen*.

Betaraya, D. M., Nasim, S., & Mukhopadhyay, J. (2018). Subsidiary innovation in developing economy: Towards a Comprehensive Model and Directions for Future Research. Manuscript submitted for publication.

Birkinshaw, J. (1996). How multinational subsidiary mandates are gained and lost. *Journal of International Business Studies, 27*(3), 467–495.

Birkinshaw, J. (1999). The determinants and consequences of subsidiary initiative in multinational corporations. *Entrepreneurship Theory and Practice, 24*(1), 9–36.

Birkinshaw, J., & Hood, N. (1997). An empirical study of development processes in foreign-owned subsidiaries in Canada and Scotland. *MIR: Management International Review, 37*(4), 339–364.

Birkinshaw, J., & Hood, N. (1998). Multinational subsidiary evolution: Capability and charter change in foreign-owned subsidiary companies. *Academy of Management Review, 23*(4), 773–795.

Birkinshaw, J., Hood, N., & Jonsson, S. (1998). Building firm-specific advantages in multinational corporations: The role of subsidiary initiative. *Strategic Management Journal, 19*(3), 221–242.

Birkinshaw, J., & Morrison, A. J. (1995). Configurations of strategy and structure in subsidiaries of multinational corporations. *Journal of International Business Studies, 26*(4), 729–753.

Björkman, I., Barner-Rasmussen, W., & Li, L. (2004). Managing knowledge transfer in MNCs: The impact of headquarters control mechanisms. *Journal of International Business Studies, 35*(5), 443–455.

Boehe, D. M. (2008). Product development in emerging market subsidiaries—The influence of autonomy and internal markets on subsidiary roles. *International Journal of Innovation and Technology Management, 5*(01), 29–53.

Bouquet, C., Morrison, A., & Birkinshaw, J. (2009). International attention and multinational enterprise performance. *Journal of International Business Studies, 40*(1), 108–131.

Brown, C., Linden, G., & Macher, J. T. (2005). Offshoring in the semiconductor industry: A historical perspective [with comment and discussion]. *Brookings Trade Forum*, 279–333. https://doi.org/10.2307/25058769.

Cantwell, J., & Mudambi, R. (2005). MNE competence-creating subsidiary mandates. *Strategic Management Journal, 26*(12), 1109–1128.

Chang, Y.-Y., Gong, Y., & Peng, M. W. (2012). Expatriate knowledge transfer, subsidiary absorptive capacity, and subsidiary performance. *Academy of Management Journal, 55*(4), 927–948.

Ciabuschi, F., Dellestrand, H., & Holm, U. (2012a). The role of headquarters in the contemporary MNC. *Journal of International Management, 18*(3), 213–223.

Ciabuschi, F., Dellestrand, H., & Martín, O. M. (2011). Internal Embeddedness, headquarters involvement, and innovation importance in multinational enterprises: Internal drivers of innovation importance in MNEs. *Journal of Management Studies, 48*(7), 1612–1639.

Ciabuschi, F., Forsgren, M., & Martín, O. (2012b). Headquarters involvement and efficiency of innovation development and transfer in multinationals: A matter of sheer ignorance? *International Business Review, 21*(2), 130–144.

Ciabuschi, F., Holm, U., & Martín, O. (2014). Dual Embeddedness, influence and performance of innovating subsidiaries in the multinational corporation. *International Business Review, 23*(5), 897–909.

Collinson, S. C., & Wang, R. (2012). The evolution of innovation capability in multinational enterprise subsidiaries: Dual network embeddedness and the divergence of subsidiary specialisation in Taiwan. *Research Policy, 41*(9), 1501–1518.

Damanpour, F. (1987). The adoption of technological, administrative, and ancillary innovations: Impact of organizational factors. *Journal of Management, 13*(4), 675–688.

Damijan, J. P., Kostevc, C., & Rojec, M. (2010). Does a foreign subsidiary's network status affect its innovation activity? Evidence from post-socialist economies. *Documentos de Trabajo= Working Papers (Instituto Complutense de Estudios Internacionales): Nueva época, 6*, 1.

Demirbag, M., & Glaister, K. W. (2010). Factors determining offshore location choice for R&D projects: A comparative study of developed and emerging regions. *Journal of Management Studies, 47*(8), 1534–1560.

Denti, L., & Hemlin, S. (2012). Leadership and innovation in organizations: A systematic review of factors that mediate or moderate the relationship. *International Journal of Innovation Management, 16*(03), 1240007.

Downes, M., & Thomas, A. S. (2000). Knowledge transfer through expatriation: The U-curve approach to overseas staffing. *Journal of Managerial Issues, 12*(2), 131–149.

Dunning, J. H., & Lundan, S. M. (2009). The internationalization of corporate R&D: A review of the evidence and some policy implications for home countries. *Review of Policy Research, 26* (1–2), 13–33.

Edström, A., & Galbraith, J. R. (1977). Transfer of managers as a coordination and control strategy in multinational organizations. *Administrative Science Quarterly, 22*(2), 248–263.

Egelhoff, W. G. (2010). How the parent headquarters adds value to an MNC. *Management International Review (MIR), 50*(4), 413–431.

Elenkov, D. S., & Manev, I. M. (2009). Senior expatriate leadership's effects on innovation and the role of cultural intelligence. *Journal of World Business, 44*(4), 357–369.

Ernst & Young. (2011). *Study on semiconductor design, embedded software and services industry.* Bangalore: Indian Semiconductor Association.

Fang, Y., Jiang, G.-L. F., Makino, S., & Beamish, P. W. (2010). Multinational firm knowledge, use of expatriates, and foreign subsidiary performance. *Journal of Management Studies, 47*(1), 27–54. https://doi.org/10.1111/j.1467-6486.2009.00850.x.

Figueiredo, P. N., & Brito, K. (2011). The innovation performance of MNE subsidiaries and local embeddedness: Evidence from an emerging economy. *Journal of Evolutionary Economics, 21* (1), 141–165.

Frost, T. S. (2001). The geographic sources of foreign subsidiaries' innovations. *Strategic Management Journal, 22*(2), 101–123.

Frost, T. S., Birkinshaw, J. M., & Ensign, P. C. (2002). Centers of excellence in multinational corporations. *Strategic Management Journal, 23*(11), 997–1018.

Fuller, D. B. (2014). Chip design in China and India: Multinationals, industry structure and development outcomes in the integrated circuit industry. *Technological Forecasting and Social Change, 81*, 1–10. https://doi.org/10.1016/j.techfore.2012.10.025.

Geiger, S. W., & Cashen, L. H. (2002). A multidimensional examination of slack and its impact on innovation. *Journal of Managerial Issues, 14*(1), 68–84.

Ghoshal, S., & Bartlett, C. A. (1988). Creation, adoption and diffusion of innovations by subsidiaries of multinational corporations. *Journal of International Business Studies, 19*(3), 365–388. https://doi.org/10.1057/palgrave.jibs.8490388.

Ghoshal, S., Korine, H., & Szulanski, G. (1994). Interunit communication in multinational corporations. *Management Science, 40*(1), 96–110.

Ghoshal, S., & Nohria, N. (1989). Internal differentiation within multinational corporations. *Strategic Management Journal, 10*(4), 323–337.

Håkanson, L., & Nobel, R. (2001). Organizational characteristics and reverse technology transfer. *MIR: Management International Review, 41*(4), 395–420.

Harzing, A.-W. (2001a). An analysis of the functions of international transfer of managers in MNCs. *Employee Relations, 23*(6), 581–598.

Harzing, A.-W. (2001b). Of bears, bumble-bees, and spiders: The role of expatriates in controlling foreign subsidiaries. *Journal of World Business, 36*(4), 366–379.

Herold, D. M., Jayaraman, N., & Narayanaswamy, C. R. (2006). What is the relationship between organizational slack and innovation? *Journal of Managerial Issues, 18*(3), 372–392. https://doi.org/10.2307/40604546.

Jayalakshmi, B., & Pramod, V. R. (2015). Total interpretive structural modeling (TISM) of the enablers of a flexible control system for industry. *Global Journal of Flexible Systems Management, 16*(1), 63–85.

Johanson, J., & Vahlne, J.-E. (1977). The internationalization process of the firm-a model of knowledge development and increasing foreign market commitments. *Journal of International Business Studies, 8*(1), 23–32.

Karna, A., Täube, F., & Sonderegger, P. (2013). Evolution of innovation networks across geographical and organizational boundaries: A study of R&D subsidiaries in the Bangalore IT cluster. *European Management Review, 10*(4), 211–226.

Keller, W. W., & Pauly, L. W. (2009). Innovation in the Indian semiconductor industry: The challenge of sectoral deepening. *Business and Politics, 11*(2).

Ke, S., & Lai, M. (2011). Productivity of Chinese regions and the location of multinational research and development. *International Regional Science Review, 34*(1), 102–131.

Kim, H. (2013). Local engineers as knowledge Liaison. *Annals of Business Administrative Science, 12*(1), 45–62.

Krishna, V. V., Patra, S. K., & Bhattacharya, S. (2012). Internationalisation of R&D and global nature of innovation: Emerging trends in India. *Science Technology & Society, 17*(2), 165–199.

Lema, R., Quadros, R., & Schmitz, H. (2015). Reorganising global value chains and building innovation capabilities in Brazil and India. *Research Policy, 44*(7), 1376–1386. https://doi.org/10.1016/j.respol.2015.03.005.

Li, X., Wang, J., & Liu, X. (2013). Can locally-recruited R&D personnel significantly contribute to multinational subsidiary innovation in an emerging economy? *International Business Review, 22*(4), 639–651.

Mahnke, V., Pedersen, T., & Venzin, M. (2005). The impact of knowledge management on MNC subsidiary performance: The role of absorptive capacity. *MIR: Management International Review, 45*(2), 101–119.

McDonald, F., Warhurst, S., & Allen, M. (2008). Autonomy, embeddedness, and the performance of foreign owned subsidiaries. *Multinational Business Review, 16*(3), 73–92.

Meyer, K. E., Mudambi, R., & Narula, R. (2011). Multinational enterprises and local contexts: The opportunities and challenges of multiple embeddedness. *Journal of Management Studies, 48*(2), 235–252.

Michailova, S., & Zhan, W. (2015). Dynamic capabilities and innovation in MNC subsidiaries. *Journal of World Business, 50*(3), 576–583.

Minbaeva, D., Pedersen, T., Björkman, I., Fey, C. F., & Park, H. J. (2003). MNC knowledge transfer, subsidiary absorptive capacity, and HRM. *Journal of International Business Studies, 34*(6), 586–599.

Miravitlles, P., Guitart-Tarrés, L., Achcaoucaou, F., & Núñez-Carballosa, A. (2013). The role of the environment in the location of R&D and innovation activities in subsidiaries of foreign multinationals. *Innovation, 15*(2), 170–182.

Mishra, C. S., & Gobeli, D. H. (1998). Managerial incentives, internalization, and market valuation of multinational firms. *Journal of International Business Studies, 29*(3), 583–597.

Molero, J., & Garcia, A. (2008). The innovative activity of foreign subsidiaries in the spanish innovation system: An evaluation of their impact from a sectoral taxonomy approach. *Technovation, 28*(11), 739–757.

Moore, K. J. (2001). A strategy for subsidiaries: Centres of excellences to build subsidiary specific advantages. *MIR: Management International Review, 41*(3), 275–290.

Mudambi, R. (2011). Hierarchy, coordination, and innovation in the multinational enterprise. *Global Strategy Journal, 1*(3–4), 317–323.

Mudambi, R., Mudambi, S. M., & Navarra, P. (2007). Global innovation in MNCs: The effects of subsidiary self-determination and teamwork*. *Journal of Product Innovation Management, 24*(5), 442–455.

Mu, S. "Carolyn," Gnyawali, D. R., & Hatfield, D. E. (2007). Foreign subsidiaries' learning from local environments: An empirical test. *Management International Review, 47*(1), 79–102.

Nasim, S. (2011). Total interpretive structural modeling of continuity and change forces in e-government. *Journal of Enterprise Transformation, 1*(2), 147–168.

Nasim, S., & Sushil. (2014). Flexible strategy framework for managing continuity and change in e-government. In *The flexible enterprise* (pp. 47–66). New Delhi: Springer.

Nobel, R., & Birkinshaw, J. (1998). Innovation in multinational corporations: Control and communication patterns in international R & D operations. *Strategic Management Journal, 19*(5), 479–496.

Nohria, N., & Gulati, R. (1996). Is slack good or bad for innovation? *Academy of Management Journal, 39*(5), 1245–1264.

Nohria, N., & Gulati, R. (1997). What is the optimum amount of organizational slack? A study of the relationship between slack and innovation in multinational firms. *European Management Journal, 15*(6), 603–611.

Noorderhaven, N., & Harzing, A.-W. (2009). Knowledge-sharing and social interaction within MNEs. *Journal of International Business Studies, 40*(5), 719–741.

Patri, R., & Suresh, M. (2017). Modelling the enablers of agile performance in healthcare organization: A TISM approach. *Global Journal of Flexible Systems Management, 18*(3), 251–272.

Phene, A., & Almeida, P. (2008). Innovation in multinational subsidiaries: The role of knowledge assimilation and subsidiary capabilities. *Journal of International Business Studies, 39*(5), 901–919.

Pogrebnyakov, N., & Kristensen, J. D. (2011). Building innovation subsidiaries in emerging markets: The experience of Novo Nordisk. *Research-Technology Management, 54*(4), 30–37.

Prasad, U. C., & Suri, R. K. (2011). Modeling of continuity and change forces in private higher technical education using total interpretive structural modeling (TISM). *Global Journal of Flexible Systems Management, 12*(3/4), 31–39.

Roth, K., & Morrison, A. J. (1992). Implementing global strategy: Characteristics of global subsidiary mandates. *Journal of International Business Studies, 23*(4), 715–735.

Sandbhor, S. S., & Botre, R. P. (2014). Applying total interpretive structural modeling to study factors affecting construction labour productivity. *Australasian Journal of Construction Economics and Building, 14*(1), 20. https://doi.org/10.5130/ajceb.v14i1.3753.

Souitaris, V. (2003). Determinants of technological innovation: Current research trends and future prospects. *The International Handbook on Innovation, 7*(07), 513–528.

Sushil. (2005). Interpretive matrix: A tool to aid interpretation of management and social research. *Global Journal of Flexible Systems Management, 6*(2), 27–30.

Sushil. (2012). Interpreting the interpretive structural model. *Global Journal of Flexible Systems Management, 13*(2), 87–106.

Sushil. (2016). How to Check correctness of total interpretive structural models? *Annals of Operations Research*, 1–15. https://doi.org/10.1007/s10479-016-2312-3.

Sushil. (2017). Modified ISM/TISM process with simultaneous transitivity checks for reducing direct pair comparisons. *Global Journal of Flexible Systems Management, 18*(4), 331–351.

UNCTAD. (2014). *World Investment Report 2014.*

Wolfe, R. A. (1994). Organizational innovation: Review, critique and suggested research directions. *Journal of Management Studies, 31*(3), 405–431. https://doi.org/10.1111/j.1467-6486.1994.tb00624.x.

Yadav, N., & Sushil. (2014). Total interpretive structural modelling (TISM) of strategic performance management for Indian telecom service providers. *International Journal of Productivity and Performance Management, 63*(4), 421–445.

Zaheer, S., & Nachum, L. (2011). Sense of place: From location resources to MNE locational capital. *Global Strategy Journal, 1*(1–2), 96–108.

Zahra, S. A., Dharwadkar, R., & George, G. (2000). Entrepreneurship in multinational subsidiaries: The effects of corporate and local environmental contexts. In *Published in Conference Proceedings, Entrepreneurship, Academy of Management.*

Zhao, H., & Luo, Y. (2005). Antecedents of knowledge sharing with peer subsidiaries in other countries: A perspective from subsidiary managers in a foreign emerging market. *MIR: Management International Review, 45*(1), 71–97.

Zhong, H. (2010). The impact of organizational slack on technological innovation: Evidence from Henan Province in China. In *2010 International Conference on Management and Service Science (MASS)* (pp. 1–4). IEEE.

Part II
Strategy and Flexibility

Chapter 8
Innovative Inventory Management for Flexible Adaptation

István Fekete and Tamás Hartványi

Abstract In this chapter, we focus on how to utilise the differential properties of the billion-year-old biochemical networks what make them so resilient against cascading failures, and in the same time, create agile adaptability to large disruptions. Those properties are the network degeneracy, the nested plasticity and the topological phase transition. Our innovative inventory management solution on creating symmetrical weak–weak-linkedness and nested plasticity in the organisation's material-subnetwork opens a new path to the supply chain management and supply chain design especially in disruptive environment.

Keywords Adaptability · Creative element · Degeneracy · Flexibility Inventory management · Plasticity–rigidity cycle · Supply chain network Topological phase transition

8.1 Introduction

Barabási (2012) pointed out that the network theory is a very powerful approach to link vastly different systems and to show the general elements of their organisation, dynamism and stability. The application of the network science approach has delivered significant breakthroughs in several disciplines, e.g. the drug design, the fight against terrorism and against cancer, the cognitive sciences, the linguistics, etc. It helped also in better understanding the resilience, adaptability, evolvability and robustness of the complex networked systems (Csermely 2009; Newman 2010; Barabási 2012). Understanding the differentiating properties of the billion-year-old viable networks, we could develop innovative solutions to increase the resilience

I. Fekete
ICG Integrated Consulting Group Kft., Budapest Sas Utca 10-12, 1051, Hungary
e-mail: fekete.istvan.pic@gmail.com

T. Hartványi (✉)
Széchenyi István University, Egyetem Tér 1, Győr 9026, Hungary
e-mail: hartvanyi@sze.hu

and agile adaptability of the organisation, the network element of the supply chain network. In this article, we discuss our innovative inventory management solution that creates the network-stabilising weak-linkedness in the material-subnetwork and smoothens the stability landscape of it. Before we discuss the developed inventory management solution, we introduce the general theories of the topological phase transition and of plasticity–rigidity cycles, i.e. the structural and functional adaptation mechanisms of the complex viable networks in a changing environment.

8.2 Topological Phase Transitions of the Networks

The viable networks adapt to environmental changes through series of topological phase transitions (Csermely 2009). As is seen in Fig. 8.1, high energy level and plethora of the resources result in random graph topology with short paths and plenty of links. The degree distribution corresponds to 'single-scale' Poisson distribution of Erdős–Rényi graph (Barabási et al. 2004). When the energy level, the available resources decrease, the network maintains its connectivity through reducing the number of links and developing longer range links to its modules, which have become relatively more isolated from each other. The network's clustering is increasing shifting from random graph to small-world networks (Watts and Strogatz 1998). The further limitation in resources requires more optimal utilisation of the available ones leading to further differentiation in the distribution of the links' strength and the nodes' degree. As a result, the network develops scale-free topology with scale-free distribution in nodes' degrees and links' weights. When the resources decrease further, a radical condensation takes place, which leads to the decrease of the weaker links and to a relative increase of the stronger ones. Lower degree hubs disappear, and few high-degree hubs remain. Consequently, the compactness of the network increases further, and it turns to star network topology. That corresponds to dictatorship and to the neighbouring topology of a strong dictating company (Fekete and Hartványi 2017). Further increase in perturbations and stress and/or decrease in resources cause the collapse of the network which falls into disconnected subgraphs—it dies.

8.3 Plasticity–Rigidity Cycles of Complex Networks Enable Adaptation

Csermely et al. (2012) and Csermely (2015) underline the agile adaptation to environmental changes is a prerequisite of the network's survival. The recursive cycles of more plastic exploring behaviour and of more rigid exploiting behaviour create the adaptation. Both extremes of rigidity and of plasticity lead to destabilisation of the system. The plasticity–rigidity cycles of different spatiotemporal

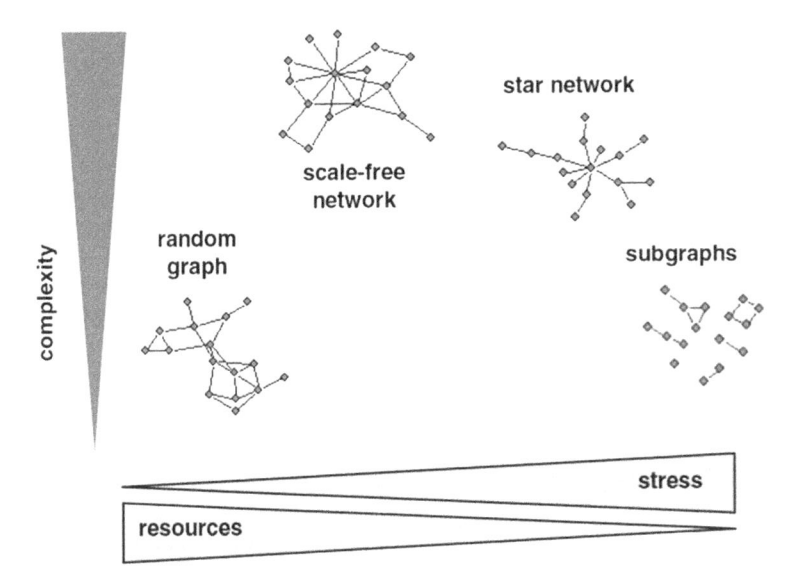

Fig. 8.1 Topological phase transitions of the networks due to environmental changes—with kind permission of Csermely (2009)

extents stabilise the networks against perturbations of different magnitudes and significantly support the success and survival of the network. Since the plasticity–rigidity cycles form an overlapping embedded complex structure, we use the symbol of yin and yang what symbolises that embeddedness (see Fig. 8.2).

The classical supply chain and operations management solutions deliver more focus, canalization, standardisation and exploitation, in other words, those create structural and functional rigidity. As it will be seen later, our innovative inventory management solution with nested plasticity enables the organisation to develop structural and behavioural plasticity in its material subnetwork to anticipate a less predictable and more turbulent overall demand pattern.

The current state and the possible states of the complex networks can be visualised by stability landscape (Csermely 2015). The local optimal minima in the stability landscape are separated by ridges and saddles of different heights causing rougher or smoother landscape. Rough stability landscapes make the transition from one state (local minimum) to another more difficult, often resulting in so-called punctuated equilibrium. The roughness of the stability landscape can be smoothened by adding weak links to the network, like water in biochemical networks, chaperone proteins in protein–protein interaction networks (Kovács et al. 2005; Antal et al. 2009; Csermely et al. 2013). By cycling between more plastic and more rigid states, the complex networks find the maximal structural and functional stability in a changing environment.

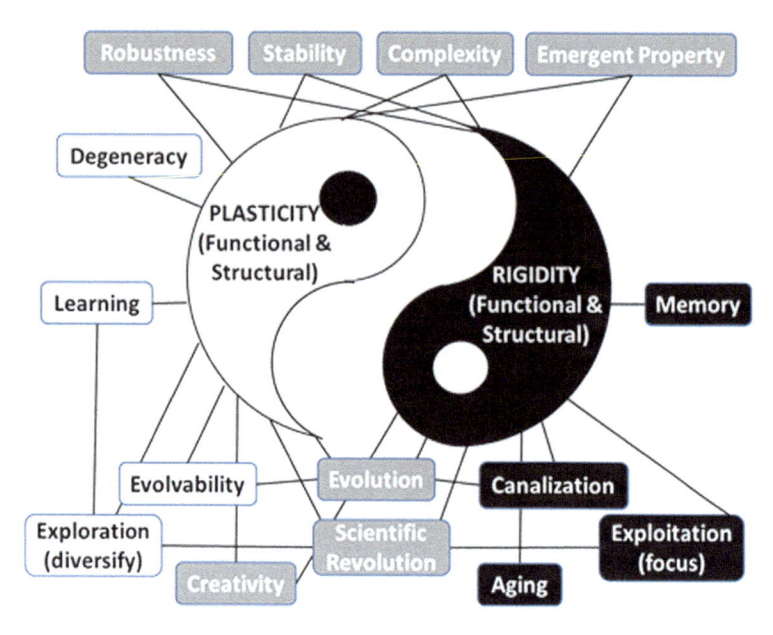

Fig. 8.2 Plasticity–rigidity cycle and its connection with key network characteristics—reconstructed with kind permission of Peter Csermely

8.4 What We Have Learned from Viable Networks?

Engineering approach expects perfect interplay between the elementary parts as designed. Csermely (2009) gives a list of distinctions between the engineering and evolutionary ('tinkerer') approaches in his fundamental monograph. Evolvability lies between the two extremes of 'error catastrophe' and 'perfection catastrophe' (Csermely 2015). We have proven empirically in different industries that it is possible to blend the engineering and evolutionary 'tinkerer' approaches in supply chain and operations management. Our suggested approach is about building predefined error tolerance in the determined parts of the organisation at different hierarchical levels.

Sushil (2017), in his eye-opener paper, pointed out that the classical flexibility with well-defined alternative options can create its own risk. That might be perceived paradoxical. The resolution of that paradox lays in the difference between flexibility and plasticity. In former case, the flexible alternatives are determined 'isolated', i.e. not in complex relationship with each other. We create plasticity and develop a smoothened stability landscape with several optima emerging as a system's property, what we call healthiness of the organisation. Since the disruptions and self-organised criticalities show fractal-like scale-free pattern (Sornette 2002), our solutions against those disruptions must correspond to such scalability, i.e. embedded plasticity both in time dimension and network extent. In supply chain management, the right product, with right quality, in the right place, at the right time, in the right quantity is required as usual. We add to these 'rights' the 'rights' of the freedom, i.e. the right freedom form, in the right place (at the right hierarchical level, in the right segment of the network), at the right time, in the right quantity (extent, magnitude).

Whitacre and Bender (2010) and Whitacre (2010) have proven that the so-called degenerative redundancy, or network degeneracy, is able to create the high level of adaptability and evolvability. Diversity in response thresholds emerges when the different sensitivity to the perturbations leads to complementing specialisation and degenerate response to environmental changes in the network, creating a large number of weak links and diverse combinations in solutions (Csermely 2009). In our below detailed inventory management approach, same product with different inventory levels may be healthy in the context of its metalevel. Different nodes of the network (finished product items) can deliver the same result while the network is resilient to environmental fluctuations and quickly adapts to those changes.

8.5 The Network Skeleton and the Behavioural Node Archetypes in the Organisation

Both our CQIG method and the matrix method are suitable for defining the network skeleton of the organisation (Fekete and Hartványi 2013; Fekete et al. 2016). We have determined seven behavioural archetypes of nodes in an organisation (Fekete and Hartványi 2017). Those seven archetypes and their internal and external links build up the network skeleton of the organisation. The large disruptive perturbations will enter in the organisation on these highways, and the cascading failure is propagating mainly within that highly connected network skeleton of the organisation (see Fig. 8.3).

When the demands for the same finished product are coming from different customers in sync (strongly correlated demands), then that transversal sync causes a demand amplification as the variabilities are adding up (Snyder and Shen 2011). In case of large demands, that finished product node will be classified by us as Disruptive Node Out (DNO). Evidently, the organisation can be protected against disruptions coming through a DNO-type finished product with buffers built from that finished product. We suggest to dissipate the disruption through the creative element motive with high reliability and low risk of obsolescence instead.

Disruptions coming from the suppliers may cause cascading failures when those destabilise either a resource node of high out-degree—Cool Hub In (CHI)—or a node of high betweenness centrality. The latter is the Priority Node In (PNI), what may possess not so high out-degree though, due to its connectedness to high importance nodes of high degree or priority, its destabilisation will fire cascading failure. A CHI type of node behaves as the date-hubs: when it is stable, then the out-links of CHI are not correlated, i.e. are in weak transversal sync. The destabilisation of a CHI leads to synchronised failure propagation towards its finished

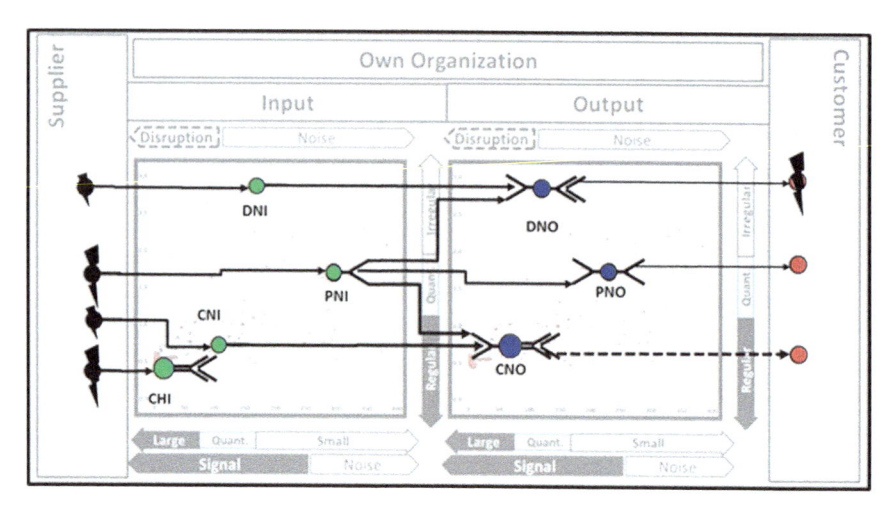

Fig. 8.3 The seven behavioural node archetypes constituting the network skeleton of the organisation and the extrinsic disruption sources

product nodes further downstream. Since CHI in the organisation is linked to the large portion of the finished products, CHI must be rather overinsured than optimised. In classical inventory management, the large number of PNI-type resources are not protected or protected by a safety stock calculated in isolation. In fact, the higher the connectedness of a disruptive finished product (DNO) to common resources (PNI) used also by Cool Node Out (CNO) and Priority Node Out (PNO) types of nodes, the better alternative is our inventory management solution.

Minor impact of failure propagation may occur when the supplier disruption destabilises a specific material of a DNO or CNO, i.e. Disruptive Node In (DNI) or Cool Node In (CNI), respectively. Those DNI and CNI can be protected through classical solutions of safety stocks and/or multi-sourcing aligned with created extra plasticity through the creative element solution described later.

8.6 The Built-In Nested Plasticity in Inventory Management

The determined freedom will be different for nodes of different behavioural archetypes, and the plasticity will occur at two hierarchical levels: at the node's level and at its metalevel. That latter metalevel may be a finished product cluster or the entire portfolio of the organisation. The aim is to reduce the intrinsic noise of our network and, in the same time, we distribute the free energy (the held inventories) so that the organisation is able to dissipate the disruption with low risk of obsolescence. For that purpose, we have designed five inventory management modes (see Fig. 8.4).

8 Innovative Inventory Management for Flexible Adaptation

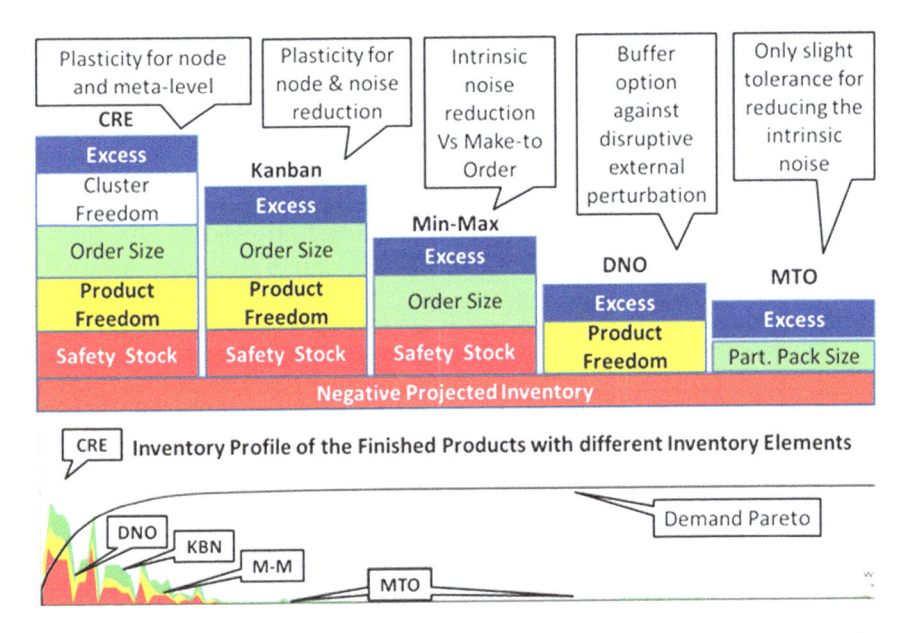

Fig. 8.4 Built-in nested plasticity in the Red-Amber-Green-White inventory elements of the five inventory management modes (automotive supplier)

The Creative Element (CRE) inventory management mode delivers metalevel plasticity. The node-level plasticity is ensured by both the CRE and Kanban inventory management modes. Managing the disruptive finished products, we may determine a buffer to partially cushion the disruptive perturbation coming from the customer, i.e. DNO inventory management mode. Min-Max and MTO inventory management modes can decrease and regulate the intrinsic noise level of our network.

The combination of the appropriate Red-Amber-Green-White Inventory Elements determines the above-mentioned inventory management modes. The inventory elements of a node are defined in line with the connectedness and network behaviour of that node. Safety stock, red inventory element (R) is calculated for Kanban, Min-Max and CRE modes in the classical ways (Snyder and Shen 2011). We use the amber inventory element (A) as node-level plasticity. That is the freedom of the supplier process either to start the replenishment or not at supplier's discretion. It occurs in CRE, Kanban and DNO modes. The other plasticity enabler is the white inventory element (W), what delivers the metalevel freedom. It is determined only in case of CRE inventory management mode (see it later). The green inventory element (G) corresponds to economic order quantity (Snyder and Shen 2011) in CRE, Kanban modes, while it equals to the pack size in Min-Max mode. The large number of make-to-order items (MTO mode) may have a tolerance on partial pack size, when the production process is not enough reliable or predictable to finish with the exact planned quantity, and the rework or scrapping would be too costly (e.g. foundry). That tolerance will define the green inventory element of the MTO mode, since the production order corresponds to the customer order.

Those R-A-G-W colours will play important role in visualising the emergent healthiness of the organisation in space-time, i.e. stability landscape of the organisation. The bottom graph in Fig. 8.4 also shows the inventory profile of all finished product items of an automotive supplier arranged in Pareto-ranking according to their weight in the organisation's demand profile. As it is expected, the distribution of the different inventory management modes depends not only on Pareto-ranking.

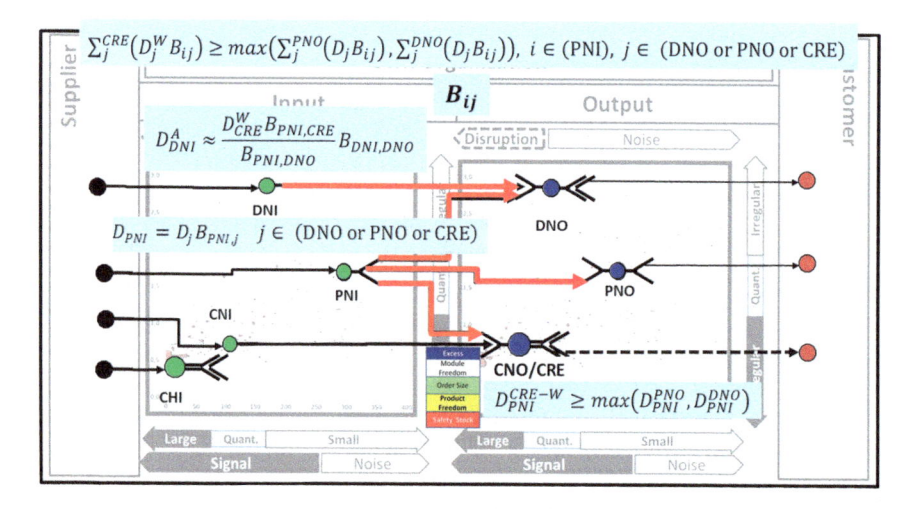

8.7 The Creative Element Motif and Its Parametrization in the Organisation

As Csermely (2008, 2009) points out, the creative elements are active centres in the network with free energy, what help the survival of the complex networks facing unprecedented challenges. Applying Csermely's theory, we could identify the creative element motif in an organisation visualised by the red arrows and the so connected behavioural node archetypes in Fig. 8.5. The large cool finished product node (CNO) is the key node in the creative element motif of the organisation. With the creative element motif, we do not focus on all common resources of PNI-type separately; rather, we build plasticity in the strongly connected network skeleton, what creates alternative intensity in the PNI-DNO and PNI-CRE pathways, keeping untouched the PNI-PNO paths (Fekete and Hartványi 2014, 2017). That is, the

Fig. 8.5 The creative element motif and its parametrization in the organisation (Eqs. 8.3 and 8.4)

demand signal of the disruptive finished product (DNO) can easily rearrange and intensify the relevant resource paths to the DNO, as the creative element (CRE) can scarify its needs on commonly used resources (PNIs).

The white inventory (W) of the Creative Element (CRE) is defined at its metalevel; in the context of several nodes, the CRE is linked to, whereas the common resource, the Priority Node In (PNI) sets the 'common language', i.e. quantities in PNI-equivalents. The affected resource quantity of Priority Node In (D_{PNI}) can be calculated through relevant bill of material ($B_{PNI,j}$) and the corresponding finished product quantity D_j:

$$D_{PNI} = D_j B_{PNI,j} \, j \in (\text{DNO or PNO or CRE}) \tag{8.1}$$

In PNI-equivalents, we expect the white inventory of CRE (D_{PNI}^{CRE-W}) to accumulate more or equal quantity than the targeted to-be-protected finished product quantity of PNO (D_{PNI}^{PNO}) or the planned to-be-dissipated perturbation quantity of DNO (D_{PNI}^{DNO}):

$$D_{PNI}^{CRE-W} \geq \max\left(D_{PNI}^{PNO}, D_{PNI}^{DNO}\right) \tag{8.2}$$

In a product cluster, we (may) have more DNO, PNO and CRE nodes—as it can be seen also in the real-life case at the bottom of Fig. 8.4. Therefore, the equation is more complex:

$$\sum_j^{CRE}\left(D_j^W B_{ij}\right) \geq \max\left(\sum_j^{PNO}(D_j B_{ij}), \sum_j^{DNO}(D_j B_{ij})\right), i \in (\text{PNI}), j$$
$$\in (\text{DNO or PNO or CRE}) \tag{8.3}$$

That is, from the entire finished product population j, we take all the CRE, PNO and DNO nodes with all the relevant PNI nodes into account, and we check the maximum PNI-equivalent quantity PNI-by-PNI. The right side of the above equation can be calculated easily, while at the left side of the equation, we may distribute the required white inventory quantity among the CRE nodes evenly, or pro rata, or according to other business consideration. Evidently, a sophisticated optimization could be also carried out. However, we follow more the approach of roughly right, since the healthy balance at the organisation-level allows the inventory levels in a wider range. It is seen in Fig. 8.4 that in a real-life situation, the white inventory (W) of a CRE node varies about 0.5–1.3 times of the R + A + G-inventories of it. That generates about 15–20% plasticity to the given product cluster.

The DNI must have also node-level plasticity (amber inventory element) aligned to the magnitude of the plasticity supplied by the white inventory of the CRE; otherwise, the latter's plasticity will be killed by the missing plasticity of the former, i.e.,

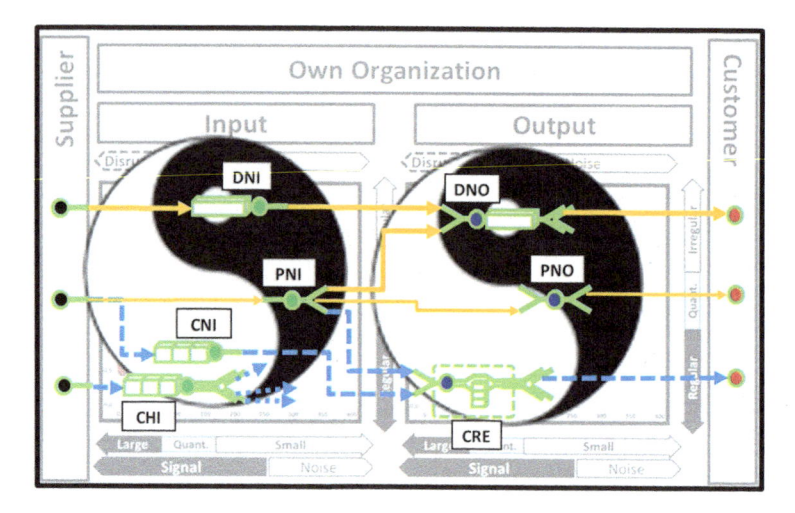

Fig. 8.6 Our innovative inventory management solution of creative element motif generates network-stabilising weak-linkedness and balance in plasticity–rigidity

$$D_{\text{DNI}}^{A} \approx \frac{D_{\text{CRE}}^{W} B_{\text{PNI,CRE}}}{B_{\text{PNI,DNO}}} B_{\text{DNI,DNO}} \quad (8.4)$$

The input nodes of the organisation are protected against upstream perturbations by classical methods, like buffer, Kanban, VMI, dual sourcing, etc. (Vitasek et al. 2003; Snyder and Shen 2011; Willems 2013, 2015).

As the yin-yang-type symbols highlight in Fig. 8.6, we keep the rigid behaviour and execution (orange arrows) in the top segment of the CQIG (in the reigns of disruption and noise), and allow node-level, partial plasticity in the top-left quarter (reign of disruption, of DNO and DNI). On the other hand, we create plasticity and symmetrical weak-linkedness in the reign of signals at node-level with Kanban mode and at metalevel through CRE inventory management mode (the blue dashed arrows represent the weak in-links and weak out-links of such nodes).

8.8 The Stability Landscape and Topological Phase Transitions in the Organisation

The complex networked systems have complex stability landscape with several local minima. The network may drift among those minima until it reaches the stable state. Figure 8.7 shows a real-life example of the stability landscape taking one product cluster from the planning board of an automotive supplier. The horizontal axis corresponds to time periods. The vertical axis (network space) visualises two hierarchical levels: of the product clusters and of the product items. The planned items were grouped in three clusters first, and within each cluster, the corresponding

8 Innovative Inventory Management for Flexible Adaptation 129

items were Pareto-ranked. The third dimension is the relative status of the projected inventory of an item versus its specific targeted inventory levels (see also Fig. 8.4). The fourth dimension is the healthiness of the network what is emerging as an overall spatiotemporal picture.

In time point 1, the organisation was in balanced state. The longer than planned maintenance hindered the production, pushing the overall state to rigid one (time point 2). After a recovery to balanced state (time point 3), the decision was made to develop the network to plastic state (time point 4) since disruptive period was expected due to factory stoppages at the customers and at own organisation (time point 5).

We determined simple rules in planning and execution:

1. at scarcity of resource(s) first all R, then A, then G target inventory levels are to be reached;
2. in plethora of resource(s) after R, A and G, the replenishment to W can be considered, especially if scarcity of resources or disruptive demand pattern is expected;

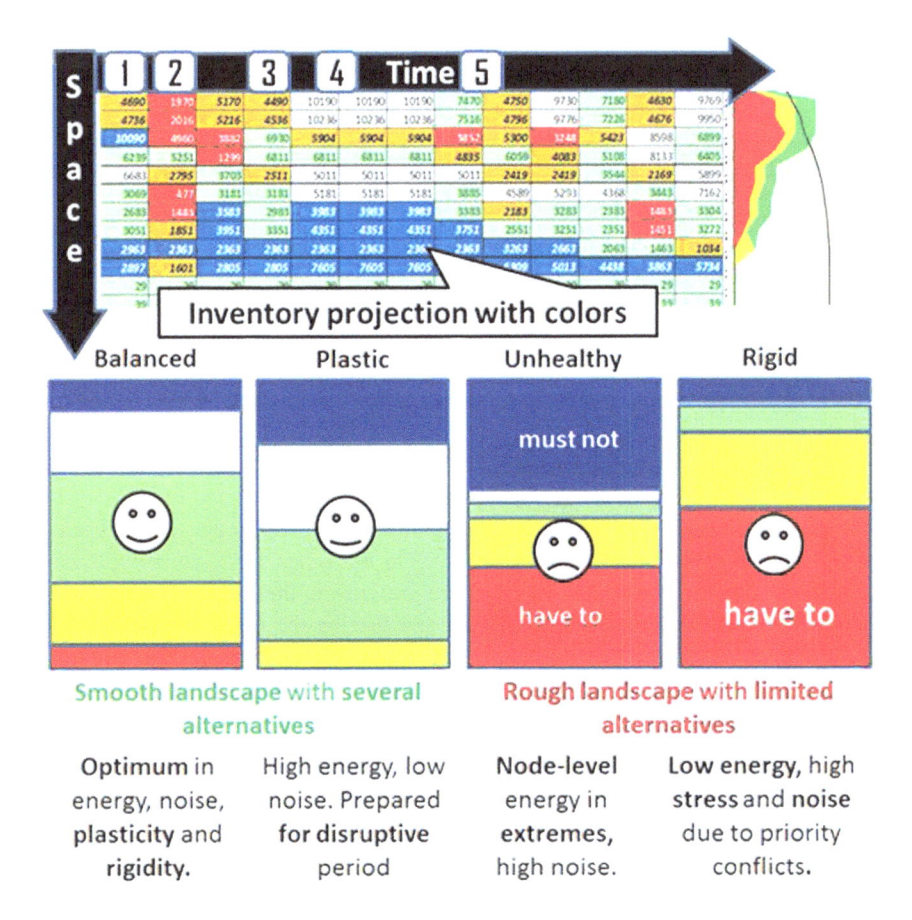

Fig. 8.7 Three dimensions of the stability landscape and the emergent healthiness in the organisation

3. overwhelmingly blue is to be avoided, especially at CRE, Kanban and DNO mode items (the high runners);
4. reach and maintain smooth landscape (balanced or plastic).

Finally, we investigate the stability landscape of the organisation (network element of the supply chain network) in wider context of Csermely (Csermely 2009)—see Fig. 8.8. If the overall picture is blue—general overstocking, then the landscape is too smooth and unstable. Nothing should be and anything could be produced, i.e. all links turn to be equally weak (statistically). That is the random graph topology as the decisions have no priorities—'any random decision can be made' (Fig. 8.8, case 1). Our plastic state corresponds to intermediate network topology between random graph and scale-free network (Fig. 8.8, case 2). The well-balanced inventories on node-level and on metalevel—the balanced state corresponds to scale-free topology (Fig. 8.8, case 3). Rigid state is an intermediate network topology between scale-free network and star-network (Fig. 8.8, case 4). When the overall picture tends to be red, then the accumulated energy is extremely low or depleted—overstretched rigid state (Fig. 8.8, case 5). That leads to frequent priority conflicts and the network becomes very noisy. The organisation may/is forced to decide to produce only some of the products (e.g. the high runners) and temporarily neglecting others (e.g. the low runners) and/or deliver to a limited circle of customers. With strict focused crisis management, we reduce the options and the noise within the organisation. The topology moves to star network direction, as a large number of weak links towards finished products and customers will disappear for the time being. Finally, the lack of prioritisation at overstretched rigid state or other wrong planning and execution decisions can lead to network fragmentation, where the items 'live their own life'. That is the unhealthy state. At extreme, the organisation may fall apart—the network dies (Fig. 8.8, case 6).

Consequently, the stability landscape may be smooth or rough. Smooth landscapes offer several planning and execution alternatives; different nodes may play same roles in network stabilisation. That is, by definition, the degenerative redundancy—similar to the buffed energy landscapes of proteins smoothen the landscape with alternatives (Plotkin and Wolyne 2003). The more turbulent the overall demand pattern is, the rougher the landscape will become (colours at the extremes). Therefore, we adjust/increase the inventory levels to plastic state before the rougher overall demand pattern arrives. On the other hand, when we face a smoother overall demand pattern, then we can lower the projected inventories keeping the alternative choices in balance and turning the network into balanced state at lower inventory/energy level.

8.9 Conclusion

In this chapter, we have described our innovative inventory management solution. In our solution, we have created the network-stabilising symmetrical weak-linkedness, nested plasticity and degeneracy. Those structural and functional differentiating properties of the billion-year-old viable networks are accountable for

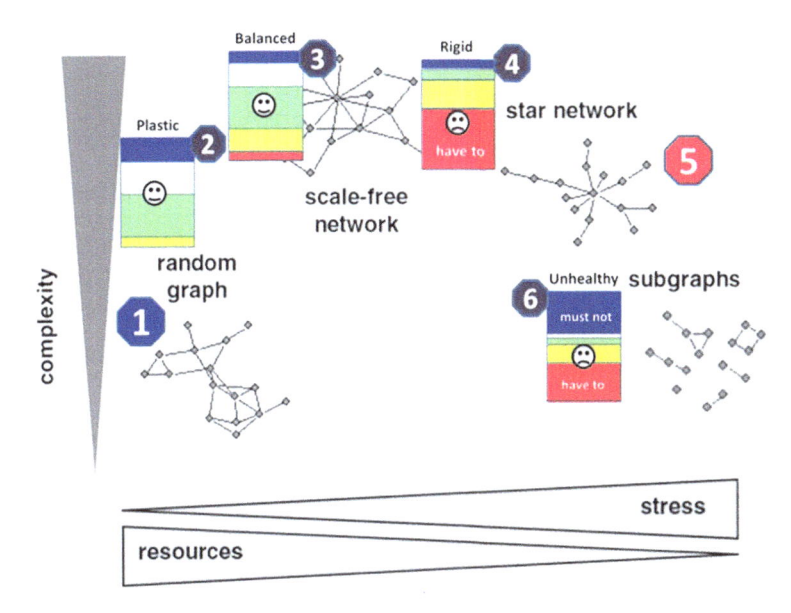

Fig. 8.8 The stability landscape and topological phase transition in the organisation—adjusted with kind permission of Csermely Péter

their outstanding robustness and adaptability. First, we introduced to network topology and topological phase transitions through what the networks maintain their integrity, connectedness in different environmental conditions and adapt to the environmental changes. As we could see, the viable networks often are cycling between plastic and rigid modes. While on the contrary, in the supply chain management, the focus is predominantly on perfecting in the rigid mode. Our innovative solution has created the missing adaptive nested plasticity in the organisations delivering outstanding results in real industrial environment (e.g. IT-telecom and automotive suppliers, foundry). Therefore, we detailed the method of determining the inventory management modes, the inventory elements corresponding to the behavioural archetypes of the nodes in the network of an organisation. In a separate section was explained the parametrization of the key inventory elements for nodes building the creative element motif of the organisation.

We see strong potential in further deploying the network science in supply chain management and in exploring additional learning opportunities from the billion-year-old successful viable networks.

References

Antal, M., Böde, Cs, & Csermely, P. (2009). Perturbation waves in proteins and protein networks: Application of percolation and game theories in signaling and drug design. *Current Protein and Peptide Science, 10*(2), 161–172.

Barabási, A.-L. (2012). The network takeover. *Nature Physics, 8*(1), 14–16.

Barabási, A. L., de Menezes, M. A., Balensiefer, S., & Brockman, J. (2004). Hot spots and universality in network dynamics. *The European Physical Journal B, 38*(2), 169–175.

Csermely, P. (2008). Creative elements: Network-based predictions of active centres in proteins and cellular and social networks. *Trends in Biochemical Sciences, 33*(12), 569–576.

Csermely, P. (2009) *Weak links. The universal key to the stability of networks and complex systems* (p. 404). Berlin: Springer.

Csermely, P. (2015) Plasticity-rigidity cycles: A general adaptation mechanism. Cornell University Library, 6 Nov 2015. https://arxiv.org/abs/1511.01239v3.

Csermely, P., Gyurkó, D. M., & Sőti, Cs. (2012). System level mechanisms of adaptation, learning, memory formation and evolvability: The role of chaperone and other networks. *Current Protein and Peptide Science*. http://arxiv.org/abs/1206.0094

Csermely, P., Korcsmáros, T., Kiss, H. J., London, G., & Nussinov, R. (2013). Structure and dynamics of molecular networks: A novel paradigm of drug discovery: A comprehensive review. *Pharmacology & Therapeutics, 138*(3), 333–408.

Fekete, I., & Hartványi, T. (2013). Value chain stabilization with combined quantity-irregularity graphs. In: T. Baltacioglu et al. (Eds.), *Value chain sustainability through innovation and design* (pp. 189–199). Izmir: Izmir University of Economics Publication.

Fekete, I., & Hartványi, T. (2014). Further analogies between biochemical networks and demand-supply networks (pp. 53–63). In *Tavaszi Szél 2014 Conference*, 21–23 March 2014, Debrecen: DOSZ.

Fekete, I., & Hartványi, T. (2017). Network science in logistics: A new way to flexible adaptation. In T. P. Singh & A. J. Kulkarni (Eds.), *Flexibility in resource management* (pp. 57–69). Singapore: Springer.

Fekete, I., Kallós, G., & Hartványi, T. (2016). Multi-partite structure of demand-supply network element. *Acta Technica Jaurinensis, 9*(3), 171–182.

Kovács, I. A., Szalay, M. S., & Csermely, P. (2005). Water and molecular chaperones act as weak links of protein folding networks: Energy landscape and punctuated equilibrium changes point towards a game theory of proteins. *FEBS Letters, 579*(11), 2254–2260.

Newmann, M. E. J. (2010). *Networks* (p. 772). Oxford: Oxford University Press Inc.

Plotkin, S. S., & Wolyne, P. G. (2003). Buffed energy landscapes: Another solution to the kinetic paradoxes of protein folding. *Proceedings of the National Academy of Sciences of the United States of America PNAS, 100*(8), 4417–4422.

Snyder, L. V., & Shen, Z.-J. M. (2011). *Fundamentals of supply chain theory*. Hoboken NJ: Wiley.

Sornette, D. (2002). Predictability of catastrophic events: Material rupture, earthquakes, turbulence, financial crashes, and human birth. *Proceedings of the National Academy of Sciences of the United States of America PNAS, 99*(1), 2522–2529.

Sushil. (2017). Does flexibility mitigate or enhance risk? *Global Journal of Flexible Systems Management, 18*(3), 169–171.

Vitasek, K. L., Manrodt, K. B., & Kelly, M. (2003). Solving the supply-demand mismatch. *Supply Chain Management Review, 7*(5), 58–64.

Watts, D. J., & Strogatz, S. H. (1998). Collective dynamics of 'small-world' networks. *Nature, 393* (6684), 440–442.

Whitacre, J. (2010). Degeneracy: A link between evolvability, robustness and complexity in biological systems. *Theoretical Biology and Medical Modelling, 7*(1), 6.

Whitacre, J., & Bender, A. (2010). Degeneracy: A design principle for achieving robustness and evolvability. *Journal of Theoretical Biology, 263*(1), 143–153.

Willems, S. P. (2013). Inventory optimization: Evolving from fad to necessity. *Supply Chain Management Review, 17*(2), 10–17.

Willems, S. P. (2015). Demystifying inventory optimization. *Supply Chain Management Review, 2015–3*, 24–30.

Chapter 9
Flexible Benchmarking Approach of Talent Management: A Case Study of MIDHANI

D. K. Likhi, C. Sabita and Akanksha Rao

Abstract 'Our assets walkout of the work place every night, and our job is to ensure that they love coming back every morning'. This sums up the way in which modern companies handle its human resources. This chapter highlights the flexible approach of talent management in one such Indian company, a Defence Public Sector Enterprise. Further, the chapter attempts to detail the various HR initiatives and schemes of the organization, so as to benchmark itself in the turbulent global era, following the case study method which is indicative and not exhaustive.

Keywords Basic pay · Benchmarking · Dearness allowance · Department of Public Enterprise (DPE) · Mishra Dhatu Nigam Limited (MIDHANI) Public Sector · Talent management

9.1 Introduction

With the introduction of automation, re-engineering, high-returns based jobs in developed markets, technology and induction of Gen Y, the public sector organizations are under pressure to acquire the best talent, and develop, engage and retain them in the organization. The challenge is even more to bridge the generation and knowledge gap. The time available for the management to groom and bridge the gap is limited. Keeping in view the aspirations of Gen X and Gen Y which are highly influenced by the strong presence of multinational and software companies, the talent management assumes enormous role especially in hardcore manufacturing sector and particularly in public sector environment. This is true of MIDHANI too in the Indian context, being in strategic sector the complexities are multifold.

D. K. Likhi (✉) · C. Sabita · A. Rao
Mishra Dhatu Nigam Limited, Hyderabad 500058, India
e-mail: dinesh_likhi@hotmail.com; cmd@midhani.com

C. Sabita
e-mail: sabita.devi@gmail.com

Various studies have been carried out to ensure better talent management, and it is brought out that the measurement of effective talent management can be measured in terms of various parameters. Attrition rate and Employee Satisfaction Index (ESI) are reported to be the critical parameters out of them.

On exploring the various parameters, it was determined that integrated talent management approach is good for getting better results on factors of attrition rate and ESI.

9.2 Case Description: MIDHANI

Mishra Dhatu Nigam Limited (MIDHANI), a Government of India Enterprise under Ministry of Defence Production, is a Mini Ratna Category I metallurgical industry engaged in the manufacture of superalloys, titanium and titanium alloys, special purpose high strength steels and other special materials to meet the requirements of critical applications in hi-tech strategic sectors of national importance such as defence, space, atomic energy and power in addition to general engineering industries.

MIDHANI is striving to recruit, retain, reward and develop its pool of employees. The biggest challenge for the company that was observed at the time of recruitment was change in mindset of young manpower who preferred typically high paying software companies as against brick and mortar companies including the public sector. It is also a challenge to recruit and retain capable individuals in the company with the widespread practice of performance management in public sector which possesses diversity of workforce, values and culture. It is indeed a daunting task for the public enterprises to achieve an inclusive growth.

MIDHANI realizes the need to have the best talent management strategies which include designing strategic recruitment plans to attract and hire the best talent, identify, train and develop leaders at all levels, and create 'great place to work'. It is also imperative to channelize and direct the positive energy and vigour of the employees to right areas so as to achieve organizational objectives.

The study is a case research of one Indian Defense Public Sector Undertaking to reflect how attrition rate and ESI have been maintained through multidimensional integrated talent management approach. The case attempts to highlight that integrated talent management approach is a good approach for lowering the attrition rate and achieving better ESI.

9.3 Talent Management at MIDHANI

The company in its endeavours focused and adopted a three-pronged mantra comprising GTT approach—Growth, Talent and Technology. The elements of integrated talent management as identified by the company are workforce planning, attracting

Fig. 9.1 Integrated talent management

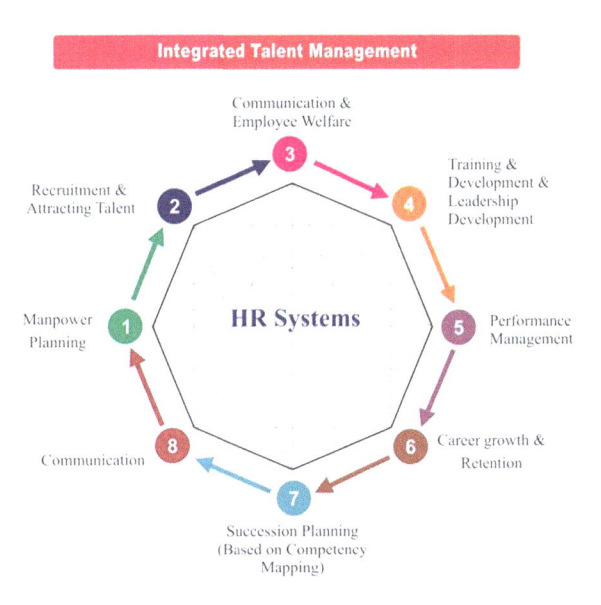

Integrated Talent Management

- 1 Manpower Planning
- 2 Recruitment & Attracting Talent
- 3 Communication & Employee Welfare
- 4 Training & Development & Leadership Development
- 5 Performance Management
- 6 Career growth & Retention
- 7 Succession Planning (Based on Competency Mapping)
- 8 Communication

HR Systems

talent, recruitment, compensation, performance management scheme, leadership development/professional development, employee engagement, employee retention, reward and recognition programme and succession planning (Fig. 9.1). These factors are aligned with the business goals of the organization. Each of these initiatives has been elaborated in subsequent sections below.

9.4 Manpower Planning

The manpower of MIDHANI is its main asset. MIDHANI is a hi-tech, knowledge-oriented and skill-based company consisting of 1500 employees till recent times. However, after three decades, the manpower started depleting due to enormous superannuations and presently stands at 800 only. Second, with strategic business plans for growth and increased capacity of production from about 3000T–5000T compelled the need for talent hunt (recruitment).

The three parameters considered for preparing the manpower plan include analysing the existing manpower, skill sets available and the gaps; additional manpower required to man the additional capacities set up and annual reduction in manpower due to superannuation/retirement, attrition/resignation or death. Based on these parameters, the manpower induction plan has been prepared for the next 5 years, and accordingly, recruitment activities have commenced, both fresh and lateral wherein about 300 employees would be inducted during 2013–2017 period.

9.5 Recruitment and Attracting Talent

MIDHANI has introduced e-recruitment process for both executives and workmen. This would enable speedy and transparent recruitment process making the right person available for the right job across different positions and levels. Management trainees/graduate engineers were recruited through campus selections till recent times. Sourcing is done from identified and reliable sources as laid down in the recruitment policy of the company which include Employment Exchanges, Directorate General of Resettlement of Ex-Servicemen, etc. In order to attract the best manpower, MIDHANI has offered financial incentives in terms of Basic pay + Dearness Allowance (DA) in place of stipend during the training period of 1 year in case of management trainees, graduate engineer trainees, senior operative technicians and junior operative technicians.

9.6 Compensation and Employee Welfare

Presently, the compensation package is attractive especially at the entry level which is at par with private sector though governed by DPE-GOI Guidelines. The package includes Basic + DA + HRA + Perks. Performance-related pay and incentives are also given to the employees. In addition, medical facilities and pension scheme are also provided. The company has also set up a school which extends excellent education to the employees' children. There are various other welfare schemes that act as enablers of talent management.

9.6.1 Comprehensive Health Checkup

As a part of the company's commitment to the overall health and well-being of its employees, the company has implemented a policy of conducting comprehensive health checkup for employees above 40 years of age. For senior employees, a scheme for health checkup of spouses has also been introduced.

9.6.2 On-Job Training

In order to give industrial exposure and experience to young graduates especially the wards of employees and to boost the morale and loyalty of employees, MIDHANI has implemented the on-job training policy. The eligibility of candidates under the policy is graduate/postgraduate in engineering/technology for technical stream and MBA for non-technical stream. The selection is based on merit. Ten trainees would be inducted every year, and the duration of training is for 2 years. The candidates are paid a hefty stipend during the training period.

9.6.3 Merit Scholarship

MIDHANI being a metallurgical company decided to promote higher education in metallurgy which is sector specific, imbibe a sense of belongingness and as an indirect incentive, the company has instituted a merit scholarship for meritorious student who is a ward of employee per academic year for pursuing Engineering Degree in Metallurgy from a recognized university. The scholarship consists of Rs. 1000/- per month from the date of commencement of course till completion of course. The student should secure 60% of the aggregate marks throughout the engineering course.

9.6.4 Merit cum Means Scholarship

In order to promote education among children of employees and as a welfare measure to motivate employees, MIDHANI has introduced education scholarship for the wards of workmen, and merit cum means scholarship for children of all employees. Rs. 300/- per month is given to the employees under education scholarship and Rs. 6000/- and Rs. 3000/- per annum to those children of employees who have stood first and second in a class from class 1 to class 10 (i.e. primary and middle level school).

9.6.5 Increment to Trainees

In order to motivate and retain the fresh workmen who have joined as trainees for a period of 1 year, they have been given an increment on completion of the training period.

9.7 Training and Development and Leadership Development

The company believes that talent management at various levels (senior level, middle level and junior level) is necessary for effective succession planning based on thorough competency mapping. The training and development needs are also mapped to ensure upskilling of individual and also to orient them towards meeting organization needs as well as attaining individual goals. The company provides extensive professional training exposure to its employees through both in-house training as well as external training programmes including national and international seminars, workshops, conferences, symposia, etc. The company also conducts statutory training programmes under provisions of Apprentice Act 1961. Executive development programmes for junior management, management development programmes for middle management and leadership programmes for senior management and top management are organized. Focused skill-based and discipline (subject)-based training is provided to workmen to hone their skills and knowledge.

Initially, when the company was set up, the engineers and technicians were trained by our collaborators in addition to providing in-house training in this hi-tech, knowledge and skill-based industry. The tradition of sharing this knowledge exists in the company. Training needs are identified based on the new concepts or technical inputs as indicated by the individual, by the senior officials in the Annual Performance Appraisal Report (APAR) and based on the task assigned from time to time. The HODs also indicate the kind of training required for the individual or group to fill the knowledge or skill gap through tailor-made in-house or external training programmes. The employees are also trained at collaborators and suppliers organizations on specific technology, equipment operation and maintenance.

Specialized/tailor-made training is also imparted in the following areas:

- Knowledge and Technology Upgradation,
- Risk Management,
- Marketing, Materials Management,
- Soft Skills Development,
- Quality of Work Life,
- Safety and Occupational Health,
- Quality Management,
- Cross-Functional/Discipline Programs and
- EDP, MDP and Leadership Programs.

9.8 Performance Management System

MIDHANI follows a robust and transparent Performance Management System (PMS) for measuring the performance of its executives at below board level and non-unionized supervisory cadre based on the guidelines issued by Department of Public Enterprises (DPE). 'Performance Management System' ensures appraisal of individuals in the organization with an ultimate object of reducing subjectivity and to introduce more and more objectivity and transparent criteria while evaluating individual's performance. The company's annual targets are fixed through Memorandum of Understanding (MOU) between the company and the Government of India. The organization's goals are then translated into departmental goals and individual goals across all functions for achieving the MOU target for the year.

The PMS process starts by fixing Mutually Agreed Targets (MATs) including key performance/result areas, of the appraise and the reporting officer along with, unit of measurement. This is followed by a periodic review and evaluation, leading to identifying the gaps, designing appropriate training for imparting knowledge. Formulation of mutually agreed targets and evaluation of performance on a five-point scale and assessment of potential and personality traits, identification of performance gaps and giving specialized training programmes based on specific needs to enhance the individual skill set and generation of innovative ideas for increasing productivity is encompassed in the performance management system.

9.9 Career Growth (Promotions) and Retention

A well-designed vacancy-based promotion policy has been framed for executives and non-unionized supervisors and a time-bound career development policy for non-executives to meet the aspirations of employees and their growth. In order to encourage and motivate employees for better performance and faster growth, the company has introduced fast track promotions for executives who are good performers and are being groomed to take up higher responsibilities.

9.9.1 Retention (Employee Engagement, and Reward and Recognition)

MIDHANI has evolved and implemented several talent management schemes in order to achieve inclusive growth of diverse workforce such as Suggestion Scheme, Young Managers Trophy and Best Employee of the Year Award. MIDHANI is engaging workforce in various social development activities which are other than routine jobs and rewarding the employees' performance for such activities such as planting of saplings, Swachh Bharat activities and CSR activities which are helping in achieving team spirit. The effectiveness of the policies can be seen from the very low attrition rate of less than 0.001% at MIDHANI. The company also has a policy of recognizing employees who have rendered 25 years of long service by felicitating them with a shawl and silver plaque on Independence Day or Republic Day.

Some of these schemes are identical yet different based on the corporate and their activities. With the study, it is observed that though MIDHANI being a small organization employing around 800 employees, its talent management policies are no way less than that of the leading Maharatna and Navratna companies such as NTPC and BHEL in the country which employ almost 100,000 employees.

9.9.2 Suggestion Scheme

MIDHANI Employees Suggestion Scheme is a formal mechanism and tool for knowledge management and creativity which would stimulate the employee's initiative to contribute concrete ideas that would be beneficial to the company. The suggestion may be something new or different application of old ideas relating to employees own job or other which may ultimately result in increase in production or productivity. The suggestions can be given by an individual or in a group which need to be specific, clear and beyond expectations of existing practice or procedure. The suggestions which are prima facie acceptable by duly constituted Suggestion Screening Committee will be eligible for a gift worth Rs. 500/- as a token of encouragement. The Apex Committee will examine the registered suggestions in detail and select the best suggestion for award. The award for best suggestion consists of prize money of Rs. 15,000/- in both executive and non-executive categories.

9.9.3 Dr. Tamhankar's Trophy for Young Managers

With a view to encourage managerial excellence among the young managers, MIDHANI has introduced a scheme known as Dr. Tamhankar's Trophy for Young Managers. The objective of the scheme is to encourage self-development through self-learning and reading and applying management concepts in an empirical situation, create enthusiasm among young managers and encourage inflow of new ideas and concepts in management of the company.

This scheme is opened to all young officers below the age of 35 years and shall participate as an individual or as a team consisting of three members. The competition is conducted annually, and the theme is announced by Chairman and Managing Director in consultation with functional directors. The papers submitted as per guidelines by the various participating teams will be screened and selected by the selection committee consisting of three senior executives. The selection committee in turn recommends five teams that have been selected to the Apex Committee consisting of C & MD as Chairman, two functional directors and two senior executives, training in charge as convener and one external expert of repute as member. The Apex Committee selects the winners who will receive the Dr. Tamhankar's Trophy for Young Managers, and the second team shall be declared as runners-up.

The award consists of a cash award as well as nomination of the team members for a seminar/conference/visit to any plant in India or abroad for three working days. The runners-up team will also receive a cash award in addition to the team members being nominated for a seminar/conference/visit to any plant in India or abroad for three working days. All the five finalists will be given certificates of merit. The papers presented by the five finalists are compiled in the form of a compendium. The awards are presented on Republic Day.

9.9.4 Best Employee of the Year Award

It is a known fact that the attrition rate in PSUs is negligible due to traditional belief of job security. It is observed that very few leave the organization for better prospects generally to another public sector and that too at middle and higher levels or for higher education. At MIDHANI, the attrition rate is insignificant, which is about 0.001%. At the same time, the company invests precious time and money to groom a new entrant to make him a corporate executive or employee. It is a loss to the company when an employee who is fully trained leaves the company. In order to retain and nurture a collaborative work culture and motivate them to perform better and develop a shade vision of the organization, a scheme for retention of employees has been formulated and titled as the Employee of the Year Award. The scheme focuses on fostering star performers. The award is given annually to the best executive, non-unionized supervisor, women employee and non-executive. The award consists of a cash prize of Rs. 10,000/- to the winner under each category and is given wide publicity.

9.10 Succession Planning

Competency mapping and assessment have been undertaken in order to assess and evaluate the employees' competencies. Based on manpower planning and assessment status, succession planning is carried out. HRD then creates an organization-wide learning calendar including specific programmes on leadership development for senior officials to take up leadership assignments. In the past 5–7 years, through continuous training and development, several officials have been posted in key positions to lead the teams.

9.11 Communication

In MIDHANI, periodic communication with employees and connecting with all employees across all levels—upward, downward and lateral is in vogue. Senior management meeting on daily basis for 15 min (before and after office hours) is conducted with an objective of improving communication and workflow within the organization. In addition, structured meetings such as Corporate Management Committee (CMC) and Production Review Meetings (PRM) are also conducted for charting plans, policies and review.

MIDHANI has been continuously leveraging technology in this regard by using its widely spread intranet portal and through bulk SMS on important occasions, announcements, etcetera which have also improved communication across the company. In addition, the company publishes a quarterly house magazine titled 'Superalloy' and an annual magazine in the official language, that is, Hindi titled 'Sankalp'.

The company's dream to become a Schedule 'A' organization in near future impacts immensely on the company's performance especially the sales turnover which should increase twofold, orders should double up and people should work twice harder than the past in order to meet the objectives and goals of the company. During the various studies conducted earlier, it was evident that the job stress/job worries, work life balance have been found as significant parameters where MIDHANI should devise suitable mechanisms to overcome such situation. It is in this context that several people's engagement initiatives were implemented as detailed above and many more are on the anvil for participation of all employees in group activities.

Second, the manpower planning and people availability have been focused at the time of recruitment, and the company realized that induction of experienced manpower would be ideal to ease the work pressures and stress. Thus, the talent management initiatives of the company have clearly indicated that there is a sense of satisfaction among employees, which is evident from the attrition rate being less than 0.001%; absenteeism has been reduced to 10% on average and the value addition per employee has increased enormously to Rs. 70 lakhs and is the best in the sector. The sales turnover has increased by 16% CAGR over the last 5 years.

9.12 Leadership

No talent management is feasible without engaged leadership. The current CEO guided and worked closely with Human Resources Department and line staff to ensure results are visible at process and outcomes level. Sense of optimism and 'go-getter' attitude allowed employees to enhance their ability and willingness to learn. They could demonstrate entrepreneurial spirit and crisis management skills. The focus was given to increase skill sets in terms of analysis, decision-making, innovation and team work. Reinforcement was done to ensure values like sincerity, integrity, work ethics, etcetera do not take a back seat.

9.13 Conclusion

From the study, it is evident that though MIDHANI is a small organization (Defence PSU) employing around 800 employees, its talent management policies are no less than that of the leading Maharatna companies in the country which employs almost a lakh of employees. The conclusion of our study also corroborates with the employee satisfaction surveys conducted during three consecutive years on 12 dimensional parameters, i.e. motivation, teamwork, work environment, career growth, decision-making, commitment, pay, supervision, fringe benefits, work life balance, co-workers and job security which are above the average mean standing at 3.9, 3.7 and 4.04 on a five-point scale. This made the company consistently achieve excellent ranking. It ranks first among all the nine Defence Public Sector Undertakings (DPSUs) in the country and plans to forge ahead with its progressive policies and approaches in future too.

Chapter 10
Strategy Alignment of Critical Continuity Forces w.r.t. Technology Strategy and Business Strategy and Their Hierarchical Relationship Using TISM

Prakash Kumar Kedia and Sushil

Abstract In the present dynamic and turbulent business environment, organizations will undoubtedly go for a flexible technology strategy and business strategy, respectively. Developing a flexible strategy w.r.t. technology and business is simple; however, their alignment is a major test for leaders. In order to retain their existing strategy or to develop a flexible strategy w.r.t. technology and business simultaneously, their respective critical characteristics must be retained and aligned, which may refer as continuity forces. Here, four critical continuity forces w.r.t. technology strategy and business strategy each were identified from the literature and verified from experts. This chapter then analyses their order and hierarchical relationship using a well-articulated mental model called total interpretive structural modelling (TISM). Finally, it will explain their importance in terms of driving forces and dependent forces.

Keywords Business strategy · Continuity forces · Hierarchical relationship
Strategy alignment · Technology strategy · Total Interpretive Structural Modelling (TISM)

P. K. Kedia (✉) · Sushil
Department of Management Studies, Indian Institute of Technology Delhi,
Vishwakarma Bhawan, Shaheed Jeet Singh Marg, New Delhi, India
e-mail: prakash.kedia@cii.in; prakash.kedia@gmail.com

Sushil
e-mail: sushil@dms.iitd.ac.in; profsushil@gmail.com

10.1 Introduction

Earlier, an organization had fixed, static or incremental strategies, depending on its present business environment. Over time, the organizations acknowledged the need for a flexible strategy due to uncertainty in the business environment. Over the last two decades, technology has evolved as a critical success factor for organizational performance, particularly in the dynamic and turbulent business environment. Because of a competitive environment and regulatory changes occurring, organizations are bound to opt for updated technology, either in-house development or deploying borrowed external solutions. Accordingly, the corresponding technology strategy and business strategy are supposed to change. In a practical sense, in order to achieve organization's objective, the new technology strategy and business strategy need to be aligned. As an example, Tata Motors simply launched a new product, i.e. Tata Nano car after making few changes to their existing assembly line. However, Nano could not be executed according to desire, because their corresponding technology strategy and business strategy were not aligned. Generally, for a new technology corresponding technology strategy and business strategy are simple. However, their appropriate alignment is truly a testing assignment for top management and leaders.

Researchers called attention to the significance of such alignment in the 80s and have developed to the point that now it is virtually difficult to do business and keep up the position in the market if their strategies are not aligned. In this way, those discussions are more relevant than ever before. An organization has to deal with a gap in the alignment of technology strategy and business strategy, otherwise it could prompt lower customer satisfaction and overall performance.

An organization has to sustain in the present and should also show growth in the future. Whenever there is any change in the technology strategy or business strategy, there are certain critical characteristics w.r.t. technology strategy and business strategy respectively, which may call for continuity forces of respective strategies. The organization is supposed to retain or maintain those continuity forces; only their order can be rearranged as per requirement. Likewise, these continuity forces are critical and crucial for the sound development of the organization both in the present and additionally in not so distant future.

The chapter will first identify four critical continuity forces w.r.t. technology strategy and business strategy each, based on available literature and verified by experts. It will then examine their order and well defined hierarchical relationship using a well-articulated mental model called total interpretive structural modelling (TISM) (Sushil 2012a, 2017). At last, it will clarify and check their significance in terms of driving forces and dependent forces.

10.2 Theoretical Background

Organizations have now developed from single function optimization of production to a multi-functional strategic orientation. In the meantime, organizations supposed to be extremely flexible and have to take care of customers demand rapidly and precisely. Earlier an organization is having a static view in the sense that organization's present technology needs to match organization's present strategy and the other way around. But, nowadays, because of vulnerability in the environment, the organization needs to have flexible strategies, i.e. must be set up for the alteration as per business condition (Volberda 1997).

Usually, an organization knows about the significance of managing technologies and its impact on overall performance. In order to achieve a significant competitive advantage, the organization needs to receive new technologies that relate particularly to their strategic business objectives (Tushman and Anderson 1986; Betz 2003). Additionally, technology has emerged as a key component in order to solve complex strategic issues and became a driving force. Thus, organizations are turning out to be more reliant on advanced technology to enhance their performance. In this way, to optimize organization's return on investments and the overall performance; a call for strategic alignment is a necessity for enterprises.

Researchers have talked about what alignment is? Why is it required? How can organizations go about getting to be aligned? And how it should best be tended? They proposed that organizations cannot be competitive if their respective technology strategy and business strategy are not aligned. Accomplishing such strategic alignment is a major concern for business leaders.

Porter (1983) stressed the need for alignment between technology strategy and business strategy and mentioned that both should be compatible with each other. Mitchell (1985) expressed that technology is an important element in any organization and its impact on the strategic management process is complex due to its quick advancements. Top management of both sides, i.e. technology and business, expected to agree on a common set of priorities to integrate technology strategy and business strategy. Usually, the business executive's perspective is that technology is seen as a subset of business, while technologist's perspective is that business is frequently seen as a subset of the general mechanical rising of individuals. The foremost vital challenges are to align these two perspectives.

Clark and Hayes (1985) mentioned that as organizations react to a worldwide rivalry, there is a developing acknowledgement of the critical part of technology in deciding organization's achievement. As a consequence of this acknowledgement, the organization has expanded its reception of cutting-edge technology and presentation of innovatively refined products. These changing practices have alarmed organization's requirement for new technology strategies that are aligned with their business strategy. This alignment guarantees the successful deployment of organization's technological capabilities and resources in the quest for the objectives of the business strategy. Such compelling arrangement of technological assets fabricates a manageable upper hand that upgrades an organization's financial performance (Porter 1985).

However, despite the far-reaching acknowledgement that technology strategy and business strategy ought to be aligned, Henderson and Venkatraman (1992) said *'The concept of alignment has been historically invoked as a metaphor to argue for the integration of technology and business strategies without adequate articulation or clarification of its characteristics'*. Later on, Itami and Numagami (1992) observed that the relationship between technology strategy and business strategy must be visible as profoundly dynamic and interactive.

Vernet and Aasti (1999) developed a model to demonstrate the relationship between technology strategy and business strategy and clarified that the overall strategy is based on technology competencies to create competitive advantage in the organization. Arasti et al. (2010) again did a literature audit on technology strategies and its alignment with business strategy at multi-business, differentiated gatherings and found that in most recent two decades, this is a critical research area in strategy and technology management fields. Khalil and Shankar (2013) further amplify this contention and said that *'integrating technology strategy and business strategy can be thought of as two sides of a coin: either side is worthless without the other'*. Thus, the organization must align its technology strategy and business strategy to concentrate on accomplishing its objectives and goals.

It is generally acknowledged that because of the new technology, huge advantages can be picked up the organization through redesigned technology strategy, which assumes to be aligned with business strategy. For such strategic alignment, the organization needs a flexible approach for better performance. So as to frame strategic alignment, the organizations assume to keep up certain critical characteristics and called continuity forces. These continuity forces are critical for the optimal operations of the organization in the present and also in not so distant future.

10.3 Critical Continuity Forces

According to Sushil (2005, 2012b, 2013), the continuity forces hold back an organization from change by creating inertia in the organization. Following critical continuity forces, both w.r.t. technology strategy and business strategy, have been classified from the literature and substantiated by the experts.

10.3.1 w.r.t. Technology Strategy

Existing Physical Infrastructure: Organizations should proceed with their existing physical infrastructure, for timely delivery. That can be considered as a point of interest and can lead to high performance if managed optimally. Any sort of changes in existing physical infrastructure is very costly affairs in nature, so it is considered as one of the major continuity forces. Because organization's current existing physical infrastructure gives continuity to the organization.

Expertise in Existing Technology: As we all know that technologies are getting obsolete and their rate of charge is turning out to be quicker and speedier. The organization needs to transform itself with acceptance of the updated technology to maintain the core competencies. But the organization is supposed to exploit the current technology completely before moving towards the updated technology. The organization as of now has invested heavily in current technology, in order to get its people prepared and trained on that technology.

Flexibility in Organization's Structure: Flexibility in organization's structure gives a leeway over organizations that are stuck in their courses because of quick technological changes. Additionally, it gives a chance to attempt new approaches, even when the old ways are working fine. Flexibility in organization's structure refines organization's strategies, which distinguishes new and better methods and fostering innovation. After some time, organization turns out to be more effective, in terms of higher profits and lower costs. The qualities of its workforce gain flexibility in organization's structure.

Core Competencies: Exercises and procedures that give a focused edge to an organization and recognizes them from its competitors and are difficult to imitate. Also, it is a key continuity force in making strategic decisions with respect to the future line of business. As an organization develops, grows and acclimatizes to the new environment, so do its core competencies likewise alter and change. Accordingly, core competencies are flexible and created with time. They do not stay rigid and fixed. The organization can make most extreme use of the given resources and relate them to new open doors tossed by the environment.

10.3.2 w.r.t. Business Strategy

Current Customer Base: Getting customers is a standout among the most troublesome parts of running a business, so it is imperative to hold the ones you have, offer more to them and consistently search for new ones. Expanding deals with your existing customers is more rewarding than winning new ones. So knowing who are your best customers can help you enhance customer loyalty and offer more to your existing customers.

Existing Culture: Culture drives or blocks the achievement of an organization and emerges as one of the parts that are imperative to sustain performance, competitive advantage and a justifiable reason or purpose behind turning into an incredible organization. An association's way of life might be one of its most grounded resources, or it can be its greatest obligation. The reason culture is so imperative is that its impact goes a long way to pass the ability in the organization and it has a significant influence on the organization's objectives. Additionally, culture affects the ability, the product, the clients and the revenue.

Legacy Database: Organizations routinely supplant their technology with the advanced one. However, scrapping legacy database and supplanting them includes huge business hazard. Most managers attempt to minimize risks and subsequently would prefer not to confront the uncertainties. Supplanting a legacy database is a dangerous business strategy in light of the fact that there is rarely a complete substitute of the legacy database. The original particular may have been lost. If a particular exists, it is impossible that it incorporates all changes that made because of the replacement of technology.

Existing Process and Services: Excellent organizations plan, oversee and enhance their existing processes and services to produce expanding esteem for customers and other stakeholders. They unmistakably characterize their existing processes and services. In the event that required any progressions, they involve their stakeholders in the improvement of inventive processes and services, which considered as a time-consuming and risky process.

10.4 Hierarchical Relationship of Continuity Forces

During the alignment of technology strategy and business strategy, few critical characteristics called as continuity forces are to be aligned with each other. Likewise, there must be some order and relationship between them. ISM (Warfield 1974) and TISM (Sushil 2012a, 2017) have been used in order to get the order and interrelation between continuity forces. TISM process has been widely applied to generate interpretive hierarchical structures (Jayalakshmi and Pramod 2015; Yadav and Barve 2016; Kumar et al. 2017; Shukla 2018; Soda et al. 2018). The process of TISM includes the following procedures:

Step I: Identify and Define Elements

To start with, the elements need to be identified and explained, whose relationships are supposed to be investigated, that can be originated from established theories or field understanding. Four critical continuity forces w.r.t. technology strategy and business strategy each, as explained in the previous section, are displayed in Table 10.1.

Table 10.1 Critical continuity forces w.r.t. technology strategy and business strategy

Elements	Description	Type
CTT1	Existing physical infrastructure	Technology strategy
CTT2	Expertise in existing technology	
CTT3	Flexibility in organization's structure	
CTT4	Core competencies	
CTB1	Current customer base	Business strategy
CTB2	Existing culture	
CTB3	Legacy database	
CTB4	Existing process and services	

Step II: Define Contextual Relationship

It is significant to express the contextual relationship between the different elements and is to be expressed according to the kind of model suppose to be developed. In theory building, the most widely recognized relationship is 'Continuity Force CTT1 will influence/enhance Continuity Force CTB1' and so on. Here, inputs have been taken from domain experts from industry and academia in the form of yes ('Y') or no ('N').

Step III: Interpretation of Relationship

Generally, another such model like ISM also captures the contextual relationship, but remains silent on their interpretation in terms of the causality like 'How Continuity Force CTT1 will influence/enhance Continuity Force CTB1?'. So, experts not just show whether 'Continuity Force CTT1 will influence/enhance Continuity Force CTB1' or not, but will also elucidate that 'How they will influence/enhance each other?'.

Step IV: Interpretive Logic of Pairwise Comparison

During the process of define contextual relationship (Step II) for each pair, the expert opinion could be 'Yes (Y)' or 'No (N)'. If the expert opinion is 'Yes', at that point, further interpretation is to be given and through this way we can develop an 'Interpretive Logic-Knowledge Base'. For paired comparison, the ith element is to be compared exclusively with other elements from $(i + 1)$th to the nth element. A specimen 'Interpretive Logic-Knowledge Base' for the elements having reaction 'Y' is shown as Exhibit 1 in the Appendix.

Step V: Reachability Matrix and Transitivity Check

The 'Interpretive Logic-Knowledge Base' is deciphered as reachability matrix by making entry 1 in the i-j cell, if the corresponding entry in 'Interpretive Logic-Knowledge Base' is 'Y', or else it ought to be entered as 0 for the corresponding entry 'N' in 'Interpretive Logic-Knowledge Base'. This reachability matrix ought to be checked for the transitivity rule to obtain the complete transitive matrix. The interpretive logic-knowledge base is likewise upgraded for each new transitive link by changing 'N' to 'Y'. Additionally, if there is any meaningful, and significant elucidation of this new transitive relationship, then that interpretation is to be updated in the interpretive logic-knowledge base alongside 'Transitive' entries or left as it is. A final post-transitivity check reachability matrix is displayed in Table 10.2.

Step VI: Level Partition on Reachability Matrix

Like ISM (Warfield 1974), the level partition is done to put the elements level-wise through determining the reachability set and antecedent sets for all the elements. Check the intersection of the reachability set and the antecedent set and if it is same as the reachability set, then the element considered to be at the top-level. The same top-level element(s) should be removed, and the same procedure to be performed till all the levels are determined. These final iterations on identified eight critical

Table 10.2 Final reachability matrix

	CTT1	CTT2	CTT3	CTT4	CTB1	CTB2	CTB3	CTB4
CTT1	1	1*	1	1*	1	1	1	1*
CTT2	0	1	0	1	0	0	0	1
CTT3	0	1*	1	1	0	1	0	1*
CTT4	0	0	0	1	0	0	0	0
CTB1	1	1*	1	1*	1	1	1	1*
CTB2	0	1	0	1	0	1	0	1
CTB3	1	1*	1	1*	1	1	1	1*
CTB4	0	1	0	1	0	0	0	1

Transitive relationship

Table 10.3 Final levels of critical continuity force

Elements	Description	Levels in TISM
CTT4	Core competencies	I
CTT2	Expertise in existing technology	II
CTB4	Existing process and services	
CTB2	Existing culture	III
CTT3	Flexibility in organization's structure	IV
CTT1	Existing physical infrastructure	V
CTB1	Current customer base	
CTB3	Legacy database	

forces w.r.t. technology and business strategy is shown as Exhibit 2 in the Appendix. The final level of eight critical continuity forces partitioned into five levels and displayed in Table 10.3.

Step VII: Developing Digraph

The final level-wise elements are to be associated graphically with the directed links according to the relationships shown in the reachability matrix. Some of the transitive links might be dropped aside from the ones whose interpretation is significant and having distinct interpretation. There may be some errors; the digraph ought to be checked for all transitive links (Sushil 2016). Likewise, the digraph is to be compared back with the reachability matrix to establish the transitivity check. The final digraph as portrayed in Fig. 10.1 can be used as a base for building up the TISM model.

Step VIII: Total Interpretive Structural Model

The TISM is deduced by utilizing the data as a part of the above digraph. The interpretation of elements is replacing the nodes in the digraph, and the interpretation of links to be delineated along the respective links in the hierarchical model. The final TISM model for critical continuity forces w.r.t. technology strategy and business strategy is delineated in Fig. 10.2.

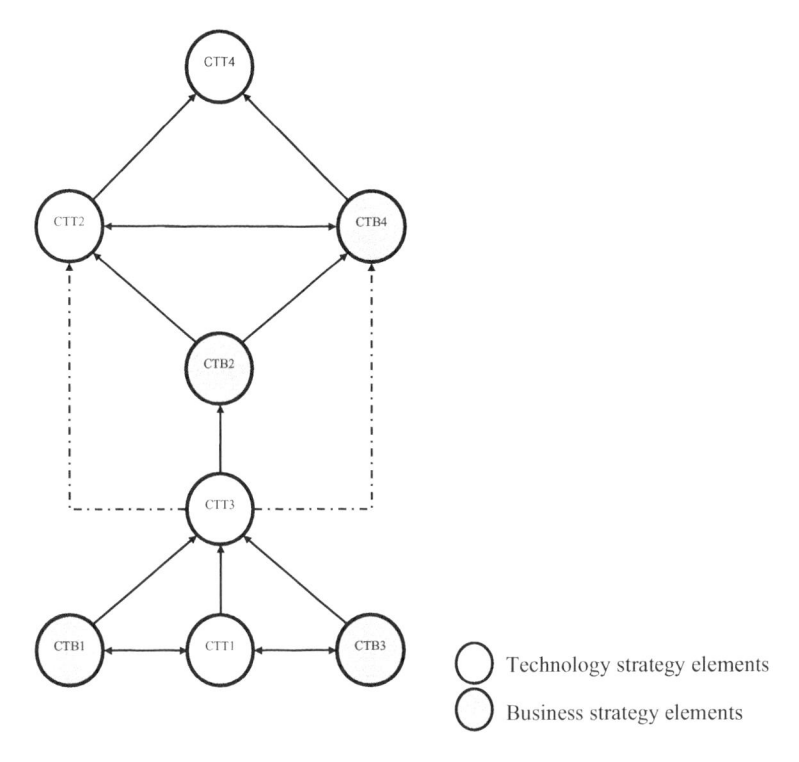

Fig. 10.1 Digraph with significant transitive links

10.5 Discussion

Four critical continuity forces, each w.r.t. technology strategy and business strategy, have been classified from the literature and substantiated from the experts through a questionnaire survey. Also, the contextual relationships among the eight critical continuity forces w.r.t. technology strategy and business strategy along with the interpretive logic were captured by conducting a questionnaire survey. Based on the survey result, the TISM model is developed, and finally, total eight continuity forces are distinctly partitioned into five levels. A technology continuity force existing physical infrastructure' and two business continuity forces 'current customer base' and 'legacy database' emerging as the most powerful driving forces in the case of alignment of technology strategy and business strategy, which determines the another one such as 'flexibility in organization's structure' and 'existing culture'. Further, it checks the expertise in existing technology and setting up process and services of an organization accordingly. The core competencies seem to be the most dependent force among all critical continuity forces in the case of alignment of technology strategy and business strategy present in the organization.

We can easily relate this model in the case of telecom service sector. If any change in strategy either related to technology or business, organizations have to

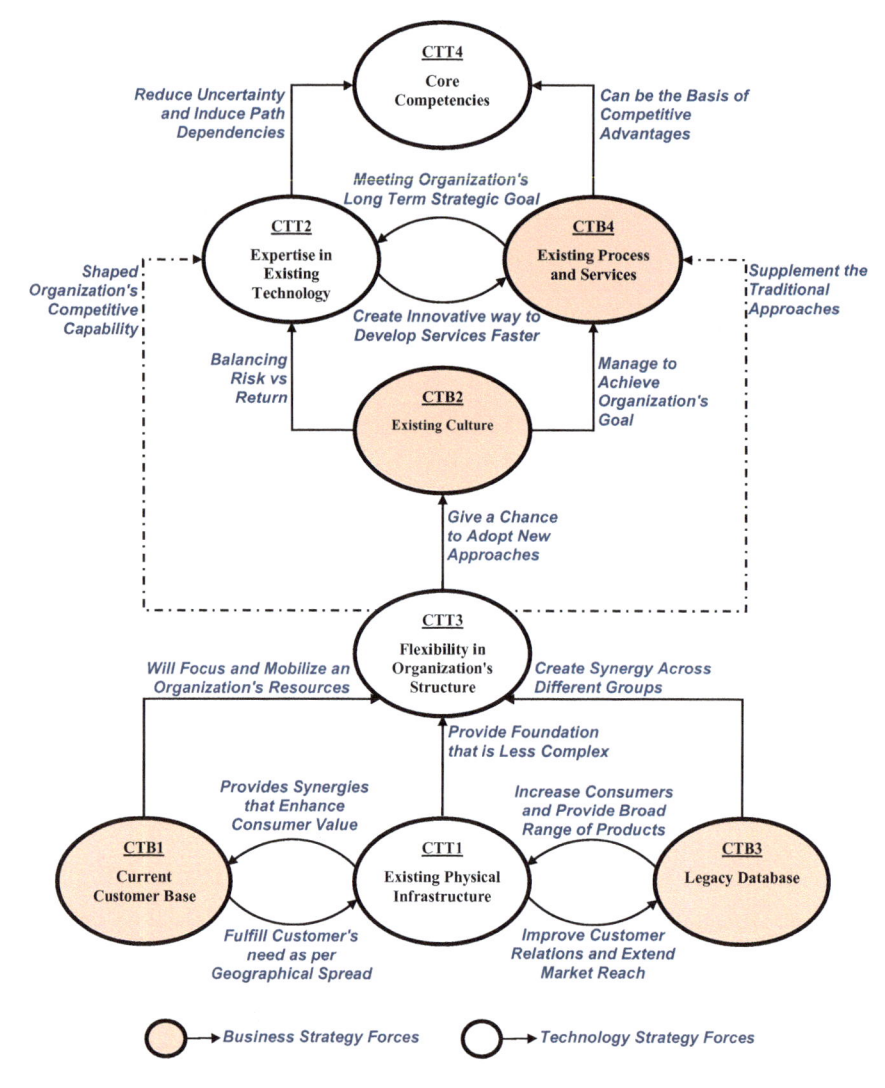

Fig. 10.2 TISM model of critical continuity forces w.r.t. technology and business strategy

continue with their present infrastructure, customer base and database together in order to maintain their core competencies. In between, organization supposed to maintain flexibility and culture, which will further align their existing processes and services along with existing technology expertise.

Out of total 13 links, two are transitive links, which clearly depicts that in the case of technology strategy and business strategy alignment, flexibility in the organization plays an important role. Here, two significant transitive links from flexibility to two other continuity forces one each w.r.t. technology strategy and business strategy, i.e. 'existing physical infrastructure' and 'expertise in existing technology' exist in order to maintain the core competencies of an organization.

10.6 Conclusion

The developed TISM model may help managers and decision-makers to know the interpretive model along with interpretive logic. The different levels also define that which continuity forces w.r.t. technology strategy and business strategy are important in the case of their alignment and also shows their relative hierarchical importance. Additionally, they can check the effect of the direct and indirect relations between continuity forces on the overall performance of the organization (Kedia and Sushil 2016). Expert's feedback in order to develop TISM model indicates that the domain experts largely accept the developed model. After seeing the importance and relationship of critical continuity forces w.r.t. technology strategy and business strategy. The senior management of an organization can formulate their strategy accordingly in another similar case context (Kedia and Sushil 2013).

The result of this research is limited by the number of experts that are used and can be improved by using a large number of experts from a wider variety of industries. Although we do not suspect that this would lead to a different model, that might bring more detail into what is found out over the course of this research. The developed model is tested against experts' opinions, and further research is needed to validate the developed model in practice either through some statistical packages like SPSS or through some case studies.

Appendix

Exhibit 1: interpretive logic-knowledge base (select relationships)

S. No.	Elements	Paired comparison of elements	Y/N	In what way elements will influence/enhance other elements? Give reason in brief
1	**CTB3-CTT1**	*Legacy Database* will influence or enhance *Existing Physical Infrastructure*	Y	Increase sophisticated consumers and provide them with a broad range of products
2	**CTB2-CTT2**	*Existing Culture* will influence or enhance *Expertise in Existing Technology*	Y	Balancing risk versus return

(continued)

(continued)

S. No.	Elements	Paired comparison of elements	Y/N	In what way elements will influence/enhance other elements? Give reason in brief
3	**CTT3-CTT2**	*Flexibility in Organization's Structure* will influence or enhance *Existing Process and Services*	Y	Transitive (*offered to supplement the traditional approaches*)
4	**CTB4-CTT4**	*Existing Process and Services* will influence or enhance *Core Competencies*	Y	*Can be the basis of competitive advantages*
5	**CTB1-CTT3**	*Current Customer Base* will influence or enhance *Flexibility in Organization's Structure*	Y	Will focus and mobilize an organization's resources

Exhibit 2: level partitioning on final reachability matrix

Iterations	Continuity forces	Reachability set	Antecedent set	Intersection set	Level
Iteration 1	CTT1	CTT1, CTT2, CTT3, CTT4, CTB1, CTB2, CTB3, CTB4	CTT1, CTB1, CTB3	CTT1, CTB1, CTB3	
	CTT2	CTT2, CTT4, CTB4	CTT1, CTT2, CTT3, CTB1, CTB2, CTB3, CTB4	CTT2, CTB4	
	CTT3	CTT2, CTT3, CTT4, CTB2, CTB4	CTT1, CTT3, CTB1, CTB3	CTT3	
	CTT4	**CTT4**	**CTT1, CTT2, CTT3, CTT4, CTB1, CTB2, CTB3, CTB4**	**CTT4**	**I**
	CTB1	CTT1, CTT2, CTT3, CTT4, CTB1, CTB2, CTB3, CTB4	CTT1, CTB1, CTB3	CTT1, CTB1, CTB3	
	CTB2	CTT2, CTT4, CTB2, CTB4	CTT1, CTT3, CTB1, CTB2, CTB3	CTB2	
	CTB3	CTT1, CTT2, CTT3, CTT4, CTB1, CTB2, CTB3, CTB4	CTT1, CTB1, CTB3	CTT1, CTB1, CTB3	

(continued)

10 Strategy Alignment of Critical Continuity Forces ...

(continued)

Iterations	Continuity forces	Reachability set	Antecedent set	Intersection set	Level
	CTB4	CTT2, CTT4, CTB4	CTT1, CTT2, CTT3, CTB1, CTB2, CTB3, CTB4	CTT2, CTB4	
Iteration 2	CTT1	CTT1, CTT2, CTT3, CTB1, CTB2, CTB3, CTB4	CTT1, CTB1, CTB3	CTT1, CTB1, CTB3	
	CTT2	**CTT2, CTB4**	**CTT1, CTT2, CTT3, CTB1, CTB2, CTB3, CTB4**	**CTT2, CTB4**	**II**
	CTT3	CTT2, CTT3, CTB2, CTB4	CTT1, CTT3, CTB1, CTB3	CTT3	
	CTB1	CTT1, CTT2, CTT3, CTB1, CTB2, CTB3, CTB4	CTT1, CTB1, CTB3	CTT1, CTB1, CTB3	
	CTB2	CTT2, CTB2, CTB4	CTT1, CTT3, CTB1, CTB2, CTB3	CTB2	
	CTB3	CTT1, CTT2, CTT3, CTB1, CTB2, CTB3, CTB4	CTT1, CTB1, CTB3	CTT1, CTB1, CTB3	
	CTB4	**CTT2, CTB4**	**CTT1, CTT2, CTT3, CTB1, CTB2, CTB3, CTB4**	**CTT2, CTB4**	**II**
Iteration 3	CTT1	CTT1, CTT3, CTB1, CTB2, CTB3	CTT1, CTB1, CTB3	CTT1, CTB1, CTB3	
	CTT3	CTT3, CTB2	CTT1, CTT3, CTB1, CTB3	CTT3	
	CTB1	CTT1, CTT3, CTB1, CTB2, CTB3	CTT1, CTB1, CTB3	CTT1, CTB1, CTB3	
	CTB2	**CTB2**	**CTT1, CTT3, CTB1, CTB2, CTB3**	**CTB2**	**III**
	CTB3	CTT1, CTT3, CTB1, CTB2, CTB3	CTT1, CTB1, CTB3	CTT1, CTB1, CTB3	

(continued)

(continued)

Iterations	Continuity forces	Reachability set	Antecedent set	Intersection set	Level
Iteration 4	CTT1	CTT1, CTT3, CTB1, CTB3	CTT1, CTB1, CTB3	CTT1, CTB1, CTB3	
	CTT3	**CTT3**	**CTT1, CTT3, CTB1, CTB3**	**CTT3**	**IV**
	CTB1	CTT1, CTT3, CTB1, CTB3	CTT1, CTB1, CTB3	CTT1, CTB1, CTB3	
	CTB3	CTT1, CTT3, CTB1, CTB3	CTT1, CTB1, CTB3	CTT1, CTB1, CTB3	
Iteration 5	**CTT1**	**CTT1, CTB1, CTB3**	**CTT1, CTB1, CTB3**	**CTT1, CTB1, CTB3**	**V**
	CTB1	**CTT1, CTB1, CTB3**	**CTT1, CTB1, CTB3**	**CTT1, CTB1, CTB3**	**V**
	CTB3	**CTT1, CTB1, CTB3**	**CTT1, CTB1, CTB3**	**CTT1, CTB1, CTB3**	**V**

References

Arasti, M. R., Khaleghi, M., & Noori, J. (2010). The linkage of technology strategy and overall strategy of multi business diversified groups: Literature review and theoretical framework. In *Proceedings of PICMET '10: Technology Management for Global Economic Growth* (pp. 1–12). Phuket: IEEE.

Betz, F. (2003). *Managing technological innovation: Competitive advantage from change.* Hoboken, USA: Wiley-Interscience.

Clark, K., & Hayes, R. (1985). Exploring factors affecting innovation and productivity growth within business unit. In K. Clark et al. (Eds.), *The uneasy alliance: Managing the productivity, technology dilemma* (pp. 425–458). Boston, MA: Harvard Business School Press.

Henderson, J., & Venkatraman, N. (1992). *Strategic alignment: A model for organizational transformation through information technology, transforming organizations.* New York: Oxford University Press.

Itami, H., & Numagami, T. (1992). Dynamic interaction between strategy and technology. *Strategic Management Journal, 13*(S2), 119–135.

Jayalakshmi, B., & Pramod, V. R. (2015). Total interpretive structural modeling (TISM) of the enablers of a flexible control system for industry. *Global Journal of Flexible Systems Management, 16*(1), 63–85.

Kedia, P. K., & Sushil. (2013). Total interpretive structural modelling of strategic technology management in automobile industry. In *Proceedings of PICMET'13: Technology Management in the IT-Driven Services* (pp. 62–71). San Jose, CA: IEEE.

Kedia, P. K., & Sushil. (2016). Hierarchy of continuity and change forces of international technology strategy. In Sushil et al. (Eds.), *Flexible work organizations: The challenges of capacity building in Asia. Flexible Systems Management*. New Delhi: Springer.

Khalil, T. M., & Shankar, R. (2013). *Management of technology: The key to competitiveness and wealth creation* (pp. 235–237). New Delhi: Tata McGraw Hill Education Pvt. Ltd.

Kumar, P., Haleem, A., Qamar, F., & Khan, U. (2017). Modelling inland waterborne transport for supply chain policy planning: An Indian perspective. *Global Journal of Flexible Systems Management, 18*(4), 353–366.

Mitchell, G. R. (1985). New approaches for the strategic management of technology. *Technology in Society, 7*(2–3), 227–239.

Porter, M. E. (1983). The technological dimension of competitive strategy, research on technological innovation. In *Management and Policy*, Greenwich, CT (pp. 1–33).

Porter, M. E. (1985). *Competitive advantage: Creating and sustaining superior performance*. New York: Free Press.

Shukla, S. K. (2018). The flexibility in product family engineering process. In Sushil, T. P. Singh, & A. J. Kulkarni (Eds.), *Flexibility in resource management, flexible systems management* (pp. 17–28). Singapore: Springer Nature.

Soda, S., Sachdeva, A., & Garg, R. K. (2018). Green supply chain management drivers analysis using TISM. In Sushil, T. P. Singh, & A. J. Kulkarni (Eds.), *Flexibility in resource management, flexible systems management* (pp. 113–135). Singapore: Springer Nature.

Sushil. (2005). A fflexible strategy framework for managing continuity and change. *International Journal of Global Business and Competitiveness, 1*(1), 22–32.

Sushil. (2012a). Interpreting the interpretive structural model. *Global Journal of Flexible Systems Management, 13*(2), 87–106.

Sushil. (2012b). Making fflowing stream strategy work. *Global Journal of Flexible Systems Management, 13*(1), 25–40. (Springer).

Sushil. (2013). *Flowing stream strategy: Leveraging strategic change with continuity*. New Delhi: Springer.

Sushil. (2016). How to check correctness of total interpretive structural models? *Annals of Operations Research*. https://doi.org/10.1007/s10479-016-2312-3.

Sushil. (2017). Modified ISM/TISM process with simultaneous transitivity checks for reducing direct pair comparisons. *Global Journal of Flexible Systems Management 18*(4), 331–351.

Tushman, M. L., & Anderson, P. (1986). Technological discontinuities and organizational environments. *Administrative Science Quarterly, 31*(3), 439–465.

Vernet, M., & Arasti, M. R. (1999). Linking business strategy to technology strategies: A prerequisite to the R&D priorities determination. *International Journal Technology Management, 18*(3/4), 293–308.

Volberda, H. W. (1997). Building flexible organizations for fast-moving markets. *Long Range Planning, 30*(2), 169–183.

Warfield, J. N. (1974). Towards interpretation of complex structural models. *IEEE Transactions: System, Man and Cybernetics, SMC, 4*(5), 405–417.

Yadav, D. K., & Barve, A. (2016). Modeling post-disaster challenges of humanitarian supply chains: A TISM approach. *Global Journal of Flexible Systems Management, 17*(3), 321–340.

Chapter 11
Manufacturing Flexibility Under Uncertain Demand by a Real Options Approach

Katsunori Kume and Takao Fujiwara

Abstract Evaluation of the optimal investment in plant modification (facility renovation and/or equipment replacement) is becoming significantly important in forecasting profits for soft drink business. The sales of soft drink have a typical seasonality; higher in summer and lower in winter. This chapter proposes a decision-making method for the optimal investment in plant expansion by treating uncertainty of potential demand, based on the real options approach (ROA) and the seasonal autoregressive integrated moving average (SARIMA). For example, the demand for soft drink in the summer can be often too high for production capacity. This chapter examines following two methods based on option theory, first one is Bermudan call options to flexibly coordinate the number of part-time workers for increase in recruitments in summer and simultaneously a decrease in winter. The second method is the American call option used to expand equipment capacity to meet not only summer demand but also long-term upside demand even at a high sunk cost. We also compare these options in binomial lattice through Monte Carlo simulation. There may be dividend like effects of seasonal demand variation on the exercise of American call options and some signaling threshold demand level just before rising wave period can be a trigger criterion for flexible investment decision if enough lead time is available.

Keywords American option · Bermudan options · Manufacturing flexibility
Real options approach · SARIMA · Soft drink manufacturing · Uncertain demand

---

K. Kume (✉)
Department of Electrical and Electronic Information Engineering, Toyohashi University of Technology, 1-1 Hibarigaoka, Tempaku, Toyohashi, Aichi 441-8580, Japan
e-mail: k119304@edu.tut.ac.jp

T. Fujiwara
Institute of Liberal Arts and Sciences, Toyohashi University of Technology, 1-1 Hibarigaoka, Tempaku, Toyohashi, Aichi 441-8580, Japan
e-mail: fujiwara@las.tut.ac.jp

© Springer Nature Singapore Pte Ltd. 2018
J. Connell et al. (eds.), *Global Value Chains, Flexibility and Sustainability*,
Flexible Systems Management, https://doi.org/10.1007/978-981-10-8929-9_11

11.1 Introduction

The sales of soft drink have a typical seasonality; higher in summer and lower in winter. Producer may have a plan to meet the necessary production capacity in the summer by means of investment in either plant (facility and equipment) modification or added temporary human power. At the time, it is uncertain whether this seasonality is repeated at the same sales level forever or not. So, the question to be addressed is: how do soft drink manufacturers provide flexibility in their manufacturing processes to deal with uncertainty in demand by using real options method?

This chapter proposes the optimal investment decision method for plant modification that copes with demand uncertainty, based on real options approach (ROA) and seasonal autoregressive integrated moving average (SARIMA). ROA is one of the methods for decision-maker concerned with irreversible investments under uncertainty, and real option is not an obligation but a right (for example, Dixit and Pindyck 1994; Copeland and Antikarov 2003; Mun 2003; Fujiwara 2012, 2013). ROA and SARIMA are applied to this industry's demand data to propose the more appropriate forecasting and decision-making methods.

In the view of ROA, the plant modification and the temporary added human power as part-time workers are, respectively, regarded as American call option and Bermudan call option. Some study works on ROA in the supply chain have already discussed with respect to the seasonality, the volume flexibility and the relation between supplier and buyer (Kume and Fujiwara 2016a, b).

By the way, a procedure of investment decision-making follows the forecasting and analysis, and the order is usually not conducted simultaneously. The reason is because the investment decision-maker generally needs some period of time for considering and examining the data from analysis till decision-making. We assume the level of monthly sales actually realized a few months ahead as *the boundary trigger* to make a decision to exercise the options. Actual data of the sales and investment expense are given by a supplier in Japan.

The main goal here is to decide on what and when is the investment needed according to information from ROA. The questions examined in the study are: (1) conducting time-series analysis for forecasting the sales by SARIMA; (2) valuating the Bermudans and American options under seasonality; (3) identifying correlations between the results of ROA and the boundary triggers as decision-making; and (4) interpreting the results of moving of the maturity of ROA. This study is carried out by using mainly Oracle Crystal Ball (Fusion Edition) and Microsoft Excel (Version 2010).

11.2 Related Works

We quantify an option value and analyze the timing and aggregate investment behavior in soft drink industry. Our study takes into account the uncertainty of demand based on seasonality. The purpose of SARIMA is to evaluate a forecasting model and to forecast future sales (Box et al. 2008).

The ROA is expected so that the investment can be improved in the future return through flexible decisions (Myers 1977). If ROA is applied for flexible decision-making to invest in the irreversible project with the sunk costs under uncertainties, the general concern is on the value of information (Pindyck 2008). However, the sunk costs should also be considered from a perspective of facility renovation and/or equipment replacement (Pindyck 2008).

In multiproduct batch plants, design and production may often be delayed in a wait-and-see mode to optimize under uncertainties (Moreno and Montagna 2012). Furthermore, when considered a general multi-period optimization model in the plants, the effect of seasonal demands is needed to considered (Moreno et al. 2007).

One of the significant problems for real options is the trigger to exercise options (Dixit and Pindyck 1994; Sarkar 2000). The hurdle rates are expected for return in excess of a required investment and three or four times larger than the cost of capital in business practice (Dixit 1992). Even if usual hurdle rate remains appropriate for investment with systematic risk exceeds the riskless rate, it simultaneously seems hard to justify intuitively such large discrepancies observed (Dixit 1992). Then, because decision-maker should smoothly and flexibly decide on his mind within the targeted durations, he needs the objective decision-trigger to identify whether the current situation is approved to invest or wait-and-see. It is important for researchers and practitioners to understand how and why this trigger is applied under demand uncertainty.

11.3 Problem Description

Producer has a plan to meet the production capacity in the summer by means of investment in either plant (facility and equipment) modification or temporary added human resources. First of all, future sales for 5 years are forecasted by SARIMA model. Second, monthly free cash flow (FCF) model is built. Third, future sales are taken in FCF model.

Monthly FCF is calculated as follows:

$$\text{FCF}_n = \text{EBIT}_n \times (1 - \text{Tax rate}) + \text{Depreciation}_n - \text{Investment expenses}_n - \Delta \text{Working capital}_n \tag{11.1}$$

where n is yearly periods, and EBIT is earning before interest and tax.

Table 11.1 Account titles and conditions for FCF

Account titles	Conditions
Sales	Stochastic process by SARIMA $(p,d,q)(P,D,Q)s$ from 2015 to 2019
EBIT	Entirely consistent in 32% of sales
Investment expense	Investment expense is paid at once in decision-making period. See investment expense in Table 11.2
Tax rate	Fixed at 40% of EBIT

Five account titles are detailed in Table 11.1. Fluctuation for working capital is not considered. We attempt that monthly FCF turns out to be yearly FCF based on each December end data point.

There are two scenarios for investment: facility and equipment for American option and human resource for Bermudan options. Relevant information for each scenario is given in Table 11.2. Effect of both investments is expected to increase sales in summer (from June to October). However, the timing of decision-making is necessary at latest in April for both options every year. Investment expenses are divided and paid by each month from June to October for the options every year. If the investment is exercised, forecasted sales are increased by 1.2 times with upper limit of monthly sales 100,000 (×1,000 JPY).

Effect of the Bermudans on sales is, on the one hand, limited within the year, so the right for the Bermudan call options is available only once per year during 5 years. On the other hand, the effect of the American call is prolonged for 5 years. Additionally, there is an allowance to change the option from the Bermudans to the Americans within 5 years. But changing the option from the latter to the former is neither financially nor physically possible.

Table 11.2 Two scenarios for investment

Scenario	Option type	Investment price (1,000 JPY)	Upper rate of multiplication (times)	Demand upper limitation (1,000 JPY/month)	Duration of option effect
Human resource	Bermudan call options	10,000/year	1.2	100,000	Within year (June to October)
Facility and equipment	American call option	50,000 at once	1.2	100,000	5 years

11.4 Forecasting Sales by SARIMA

We conduct time-series analysis for forecasting the sales by SARIMA model which is widely used to deal with seasonal data for the time-series analysis and forecasting. In a seasonal time-series $\{Z_t | t = 1, 2, \ldots, k\}$, SARIMA$(p, d, q)(P, D, Q)s$ can be depicted if:

$$\varphi_p(B)\Phi_P(B^s)(1-B)^d(1-B^s)^D Z_t = \theta_q(B)\Theta_Q(B^s)a_t \qquad (11.2)$$

where k is the number of observations, p, d, q, P, D, Q, B, and s are integers, B and B^s are lag operator, s is the seasonal period length, d is the number of non-seasonal differences, D is the number of seasonal differences, and a_t is white noise and the estimated residual at period t is identically and independently distributed as a normal random variable with $\mu = 0$ and $\sigma^2 = 1$ (Bouzerdoum et al. 2013). $\varphi_p(B)$, $\Phi_P(B^s)$, $\theta_q(B)$, and $\Theta_Q(B^s)$ are the nonseasonal autoregressive (AR) operators of order p, the seasonal AR (SAR) operator of order P, the nonseasonal moving average (MA) operator of order q, and the seasonal MA (SMA) operator of order Q, respectively.

Suppose the only available historical data on sales are 84 monthly data equal to 7 years, forecast is created for 60 months equal to 5 years. We attempt to prolong forecast years over 5 years, but do not get statistical confidence. For each of the 60 forecast months, predictor automatically creates the expected sales value forecasts with the relevant distributional assumptions.

Results of monthly point forecasts are based on SARIMA $(2, 1, 2) (1, 0, 1)_{12}$ model as the best fitting line in the gallery of time-series approaches. We get confident and lowest value 17.84 for Akaike's information criterion (AIC) of this model. The forecasted sales have a tendency to be cyclic movements with the highest and the lowest in summer and winter of each year, respectively.

11.5 ROA

We apply ROA to the American and Bermudan options with seasonality and make a reference to four step processes for valuing real options (Copeland and Antikarov 2003; Mun 2003). Following four steps are referred by Copeland and Antikarov (2003). First, a standard net present value (NPV) of this project using discounted cash flow (DCF) is estimated by the entire FCF over the life of the project. Second, a binomial lattice is based on the set of recombined uncertainties and is built by varying the volatility of the demand. Third, the decision-making, if combined into the nodes of the event tree, are shown as a decision tree. Fourth and finally, valuation of the payoffs using risk-neutral probabilities method is calculated as option value. ROA includes the basic present value (PV) plus the option value as flexible decision value.

Some different points from Copeland and Antikarov (2003) are to incorporate Monte Carlo simulation by the four step processes, yield simulated monthly sales repeatedly according to SARIMA (2, 1, 2) (1, 0, 1)$_{12}$ model for 5 years, and calculate option value. Monthly sales are converted to yearly sales at each December. As we use Monte Carlo simulation yielding monthly sales, the option value is evaluated by the improvement calculated as follows:

$$\text{Improvement } (\%) = \frac{\text{Option Value}}{\text{PV}} \times 100 \qquad (11.3)$$

Next, we test the effect of symbiotic American and Bermudan options. We assume each Bermudan and American are independent. Until exercising a right of American option, soft drink producer keeps a right to exercise Bermudan options which can be exercised once every year. But once exercising American option, Bermudan options are no more allowed to exercise. The values of American option and Bermudan options are summed and make a total option value. Such option value is also expressed as the improvement.

11.6 Trigger for Exercising Options

We propose that the trigger is conditional upon some monthly sales in April for the option exercise if considering the lead time for summer demand-peak season. If the forecasted sales meet the target criteria, it is an opportunity to exercise options. That is, as the criteria of conditional sales are lower than forecasted sales in targeted duration, the orbit of SARIMA can move up. The trigger is assumed as monthly sales in April without options; over 30,000 ($\times$1,000 JPY). Conditional value as the 30,000 is calculated to meet positive NPV even if option expenses are paid. For example, the probability of investment is higher in case of lower sales criteria, but the failure rate is also increased. Then moderate criterias are needed to invest based on the trigger. The correlation between the results by ROA and the trigger is also evaluated by 10,000 runs of simulations.

11.7 Interpretation of the Results Within Periods and After the Periods of ROA

After the periods of ROA, finite annuity improvement for American option and Bermudan options are calculated on December of sixth year using Eq. (11.3). To get accuracy, 10,000 simulations are conducted.

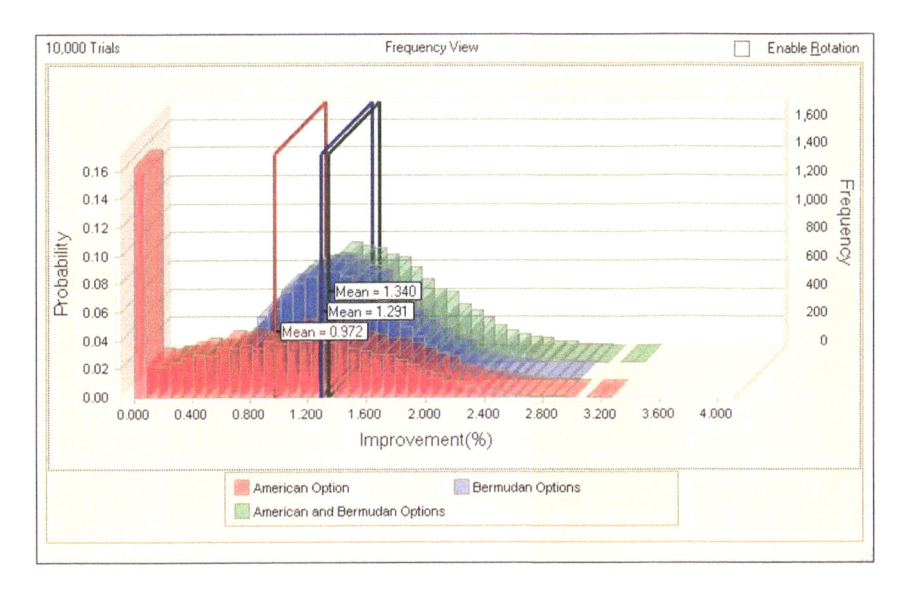

Fig. 11.1 Probability distribution of each improvement of American, Bermudan, and symbiotic American and Bermudan options

11.8 Results

Results are shown as following probability distribution as Fig. 11.1 because of 10,000 simulations.

11.8.1 Valuation for ROA

Figure 11.1 indicates that the improvement effects by independent American, Bermudan, and symbiotic American and Bermudan options. The highest improvement of the expected value is gained by the symbiotic American and Bermudan options, and then the Bermudans and the American options are following. The expected value of 1.340 in the symbiotic American and Bermudan options is slightly superior to the 1.291 in the Bermudan options; it means that the American and the Bermudan options yield synergy effect. The expected value of 0.972 for the American options is lowest and the probability of no improvement is 0.15; thus, it is risky and not so flexible for decision-makers to use independent American options only. To get higher improvement, it is rational choice to use the symbiotic American and Bermudan options in this condition.

Figure 11.2 shows the probability distribution for exercise timing of American option including both the independent American call option and the symbolic American and Bermudan call options with profitability until fifth year time horizon.

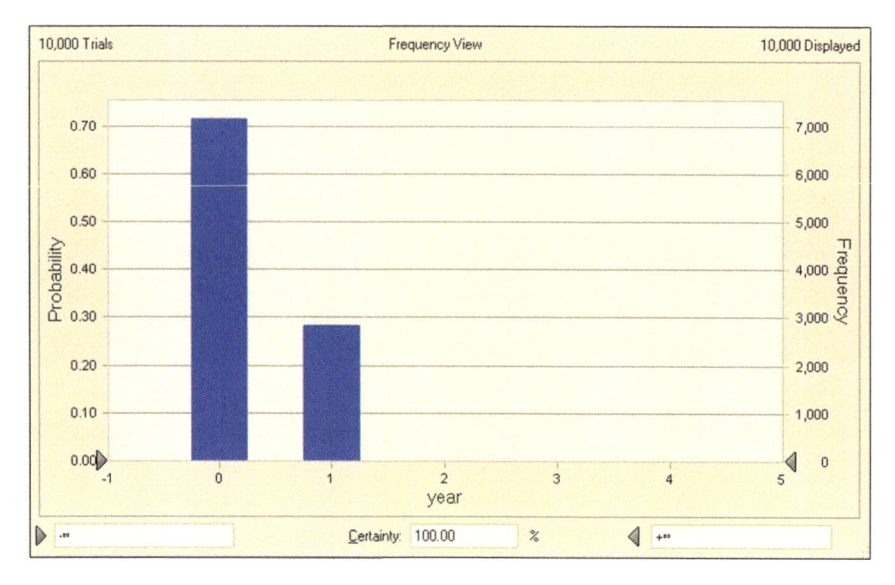

Fig. 11.2 Probability distribution of timing of exercise of American option

Year 0, for the sake of convenience, it shows the case not to exercise the option at all during the periods. From the results of probability distribution, the American call option had better be exercised only at first year (it means different from the usual rule for American call option without dividends as "wait the decision until maturity") or wait until maturity (not exercise cases are also included in this class). But, after first year, there is no opportunity to exercise American option. Then, it can be considered that each rising wave in the seasonal variation of annual demand can play the role of potential dividend.

11.8.2 Trigger for Option Exercises

A correlation for improvement between ROA and trigger is analyzed in order to validate each monthly FCF of April as the trigger index. Improvement based on trigger is coming from investment unrelated with the ROA, if the trigger value exceeds the criterion. However, as shown in Fig. 11.3 and expected from SARIMA model, the value of improvement based on trigger is highly proportional to the improvement based on ROA in 0.9447 of R^2 determination coefficient. This means that the trigger is valid, but it has somewhat downside risk because the criteria of trigger can be a little overestimated. Although the trigger may have some defect in accuracy, decision-maker can receive the signal to invest or not considerably well before executing investment.

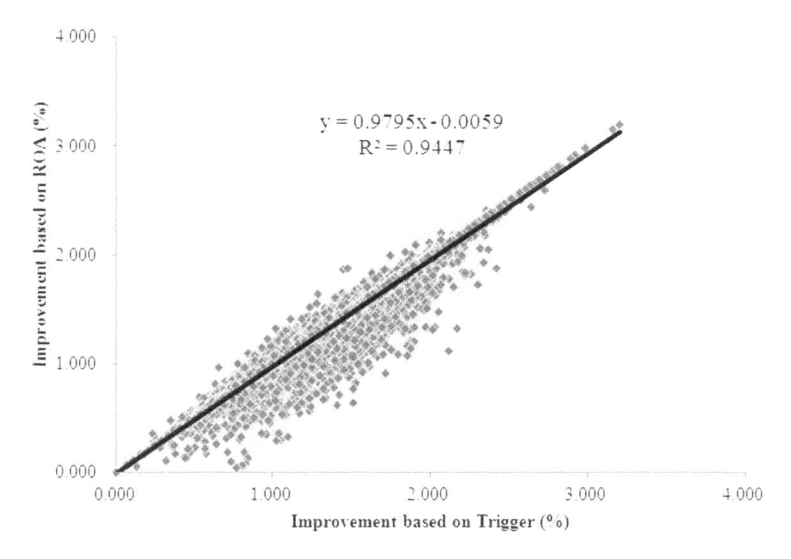

Fig. 11.3 Correlation of the results between ROA and the trigger

11.8.3 Valuation of Finite Annuity of Extended ROA Duration

Figure 11.4 shows the effect of some extension of the base case maturity of ROA. This figure includes the results between American and Bermudan options with extended maturity until 10th year.

Although base case duration of American and Bermudan options is 5 years, we evaluate independent effect of improvement of the extended maturity even after fifth year by applying finite life annuity method. In opposite to prior results within 5 years in Fig. 11.1, these results show that mean improvement rate of the American option 4.462% is higher than that of the Bermudan options 0.646%. If American option as facility replacement is exercised at sixth year, effect of investment is assumed to be effective for residue depreciation years according to this renewed maturity. On the contrary, even though Bermudan option as annual part-time manpower procurement is exercised at sixth year, the effect of investment is not effective so long but just annually. Although it is self-evident by definition, Bermudan options need its expense recovery at each year.

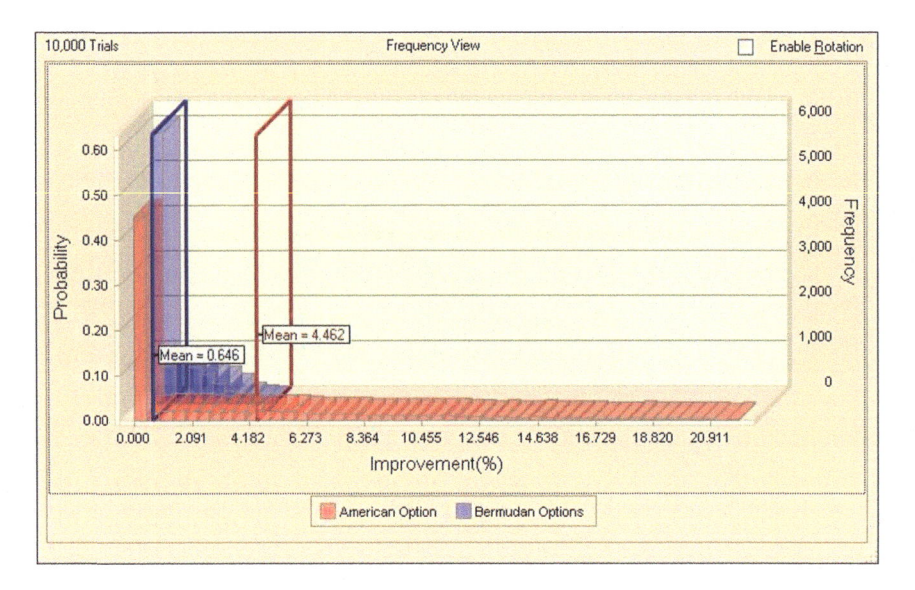

Fig. 11.4 Probability distribution of independent American and Bermudan options with extended maturity

11.9 Conclusion

This chapter proposes a decision-making method for the optimal alternative investment in plant capacity expansion by treating seasonal uncertainty of demand with ROA and SARIMA. Here two options based on option theory are considered for production capacity in summer. First one is Bermudan options to flexibly coordinate the number of part-time workers for increase in summer and decrease in winter. The other is American option to expand equipment capacity to meet not only one summer demand but also long-term demand in spite of a high sunk cost.

We propose such new ROA methods that binominal lattice is repeated by Monte Carlo simulation. In this process, time-series analysis by SARIMA can be helpful to forecast the sales in ROA. The ROA on the Bermudan and American options under seasonality is applied by using yearly sales in spite of focusing on seasonal option effects in summer. Furthermore, the correlation coefficient between the ROA and the trigger as targeted monthly sales is strongly positive, and thus, the trigger is considered as helpful to exercise option with enough time allowance for lead time. Our results show that the Bermudan options are more excellent in short-term flexible improvement than the American option. But in 28% of 10,000 simulations, the American option can be given priority and exercised at first year. Then, it is considered that a rising wave in each seasonal variation may play the role of "divided" to American call option.

The exercise-timing distribution of the American call option can be changed by applying finite life annuity method if maturity is extended until 10th year from 5th year. Then, it is necessary to make a balance between the dividend effects of seasonal variation and its reduction with the extension of time horizon. Additionally, Bermudan call option with annual maturity is more flexible than American call option regardless of the dividend with 5th or 10th year maturity. Then, some combination between shorter maturity Bermudan call and longer American call options is also a reasonable method.

We here demonstrated a quantitative decision method on what and when is the reasonable capacity expansion investment to uncertain seasonal demand variation according to information from ROA. Next challenge is to make much clearer about the dividend effects of rising seasonal demand variation to exercise the American call option.

References

Bouzerdoum, M., Mellit, A., & Pavan, A. M. (2013). A hybrid model (SARIMA-SVM) for short-term power forecasting of a small-scale grid-connected photovoltaic plant. *Solar Energy, 98*(Part C), 226–235.

Box, G. E., Jenkins, G. M., & Reinsel, G. C. (2008). *Time series analysis forecasting and control* (4th ed.). Hoboken, NJ: Wiley.

Copeland, T., & Antikarov, V. (2003). *Real options: A practitioners guide*. New York: Texere LLC.

Dixit, A. (1992). Investment and hysteresis. *Journal of Economic Perspectives, 6*(1), 107–132.

Dixit, A. K., & Pindyck, R. S. (1994). *Investment under uncertainty*. Princeton, NJ: Princeton University Press.

Fujiwara, T. (2012). On growth option for R&D continuity of biotech start-ups under uncertainty. *Global Journal of Flexible Systems Management, 13*(3), 129–139.

Fujiwara, T. (2013). Real options analysis on strategic partnership dealing of biotech start-ups. *Global Journal of Flexible Systems Management, 14*(1), 17–31.

Kume, K., & Fujiwara, T. (2016a). Production flexibility of real options in daily supply chain. *Global Journal of Flexible Systems Management, 17*(3), 249–264.

Kume, K., & Fujiwara, T. (2016b). Effects of the exercisable duration and quantity of real options in multi-stages. *Technology Transfer and Entrepreneurship, 3*(2), 107–118.

Moreno, M. S., Montagna, J. M., & Iribarren, O. A. (2007). Multiperiod optimization for the design and planning of multiproduct batch plants. *Computers & Chemical Engineering, 31*(9), 1159–1173.

Moreno, M. S., & Montagna, J. M. (2012). Multiperiod production planning and design of batch plants under uncertainty. *Computers & Chemical Engineering, 40*, 181–190.

Mun, J. (2003). *Real options analysis course: Business cases and software applications*. Hoboken NJ: Wiley.

Myers, S. (1977). Determinants of corporate borrowing. *Journal of Financial Economics, 5*(2), 147–175.

Pindyck, R. S. (2008). Sunk costs and real options in antitrust analysis. In W. D. Collins (Ed.), *Issues in competition law and policy* (pp. 619–640). Washington, DC: American Bankers Association Press.

Sarkar, S. (2000). On the investment-uncertainty relationship in a real options model. *Journal of Economic Dynamics & Control, 24*(2), 219–225.

Chapter 12
Resistance to Integrate Information Systems in Healthcare Service: A Study on Developing Country

Nusrat Jusy Umme and Md. Maruf Hossan Chowdhury

Abstract Information systems are vital for meeting the service expectations of customers and stakeholders. However, integration of information systems in health service is inhibited due to numerous resistance factors which need to be addressed in order to ensure a quality healthcare service. Despite its significance, there is a paucity of research in addressing the resistance to information technology adoption in the healthcare industry. This relates to two domains: (i) factors contributing to resistance to health information systems (HIS) in developing country contexts and (ii) strategies to mitigate the resistances. This chapter sets out to develop a methodology to address the aforementioned gaps in the literature using an analytical hierarchy process (AHP) integrated quality function deployment (QFD) approach. The developed methodology will be used in a healthcare service providing organization in Bangladesh to identify the factors contributing to resistance to health information systems (HIS) and to determine the most significant strategies to mitigate those resistance factors. This research has significant theoretical, methodological and managerial implications.

Keywords Health service · Information systems · Mitigation strategies Optimization · QFD resistance

---

N. J. Umme
School of Information Systems, Curtin Business School, Perth, Australia
e-mail: Umme.nusrat@yahoo.com

Md. M. H. Chowdhury (✉)
Management Discipline Group, UTS Business School, 15 Broadway,
Ultimo, NSW 2007, Australia
e-mail: maruf.chowdhury@uts.edu.au

12.1 Introduction

ICT is an avenue for change, offers effectiveness and efficiency in many facets of the society. By implementing health information systems (HIS), the health sector has been able to improve its health service quality and lessen medical errors (Menachemi and Collum 2011). In the contemporary world, HIS has been successfully adopted by many developed countries in their health service organizations (Mutale et al. 2013). Yet, the HIS in developing countries has not been widely adopted. There are numerous factors that influence the resistance to HIS implementation in developing countries. A review of the relevant, extant literature reveals that issues responsible for reluctance to HIS in developing countries are still underexplored.

Akter et al. (2013) posit that ICT is a leading issue for ensuring health service quality. Likewise, it has been asserted by Chowdhury and Quaddus (2016) that information technology enabled health service design is supportive for sustainable health service systems. They also focused on the significance of information systems (IS) in health service to ensure improved service delivery processes in Bangladesh. Similarly, studies by Braa et al. (2004, 2007) and Lucas (2008) informed the health information systems in developing countries.

The health service industry in Bangladesh still lags behind in the adoption of information technology in delivering their healthcare service, although the advantages of ICT usage in health service are well explored. The reluctance to non-adoption of information and communication technology to deliver and manage health service is contributed by many factors. If such resistances cannot be mitigated, improving health service delivery process is not easy. As a result, it is important to examine the factors responsible for reluctance to HIS implementation in order to identify and mitigate them.

Although the extant literature finds that a lack of ICT infrastructure (Gichoya 2005) is the salient factor contributing to the resistance of IS, the literature on resistance shows that the HIS resistance in a developing country context is still under investigated. This gap in the literature encourages the researchers to investigate the following research questions:

1. What are the factors responsible for resistance to HIS in the developing countries?
2. What are the most significant strategies to mitigate the resistance factors?

12.2 Literature Review

The following sections include a thorough review of existing literature to identify the factors responsible for resistance to the adoption of health information systems and strategies to mitigate that resistance.

12.2.1 Importance of Health Information Systems

Because of the efficiency, effectiveness, productivity and accuracy gained through technology in business and society, technological dependencies are becoming exponential. In order to satisfy the current business needs, more and more businesses are now keen to utilize technology (Mohammad Alamgir 2012). For improving the service quality in the service industry, technological excellence has also made a substantial contribution (Brynjolfsson 1993). Technological excellence is a vital enabler for service quality which is highly evident in the healthcare industry (Chowdhury and Quaddus 2016). The healthcare industry includes a broad spectrum of areas which includes primary health care, medical research, pharmaceuticals, etc. (Seninger 1996). Of those, primary health care is one of the most important areas since it provides a direct medical service to a large number of people. The technology used in the healthcare environment is often referred to as health information systems (Hirdes et al. 2008), computerized health information systems (Metsemakers et al. 1992) and hospital information systems (Cline and Luiz 2013; Anderson 1997) by the health service institutions.

It is crucial to implement HIS in the health service organizations. The health service institutions have been able to achieve improved health service, more efficiency, less medical errors and more accuracy with the increased adoption of HIS use (Buntin et al. 2011). Despite the benefits achieved through HIS adoption, it has not yet been diffused in all regions at the same rate. It is evident that the higher adoption of HIS is seen in most developed countries such as the USA, Canada and Australia (Jha et al. 2008; Ludwick and Doucette 2009; Buntin et al. 2011). Developed countries have improved their health services by implementing HIS. However, developing countries such as India, Bangladesh and Nepal are still far from adopting HIS across the broader spectrum. There are many important issues which are responsible for the non-adoption of HIS by health service providers in developing countries. Among there are many reasons for the slow adoption of HIS in developing countries, resistance to accept the technology is one of the most significant ones (Kapurubandara and Lawson 2006). The following section enumerates the resistance factors responsible for the non-adoption or slow adoption of HIS.

12.2.2 Factors Responsible for Resistance to Health Information Systems

Different studies find that people show resistance to accept new technology both in the context of developing (Knol and Stroken 2001; Kapurubandara and Lawson 2006) and developed countries (Lapointe and Rivard 2005; Bhattacherjee and Hikmet 2007). Existing literature reveals that lack of telecommunication infrastructure, financial constraints (Blaya et al. 2010), lack of IT knowledge and training (Knol and Stroken 2001), lack of skilled human resources (Kapurubandara and

Lawson 2006) and a few other factors are important drivers towards resistance to technology in the context of developing country. On the other hand, in developed countries, the significant drivers of resistances are related to compatibility, IT-related knowledge (Bhattacherjee and Hikmet 2007) and perceived threat (Lapointe and Rivard 2005). Table 12.1 lists the factors responsible for resistance to HIS.

The lack of an integrated framework to address the possible factors contributing to resistance in the healthcare industry is realized specifically in the context of developing countries, although resistance to technology has caught the attention of scholars for many years. This study, therefore, aims to examine the factors contributing to the resistance of implementing HIS in developing countries.

It is imperative to address the factors responsible for resistance to health information systems, especially in the case of developing countries. Failure to address the factors responsible for resistance to Health Information Systems results in the non-adoption or ineffective implementation of HIS. Therefore, it is crucial to identify the strategies which can mitigate the current resistance problems. Current studies identify a number of strategies to mitigate HIS resistance. It is revealed that ICT Infrastructure development (Detmer 2003), ICT training (Gagnon et al. 2012), Investment in ICT projects (Detmer 2003); effective change management (Markus 2004) and compatible systems (Tung et al. 2008) can mitigate the resistance to integrate the HIS in a developing country context. Table 12.2 presents various strategies for addressing resistance to HIS.

Table 12.1 Factors responsible for resistance to HIS in developing countries

Resistance factors	Sources
Lack of interest and awareness	Lapointe and Rivard (2005), Kim and Kankanhalli (2009)
Lack of tendency to take responsibility	Lapointe and Rivard (2005), Kim and Kankanhalli (2009)
Lack of Internet coverage	Azam (2014)
Lack of required hardware, software	Azam (2014)
Inadequate Internet speed	Azam (2014)
Power supply interruption	Azam (2014)
Lack of IT knowledge	Venkatesh et al. (2003), Mohammad Alamgir (2012), Azam (2014)
Lack of change management	Anderson (1997), Lorenzi and Riley (2000), Umble et al. (2003)
Lack of compatibility with existing systems	Venkatesh et al. (2003), Azam (2014)
Feeling uncertainty of output	Ali et al. (2016)

Strategies to mitigate resistance to Health Information Systems

Table 12.2 Strategies for addressing resistance to HIS

Strategies	Sources
ICT infrastructure development	Detmer (2003)
Imparting ICT training	Gagnon et al. (2012)
Investing in access to high speed internet	Chowdhury and Quaddus (2016)
Investing in hardware and software	Azam (2014)
Awareness creation	Chowdhury and Quaddus (2016)
More ICT projects	Detmer (2003)
Arranging alternative power supply	Chowdhury and Quaddus (2016)
Effective change management	Markus (2004)
Compatible system	Tung et al. (2008)
Government policy	Azam (2014)
Recruiting IT skilled people	Chowdhury and Quaddus (2016)

12.3 Methodology

This research adopts mixed methods to increase the validity and reliability of data (Creswell and Tashakkori 2007). Aligned with the research objectives, our study adopts both qualitative and quantitative methods. Table 12.3 depicts a summary of the research design. In the qualitative stage, it uses interviews with respondents to identify the resistance factors and the strategies to mitigate resistance to adopt HIS. Data were collected from two decision-makers and three employees of a large public hospital. The average interview time was around 40–60 min. Data collected from the interviews were analysed using content analysis technique.

Table 12.3 Summary of the research design

Research objectives	Data collection	Data analysis
– Identifying the factors responsible for resistance to HIS and – Prioritizing the resistance factors	– Review of literature on resistance to HIS – Interviewing decision makers and employees using semi-structured interview for identifying resistance factors (WHATs in QFD matrix) – Comparing the resistance factors using AHP	– Using content analysis for literature and field study data – AHP analysis
– Identifying the strategies to mitigate the resistance factors and selecting the most important strategies among them	– Review of existing literature on mitigation strategies – Using interview protocol (semi-structured) to identify mitigation strategies (HOWs in QFD matrix) – Using structured questionnaire for determining WHAT-HOW relationship matrix	– Using content analysis technique of literature and field study data – QFD analysis

Fig. 12.1 Weighting of WHATs using AHP (Saaty 1980)

$$\mathbf{A} = \begin{array}{c} \\ A_1 \\ A_2 \\ \\ \\ A_n \end{array} \begin{array}{|cccc} A_1 & A_2 & \ldots & A_n \\ \hline W_1/W_1 & W_1/W_2 & \ldots & W_1/W_n \\ W_2/W_1 & W_2/W_2 & \ldots & W_2/W_n \\ & & & \\ & & & \\ W_n/W_1 & W_n/W_2 & \ldots & W_n/W_n \end{array}$$

In the quantitative stage, it uses AHP integrated QFD. The analytic hierarchy process (AHP), developed by Saaty (1980), is a widely used multi-criteria decision modelling technique which deploys a paired comparison method of hierarchical structuring of a decision problem to rank alternative solutions. Figure 12.1 depicts the weighting scheme of decision criteria using AHP.

QFD is an effective technique to translate the customer needs into suitable design requirements/strategies (Kuo et al. 2009). QFD is also used to address specific problems of companies by finding the relationships between organizational problems and strategies to solve those problems (Chowdhury and Quaddus 2015, 2016). In this chapter, QFD is used to identify the factors responsible for resistance to HIS and develop design requirements/strategies to mitigate those resistance factors. In a typical QFD model, 'design requirements/strategies are referred to as 'WHATs' and 'how to fulfil requirements/solve problems' are referred to as 'HOWs' (Fig. 12.2). In this chapter, WHATs are the resistance factors and HOWs are the strategies to mitigate the resistance factors. A typical QFD model includes some basic inputs such as: (a) requirements/problems—WHATs; (b) importance of WHATs; (c) design requirements/strategies—HOWs; (d) WHAT-HOW relationship matrix; (e) roof matrix (interrelationship among HOWs/Strategies.

The relationship between the resistance factors (WHATs) and corresponding strategies (HOWs) to mitigate the resistance factors is measured as 'no', 'very weak', 'weak', 'moderate', 'strong' and 'very strong' a relationship that is later replaced by the scale 0, 1, 3, 5, 7 and 9. These weights are used to represent the degree of significance attributed to the relationship. The importance of each strategy is determined by the following equation:

$$\mathrm{AI}_j = \sum_{i=1}^{m} w_i R_{ij} \quad \forall_j, \ j = 1, \ldots, n \tag{12.1}$$

Fig. 12.2 QFD layout

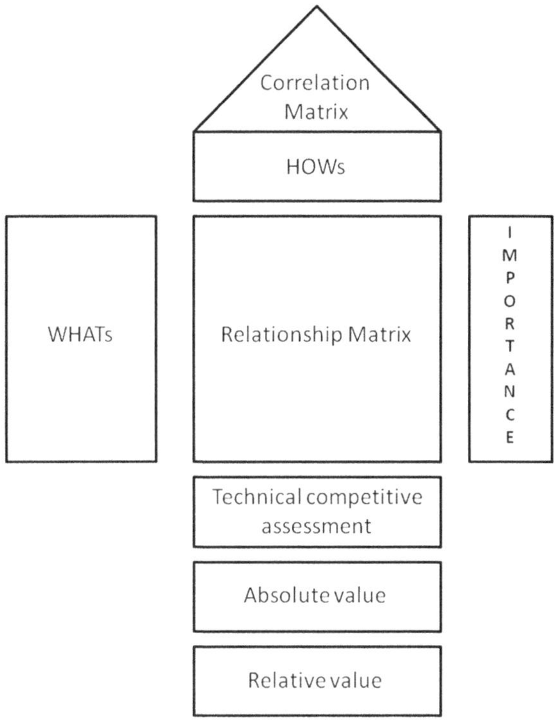
Correlation Matrix
HOWs
WHATs
Relationship Matrix
IMPORTANCE
Technical competitive assessment
Absolute value
Relative value

where,

AI_j absolute importance of jth strategy.
w_i weight of the ith resistance factor.
R_{ij} relationship value; extent of mitigating ith resistance factor by jth strategy scaled as 9, 7, 5, 3, 1, or 0.
n number of strategies.
m number of resistance factors.

The relative importance of strategy j is:

$$RI_j = \frac{AI_j}{\sum_{j=1}^{n} AI_j} \tag{12.2}$$

12.4 Case Study

The method as outlined in Table 12.3 was applied in the case of the healthcare industry in Bangladesh. Bangladesh is one of the developing countries in the South-East Asian region with a high density population. According to the

Population Census Bangladesh 2011, it has a population of 150 million people and among those, 72% live in rural areas. It is apparent that among 10,000 individuals, there are only 3–4 doctors and the numbers are even less in the rural areas (World Health Organization 2015). Similar to other developing nations, the problem of inadequate information infrastructural facilities in the healthcare service is acute in Bangladesh. The quality and accessibility of health service is poor, although health service facilities are available in different locations, including the remote areas. Health service efficiency is important to provide health services to people in a highly populated country like Bangladesh and, it is evident that ICT implementation contributes significantly to the health service efficiency (Buntin et al. 2011). Health service organizations can not only improve their operational efficiency but also its long-term viability with the use of ICT. Therefore, ICT-enabled healthcare service has huge potential in improving healthcare service in developing countries. This is supported by the findings of Chowdhury and Quaddus (2016). Despite the benefit of using health information systems, the adoption, implementation and use of health information systems in Bangladesh are inhibited due to a number of resistance factors. Therefore, this study develops a model that identifies the resistance factors to HIS and strategies to mitigate those resistance factors. Application of the model is operationalized below.

12.4.1 Identifying the Resistance Factors (WHATs)

As mentioned earlier, this study adopts a mixed method research where the resistance factors identified from the literature (Table 12.1) were compared with the field study findings to contextualize the resistance factors. Based on the comparison, a list of resistance factors are selected which are presented in Table 12.4 and were finalized for further analysis. Once the list of resistance factors was selected, the importance weights of the resistance factors were then determined using AHP. Table 12.4 presents the resistance factors and their weights. It is apparent from Table 12.4 that lack of awareness about the benefits of HIS is the most important factor creating resistance to HIS, followed by lack of telecommunication infrastructure and lack of IT knowledge and training.

Table 12.4 Resistance factors and their weights

Resistance factors	AHP weight
Lack of IT knowledge and training	0.188
Implementation cost	0.100
Maintenance cost	0.034
Lack of telecommunication infrastructure	0.213
Interruption in utility supply	0.056
Lack of awareness about the benefits of HIS	0.409

Table 12.5 Importance score of mitigation strategies

Mitigation strategies	Importance score from QFD matrix
St1—Awareness building	0.2596
St2—Imparting training	0.2145
St3—Investing in ICT infrastructure	0.1437
St4—Effective change management	0.1937
St5—Recruiting IT skilled people	0.1886

12.4.2 Strategies to Mitigate Resistance Factors (HOWs)

In line with the research objective, after determining the importance of resistance factors weights, strategies to mitigate those resistance factors were identified from the interview with the decision makers. The strategies—as identified from the field study—were compared with the strategies identified from the literature (Table 12.2) to determine the final list of strategies as relevant with the context. Table 12.5 presents the strategies relevant to our research context. Once the strategies to mitigate the resistance factors were identified, the decision-makers were then asked to determine the relationship between resistance factors and the corresponding strategies. Figure 12.3 presents the relationship matrix. The relationship matrix is used to determine the most important 'HOWs' or strategies. The relationship between WHATs and HOWs can be measured using the scale 9, 7, 5, 3, 1 and 0 which stand for very strong, strong, moderate, weak, very weak or no relation, respectively. Once the relationship between WHATs and HOWs is determined, the relationship score (in the scale of 9, 7, 5, 3, 1 and 0) is multiplied by the weight of corresponding WHAT to derive the final value of each cell in the relationship matrix. For example,

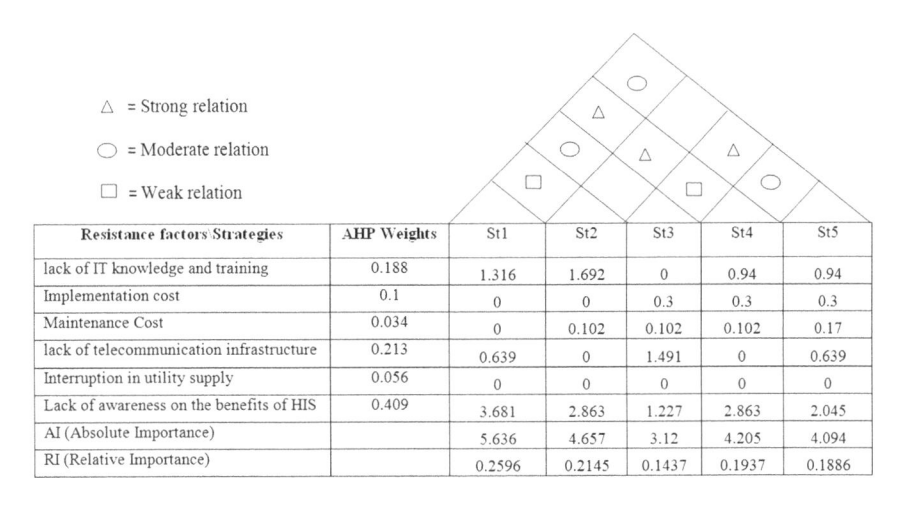

△ = Strong relation
○ = Moderate relation
□ = Weak relation

Resistance factors\Strategies	AHP Weights	St1	St2	St3	St4	St5
lack of IT knowledge and training	0.188	1.316	1.692	0	0.94	0.94
Implementation cost	0.1	0	0	0.3	0.3	0.3
Maintenance Cost	0.034	0	0.102	0.102	0.102	0.17
lack of telecommunication infrastructure	0.213	0.639	0	1.491	0	0.639
Interruption in utility supply	0.056	0	0	0	0	0
Lack of awareness on the benefits of HIS	0.409	3.681	2.863	1.227	2.863	2.045
AI (Absolute Importance)		5.636	4.657	3.12	4.205	4.094
RI (Relative Importance)		0.2596	0.2145	0.1437	0.1937	0.1886

Fig. 12.3 Relationship between resistance factors and corresponding strategies

corresponding to strategy 1 and resistance factor 1, the cell value 1.316 in the relationship matrix has derived from the multiplication of the AHP weight of resistance factor 1 (0.188) with the 'WHATs and HOWs' correlation score 7 (in the scale of 9, 7, 5, 3, 1 and 0). After determining all the cell values as mentioned, the value of absolute importance (AI) and relative importance (RI) can be determined using Eqs. 12.1 and 12.2 as presented in Fig. 12.3. It is inferred from Fig. 12.3 that the importance weight of awareness building (strategy 1) is highest (0.2596), followed by imparting training (strategy 2) (0.2145) and effective change management (strategy 4) (0.1937).

12.5 Discussion and Implications

This study finds that 'lack of awareness' about the benefits of health information systems is the most important factor (40.9%), resisting the adoption and implementation of HIS. Usually, health service staffs in the less developed countries are reluctant to use new technology as they have limited knowledge about the technology and its benefits to improve services to patients—which is consistent with the study of Chowdhury and Quaddus (2016). In their study on sustainable service design for m-health (mobile health) services in Bangladesh, Chowdhury and Quaddus (2016) find that the service providers are not very aware about the customer requirements and some of the health staffs have a lack of knowledge to provide technology enabled services. The second most important resistance factor is a lack of telecommunication infrastructure which accounts for 21.3% weight. The telecommunication infrastructure is essential to information technology. Most of the cases concerning telecommunication infrastructure in the developing and under developed countries are not well built. As a result, it is difficult to adopt and implement HIS which creates resistance among the managers and the employees to adopt HIS. This finding is consistent with the findings of Azam (2014). This study also finds that the third most important factor resisting HIS is a lack of IT knowledge and training—which accounts for 18.8% of the total weight. This finding is highly relevant as found in previous studies. Azam (2014), Mohammad Alamgir (2012) and Venkatesh et al. (2003) found that people with a lack of IT knowledge are reluctant to adopt and implement information systems. Similarly, our study also found that implementation costs, maintenance costs and interruptions in utility supply were the other factors in relation to the resistance of HIS in Bangladesh.

Corresponding to the resistance factors, our study found a number of mitigation strategies. Among the strategies, awareness building was found to be most significant which accounts for 25.96% of the total weight. In line with this finding, it can be inferred that building awareness among employees and managers is very important to adopt HIS and to create readiness to implement HIS. Previous studies (Kim and Kankanhalli 2009; Lapointe and Rivard 2005) also found that awareness building is salient in mitigating the resistance to adopt information systems. The findings also reveal that a strategy for building awareness is effective for mitigating vital challenges such as lack of IT knowledge and training, lack of telecommunication infrastructure and lack of awareness about the benefits of HIS. This is highly relevant, because building awareness about the uses and the benefits of HIS will create interest and expectations among the users and decision-makers to use the systems, develop infrastructure for proper implementation of the systems and train people to run the systems effectively and efficiently. The second most important strategy (21.45%) was found to be imparting training—which is effective for mitigating the resistance factors such as: lack of IT knowledge and training, maintenance cost and lack of awareness about the benefits of HIS. Our findings also reveal that the third most important strategy is effective change management which can assist in mitigating most of the resistance factors, except lack of telecommunication infrastructure and interruption in utility supply.

The findings of this study contribute to the existing literature on the health information systems literature—particularly resistance to adopt health information systems in the case of developing countries. The findings of this study identify the most important resistance factors to adopt and implement health information systems in a developing country context. To our knowledge, this has not been studied before and consequently, can make a useful addition to existing literature. This study also determines the strategies to mitigate resistance to health information systems and determines the weight of the strategies to identify the most significant strategies to mitigate the resistance. Previous studies fall short of identifying strategies to mitigate resistance to adopt health information systems in general and in the case of developing countries in particular. With regard to managerial implications, it is proposed that our study outcomes will help health service managers to identify the most important resistance factors to be aware of with regard to the adoption of health information systems in a developing country context. Identifying significant resistance factors will help them to prepare and to mitigate the resistance factors. Further, this study will help managers to determine the most important strategies to mitigate the resistance to adopt health information systems.

12.6 Conclusion

This study aims to identify the factors contributing to the resistance to health information systems and strategies to mitigate that resistance. As there is a paucity of current research in addressing the resistance to information technology adoption in the healthcare industry, this study adds value to the existing body of knowledge in health information systems. First, it identifies the most important factors resisting the health information systems. Second, it determines the strategies to mitigate resistance to health information systems. The findings of this study reveal that lack of awareness about the benefits of HIS, lack of telecommunication infrastructure and lack of IT knowledge and training are the most important resistance factors. On the other hand, the study finds that awareness building, imparting training and effective change management are the most important mitigation strategies. This study also has limitations that can provide opportunities to pursue further research. The study is conducted on few sample cases, thus empirical verification is needed by operationalizing survey research to ensure the external validity of the findings. Finally, it opens the avenue for further research based on surveys to explore the relationship between the resistance factors and the mitigation strategies. Though this study considers the healthcare service of Bangladesh as a case study, it is proposed that the findings and implications have significance for the healthcare services of other developing countries.

References

Akter, S., D'Ambra, J., & Ray, P. (2013). Development and validation of an instrument to measure user perceived service quality of mHealth. *Information & Management, 50*(4), 181–195.

Ali, M., Zhou, L., Miller, L., & Ieromonachou, P. (2016). User resistance in IT: A literature review. *International Journal of Information Management, 36*(1), 35–43.

Anderson, J. G. (1997). Clearing the way for physicians' use of clinical information systems. *Communications of the ACM, 40*(8), 83–90.

Azam, M. S. (2014). *Diffusion of ICT and SME performance: The mediating effects of integration and utilisation*. Doctoral dissertation, Ph.D. Curtin University, Graduate School of Business.

Bhattacherjee, A., & Hikmet, N. (2007). Physicians' resistance toward healthcare information technology: A theoretical model and empirical test. *European Journal of Information Systems, 16*(6), 725–737.

Blaya, J. A., Fraser, H. S., & Holt, B. (2010). E-health technologies show promise in developing countries. *Health Affairs, 29*(2), 244–251.

Braa, J., Hanseth, O., Heywood, A., Mohammed, W., & Shaw, V. (2007). Developing health information systems in developing countries: The flexible standards strategy. *MIS Quarterly, 31*(2), 381–402.

Braa, J., Monteiro, E., & Sahay, S. (2004). Networks of action: Sustainable health information systems across developing countries. *MIS Quarterly, 28*(3), 337–362.

Brynjolfsson, E. (1993). The productivity paradox of information technology. *Communications of the ACM, 36*(12), 66–77.

Buntin, M. B., Burke, M. F., Hoaglin, M. C., & Blumenthal, D. (2011). The benefits of health information technology: A review of the recent literature shows predominantly positive results. *Health Affairs, 30*(3), 464–471.

Chowdhury, M. M. H., & Quaddus, M. A. (2015). A multiple objective optimization based QFD approach for efficient resilient strategies to mitigate supply chain vulnerabilities: The case of garment industry of Bangladesh. *Omega, 57*(Part A), 5–21.

Chowdhury, M. M. H., & Quaddus, M. A. (2016). A multi-phased QFD based optimization approach to sustainable service design. *International Journal of Production Economics, 171* (Part 2), 165–178. https://doi.org/10.1016/j.ijpe.2015.09.023.

Cline, G. B., & Luiz, J. M. (2013). Information technology systems in public sector health facilities in developing countries: The case of South Africa. *BMC Medical Informatics and Decision Making, 13*(1), 1–12.

Creswell, J. W., & Tashakkori, A. (2007). Developing publishable mixed methods manuscripts. *Journal of Mixed Methods Research, 1*(2), 107–111.

Detmer, D. E. (2003). Building the national health information infrastructure for personal health, health care services, public health, and research. *BMC Medical Informatics and Decision Making, 3*(1), 1–12.

Gagnon, M. P., Desmartis, M., Labrecque, M., Car, J., Pagliari, C., Pluye, P., et al. (2012). Systematic review of factors influencing the adoption of information and communication technologies by healthcare professionals. *Journal of Medical Systems, 36*(1), 241–277.

Gichoya, D. (2005). Factors affecting the successful implementation of ICT projects in government. *The Electronic Journal of e-Government, 3*(4), 175–184.

Hirdes, J. P., Ljunggren, G., Morris, J. N., Frijters, D. H., Soveri, H. F., Gray, L., et al. (2008). Reliability of the InterRAI suite of assessment instruments: A 12-country study of an integrated health information system. *BMC Health Services Research, 8*(1), 277.

Jha, A. K., Doolan, D., Grandt, D., Scott, T., & Bates, D. W. (2008). The use of health information technology in seven nations. *International Journal of Medical Informatics, 77*(12), 848–854.

Kapurubandara, M., & Lawson, R. (2006). Barriers to adopting ICT and e-Commerce with SMEs in developing countries: An exploratory study in Sri Lanka. *University of Western Sydney, Australia*, 2005–2016, [online]. http://www.collecter.org/archives/2006_December/07.pdf. August 30, 2016.

Kim, H. W., & Kankanhalli, A. (2009). Investigating user resistance to information systems implementation: A status quo bias perspective. *MIS Quarterly, 33*(3), 567–582.

Knol, W. H. C., & Stroeken, J. H. M. (2001). The diffusion and adoption of information technology in small-and medium-sized enterprises through IT scenarios. *Technology Analysis & Strategic Management, 13*(2), 227–246.

Kuo, T. C., Wu, H. H., & Shieh, J. I. (2009). Integration of environmental considerations in quality Function deployment by using fuzzy logic. *Expert Systems with Applications, 36*(3), 7148–7156.

Lapointe, L., & Rivard, S. (2005). A multilevel model of resistance to information technology implementation. *MIS Quarterly, 29*(3), 461–491.

Lorenzi, N. M., & Riley, R. T. (2000). Managing change: An overview. *Journal of the American Medical Informatics Association, 7*(2), 116–124.

Lucas, H. (2008). Information and communications technology for future health systems in developing countries. *Social Science and Medicine, 66*(10), 2122–2132.

Ludwick, D. A., & Doucette, J. (2009). Adopting electronic medical records in primary care: Lessons learned from health information systems implementation experience in seven countries. *International Journal of Medical Informatics, 78*(1), 22–31.

Markus, M. L. (2004). Technochange management: Using IT to drive organizational change. *Journal of Information Technology, 19*(1), 4–20.

Menachemi, N., & Collum, T. H. (2011). Benefits and drawbacks of electronic health record systems. *Risk Management and Healthcare Policy, 4*, 47–55.

Metsemakers, J. F., Höppener, P., Knottnerus, J. A., Kocken, R. J., & Limonard, C. B. (1992). Computerized health information in The Netherlands: A registration network of family practices. *British Journal of General Practice, 42*(356), 102–106.

Mohammad Alamgir, H. (2012). *Adoption, continued, and extended use of radio frequency identification (RFID) technology: Australian livestock industry*. Doctoral dissertation. Curtin University.

Mutale, W., Chintu, N., Amoroso, C., Awoonor-Williams, K., Phillips, J., Baynes, C., et al. (2013). Population health implementation and training-Africa health initiative data collaborative. Improving health information systems for decision making across five Sub-Saharan African countries: Implementation strategies from the African health initiative. *BMC Health Services Research, 13*(Suppl 2), S9.

Population Census Report Bangladesh. (2011). Available at 〈http://www.sid.gov.bd/wp-content/uploads/2013/01/BANGLADESH-at-a-glance-Census-2011.pdf〉. URL (Accessed May 1, 16).

Saaty, T. L. (1980). *The analytic hierarchy process*. NY, USA: McGraw-Hill. Cook, W. D. & Seiford, L. M. (1978). Priority ranking and consensus formation. *Management Science, 24*, 1721–1732.

Seninger, S. F. (1996). Health service industry highlights. *Montana Business Quarterly, 34*(1), 23–24.

Tung, F. C., Chang, S. C., & Chou, C. M. (2008). An extension of trust and TAM model with IDT in the adoption of the electronic logistics information system in HIS in the medical industry. *International Journal of Medical Informatics, 77*(5), 324–335.

Umble, E. J., Haft, R. R., & Umble, M. M. (2003). Enterprise resource planning: Implementation procedures and critical success factors. *European Journal of Operational Research, 146*(2), 241–257.

Venkatesh, V., Morris, M. G., Davis, G. B., & Davis, F. D. (2003). User acceptance of information technology: Toward a unified view. *MIS Quarterly, 27*(3), 425–478.

World Health Organization. (2015). https://www.who.int/gho/countries/bgd.pdf.

Chapter 13
Towards an Effective Agricultural e-Trading System in India

P. K. Suri

Abstract The Indian Government has boldly announced its intent of doubling the income levels of farmers in next five years while presenting the last Union Budget 2016–17. The Government then promptly launched an electronic National Agriculture Market (eNAM) during April, 2016 to create more options for farmers for getting better returns for their agricultural produce. Several years before launching of eNAM, the central Department of Agriculture Co-operation and Farmers Welfare took an initiative to network various agricultural produce wholesale markets under Agricultural Marketing Information Network (AGMARKNET) project. So far, the AGMARKNET project has remarkably networked about 3000 markets in India and daily market information is being disseminated in several geographically spread markets for the use of farmers and other stakeholders. In this chapter, the eNAM and AGMARKNET projects are analyzed from the perspective of their integration for the purpose of creating better value for both buyers and sellers. Situation, actors, and process-related gaps in AGMARKNET are identified for taking corrective measures for its improvement and integration with eNAM. Based on learning issues, a few strategic recommendations are brought out for eNAM system to eventually deliver as per its mandate.

Keywords AGMARKNET · Agricultural marketing · Digital India
e-governance · e-NAM · Marketing reforms · SAP-LAP

13.1 Introduction

Agriculture continues to play a significant role in Indian economy as about two-third of its population earns livelihood from Agriculture and allied sectors. For safeguarding the interest of farmers, about 7000 Agricultural Produce Wholesale Markets

P. K. Suri (✉)
Delhi School of Management, Delhi Technological University, New Delhi, India
e-mail: pksuri@dtu.ac.in; pks.suri@gmail.com

P. K. Suri
NIC, Govt. of India, New Delhi, India

(APWMs) have been set up in different parts of the country over the years. The farmers are expected to realize better returns by selling their surplus produce in these markets. Agriculture being a state subject in India, these wholesale markets operate under the respective State Marketing Boards/Directorates. As per the traditionally established system, the markets in a state are governed under a state-specific Agricultural Produce Marketing Committee Act (APMC Act). Despite the variation in the Acts implemented across the states, the essence of these Acts is to progressively develop a farmer-friendly environment for trading based on a transparent mechanism for price discovery. In practice, however, the system in most of the markets has deteriorated over the years. Apart from underreporting of commodity transactions by traders to save market charges and taxes, the revenue being generated by markets is often diverted for other purposes instead of utilizing the same for strengthening the market infrastructure. This is against the spirit of APMC Act. Further, due to vested interests of dominant players in market operations, farmers are generally deprived of an enabling environment to negotiate better prices for their produce. Realizing the lacunae in the existing system of agricultural marketing in terms of weak marketing infrastructure and restrictive legal bindings on selling of agricultural produce, the Government of India had set up an Inter-Ministerial Task Force on Agricultural Marketing Reforms in July, 2001. The committee took stock of many challenges in post-harvest operations related to agricultural produce and made several recommendations for strengthening agricultural marketing in the country. One of the key areas identified by the task force was to empower farmers with latest market information. Accordingly, a plan scheme was formulated by the Directorate of Marketing and Inspection, Ministry of Agriculture (now Ministry of Agriculture and Farmers' Welfare) to support setting up of an Information and Communication Technology (ICT) based Agricultural Marketing Information Network (AGMARKNET) System. The project aims at collecting daily commodity prices and arrivals information from various APWMs and disseminating the same for the use of farmers and other stakeholders. The AGMARKNET project (www.agmarknet.gov.in), launched during October, 2000 has incrementally networked about 3000 wholesale markets.

AGMARKNET is a unique kind of e-governance system where a large number of autonomous markets are sharing daily market information for the use of farmers. The scope of the ongoing national level project could have been enhanced by facilitating e-trading of agricultural commodities. However, the Government has decided to launch a new e-platform, viz., e-NAM (www.enam.gov.in) to establish a national agriculture market. There are inherent limitations in both the projects which are discussed in this chapter in order to suggest a few corrective measures for developing an effective e-trading system for agricultural commodities.

The chapter:

- presents an overview of the AGMARKNET system and the recently launched electronic National Agriculture Market (eNAM) system, and identifies the challenges being faced; and
- conducts a gap analysis of the already implemented national level AGMARKNET system from the perspective of leveraging the capability built over the years to support an effective electronic trading system for agricultural commodities.

The chapter has eight sections. After the introductory remarks in Sect. 13.1, methodology adopted is explained in Sect. 13.2. This is followed by a brief review of literature brought out in Sect. 13.3. Section 13.4 presents an overview of eNAM, its intended outcomes, conceptual and implemented process flow and challenges ahead. The need for integration of AGMARKNET and eNAM is discussed in Sect. 13.5. Section 13.6 presents a Situation-Actor-Process analysis of AGMARKNET service and a gap analysis related to situation, actors, and processes. Section 13.7 brings out key learning issues based on which a few strategic recommendations are made to strengthen e-trading of agricultural commodities. Finally, the chapter is concluded in Sect. 13.8.

13.2 Methodology

The chapter is based on:

- Practical experience gained as National Coordinator during execution and recent review of AGMARKNET project as part of a study conducted by Food and Agriculture Organization of the United Nations. This involved visits to several agricultural produce wholesale markets to understand their marketing environment and prevailing practices of commodity transactions.
- Learning from studies conducted on AGMARKNET and eNAM systems.
- Study of operational guidelines of AGMARKNET and policy initiatives on reforms in agricultural marketing (DMI 2003; DAC 2013; NIC 2014) and eNAM projects.
- Interactions held with key stakeholders including farmers, traders, commission agents, center and state government officials, etc.
- Comparative analysis of market information being disseminated through AGMARKNET and eNAM websites.
- Gap analysis of AGMARKNET project by identifying situation, actor, and process-related gaps. This is followed by the synthesis of learning to bring out actions in terms of strategic recommendations for improving performance using SAP-LAP framework (Sushil 2000, 2001, 2009, 2017).

13.3 Literature Review

In the recent past, Government of India has undertaken several initiatives for transforming government functioning with the intent of strengthening interfaces with different sections of society. Recognizing that Information and Communication Technology (ICT) can play a big role in extending Government services to the doorsteps of citizens, the Government of India announced a mega plan titled National e-Governance Plan (NeGP) in May, 2006. Several mission mode projects were conceptualized for implementation by different departments in order to equip them to serve citizens as per their respective organizational mandates (www.mit.gov.in). While many projects could be launched in urban areas, their performance was considered suboptimal (DIT 2015, p. 6). A few projects either progressed at a slow pace or could not be initiated at all. NeGP has subsequently been subsumed in the "Digital India Programme" announced by the new Government. Agriculture is one such area, where several of the services envisaged under the corresponding Mission Mode Project of NeGP are yet to be implemented. Well before the approval of Mission Mode Project on Agriculture in 2010, the Department of Agriculture and Co-operation (DAC) under the erstwhile Union Ministry of Agriculture initiated AGMARKNET project in the year 2000 to empower farmers with market information. In 2001, the DAC set up an Inter-Ministerial task force to bring out recommendations for reforming the area of agricultural marketing. The committee reviewed the challenges related to post-harvest management of agricultural produce and made several recommendations with respect to nine key areas for strengthening agricultural marketing in the country (DAC 2002). The areas identified for improving the marketing system were (a) Legal reforms; (b) Direct marketing; (c) Market infrastructure; (d) Pledge financing; (e) Warehousing receipt system; (f) Forward and futures markets; (g) Price support policy; (h) IT in agricultural marketing; and (i) Marketing extension, Training and Research.

The progress of reforms in the identified areas has not been satisfactory due to lack of interest at the level of state governments to adopt reforms (DAC 2013, 2014). For example, even though AGMARKNET project has expanded to about 3000 markets spread across the country, there are still many operational and organizational challenges which are yet to be overcome (Suri 2005). Of particular significance is the challenge of forming cross-organizational strategic alliances for creating better value for the farming community and other stakeholders (Suri and Sushil 2017). Despite AGMARKNET emerging as a unique web-based service for sharing market information, it is reported that farmers continue to rely on conventional sources for accessing agriculture related information (NSSO 2003, 2014). The Government has recently launched another project, viz., eNAM to provide a common electronic platform for enabling commodity transactions by buyers and sellers (www.enam.gov.in). The project is being viewed upon as a game changer in the area of agriculture provided it can overcome the underlying challenges (Chand 2016). The idea of eNAM has roots in the initiative taken in the Karnataka state to establish a common market across the state by introducing online trading of agricultural produce. The state-level project, however, is yet to roll out fully and deliver as per expectations of various stakeholders. As per a recent study, while market officials and major markets where trading is dominated by farmer marketing cooperatives have welcomed this reform initiatives, the progress in most other markets is unsatisfactory. The key issues being faced during execution are: continued preference of farmers to trade through commission agents due to past relations, reluctance of farmers for assaying of their produce due to procedural delays and costs involved, nonparticipation by distant traders due to lack of trust on assaying mechanisms, operational issues related to connectivity and IT equipment and inadequate banking facilities (Aggarwal et al. 2016). Such practical issues being faced in the state-level project reflect upon several complexities associated with the national level eNAM project. Keeping in view high failure rate of e-governance projects in developing countries, both AGMARKNET and eNAM projects need to possibly integrate for removing information asymmetry and thus contribute for creation of better value from the perspective of farmers as well as other stakeholders.

13.4 An Overview of eNAM

The conventional agricultural marketing set up in India is based on physical wholesale markets established in each state. Farmers bring their surplus produce to the markets with the expectation of getting better returns for their produce. However, farmers are often deprived of the expected benefits as the traders tend to collude and dictate the buying price to their advantage. In such situations, farmers are left with no option but to sell the produce at offered prices. The traditional system of commodity transactions is also a closed system in the sense that only a limited number of traders, who are issued licenses by a particular market, are authorized for trading with the farmers visiting the market. Such a system, with limited options with farmers, curtails the bargaining power of farmers. The electronic National Agriculture Market (eNAM) initiative launched by the Prime Minister on April 14, 2016 aims at using technology for establishing an effective and transparent price discovery mechanism by overcoming the limitations of the conventional system. The project is being implemented with an incremental approach by the Department of Agriculture, Co-operation and Farmers Welfare. As of October 31, 2017, 470 APMC of 14 States (Andhra Pradesh, Chhattisgarh, Gujarat, Haryana, Himachal Pradesh, Jharkhand, Madhya Pradesh, Maharashtra, Odisha, Rajasthan, Tamil Nadu, Telangana, Uttar Pradesh, and Uttarakhand) have been integrated in NAM Platform (www.enam.gov.in, last accessed on 28.3.2018). The project is expected to be implemented in 585 markets by 31.3.2018 in the states which are desirous of joining the network. The key features of the eNAM system are:

- Pan-India electronic trading portal to create a unified national market of agricultural commodities
- Uniform license for traders to transact across all markets in a state
- Single point levy of market fee at the time of purchase from farmer
- Transparent auction process
- Quality assessment of produce
- Instant online payments

13.4.1 Intended Outcomes of eNAM

The following are the intended outcomes of eNAM initiatives:

- Nation-wide market for farmers for realization of better prices for their produce
- Reduction in transaction costs
- Elimination of information asymmetry between buyers and sellers
- Real-time price discovery
- An actual transaction-based early warning system enabling need-based market intervention by the Government

13.4.2 Farm to Market Process Flow: A Conceptual Framework

The eNAM national level system is designed on the lines of an electronic auction system already under implementation in the state of Karnataka. In Karnataka, the Department of Agricultural Marketing has created a Special Purpose Vehicle in the form of Rashtriya eMarket Services (ReMS) to implement electronic auction system in 105 markets dealing with nonperishable agricultural commodities. When fully implemented, farmers shall be able to do trading through warehouses set up near their villages or in markets.

The chain of activities in marketing of agricultural produce involves: harvesting, drying, cleaning and classifying, packing, getting price information, deciding to store the crop in warehouse and to sell the same depending on the price, transit of crop to warehouse, storing the product in the warehouse; issuing of receipt for storing the produce, farmer taking loan from bank on the commodities stored/stocked in the warehouse as per needs, giving consent for selling after getting market price information, bidding, farmers receiving information through SMS about prices for their produce, consent for selling, and finally payment through bank.

13.4.3 The Implemented Process Flow

Implementation of the flow of commodities for trading purpose, as discussed above, is highly challenging due to lack of required marketing infrastructure in the vicinity of farmers. Creation of such infrastructure at the market level also seems to be unrealistic in the near future. Keeping such operational constraints into view, the scope of eNAM is presently restricted to only partial implementation of the proposed marketing system in select markets. This is in line with the implementation approach adopted by Karnataka. The processes encompassing the system, which is yet to be fully implemented, are summarized as follows:

- Recording of farmer's details at the entry gate. The details include name, address, mobile number, type of vehicle used for transporting produce, registration number of vehicle (if applicable), approximate quantity of produce and its type, and name of the trader through whom the farmer shall be selling produce. The farmer is issued computerized receipt containing these details and a code for the lot of produce.
- Unloading of produce at the auction platform where the produce is cleaned.
- Collection of sample by the designated official. The sample collected is tested in lab for assessing the quality of produce. The result of quality test is prominently displayed on the lot of produce. For example, in case of wheat, the outcome of quality test is displayed in terms of Normal/Medium/Poor.
- The sample collected is divided into three equal parts to form three packets. In each packet, result of quality test is placed and the packets are sealed. The sealed packets are given to farmer, grading inspector, and the buyer to facilitate reverification of quality in case of any dispute.
- Auction of produce is held electronically in a transparent manner. Farmer has the right to reject the price offered if he is not satisfied with the outcome of bidding. In such a case, he can again particpate in bidding at a later date.
- The trader through whom the produce is sold, weighs the produce, enters the quantity in computer, and makes payment electronically to the farmer as per the highest bid.
- The trader ties up with the firm which offered highest bid for collecting charges related to weighment, filling of bags, commission, mandi cess, and transportation cost (in case the buyer asks for produce to be transported to outside market).

13.4.4 Key Challenges

eNAM may appear to have addressed the issue of transparency in commodity transactions in markets. However, its effective implementation in all the states is likely to take quite some time; particularly in terms of resolving of legal complexities and huge requirement of funds for establishing desired marketing infrastructure across the country.

Based on literature review including study of electronic auction system introduced in Karnataka, the major challenges in the implementation of eNAM are identified as follows:

- Access of buyers and sellers to a reliable market information system
- Amendment of APMC Act by states for promoting e-trading
- Harmonization of quality standards of agricultural produce across markets [tradable parameters developed for 90 commodities so far (www.enam.gov.in, last accessed on 28.3.2018)]
- Acceptability of quality standards by farmers traders in terms of trust and cost effectiveness of testing procedures
- Setting up of quality testing infrastructure in markets and warehouses
- Accrediting of warehouses as per Warehousing (Development and Regulation) Act 2007 and giving option to farmers to trade from warehouses
- Sensitization of farmers, traders, and other related functionaries
- Capacity building of farmers to enable their direct participation in electronic trading
- Opening-up of bank accounts of farmers for direct transfer of payments

13.5 Need for Integration of eNAM and AGMARKNET

As discussed in Sect. 13.3, the central government initiated the process of reforms in agricultural marketing way back in the year 2001. As part of the reforms process, various actions were taken in the direction of overcoming these challenges. While the progress of various other reforms initiatives has been slow (DAC 2013), the Union Ministry of Agriculture has been able to sensitize various APWMs through their respective state governments to participate in the setting up of an Internet-based country-wide network of agricultural markets in the form of AGMARKNET. As the next logical step, scope of AGMARKNET could have been extended to progressively enable electronic trading of commodities. However, the authorities have decided to promote electronic trading through a new platform by launching eNAM. As a result, market information is now accessible from two different government-funded national level projects. This can often lead to indecisiveness among buyers and sellers while trying to trade online. Monitoring of commodity prices by the concerned government departments has also become more difficult.

A comparison of markets with respect to trading of Maize as reported on eNAM and AGMARKNET is presented in Table 13.1. The state-wise price spread in respect of maize transacted in different AGMARKNET markets is shown in Table 13.2.

Table 13.1 Trading of maize on AGMARKNET and eNAM as reported on 30.8.2017

S. No.	State	Market	Maximum price (Rs./Quintal)	Minimum price (Rs./Quintal)	Remarks
1	Chhattisgarh	Rajnandgaon	100	100	Appears incorrect; not reported on AGMARKNET
2	Gujarat	Jhalod	1200	1200	Not reported on AGMARKNET
		Bhiloda	1465 (1450)	1465 (1350)	
3	Haryana	Ladwa	2295	1150	Not reported on AGMARKNET
4	Madhya Pradesh	Dewas	2910 (1425)	1328 (1375)	
		Dhar	1248 (1276)	1238 (1238)	
		Harda	1361 (1361)	1296 (1343)	
		Jabalpur	1260 (1280)	1260 (1280)	
		Khirkiya	1155 (1145)	1155 (1106)	
5.	Uttar Pradesh	Banda	600	600	Not reported on AGMARKNET
		Bangarmau	1251 (1165)	1125 (1115)	
		Bilsi	1335 (1350)	1230 (1250)	
		Chandausi	1100	1070	Not reported on AGMARKNET
		Chaubepur	1300	1295	Not reported on AGMARKNET
		Chibramau	1195	1150	Not reported on AGMARKNET
		Farrukhabad	1200 (1220)	1100 (1125)	
		Ghajiabad	1250	1250	Not reported on AGMARKNET
		Jahangirabad	1220 (1300)	1100 (1150)	
		Kannauj	1200 (1275)	1100 (1210)	
		Kasganj	1200 (1250)	1150 (1125)	
		Madhoganj	1240 (1300)	1200 (1180)	

(continued)

Table 13.1 (continued)

S. No.	State	Market	Maximum price (Rs./Quintal)	Minimum price (Rs./Quintal)	Remarks
		Mainpuri	1200 (1165)	1200 (1110)	
		Sirsaganj	1215 (1260)	1185 (1220)	
6	Rajasthan	Bundi	1237 (1275)	1211 (1211)	
7	Telangana	Jagtial	911	911	Not reported on AGMARKNET
		Kesamudram	1259	911	Not reported on AGMARKNET

Source www.agmarknet.gov.in, www.enam.gov.in; (figures inside parentheses are prices reported on AGMARKNET, last accessed on 10.9.2017)

Table 13.2 Country-wide prices of maize on AGMARKNET as reported on 30.8.2017

S. No.	State	No. of markets which reported	Maximum price (Rs./Quintal)	Minimum price (Rs./Quintal)
1	Chhattisgarh	14	1525	1200
2	Gujarat	17	1725	1250
3	Haryana	1	1175	1150
4	Madhya Pradesh	29	1625	1106
5	Uttar Pradesh	60	1550	850
6	Rajasthan	20	1800	1161
7	Telangana	17	1600	1058

Source www.agmarknet.gov.in, last accessed on 10.9.2017

It is reflected from Tables 13.1 and 13.2:

- Commodity transactions reported over eNAM form only a small proportion of the transactions reflected on AGMARKNET.
- There are instances where markets have reported over eNAM but not on AGMARKNET.
- There are differences in the market prices information being disseminated through the two parallel services.
- There are differences in variety names of the commodities transactions reflected over eNAM and AGMARKNET.

It is, therefore, important to methodically integrate AGMARKNET with eNAM to enable improved decision making by buyers and sellers based on knowledge about market prices prevailing across the nation.

In the following section, a review of AGMARKNET is undertaken to identify gaps prevailing in the ongoing system from the perspective of taking corrective measures so that it can effectively serve the market information needs of buyers and sellers who trade over eNAM.

13.6 The AGMARKNET Service—A Situation-Actor-Process Analysis

The AGMARKNET e-governance project was launched during October, 2000 with the intent of empowering farmers with market information by networking various wholesale markets (Dhankar 2003). The ongoing project is funded by central Department of Agriculture, Co-operation and Farmers' Welfare and implemented with the technical support of the National Informatics Centre (NIC) (Readers are referred to Suri (2005) and Suri and Sushil (2006) for a detailed Situation-Actor-Process-Learning-Action-Performance (SAP-LAP) based analysis of AGMARKNET project). A summary of the S-A-P analysis is presented here for quick reference and better understanding of the readers. This is followed by a gap analysis of AGMARKNET system based S-A-P components in order to suggest corrective measures for transforming the project into an authentic market information service for farmers. A reliable AGMARKNET service shall enable farmers to take informed decisions before they venture into electronic trading of their produce on eNAM platform.

13.6.1 Situation Analysis

The pre-AGMARKNET and post-AGMARKNET situation of Agricultural Marketing Information Service is summarized as follows:

13.6.1.1 Pre-AGMARKNET Situation (Before the Year 2000)

- The market prices and arrival information were maintained manually in the form of registers. There was no mechanism of sharing daily market information across markets or for the use of farming community and other stakeholders
- Only limited market information could be disseminated through mass media channels like radio, television, and newspapers
- There used to be considerable gap between generation and dissemination of market information
- Markets were not familiar with use of computers

13.6.1.2 Post-AGMARKNET Situation

- About 3250 APWMs have been equipped with computers and Internet connectivity
- More than 5000 market personnel have been trained to use a software application developed by the National Informatics Centre for reporting daily market information
- A commodity directory of about 300 commodities and 2000 varieties has been built over the period
- The daily market information in respect of connected markets can be accessed at www.agmarknet.gov.in
- Market information can be downloaded for past period also for analyzing commodity prices and arrival trends
- Market information is disseminated in the form of several national and state-level bulletins
- Daily market information can be accessed in 11 Indian languages besides English
- Daily market information is also disseminated through SMS over mobile phones to the registered farmers
- Apart from prices and arrivals, the AGMARKNET service also disseminates other marketing related information in the form of market profiles and commodity profiles

13.6.2 Gap Analysis

13.6.2.1 Situation-Related Gaps

Mismatch Between Market Data Being Captured and Changed User Expectations
The initial scope of the software application developed by NIC was limited to daily reporting of basic market information, viz., minimum price, maximum price, modal price, arrivals, source, and destination. The scope of data entry was purposely kept small to enable market personnel to get acquainted with the IT-based reporting system. However, the scope of the data reporting module has not been enhanced even after several markets started reporting data regularly.

Lack of a Unified Market Information System With the passage of time, multiple independent initiatives have emerged at center and state government levels to collect and disseminate market information. With the emergence of many new user types over the years, the need for a comprehensive market information system is increasingly being felt.

Lack of Performance Measures Since the start of project, the performance of project continues to be measured in terms of number of reporting markets with lesser emphasis being put on quality of data reported.

Lack of Collaborative Linkages It was required to establish a web of strategic alliances with related organizations to achieve wider dissemination of relevant market information among millions of farmers and other stakeholders (Suri 2005). Such synergetic linkages could not be developed to the desired extent.

Slow Pace of Market Reforms The progress of reforms suggested by the Inter-Ministerial Task Force on agricultural marketing (DAC 2002) has been quite slow. AGMARKNET has not yet been integrated with other marketing related initiatives such as National Warehousing Receipt System for promoting electronic trading of agricultural commodities.

Non-Updating of Market Profiles It is observed from the website that the market profiles (available at http://agmarknet.gov.in/MarketProfile/MarketProfile.aspx, last accessed on 5.9.2017) are not being updated by many markets due to which the contents being disseminated may be misleading.

Non-Updating of Commodity Profiles DMI has published profiles for about 20 commodities so far (http://agmarknet.gov.in/CommodityProfiles/Default.aspx, last accessed on 5.9.2017). However, most of these profiles were prepared a few years back and thus need to be updated to make them relevant in the present context.

13.6.2.2 Actor-Related Gaps

Lack of required resources with DMI Due to limited resources, the DMI field offices are not able to get actively involved in preparing marketing related advisories for farmers.

Lack of Shared Ownership by Markets The irregular and inconsistent reporting of daily information by many markets and non-updating of market profiles is a reflection on lack of project ownership by markets.

Lack of Shared Ownership by States Many states have developed their own websites to disseminate market information on the lines of AGMARKNET. A list of these can be seen at http://agmarknet.gov.in/MarketingBoards/Default.aspx (last accessed on 5.9.2017). Such duplication of work should be avoided to save resources. States need to play a larger role in effective monitoring of the markets and ensure regular reporting of quality market data to AGMARKNET.

Parallel Central Level Systems Apart from AGMARKNET system of DMI, three other central level organizations, viz., the Directorate of Economics and Statistics (DES), the Department of Consumer Affairs (DCA) and the National Horticulture Board (NHB) are maintaining separate market information systems on agricultural commodities. It is difficult for the end users to comprehend market information from multiple sources.

13.6.2.3 Process-Related Gaps

For the purpose of this paper, a detailed gap analysis is conducted with respect to the processes of market data collection, reporting, and dissemination. The key gaps are identified as follows:

Manual Data Compilation Commodity prices and arrivals are to be compiled from receipts collected from traders operating in the market. It is impractical to manually derive daily prices and arrivals related statistics from these receipts as per the scope of present system.

Lack of Standardized Data Definitions The data entry operators in the markets have been provided with a standard application user manual to use the software for data reporting. However, the markets have not been provided with a conceptual document defining the methodology for data collection. As a consequence, the quality of data reported can differ from market to market.

Issues in Reporting of Arrivals The arrivals statistics reported by markets could be misleading due to issues such as difficulty in compiling daily arrivals data, reporting of commodity-wise but not variety-wise arrivals, possible errors in conversion from local units to standard units before reporting arrivals, lack of mechanism to match arrivals recorded at entry gate of markets and the arrivals reported to AGMARKNET.

Issues in Reporting of Prices Quite a few instances have been observed where markets are constantly reporting same minimum, maximum, and modal prices for successive days. The instances of modal price being reported as average of minimum and maximum prices are also quite common as may be seen on any commodity specific report for several markets on AGMARKNET portal.

Lack of Standard Commodity Specifications Markets are generally assigning FAQ (Fair, Average, Quality) grades for data reported for cereals. In practice, buying decisions are based on perception of buyers about the specific characteristics of produce.

Inconsistent Reporting by Markets There are instances where certain markets are irregular in reporting. During the period of study, about 40% of the markets were found to be not reporting on daily basis. Inconsistencies have also been observed between data reported on state-level websites and the AGMARKNET.

13.7 Key Learning Issues, Strategic Recommendations, and Expected Benefits

Based on the above analysis, the key learning issues are summarized as follows:

13.7.1 Learning Issues

- Agriculture being a state subject in India, there are state specific marketing laws and restrictions on interstate movement of agricultural produce. Due to such trade barriers and lack of adequate agricultural marketing infrastructure, agricultural marketing trade flows are fragmented and disadvantageous to the farming community.
- The central Department of Agriculture and Farmers' Welfare is actively pursuing for reforms in agricultural marketing. However, the progress of reforms is quite slow due to lack of active participation by several states.
- Government has been trying to utilize convergence potential of ICT to bring cohesiveness among states for uplifting the farming community. About 3000 wholesale markets have been networked under AGMARKNET project with the aim of empowering farmers with market information. The eNAM is another major initiative which aims at establishing a common platform to promote agro-trading.
- Both the services have a few inherent limitations which need to be removed. A number of states are yet to participate in eNAM due to which only a small proportion of commodity transactions are reflected on eNAM as compared to AGMARKNET.

13.7.2 Strategic Recommendations and Expected Benefits

Based on learning issues, a few strategic recommendations for establishing a sound e-trading system for agricultural commodities along with the corresponding expected benefits are brought out as follows:

- The market information base of AGMARKNET project needs to be leveraged for strengthening of eNAM through integration of both the initiatives. *(Expected Benefit: Removal of market information asymmetry among buyers and sellers)*
- The commodity-variety directories being used by AGMARKNET and eNAM need to be standardized in the form of a common directory. *(Expected Benefit: Reliable information base to develop an effective decision support system for buyers, sellers as well decision-makers in government at various levels)*

- A unified agricultural market information service through reengineering of processes at state and central level need to be promoted. *(Expected Benefit: Effective utilization of resources through removal of redundant efforts)*
- The identification of select markets, where eNAM is being implemented in participating states, should preferably be based on the quantity traded, i.e., major markets in terms of commodity trade. *(Expected Benefit: Coverage of relatively much larger proportion of commodity trade)*
- Farmers need to be sensitized about recommended quality norms of produce to be sold through eNAM and capability improvement programmes need to be organized for farmers, traders, and market officials. *(Expected Benefit: Effective utilization of eNAM platform)*
- Farmers need to be empowered for direct trading of their produce. *(Expected Benefit: Elimination of dependence on traders and markets, better price realization benefitting both farmers and consumers)*
- Establishment of private markets similar to APMCs needs to be incentivized. *(Expected Benefit: Removal of monopoly of APMCs, who have become more powerful now as traders willing to participate through eNAM for trading in a particular market, has to register with that APMC)*
- Agricultural Marketing related contents such as commodity profiles available on AGMARKNET need to be regularly updated for dissemination in local languages through eNAM. *(Expected Benefit: Enhanced competitiveness of agricultural produce through adoption of good marketing practices by farmers)*

13.8 Conclusion

The recently launched eNAM service is a transformational initiative to reform the conventional physical markets based agricultural marketing system in India. There are, however, several challenges to be overcome before eNAM can deliver anticipated benefits to the farmers and consumers. Apart from active cooperation by states, it is required for eNAM to integrate with related services such as Agricultural Marketing Information Service already implemented under AGMARKNET project. In parallel, the AGMARKNET service needs to be improved and effectively utilized for removing prevailing information asymmetry among buyers and sellers. Its integration with eNAM shall enable informed trade related decisions by buyers and sellers who intend to use eNAM platform for trading of agricultural produce. Implementation of a few strategic recommendations, as brought out in the chapter based on analysis of eNAM and AGMARKNET, is expected to strengthen the agricultural e-trading platform for the benefit of all stakeholders.

References

Aggarwal, N., Jain, S., & Narayanan, S. (2016). The long road to transformation of agricultural markets in India: Lessons from Karnataka, WP-2016-026. Available at https://ifrogs.org/PDF/WP-2016-026.pdf, last accessed on August 30, 2017.

Chand, R. (2016). e-Platform for national agricultural market. *Economic and Political Weekly, L1* (28), 15–18.

DAC. (2002). *Report of inter-ministerial task force on agricultural marketing reforms*. Department of Agriculture and Cooperation, Ministry of Agriculture, Government of India.

DAC. (2013). *Final report of the committee of state ministers, in-charge of agriculture marketing to promote reforms*. Department of Agriculture and Co-operation, Government of India.

DAC. (2014). *Operational guideline—marketing research and information network*. Department of Agriculture and Co-operation, Government of India. Available at http://agmarknet.gov.in/Others/final_guidelines_2014.pdf, @@62–73, last accessed on September 6, 2017.

Dhankar, G. H. (2003). Development of internet based agricultural marketing information system in India. *Agricultural Marketing Journal, 45*(4), 7–15.

DIT. (2015). *E-governance policy initiatives under digital india programme*. Department of Electronics and Information Technology, Government of India. Available at http://digitalindia.gov.in/writereaddata/files/new-policy-book/index.html, last accessed on September 6, 2017.

DMI. (2003). *Operational guidelines: AGMARKNET*. Department of Agriculture and Co-operation, Ministry of Agriculture, Government of India.

NIC. (2014). *AGMARKNET user manual*. National Informatics Centre, Government of India. Available at http://agmarknet.nic.in/market_online/UserManual.pdf, last accessed on June 23, 2016.

NSSO. (2003). *Access to modern technology on farming: NSS 59th round*. National Sample Survey Organization, Government of India.

NSSO. (2014). *Key indicators of situation of agricultural households in India*. National Sample Survey Organization, Government of India.

Suri, P. K. (2005). Strategic insights into an E-governance project—a case study of AGMARKNET based on SAP-LAP framework. *Global Journal of Flexible Systems Management, 6*(3&4), 39–48.

Suri, P. K., & Sushil, (2006). E-governance through strategic alliances—a case of agricultural marketing information system in India. *IIMB Management Review, 18*(4), 389–401.

Suri, P. K., & Sushil, (2017). *Strategic planning and implementation of E-governance*. Singapore: Springer Nature.

Sushil. (2000). SAP-LAP models of inquiry. *Management Decision, 38*(5), 347–353.

Sushil. (2001). SAP-LAP framework. *Global Journal of Flexible Systems Management, 2*(1), 51–55.

Sushil, (2009). SAP-LAP linkages—a generic interpretive framework for analyzing managerial contexts. *Global Journal of Flexible Systems Management, 10*(2), 11–20.

Sushil. (2017). Theory building using SAP-LAP linkages: An application in the context of disaster management. *Annals of Operations Research*, 2017. https://doi.org/10.1007/s10479-017-2425-3.

Web URLs

www.agmarknet.gov.in.
www.enam.gov.in.
http://wdra.nic.in/.

Chapter 14
Impact of Behavioral Flexibility on Flexible HR System and Organizational Role Stress

Priyanka Jaiswal

Abstract In the current dynamic business environment, where there is an overlapping of organizational roles, it is extremely challenging for employees to focus on professional success to achieve as well as accomplish a specific career objective. In an organization, employees make some behavioral changes and try to adopt behavioral flexibility to adjust with the situation. As flexibility is known as the capacity to react to different demanding, dynamic, and competitive conditions which brings a change in an individual's regular behavior. This change in behavior is not only for adjusting with the culture of the organization; individuals show flexible behavior also for the purpose of managing their organizational role stress. The behavioral flexibility of an employee demonstrates broad range of behavior traits that could be used in different situation-focused demands. These traits are easy to adapt as compared to the changes in routine behaviors. At the firm level, human resource adaptability is the dynamic capacity of a firm centered on adjusting employee characteristics, and behavioral flexibility is one of the attributes. This article investigates the links between employees' behavioral flexibility at workplace, flexible HR systems, and organizational role stress. This study has been conducted on middle management employees in India. A well-constructed questionnaire with standard scales was used for data collection. Hypotheses were tested through statistical analysis after building psychometric properties of the scales. The results show that behavioral flexibility is significantly associated with HR flexibility and organizational role stress. Results have been further analyzed for their practical implications and future direction.

Keywords Behavioral flexibility · Flexible human resource system Organizational role stress

---

P. Jaiswal (✉)
FORE School of Management, New Delhi 110016, India
e-mail: priya.jais26@gmail.com; p.jaiswal@fsm.ac.in

© Springer Nature Singapore Pte Ltd. 2018
J. Connell et al. (eds.), *Global Value Chains, Flexibility and Sustainability*,
Flexible Systems Management, https://doi.org/10.1007/978-981-10-8929-9_14

14.1 Introduction

Organizations contain individuals who have been appointed with authority, power, and status, as indicated by their position in the levels of hierarchy. Everyone contemplates his/her professional success to get achievement or to accomplish a specific goal. Employees display behavioral changes and try to adjust their conduct to make it adaptable to a particular situation easily. Flexibility has been stated as the ability to react to different demands of a dynamic and competitive environment (Sanchez 1995). It is a change in individual's regular behavior which is not merely to adjust to the culture of the organization but also to manage one's job responsibility through flexible behavior, particularly in the present dynamic business world where various overlaps in organizational role exists. The behavioral flexibility may help employees to manage organizational role stress. The behavioral flexibility of an employee demonstrates versatility rather than routine practices. It is the degree to which workers have an expansive scope of behavioral changes that can be adjusted according to demands of the situation (Bhattacharya et al. 2005). At the firm level, researchers (Teece et al. 1997; Eisenhardt and Martin 2000; Zollo and Winter 2002) have described HR flexibility as a dynamic capability of a firm that is centered on adjusting characteristics of the worker like knowledge, aptitude, skills, and behavior changing conditions. According to Wright and Snell (1998), the HR flexibility is considered an inside feature of any organization. Over the last few decades, scholars have undertaken several researches to map out numerous determinants of flexibility at diverse levels: individual, group, and organizational. However, limited interest has been paid to role stress and understanding individual flexibility. This study aims to fill this gap and seeks to inquire the links between employees' behavioral flexibility at workplace, HR flexibility, and organizational role stress.

14.2 Background and Hypothesis Development

14.2.1 Behavioral Flexibility

In this dynamic, fast changing business world where employees are dealing with multiple roles to optimize the business, the concept of behavioral flexibility plays a vital role for every person. According to Sushil (1997), the concept of flexibility is associated with various connections depending on different situations. Environment adaptiveness, positive response to change, openness in thinking and versatile action taking are few of the connections that employees apply to deal with various situations. Jaiswal and Bhal (2014) explained that employees make some behavioral changes to handle different situations efficiently. Paulhus and Martin (1987, 1988) operationalized the term behavioral flexibility in terms of capabilities. Similarly, Gibbons and Rupp (2009) described behavioral flexibility as employees' ability to adjust their behavior in order to cope with the situation. Wright and Snell (1998) have explored the concept of behavioral flexibility and stated that employees have a broad repertoire of behavioral scripts and they may use these scripts according to the demands of the situation. Similarly, Lindberg and Kaiser (2004) suggested that behavioral flexibility involves proper identification of the behavioral approach and skills for different demands; when to use what in response to various demands. However, if the employee has the ability to apply a specific script accurately as per the need of the situation without following the regular work routine, then the overall organization would be able to react and manage the various changing situations that would lead toward organizational sustainability and effectiveness. Individuals who can manage a more extensive scope of fitting behavior when opposed to various situations are high on behavioral flexibility (Jaiswal and Bhal 2014). The concept of behavioral flexibility follows beyond the fixed routine work culture as researchers (Bhattacharya et al. 2005; Ericksen and Dyer 2005) explained that employees apply different actions to handle their routine situations or challenge-specific situations and these actions would be different from their fixed routine actions. Zaccaro (2002) has suggested that leaders should also display high behavioral flexibility in order to adopt to the social situation and to deal with the work group dynamics. During the implementation and execution of a major organizational change, leaders' behavioral flexibility may play a great role for other members (Groves 2005). Individuals with behavioral flexibility also develop good relations with other members and have the ability to manage situation-specific tasks appropriately with higher impact (Ferris et al. 2007).

However, the behavioral flexibility has a major impact on employees' emotions and decision-making which reflects in the organizational outcome. Therefore, this concept needs to be explored; how it affects employees' emotions in terms of handling organizational stress and various HR functions.

14.2.2 Flexible HR Systems

In organization, flexibility has been studied in various organizational functions. The main focus of flexibility is on optimum utilization of recourses and to maximize the organizational productivity. According to Sushil (2000) "Flexibility offers freedom of choice and is highly context specific". Organizations are adopting the flexibility concept in a different functional area in order to achieve organizational excellence and competitive advantage over others. According to Sanchez (1995), flexibility refers to organizational capabilities in order to respond to various environmental demands and challenges. The human resource being the essential component of an organization, controls organizational capabilities. Application of flexibility concept in human resource triggered the research interest. A flexible human resource system facilitates an organization to respond to various external dynamic environmental changes (Snow and Snell 1993; Wright and Boswell 2002). Many researchers (Milliman et al. 1991; MacDuffie 1995; Wright and Snell 1998; Milliman et al.

2002) recommended that a flexible HR system specifically is one of the most essential organizational capabilities. Previous researches (Wright and Snell 1998; Ketkar and Sett 2010) have shown that an organization with more flexible HR systems can respond to and handle a complex and dynamic environment in a much better way. Researchers (Sanchez 1995; Hitt et al. 1998; Ngo and Loi 2008; Ketkar and Sett 2009) have also suggested that in the current business scenario, where organizations are facing a strategic shift and economic change, flexible human resource systems assist organizations to achieve competitive advantage and lead them toward positive performance. Bhattacharya et al. (2005, p. 624) defined flexible HR systems as "the extent to which the firm's HR practices can be adapted and applied across a variety of situations, or across various sites or units of the firm, and the speed with which these adaptations and application can be made". They conceptualized HR flexibility as a multidimensional construct with behavioral flexibility as one of its dimensions. However, in this study, flexible HR system has been conceptualized as a flexible HR function at the firm level. It only focuses on the flexible HR practices which have been strategically implemented in the organization's HR system. It was seen that employees working in a flexible HR system are more involved in the task and enhance the organizational productivity (Beltrán-Martín et al. 2008). This may not be possible in all the cases. There are various individual and organizational factors which affect the effectiveness of flexible HR systems. The employee behavioral flexibility is one of the factors that can diminish the effectiveness of a flexible HR system. Since employees are the ones who are going to face different challenging situations and respond to them, if employees are not ready to change their behavior, it would be difficult to implement an effective flexible HR system in any organization. Therefore, the motive behind this study is to throw light on the impact of employees' behavioral flexibility on the flexible HR systems.

The following hypothesis has been proposed based on the discussion.

H1. *Higher employee behavioral flexibility leads to Flexible HR systems in the organization*

14.2.3 Organizational Role Stress

As the economy is transforming, organizations are shifting their structure from being functional to matrix. With the changing organizational structure, the responsibility of individuals at workplace has taken a different shape altogether. The current job scenario has a huge overlapping of roles. Individuals are expected to handle various roles and respond to various demands of the competitive environment. Therefore, individuals need to balance these multiple aspects of their work role. When there is a mismatch between the individual and his or her environment and the person cannot cope up with the demands, it results in work stress (Goyal and Kashyap 2010). "Stress" is one of the most researched concepts. Initially, this concept was studied by physicists and later on it shifted to social scientists (Cooper and Marshall 1978). Researchers then linked stress with organizational roles and their pressure. According to Michie (2002), stress is the psychological and physical state of an individual. Nowadays, organizational role stress has become a serious issue and this has an indirect and direct effect on organizational performance (Matteson and Ivancevich 1987). The concept of organizational role stress was pioneered by Pareek (1983). He identified ten types of organizational role stress: (1) Inter-role distance: It reflects the problems between non-organizational and organizational roles. (2) Role stagnation stress: In this kind of stress, an individual generates a feeling that he or she has been stuck in a similar role. (3) Role expectation stress: This stress arises from contradictory demands coming from superiors, colleagues, peers, and subordinates in an organization. (4) Role erosion stress: This stress comes when a position has come to be less critical than it used to be, or when someone receives the credit score for doing what desires to be completed in a single's very own role. (5) Role overload stress: In this stress, an individual feels that the job requires too much effort or all the job activities are considerably important. (6) Role isolation stress: This kind of stress is described as a feeling of an individual with which others do not connect easily, indicating absence of strong linkage of own role with other roles. (7) Personal inadequacy stress: This stress shows that the individual is not having the relevant knowledge, competency, skills, or training, in order to respond to the demanding organizational role. (8) Self-role distance stress: This kind of stress comes up with a vacuum existing between one's ideas of self and the demands of his or her role. (9) Role ambiguity stress: An individual experiences this stress when there is an absence of clarity about a role and its demands. (10) Resource inadequacy stress: This type of stress develops when there is a lack of resources such as human or material, or the given resources are insufficient to fulfill the demands of the role.

The organizational stress may prevail in any work (Bhattacharya and Basu 2007; Dasgupta and Kumar 2009). It is not caused by work responsibility only, there may be different reasons also for role stress. Researchers (Aasland and Forde 2005; Bateman 2009; Correa and Ferreira 2011) have explained that individual variables are also responsible for stress. Many researchers have worked on how to cope with organizational role stress. Researchers (La Rocco et al. 1980; Fisher 1985; Ganster et al. 1986; Kaufman and Beehr 1986) have suggested that social support can be one of the ways to manage organizational role stress. Most of the researches have mainly focused on organizational factors such as support from coworkers, supervisors, provide adequate resources, provide a standard job description, etc., to manage or minimize the organizational role stress. Still, literature lags behind in exploring individual factors to cope with the stress of organizational role. In this research, behavioral flexibility has been taken as a separate characteristic of an individual to help cope with the stress of organizational role. Researchers (Bhattacharya et al. 2005; Gibbons and Rupp 2009) have described behavioral flexibility as employees' broad range of behaviors and that they adjust their behavior in order to cope with or adapt to situation-specific demands. Similarly, Bamel et al. (2013, 2014) have suggested that people flexibility plays a vital role in

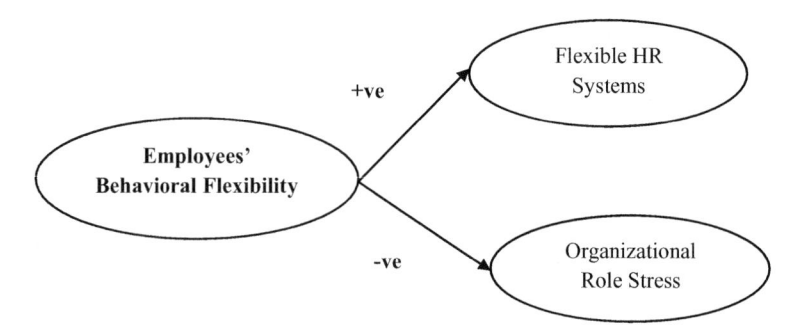

Fig. 14.1 Research model

individual role efficacy. Thus, behavioral flexibility may also help an individual to understand high priority and low priority work and according to that he or she will change behavior to respond to the situation. Moreover, if an employee is able to manage specific demand then automatically organizational role stress would reduce.

Based on above discussion, following hypothesis has been proposed.

H2. Higher employee behavioral flexibility leads to lower organizational role stress.

Overall, the impact of employees' behavioral flexibility has been explored in this study on flexible HR system and organizational role stress. Based on the discussion and literature, the following research model has been developed as shown in Fig. 14.1.

14.3 Methodology

14.3.1 Sample and Collection of Data

This is not a survey study. Data was collected from middle management people working in different organizations. A total of 383 management employees participated from organizations of various sectors, including IT, banking, BPO and manufacturing sectors, located in National Capital Region. The data was collected by administering a structured questionnaire. Only 322 of them were considered in the final analysis after dropping the incomplete and inconsistent responses. Total 194 males and 128 females with an average age of 36.4 years participated in this survey. The participants of the survey were mainly the middle management people who were looking for career growth.

14.3.2 Measures

Employee Behaviorial Flexibility

Employee behavioral flexibility variable was measured by a scale having three items. These three items were chosen from the original scale of Bhattacharya et al. (2005). These items include: (1) "The flexibility of our employees' work habits helps us to change according to market demands", (2) "Our employees respond to changing situations within a short time" and (3) "Most of our employees are flexible enough to adjust to dynamic work requirements". All items were measured on a five-point Likert scale (Where 1 = Strongly Disagree and 5 = Strongly Agree).

Flexible HR Systems

To measure Flexible HR System variable, again a three-item scale was used. Only those three items have been selected, which were highest on factor loadings and validity in the original scale developed by Bhattacharya et al. (2005). Items are: (1) "Flexibility of our HR practices helps us to adjust to the changing demands of the environment", (2) "Our firm modifies its HR system to keep pace with the changing competitive environment", (3) "Our HR practices are designed in such a way that they can adjust quickly to the changes in business conditions". All items were measured on a five-point Likert scale (Where 1 = Strongly Disagree and 5 = Strongly Agree).

Organizational Role Stress

To measure organizational role stress, an established standard Organizational Role Stress scale was used which was constructed by Pareek (1983). This Organizational Role Stress scale is used in measuring 10 role stresses. It is a five-point scale with a total of 50 statements to measure all 10 role stresses—(1) Inter-role distance (IRD), (2) Role stagnation, (RS) (3) Role expectation conflict (REC), (4) Role erosion (RE), (5) Role overload (RO), (6) Role conflict (RC), (7) Personal inadequacy (PI), (8) Self-role distance (SRD), (9) Role ambiguity (RA), and (10) Resource inadequacy (RIn). All items were measured on a five-point Likert scale (Where 1 = Strongly Disagree and 5 = Strongly Agree).

14.4 Analysis and Results

14.4.1 Psychometric Properties

Scale validation and psychometric properties were checked with confirmatory factor analysis (CFA) using AMOS 20 and reliability testing through SPSS 20. To evaluate the first model, multiple fit indices were compared with the nested model (one factor) and the null model. The proposed CFA model is also assumed to be the default model

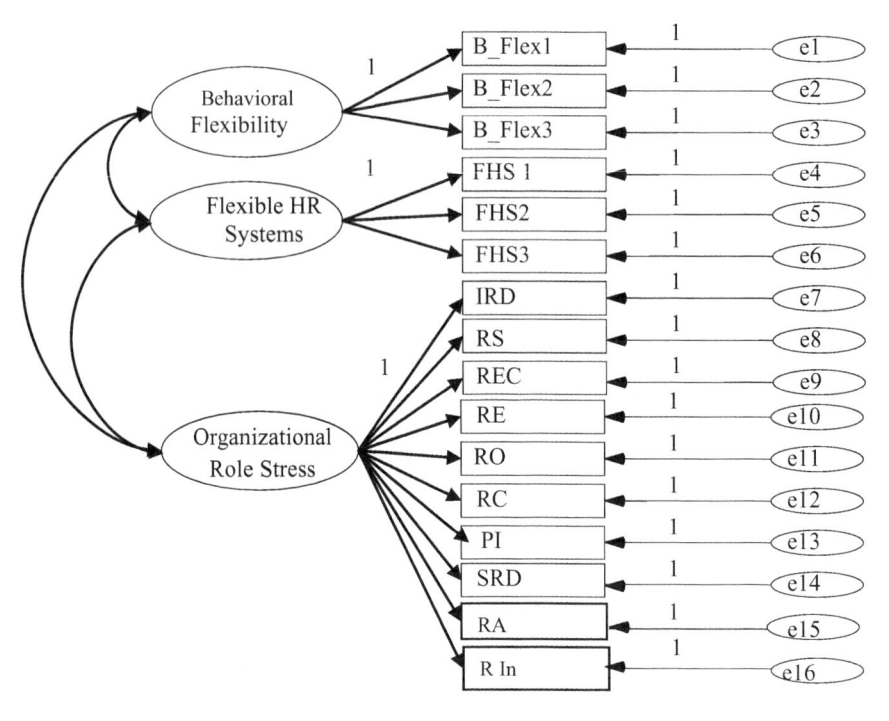

Fig. 14.2 CFA 3 factor model for all variables

and almost always fits better than the independence model, with which it is compared using goodness-of-fit measures. The nested model is usually the one-factor model. The null model is also known as the independent model. It assumes the relationship among the various variables to be 0. It is an uncorrelated construct model. Figures 14.2 and 14.3 show the three-factor and one-factor models. The fit indices were considered for testing absolute, comparative, and parsimonious fitness of the model as shown in Table 14.1. The following fit indices were assessed; the three- and one-factor model fit for three-factor model (CMIN = 739.02, $p < 0.000$; CMIN/DF = 2.6) which exceeds the recommendation cutoff level 3 recommended by Hair et al. (1998), other fit for the measurement model. The goodness-of-fit index (GFI) is at >0.8, the recommendation cutoff at >0.8 by Hsu and Lu (2004). Adjusted goodness-of-fit index (AGFI) is >0.8, which meets the recommended cutoff level 0.8 by Taylor and Todd (1995), Chau and Hu (2001). Bollen (1989) Incremental fit index (IFI) is 0.901, and comparative fit index (CFI) is 0.903, >0.9 recommended by Chau and Hu (2001), Bentler (1990), Bentler and Bonett (1980). Root mean square error of approximation (RMSEA) is 0.06, exceeding the recommendation cutoff level of 0.08 by Browne and Cudeck (1993). The combinations of these outcomes propose that the demonstrated measurement model fits the data well. Thus, the goodness-of-fit measurement should be acceptable. The fit indices for hypothesized (3 factor), nested (1 factor), and null model are contained in Table 14.1. It can be seen that three-factor

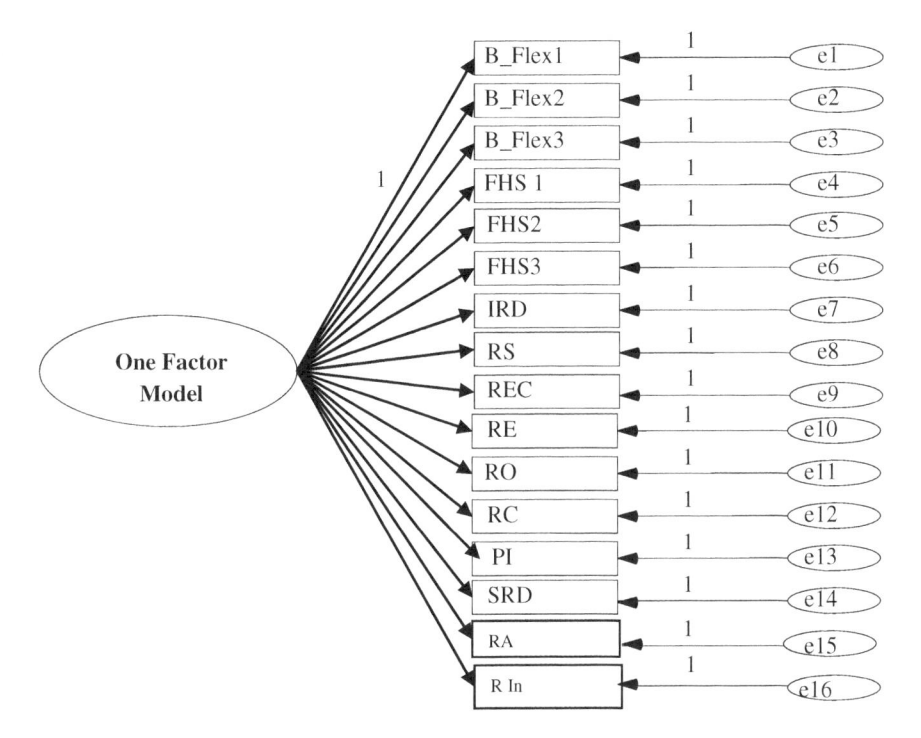

Fig. 14.3 CFA 1 factor model for all variables

Table 14.1 Multiple fit indices of measurement model compared with the nested model (one factor) and the null model for all variables

Model	χ^2/df	GFI	AGFI	NFI	IFI	CFI	RMSEA
Default model (3 factor)	2.6	0.936	0.902	0.856	0.901	0.903	0.06
Nested model (1 factor)	5.7	0.849	0.782	0.667	0.628	0.624	0.11
Null model	7.2	0.446	0.406	0.00	0.00	0.00	0.13

model not only meets the cutoff criteria for all indicators but is also the best fitting model, far superior to the one-factor or null models.

The variables were further assessed for convergent and discriminant validity with confirmatory factor analysis. We estimated the convergent validity of measurement items by composite reliability, average variance extracted, and factor loading. The factor loadings of all items in each variable were significant. The composite reliabilities for all the dependent variables were above 0.70 and average variance extracted was more than 0.50. Internal consistency was assessed by Cronbach's coefficient alpha, which was above 0.70 for all the dependent variables. The results are displayed in Tables 14.2 and 14.3.

Table 14.2 Inter-correlation table with discriminant validity

		Mean	SD	1	2	3	4	5
1	Age	36.4	8.14	**(0.86)**				
2	Experience	8.5	3.60	0.482**	**(0.84)**			
3	Behavioral flexibility	3.89	1.82	0.566**	0.479**	**(0.76)**		
4	Flexible HR systems	3.82	1.36	0.477**	0.577**	0.591**	**(0.73)**	
5	Organizational role stress	4.01	1.70	0.264**	0.476**	−0.662**	−0.538**	**(0.84)**

**Correlation is significant at the 0.01 level (2-tailed)
*Correlation is significant at the 0.05 level (2-tailed)

Table 14.3 Descriptive statistics: composite reliability, average variance extracted, and Cronbach alpha of all variables

Constructs	Composite reliability (CR)	Average variance extracted (AVE)	Cronbach α
Behavioral flexibility	0.926	0.734	0.917
Flexible HR systems	0.946	0.709	0.902
Organizational role stress	0.872	0.640	0.896

14.4.2 Hypothesis Testing

Regression analysis was conducted to check the hypothesis H1, i.e., to see the impact of employee behavioral on flexible HR systems. Table 14.4 reports the results of regression analysis. The results show that the impact was significant, as indicated by the F-statistic (23.157) and other parameters. Figure 14.4 and Table 14.4 show that employee flexibility ($\beta = 0.763$, $r^2 = 0.534$) has a significant ($p < 0.001$) and positive effect on flexible HR systems.

The regression line, as indicated in Fig. 14.5, represents that if employee's behavioral flexibility is low, the organization would be low on flexible HR systems. When employees' behavioral flexibility is high, the organization would be able to maintain a high flexible HR system. Therefore, employee behavioral flexibility plays a significant role in flexible HR systems. Taken together with the graph and results, our findings provided support for Hypothesis 1. Accordingly, the Hypothesis 1 got accepted.

To test the hypothesis H2, the regression analysis was again constructed to see the impact of employee behavioral flexibility on organizational role stress.

Table 14.4 Regression results: impact of employees behavioral flexibility on flexible HR systems

DV	β	R^2	F	t	sig
Flexible HR systems	0.762	0.534	23.157	4.812	0.000

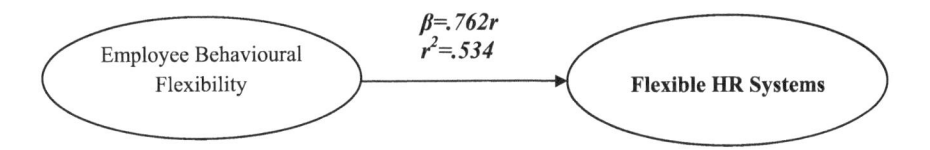

Fig. 14.4 Employee behavioral flexibility relation with flexible HR systems

Employee Behavioural Flexibility → Flexible HR Systems

$\beta = .762r$
$r^2 = .534$

Fig. 14.5 Regression line representing the relation of employee behavioral flexibility with flexible HR system

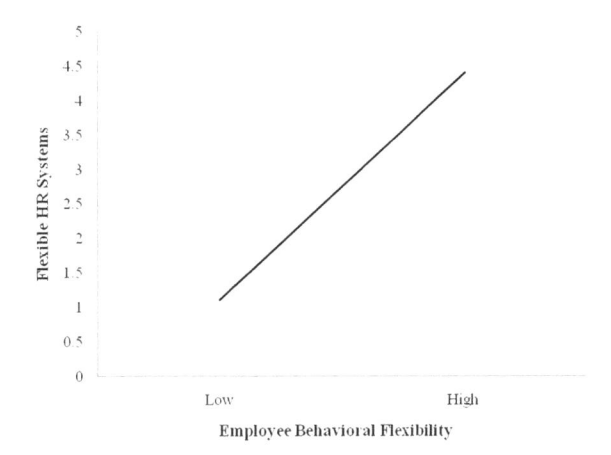

Table 14.5 Regression results: impact of employees behavioral flexibility on organizational role stress

DV	β	R^2	F	t	sig
Organizational role stress	−0.664	0.519	21.183	4.812	0.000

Table 14.5 reports the results of regression analysis. The results show that the impact was significant as indicated by the F-statistic (21.187) and other parameters. Figure 14.6 and Table 14.5 show that employee behavioral flexibility has a significant but negative effect on organizational role stress, sit's beta coefficient and standardized regression coefficients were $\beta = -0.664$, $r^2 = 0.519$, demonstrating a significant ($p < 0.001$) impact on organizational role stress.

The regression line, as indicated in Fig. 14.7, represents that if employees' behavioral flexibility is low, employees' organizational role stress would be high. When employees' behavioral flexibility is high, organizational role stress of employee would be low. Therefore, employees' behavioral flexibility plays significant role in minimizing the employee's organizational role stress. Taken together with the graph and results, findings provided support for Hypothesis 2 also. Accordingly, the Hypothesis 2 also got accepted.

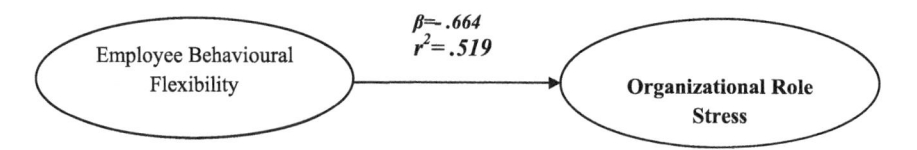

Fig. 14.6 Employee behavioural flexibility relation with organizational role stress

[Diagram: Employee Behavioural Flexibility → Organizational Role Stress, with $\beta = -.664$, $r^2 = .519$]

Fig. 14.7 Regression line representing the relation of employee behavioural flexibility with organizational role stress

[Graph: Organizational Role Stress (y-axis, 0 to 5) vs Employee Behavioral Flexibility (x-axis, Low to High), showing a downward sloping regression line]

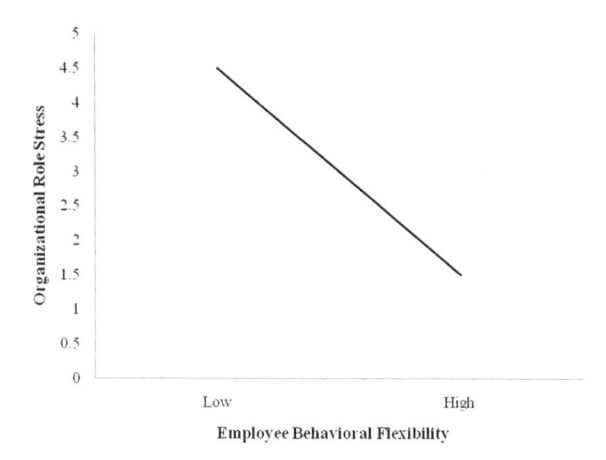

14.5 Discussion

In this study, the focus was on employees' behavioral flexibility. It was an attempt to explore how behavioral flexibility continuously supports the flexible HR system in any organization and its role in setting up a flexible HR system. This study examines two components of an organization. One component represents the strategic side of an organization, which is the flexible HR system. The second component represents the human behavior related issues at workplace that is organizational role stress. For each of the components, hypothesis was developed, tested, and got accepted. For the first hypothesis, it was proved that employee behavioral flexibility has positively impacted the flexible HR system. It shows that flexible HR system would be successful in any organization when the employee would have a flexible behavior. In this situation, the acceptance of change would be high and employees would like to have some level of autonomy so that they can take a call to meet the demands of the situation. When we look at the second component, the Hypothesis 2 is also accepted. This hypothesis examines that employee behavioral flexibility helps in reducing employees' organizational role stress. It shows that when employees would be able to manage the change, they would respond to the situation through changing their flexible behavior. Researchers (Bhattacharya et al. 2005; Gibbons and Rupp 2009) described behavioral flexibility as the employees' broad range of behaviors and adjustment in their behavior in order to cope with or adapt to situation-specific demands. Similarly, with this flexible behavior characteristic, employee would be able to handle various organizational roles which will minimize employees' organizational role stress.

14.6 Implications, Future Directions, and Limitations

With the expansion of global economy, there has been a huge change in the nature of job. The job has become more dynamic, complex, and unpredictable. The flexibility has always been a key solution to manage the unpredictable situation. The present study will help the employees and the organizations, as the concept of behavioral flexibility plays role in both, the strategic HR at the organizational level and the role stress at the individual level. Therefore, behavioral flexibility has emerged as a key component of any organization. The results of this study are generalizable across situations. One of the areas where behavioral flexibility is used extensively is the job interviews and selection process. For any organization, it is very important to hire a candidate who can manage various roles. At the time of the selection process, the behavioral flexibility component can be added to recruit an employee with high behavioral flexibility skill. This would automatically contribute toward organizational productivity. For the existing employees, training can be given on behavioral flexibility. This training would help the employees in managing complex tasks and reducing organizational role stress. Overall, this behavioral flexibility training may help the organization to manage human resources successfully. It has been seen that an effective and flexible HR system improves the competence of the organization when it comes to competing with others based on innovation and market responsiveness. This may, likewise, encourage an organization to be more efficient in its human resource management framework as far as employee commitment, employee turnover, employee engagement, and employee satisfaction are concerned, which prompts better performance and enhanced productivity and effectiveness of the organization. Though the study has significantly contributed to understand the role of employee behavioral flexibility in flexible HR systems and organizational role stress, there are some limitations that need to be addressed. First limitation is that this study did not measure the impact of behavioral flexibility on the various dimensions of organizational role stress individually. The future studies need to explore all these dimensions individually. Second, this study examines the impact of behavioral flexibility on only organizational HR flexibility and role stress; it does not explore how it impacts the individual performance, employee efficiency, and organizational productivity. Therefore, the future research should focus on these factors. This study has not been conducted on a particular industry, so the results may vary from industry to industry, which is one of the limitations. The future research can be conducted by incorporating some mediator and moderator like experience, gender, and age. The future research can also be conducted on the consequences of behavioral flexibility, such as organizational citizenship behavior, employee trust, ethics and commitment.

14.7 Conclusion

In this changing environment, it is imperative to understand the significance of employee behavioral flexibility. With the growth of organization, the capacity of any organization can be enhanced by flexible human resource system. Therefore, it is necessary to look into the importance of behavioral flexibility to understand the role of human resource management in this fast changing and dynamic era. In the current scenario, when employees are facing huge challenges in highly complex job roles, behavioral flexibility would play a great role in coping with these challenges. The effective utilization of human resource and with the assistance of a flexible HR system can lead to increased market responsiveness and innovation of an organization. Therefore, managers should give adequate importance to behavioral flexibility and flexible HR systems. Overall, flexibility is one of the most important components for both, the organization and its employees.

References

Aasland, O. G., & Forde, R. (2005). Impact of feeling responsible for adverse events on doctors' personal and professional lives: The importance of being open to criticism from colleagues. *Quality and Safety Health Care, 14*(1), 13–17.

Bamel, U. K., Rangnekar, S., & Rastogi, R. (2014). Do gender, position, and organization shape human resource flexibility? In M. K. Nandakumar, S. Jharkharia, & A. S. Nair (Eds.), *Organizational flexibility and competitiveness, flexible systems management* (pp. 123–134). New Delhi: Springer.

Bamel, U. K., Rangnekar, S., Rastogi, R., & Kumar, S. (2013). Organizational process as antecedent of managerial flexibility. *Global Journal of Flexible Systems Management, 14*(1), 3–15.

Bateman, G. (2009). *Employee perceptions of co-worker support and its effect on job satisfaction, work stress and intention to quit* (Unpublished dissertation). University of Canterbury.

Beltrán-Martín, I., Roca-Puig, V., Escrig-Tena, A., & Bou-Llusar, J. C. (2008). Human resource flexibility as a mediating variable between high performance work systems and performance. *Journal of Management, 34*(5), 1009–1044.

Bentler, P. M. (1990). Comparative fit indexes in structural models. *Psychological Bulletin, 107*(2), 238.

Bentler, P. M., & Bonett, D. G. (1980). Significance tests and goodness of fit in the analysis of covariance structures. *Psychological Bulletin, 88*(3), 588–606.

Bhattacharya, M., Gibson, D. E., & Doty, D. H. (2005). The effects of flexibility in employee skills, employee behaviors, and human resource practices on firm performance. *Journal of Management, 31*(4), 622–640.

Bhattacharya, S., & Basu, J. (2007). Distress, wellness and organizational role stress among it professionals: role of life events and coping resources. *Journal of the Indian Academy of Applied Psychology, 33*(2), 169–178.

Bollen, K. A. (1989). A new incremental fit index for general structural equation models. *Sociological Methods and Research, 17*(3), 303–316.
Browne, M. W., & Cudeck, R. (1993). Alternative ways of assessing model fit. In K. A. Bollen & J. S. Long (Eds.), *Testing structural equation models* (p. 136). Newbury Park, CA: Sage.
Chau, P. Y., & Hu, P. J. H. (2001). Information technology acceptance by individual professionals: A model comparison approach. *Decision Sciences, 32*(4), 699–719.
Cooper, C. L., & Marshall, J. (1978). *Understanding executive stress*. New York: Springer.
Correa, A. P., & Ferreira, M. C. (2011). The impact of environmental stressors and types of work contract on occupational stress. *The Spanish Journal of Psychology, 14*(1), 251–262.
Dasgupta, H., & Kumar, S. (2009). Role stress among doctors working in a government hospital in Shimla. *European Journal of Social Sciences, 9*(3), 356–370.
Eisenhardt, K. M., & Martin, J. A. (2000). Dynamic capabilities: What are they? *Strategic Management Journal, 21*(10–11), 1105–1121.
Ericksen, J., & Dyer, L. (2005). Toward a strategic human resource management model of high reliability organization performance. *The International Journal of Human Resource Management, 16*(6), 907–928.
Ferris, G. R., Zinko, R., Brouer, R. L., Buckley, M. R., & Harvey, M. G. (2007). Strategic bullying as a supplementary, balanced perspective on destructive leadership. *The Leadership Quarterly, 18*(3), 195–206.
Fisher, C. D. (1985). Social support and adjustment to work: A longitudinal study. *Journal of Management, 11*(3), 39–53.
Ganster, D. C., Fusilier, M., & Mayes, B. T. (1986). Role of social support in the experience of stress at work. *Journal of Applied Psychology, 71*(1), 102–110.
Gibbons, A. M., & Rupp, D. E. (2009). Dimension consistency as an individual difference: A new (old) perspective on the assessment center construct validity debate. *Journal of Management, 35*(5), 1154–1180.
Goyal, S., & Kashyap, V. (2010). Organizational role stress: An empirical study among insurance employees. *Asia Pacific Business Review, 6*(4), 105–113.
Groves, M. (2005). Problem-based learning and learning approach: Is there a relationship? *Advances in Health Sciences Education, 10*(4), 315–326.
Hair, J. F., Black, W. C., Babin, B. J., Anderson, R. E., & Tatham, R. L. (1998). *Multivariate data analysis* (Vol. 5, No. 3, pp. 207–219). Upper Saddle River, NJ: Prentice Hall.
Hitt, M. A., Keats, B. W., & DeMarie, S. M. (1998). Navigating in the new competitive landscape: Building strategic flexibility and competitive advantage in the 21st century. *The Academy of Management Executive, 12*(4), 22–42.
Hsu, C. L., & Lu, H. P. (2004). Why do people play on-line games? An extended tam with social influences and flow experience. *Information and Management, 41*(7), 853–868.
Jaiswal, P., & Bhal, K. T. (2014). Behavioural flexibility: The use of upward impression management tactics by subordinates for good performance rating from leader and impact of organizational and leader's machiavellianism. *Global Journal of Flexible Systems Management, 15*(4), 313–326.
Kaufman, G. N., & Beehr, T. A. (1986). Interactions between job stressors and social support: Some counterintuitive results. *Journal of Applied Psychology, 71*(3), 522–526.
Ketkar, S., & Sett, P. K. (2009). HR flexibility and firm performance: Analysis of a multi-level causal model. *The International Journal of Human Resource Management, 20*(5), 1009–1038.
Ketkar, S., & Sett, P. K. (2010). Environmental dynamism, human resource flexibility, and firm performance: Analysis of a multi-level causal model. *The International Journal of Human Resource Management, 21*(8), 1173–1206.
La Rocco, J. M., House, J. S., & French, J. R. P., Jr. (1980). Social support, occupational stress and health. *Journal of Health and Social Behavior, 21*(3), 202–218.
Lindberg, J. T., & Kaiser, R. B. (2004) Assessing the behavioral flexibility of managers: A comparison of methods. In Poster session presented at the 19th annual meeting of the society for industrial and organizational psychology in Chicago, IL, April 2004.

MacDuffie, J. P. (1995). Human resource bundles and manufacturing performance: Organizational logic and flexible production systems in the world auto industry. *Industrial and Labor Relations Review, 48*(2), 197–221.

Matteson, M. T., & Ivancevich, J. M. (1987). *Controlling work stress: Effective human resource and management strategies*. Wiley, New York: Jossey-Bass.

Michie, S. (2002). Causes and management of stress at work. *Occupational and Environmental Medicine, 59*(1), 67–72.

Milliman, J., Von Glinow, M. A., & Nathan, M. (1991). Organizational life cycles and strategic international human resource management in multinational companies: implications for congruence theory. *Academy of Management Review, 16*(2), 318–339.

Milliman, J., Taylor, S., & Czaplewski, A. J. (2002). Cross-cultural performance feedback in multinational enterprises: Opportunity for organizational learning. *People and Strategy, 25*(3), 29.

Ngo, H. Y., & Loi, R. (2008). Human resource flexibility, organizational culture and firm performance: An investigation of multinational firms in Hong Kong. *The International Journal of Human Resource Management, 19*(9), 1654–1666.

Pareek U (1983) *Role analysis for human resources development, Indian management* (pp. 13–16).

Paulhus, D. L., & Martin, C. L. (1987). The structure of interpersonal capabilities. *Journal of Personality and Social Psychology, 52*(2), 354–365.

Paulhus, D. L., & Martin, C. L. (1988). Functional flexibility: A new approach to interpersonal flexibility. *Journal of Personality and Social Psychology, 55*(1), 88–101.

Sanchez, R. (1995). Strategic flexibility in product competition. *Strategic Management Journal, 16*(S1), 135–159.

Snow, C. C., & Snell, S. A. (1993). Staffing as strategy in personnel selection in organizations (pp. 448–479). In N. Schmitt & W. Borman (Eds.), San Francisco, CA: Jossey-Bass.

Sushil. (1997). Flexible systems management: An evolving paradigm. *Systems Research and Behavioral Science, 14*(4), 259–275.

Sushil. (2000). Concept of systemic flexibility. *Global Journal of Flexible Systems Management, 1*(1), 77–80.

Taylor, S., & Todd, P. A. (1995). Understanding information technology usage: A test of competing models. *Information Systems Research, 6*(2), 144–176.

Teece, D. J., Pisano, G., & Shuen, A. (1997). Dynamic capabilities and strategic management. *Strategic Management Journal, 18*(7), 509–533.

Wright, P. M., & Boswell, W. R. (2002). Desegregating HRM: A review and synthesis of micro and macro human resource management research. *Journal of Management, 28*(3), 247–276.

Wright, P. M., & Snell, S. A. (1998). Toward a unifying framework for exploring fit and flexibility in strategic human resource management. *Academy of Management Review, 23*(4), 756–772.

Zaccaro, S. J. (2002). Organizational leadership and social intelligence, In *Kravis-de Roulet Leadership Conference, 9th, Apr, 1999, Claremont McKenna Coll, Claremont, CA, US*. Lawrence Erlbaum Associates Publishers.

Zollo, M., & Winter, S. G. (2002). Deliberate learning and the evolution of dynamic capabilities. *Organization Science, 13*(3), 339–351.

Part III
Sustainability

Chapter 15
Organizational Sustainability—Why the Need for Green HRM?

Christina Kirsch and Julia Connell

Abstract The purpose of this study was to examine the impact of change when sustainability programs were implemented, in addition to the drivers of sustainability initiatives and organizational performance. The large, Asia-Pacific based professional services company where the study was undertaken had introduced a number of sustainability initiatives prior to this investigation. An employee survey concerning the company's sustainability program and change processes was conducted consisting of 70 questions. The sample comprised 2557 respondents representing every hierarchical level. Opportunity was also provided for open ended comments. Findings showed that while employee involvement, accountability, leadership support and commitment were important drivers of sustainability initiatives, they were perceived as lacking in this organization. Moreover, teams lacked the ability to change business practices and there was a lack of recognition and reward related to any sustainability improvements. The implications of the study are that, despite environmental sustainability being of great concern to employees personally, it did not translate to the corporate agenda, which was mainly focused on 'compliance'. This led to frustration amongst some employees who were undertaking sustainability initiatives at home but were unable to translate them to their workplaces, reportedly because there was an apparent absence of any sustainable leadership or promotion of any Green HRM initiatives in this organization. This value of this study is that it emphasises that, if senior management introduces sustainability initiatives without any attempt to embed them within company practice/client relationships, reward systems and more, they are likely to fail and attempts to introduce a circular economy need to be accompanied by 'Green HRM' policies and practices.

Keywords Change management · Green HRM · Sustainable leadership

C. Kirsch
E2Q Consulting Sydney, Sydney, NSW, Australia
e-mail: ckirsch@optusnet.com.au

J. Connell (✉)
University of Newcastle, Newcastle, NSW, Australia
e-mail: julia.connell@newcastle.edu.au

15.1 Introduction

The concept of sustainable development is critical to understanding the relationship between Human Resource Management (HRM) and sustainability. The Brundtland Commission (Brundtland 1987) originally defined 'sustainable development' as development that 'meets the needs of the present without compromising the ability of future generations to meet their own needs.' Elkington (1998) attempted to translate the Brundtland Commission's definition of sustainable development into a usable business metric and introduced the notion of the 'Triple Bottom Line (TBL)'—economic, social and environmental performance. Environmental management studies span disciplines such as marketing, accounting, operations management and management (Zoogah 2011). However, to date there has been a scarcity of research linking the field of human resource management (HRM) and environmental management (EM) which is surprising given that organizational responses to environmental concerns must involve decisions made and actions taken by an organization's employees. Nonetheless, although the need for HR policies that focus on environmental management and the requisite capability development have been recognized by some researchers (Daily and Huang 2001; Wilkinson et al. 2001; Benn and Dunphy 2007; Renwick et al. 2008; Zoogah 2011). Kramar (2014) argues that many of these studies focus on the practice of environmental management rather than managerial decisions and behaviours. Specifically, she maintains that Green HRM (the integration of environmental management (EM) in HRM (Sharma et al. 1999) depends on the patterns of green decisions and behaviours of HR managers (referred to as green signatures) that lead to the relevant HRM policies, philosophies and practices to promote the sustainable use of resources and prevent environmental harm. Further, Zoogah proposes that there are two types of green signatures: promotive (the behaviours that promote EM) and preventive (the behaviours that prevent negative environmental outcomes). To support such initiatives, a stream of literature focusing on sustainable leadership practices has identified the need for a management approach that supports stakeholders behaving ethically and responsibly within their organizations and towards the environment and the community. Avery and Bergsteiner (2011, 6) maintain that while such management approaches are not new, what is new is the understanding that these practices form a 'self-reinforcing leadership system that enhances the performance of a business and its prospects for survival. What is also significant is that sustainable leadership practices are diametrically opposed to the typical shareholder-first approach...' Hargreaves and Fink (2004: 3) define sustainable leadership as follows:

> Sustainable leadership matters, spreads and lasts. It is a shared responsibility, that does not unduly deplete human or financial resources, and that cares for and avoids exerting negative damage on the surrounding educational and community environment. Sustainable leadership has an activist engagement with the forces that affect it, and builds an educational environment of organizational diversity that promotes cross-fertilization of good ideas and successful practices in communities of shared learning and development.

Recent developments (some now defunct) with regard to regulations and legislation that include carbon taxes, carbon trading schemes and increasing environmental standards, have forced companies to include their environmental and social impact in strategic planning (Australian Government Department of Climate Change 2008). A company's sustainability is increasingly recognized as a fundamental platform for success by stakeholders: consumers, employees, shareholders and suppliers (Brower and Leon 1999; Epstein and Roy 2001; Sharma and Henriques 2005; Speth 2008) with the potential to create long-term value, harness new opportunities and help to manage future risks from economic, environmental and social developments (Daly 1996; Dunphy et al. 2007). Moreover, organizational sustainability is a value proposition with the potential to improve the corporate engagement of employees (Kramar and Jones 2010).

Epstein and Roy (2001) distinguish three types of activities that are required to increase sustainability: (a) the formulation of a sustainability strategy, (b) development of plans and programs and (c) the design of appropriate structures and systems. We suggest that all of these activities should be integrated within a Green HRM framework (see Table 15.1) which includes the promotive and preventive signatures of HR managers.

The plans and programs aimed at improving sustainability can range from minor changes to existing routines to radical, transformational change concerning the way in which a company operates. The implementation of a sustainability program, like any change process, is a substantial challenge (Epstein and Roy 2001). Some businesses successfully accomplish the transition towards more sustainable operations, but many others do not. The issue with change projects—including sustainability projects—is that generally change is managed poorly. Despite good intentions, change projects take longer, cost more, and achieve less than planned (Sauer and Cuthbertson 2003). The leading cause of failure is generally not found to relate to the technical side of the system, but can be traced back to poor management, miscommunication, a lack of training or other factors related to the social and organizational aspects of the system (Jorgensen et al. 2008). Epstein and Roy (2001) argue that a careful analysis of the key drivers of performance is needed in order to provide managers with a better understanding of how to implement sustainability strategies and what actions and decisions are required for success.

The purpose of this study was to examine the impact of change when sustainability programs are implemented, to understand the drivers of sustainability initiatives and organizational performance, and the linkages between them. The large professional services company where the study was undertaken had introduced a number of sustainability initiatives and the survey was conducted as a means of assessing the effectiveness of those initiatives. The chapter begins by discussing sustainability initiatives and organizational performance, before moving to the method, results, discussion and conclusions.

Table 15.1 HR processes and Green HRM—entry to exit

Recruitment	Performance management and appraisal	Training and development	Employment relations	Pay and reward	Exit
HR managers promotive signatures					
Attraction benefits	Assessment of Green incidents	EM training needs analysis	Employee involvement schemes	Green pay/reward systems	Gauge perceptions of firm initiatives
Green job descriptions	Green KPIs	Training on EM	Helpline for green matters	Reward green skills	Reasons for leaving related to green EM?
Recruitment of green aware employees	Green schemes as motivators	EM competence building	Green workplace agreements	Monetary and non-monetary premiums and recognition	
Green employer branding	Managers set green targets	EM socialization	Green elements into OHS matters	Green career gains	
Green inductions	Green criteria in appraisals	Green teams	Low carbon leaders to increase EM	Tax breaks and other motivators	
HR managers preventive signatures					
Non-compliant applicants not recruited	Penalties for non-compliance	Re-training of staff not achieving green goals	Green whistle-blowing lines, disciplinary actions	Warnings and suspensions for breaches	Debriefing if related to EM dismissals

Source Renwick et al. (2013)

15.2 Measuring Drivers of Sustainability Initiatives

Sustainability reporting and the analysis and evaluation of organizations in terms of the triple bottom line have become increasingly widespread and there is now a vast number of sustainability indicators and reporting procedures (Holmberg et al. 1999; Holmberg and Robert 2000; Paehlke 2005; Hak et al. 2007). The problem is that many of the available analytical instruments focus on the 'reporting' of sustainability indicators, but not on the 'management' of the process aimed at improving those sustainability indicators (Doppelt 2003). Establishing indicators and reporting on them does not necessarily lead to improvements in sustainability (Adams and Frost 2008); in fact it might just lead to compliance. Managers that are intent on implementing sustainability initiatives need to know what actions need to be taken to ensure that the projects are managed successfully (Epstein and Roy 2001).

Sustainability initiatives have the potential to provide a clear competitive advantage but they do not happen in isolation, generally being introduced whilst the company is still dealing with ongoing day-to-day operations. In order to assess the success of sustainability initiatives, companies must incorporate items relating to the success of the sustainability initiative and items relating to overall organizational performance. Also, environmental and social sustainability are unlikely to come into play if they come at the expense of economic performance. Studies of the relationship between corporate social responsibility, environmental sustainability and organizational performance are inconclusive. Some studies point to a positive return from social responsibility (Orlitzky et al. 2003) and environmental performance (Judge and Douglas 1998; Gilley et al. 2000; Pujari et al. 2003). A survey by PriceWaterHouseCoopers (2009) revealed a positive relationship between corporate sustainability and financial performance, as measured by stock returns. Weber et al. (2005) found a positive correlation between sustainability activities, the impact on sustainable development and the financial performance of companies. Russo and Fouts (1997) confirmed the hypothesis that a company's environmental performance and economic performance are positively correlated and that this relationship strengthens with industry growth. Other studies found that although sustainable management had a positive impact on social and environmental sustainability indicators, it did not impact on organizational performance (Enticott and Walker 2008). The relationship between social, environmental and economic performance, especially at the level of the organizational unit, deserves further analysis. Therefore, this research tests the hypothesis that sustainability initiatives have a positive impact on organizational performance in terms of improvements in effectiveness, customer service and cost management:

> H1: Sustainability initiatives have a positive impact on organizational performance and are related to improvements in effectiveness, customer service and cost management.

Previous empirical studies found that in order to establish sustainability programs and improve environmental performance companies need to have the capability, resources and abilities for managing organizational change and mobilizing their people (Doppelt 2003; Judge and Elenkov 2005). Although managers may undertake promotive or preventative EM decision-making (Zoogah 2011), it is also necessary to engage line managers as line support is considered an important aspect of generating employee environmental problem solving (Ramus 2002). Epstein and Roy (2001) suggest a series of actions and interventions that are required to successfully manage sustainability projects, but the outline of what needs to be done to 'drive a sustainability strategy through an organization' is limited to certain HR aspects, such as evaluating employee performance and providing rewards and incentives, and does not provide empirical data that reveals what actions and decisions managers and leaders need to pursue to successfully implement a sustainability program. Doppelt (2003) found that a clear vision and leadership, as well as opportunities for learning, encouragement and rewards for innovation are the key elements to the success of sustainability projects. Others have pointed out the need for a stakeholder approach to sustainability which recognizes the interconnection and interaction of stakeholders' organizational systems and subsystems, social systems and the environment in which these systems operate (Benn and Bolton 2011, p. 218). Given this approach, Kramar (2014) points out that members of organizations are required to engage a variety of stakeholders who will have different perspectives and values. Moreover, such approaches will need the support of sustainable leadership practices which are 'diametrically opposed to the typical shareholder-first approach, which business schools, management journals, the media, and many practitioners continue to promote' (Avery and Bergsteiner 2011: 6). A more detailed analysis of the various aspects of change processes, such as the availability of resources, the impact of leadership styles, work design and emotions at work would be beneficial in order to advance the understanding of the drivers of successful change towards improved sustainability. Previous studies of organizational change projects have found that the main drivers of successful management of change initiatives (Fig. 15.1) are: (a) a clear vision and direction, (b) sufficient and adequate resources, (c) change management and leadership, (d) adequate work roles, including involvement and accountability and (e) emotional energy (Parry 2008).

A key question is whether the factors that are driving change projects are also impacting on the success of sustainability initiatives. The purpose of this study is to determine what needs to be in place and what managers need to do in order to keep sustainability initiatives on track and achieving intended goals. The objective of the study was to investigate the variables that impact on the success of sustainability initiatives and provide empirical insights in the management and HRM aspects of sustainability initiatives. Thus, hypothesis two is:

> H2: The way in which change is managed affects the implementation of sustainability initiatives as well as overall organizational performance (Fig. 15.1).

In order to drive organizational change, it is important to mobilize employees' passion for it. As a result, it is hypothesized that, in order to harness the emotional energy and passion of employees, managers need to ensure that they are involved in the planning and implementation of the initiative, have sufficient resources and

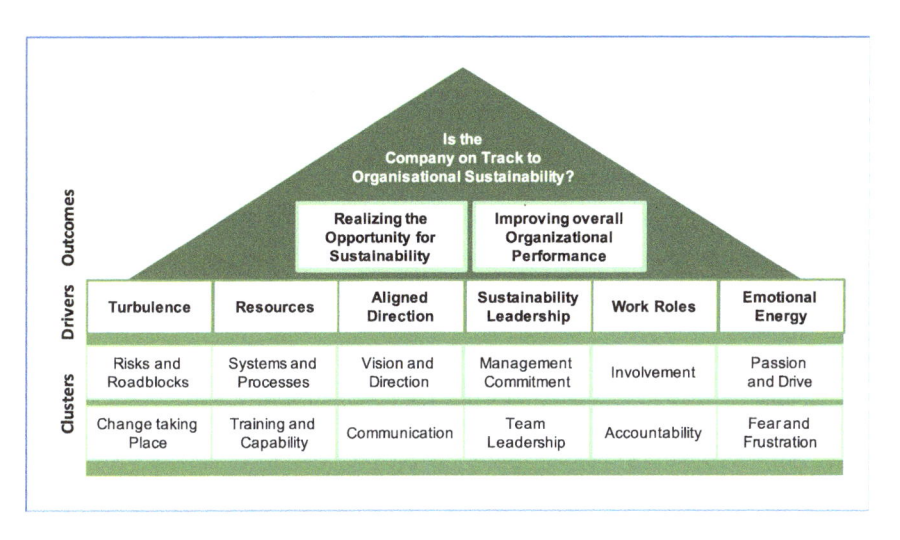

Fig. 15.1 Model for the drivers and outcomes of organizational sustainability initiatives. *Source* Adapted from Parry et al. (2013)

support from management, and are held accountable, recognized and rewarded for achieving the objectives.

> H3: Characteristics of the way in which sustainability initiatives are managed, for example a clear vision and direction, sufficient resources, opportunities for involvement, accountability, incentives, and leadership support, and impact on employees' passion for the sustainability initiatives.

15.3 Method

A survey was developed that monitored the characteristics related to the management of the change process and the impact of the sustainability initiatives on environmental performance and business outcomes (Parry 2008). The survey consisted of 70 questions that investigate company-specific opportunities for sustainability improvements, implemented initiatives and the organizational characteristics that impact on organizational change projects and organizational performance. The items were based on a questionnaire used to evaluate and optimize organizational change projects (Parry 2008) and addresses the following areas:

Outcome or Dependent Variables

1. **Performance Improvements** in customer service, cost management and effectiveness
2. **Realizing Opportunities for Sustainability**: Implemented sustainability initiatives

Drivers or Independent Variables

3. **Turbulence**: The overall amount of change happening within the organizational unit, and risk and roadblocks to change
4. **Resources**: Skills and capabilities, process and procedures, time and budget, autonomy
5. **Aligned Direction**: Employee's understanding and agreement with the company's vision and direction and how information is communicated
6. **Sustainability Leadership**: Management commitment and team leadership
7. **Work Roles**: Employee involvement and accountability
8. **Emotional Energy**: Passion and drive and disturbance

In order to determine the extent to which sustainability initiatives had been implemented, survey respondents were asked about the recently implemented sustainability initiatives, ranging from (a) fostering environmental awareness and responsibility, to (b) identifying environmental aspects of operations and implementing programs to reduce environmental impacts, (c) conducting operations in a manner that minimizes consumption of natural resources, (d) responsible reuse, recycling and disposal of materials, (e) consideration of environmental factors in procurement processes, (f) addressing environmental concerns and standards within company facilities, (g) compliance with legal and other requirements and (h) ongoing monitoring and reviewing of sustainability objectives and targets. The survey questions were divided into (a) drivers or independent variables, and (b) performance outcomes/dependent variables based on the model in Fig. 15.1.

The survey was administered to staff at all hierarchical levels across teams and divisions within a business area of a large professional services company based in the Asia Pacific. The sample size consisted of 2557 respondents, of which 179 were 'Baby Boomers' (born 1946–1965), 946 were 'Gen X' (born 1966–1977), and the majority of respondents, with 1432, were 'Gen Y' (born 1978–2000). Three hundred and forty three respondents had worked for the company less than a year; 1609 between 1 and 5 years; 407 between 6 and 10 years; 142 between 11 and 15 years; and 56 had over 15 years with the company. Five per cent of responses were from Senior Executives, 14% from Senior Managers, 23% from Managers and 58% from Employees.

15.4 Results

Environmental sustainability was found to have the highest importance for employees, followed by the company and, to a lesser degree, by clients. At the company level, environmental sustainability was considered to be of great importance, but respondents were not convinced that their clients saw the company's sustainability approach as a differentiator (Fig. 15.2). The main opportunities for improving the company's environmental sustainability were seen to be in the

15 Organizational Sustainability ...   231

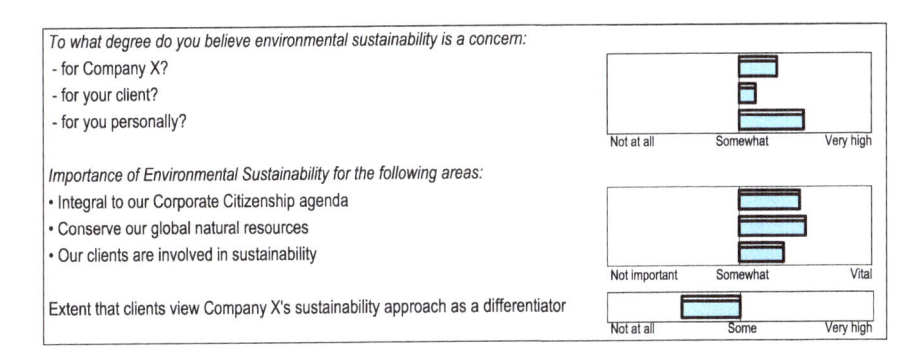

Fig. 15.2 Importance of environmental sustainability for employees, company and clients

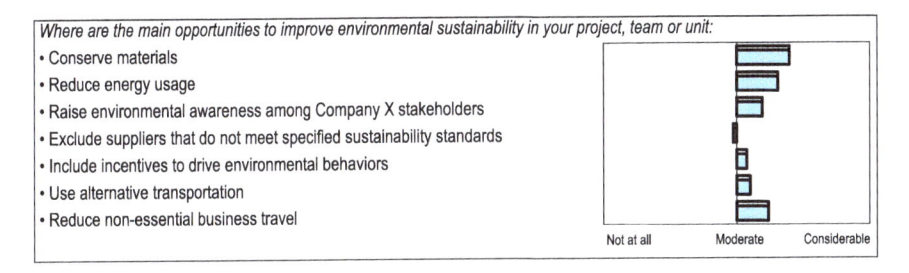

Fig. 15.3 Opportunities for improving environmental sustainability

conservation of materials, reduction of energy usage, the reduction of non-essential business travel, and the raising of awareness of this factor among their stakeholders (Fig. 15.3). This latter point relates to the fact that the company is in the professional services industry, which involves a large amount of business travel.

Despite the opportunities for sustainability improvements and employees' interest in environmental sustainability, the company only put a moderate amount of efforts into the reduction of resource consumption, programs to monitor and reduce environmental impacts and the raising of awareness amongst stakeholders. The main effort was focused on compliance with legal requirements (Fig. 15.4).

The key obstacles to the implementation of effective sustainability initiatives were seen to be the 'limited ability of teams to change business practice', followed by a 'lack of awareness' and a 'lack of resources'. The fact that 'getting the job done takes precedence over environmental sustainability' was another major obstacle (Fig. 15.5). A closer scrutiny of the organizational characteristics that may have impacted on employee attitudes towards the sustainability initiatives revealed a lack of 'support from company leadership', a lack of 'involvement in planning and implementing actions to improve sustainability in their team' and a lack of 'reward and recognition for sustainability initiatives' (Fig. 15.6).

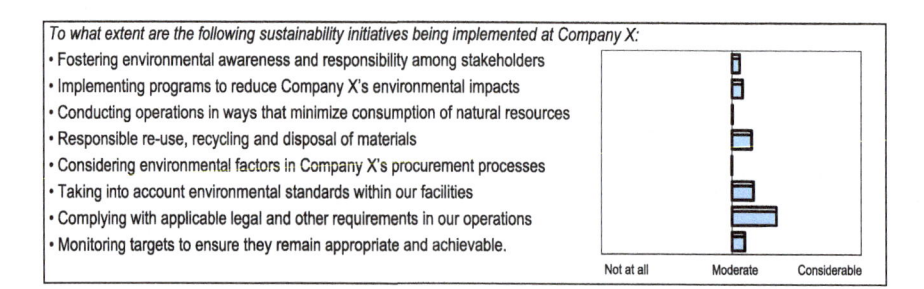

Fig. 15.4 Sustainability initiatives being implemented at the company

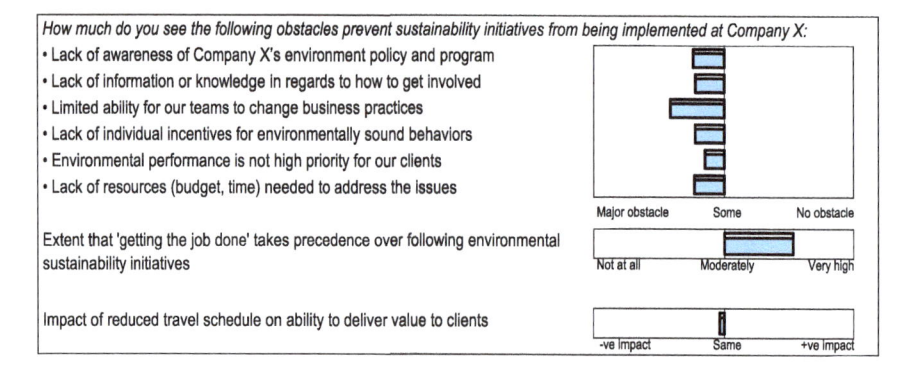

Fig. 15.5 Obstacles preventing sustainability initiatives from being implemented

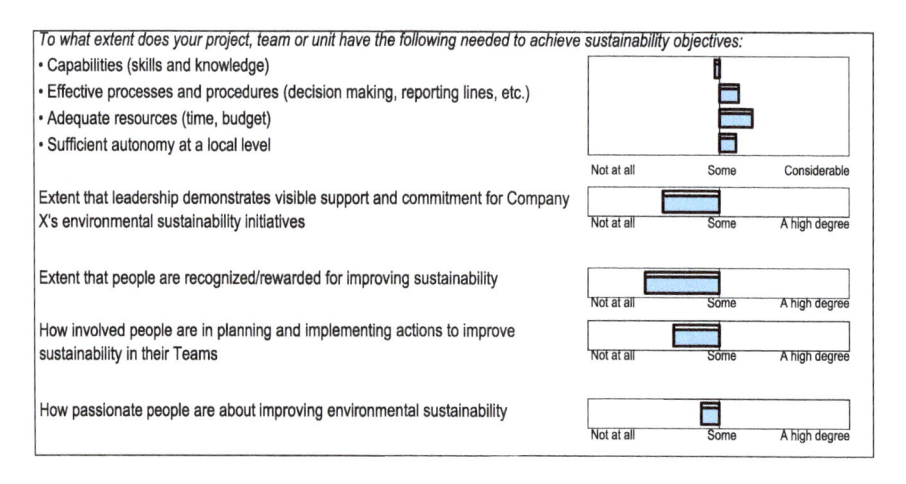

Fig. 15.6 Organizational characteristics and employee attitudes

Organizational effectiveness was mainly impacted positively by the overall amount of change taking place. The main obstacle to improved EM effectiveness was the 'inability to change business practices'. Initiatives to 'reduce resource consumption' had a positive impact on customer service and on cost-effectiveness, while initiatives aimed at 'compliance with legal and other requirements' and the 'consideration of environmental factors in procurement processes' had a positive impact on cost management. The 'identification of environmental aspects associated with operations, and implementing programs to reduce environmental impacts' had a negative impact on improvements in customer service and in cost management. 'Supervisor's performance management' skills and 'accountability' were significant drivers of improvement in all aspects of performance, from customer service to cost management. Improvements in effectiveness were also impacted by leadership support and employees' passion for the sustainability initiative. Customer service was impacted by agreement with the company's sustainability approach, information from compulsory training, skills and capabilities within the team, and people feeling passion.

A stepwise regression analysis (not reported here due to lack of space) of the drivers of employees' 'passion for improving environmental sustainability' revealed that the most important driver was 'employee involvement in planning and implementing actions to improve sustainability', followed by 'leadership support' (project or team leadership). A significant positive impact came from the employees' personal interest in sustainability issues and their clients interest in sustainability. Overall, the extent to which sustainability initiatives were implemented in the organizational units was significantly impacted by the employees' perception that sustainability is of concern to the company and employees agreeing with the company's sustainability approach. Extensive communication was a significant driver, as well as 'leadership support and commitment', 'effective processes and procedures' in the teams and 'accountability'. The main hindrances were a 'lack of incentives', the 'impact of reduced travel schedules on clients' and a 'lack of information on how to get involved'.

Respondents were also asked to provide comments on the survey questionnaire and 102 comments were provided. The comments were coded according to the key themes that emerged. These themes were: leadership, management/organization; travel; office environment; concerns that initiatives will harm the business; impact on clients; working from home; teleconferencing and need for rewards. A sample of the comments provided is shown in Table 15.2. Most frequent comments were related to the need for support to work at home one day a week/one week a month or similar or to be supported to engage clients through remote communication (videoconferencing or similar) and more effective use of travel—such as support for cycling; taking a train. There were many good ideas provided regarding how to be more sustainable both personally and as a company but all require the support of leadership/management to initiate.

Table 15.2 Responses to survey question—how could we improve our sustainability? ($n = 102$)

Theme	Key comments
Leadership	Leadership a key theme in terms of support for initiatives Need support to work at home at least 1 day/week and 1 week/month. Need to encourage discussion (driven by the project manager) on how to address this
Management/organization	Staff people close to their home-office, subject to skill match. Company often staffs people from the opposite end of the country. Encourage programs, i.e. pay to ride program (i.e. London office) if you bike to work company pays for your kilometres. Provide incentives
Travel	Couples that work for the company should be on the same project when feasible, avoiding unnecessary flybacks every week. Could be a 'green points' system that gives back some of the money saved by renting smaller cars/taking public transport. Same goes for air travel
Office environment, i.e. lighting, disposable cups etc.	Provide compost bins in all break rooms and recycling bins for cans, plastic, electronics, eyeglasses. Need showers at the office so we can cycle in. Our office has a standard like the 1970s but zero emission buildings are a spreading reality
Concerns that initiatives will harm the business	The environmental tail should not wag the business dog. F2F interaction is important, especially when teams are new. Concerned about limiting travel—many projects have a focus on generating money and sustainability is not part of the discussion. Business/sustainable actions most valuable for clients, i.e. minimize supply chain carbon emissions
Impact on clients	Demonstrate behaviour to clients. Engage them to ensure it is OK to work remotely. Provide company resources with mugs/thermos so they stop using the Styrofoam/paper cups. Only a few team members have those. Clients notice when we use disposable cups instead of reusable/washable cups
Working from home/remotely very frequently mentioned	Flying has largest impact. If we had a 'stay home and focus on deliverables' 1 week/month, make a big impact to carbon footprint/reduce project costs and improve engagement; reduce burnout, increase productivity (less time in meetings)
Teleconferencing/video conferencing	We could use savings to invest in enhanced communications technology to make non-face time even more effective
Need for incentives/rewards and vice versa?	Have everyone work on their own home—bulbs, power strips, insulation, and thermostats—promote like crazy. Intra-company CO_2-trading among projects, i.e. what is another project willing to pay for my savings (i.e. Taking a train). Need incentives/rewards—Carbon credits, plant trees

15.5 Discussion

All of the hypotheses were confirmed as positive. With regard to hypothesis 1 (that sustainable management has a positive impact on certain aspects of organizational performance) it was revealed that there needs to be a differentiation between the various sustainability initiatives. Improvements in customer service and cost management were impacted by initiatives to 'reduce the consumption of natural resources'. Conversely, the 'investigation of the company's environmental impact and implementation of programs to reduce it' had a negative impact on improvements in customer service and cost management. The data also confirmed hypothesis 2, that project characteristics affect the overall implementation of sustainability initiatives as well as overall organizational performance. The overall amount of change taking place, agreement with the company's sustainability approach, information from compulsory training, leadership support and commitment, and accountability, all had a significant impact, not only on the implementation of sustainability initiatives, but also on performance improvements. This shows that people not only need to have a clear vision (Doppelt 2003) but, more importantly, they need to agree with the company's vision and approach to sustainability. Other factors that impacted on the implementation of sustainability initiatives were a lack of information on how to get involved, a lack of incentives, and ineffective processes and procedures within the team. Despite employees recognizing that environmental sustainability is important to the company's agenda, the conservation of natural resources, and to clients who are involved in sustainability, it was not seen to be a 'major differentiator' in the market. The company introduced only a moderate level of sustainability initiatives, with the main focus on compliance. Other obstacles on the path to sustainability included low levels of involvement in planning and implementing actions aimed at improving sustainability; lack of employee resources, incentives and information on how to get involved; poor communication processes; and an awareness of the need for sustainability.

The data also confirmed hypothesis 3 that employee involvement, management support, accountability and resources are crucial to instil passion for sustainability initiatives in employees. Overall, sustainability was found to be of great concern to employees, but to a lesser extent to the company leaders and clients. Although they were found to be interested in sustainability, employees were not very passionate about improving environmental sustainability within the organizational context, mainly due to the lack of opportunities for involvement and lack of support and commitment from senior management. Other factors that undermined employee's passion for sustainability initiatives were the perception that sustainability is of little concern to the client, limited abilities to change business practices, and a lack of information on how to get involved. The teams lacked the skills, capabilities and accountability required to support any sustainability initiatives. Consequently, the company needs to fundamentally change the way in which it leads and manages to increase employee involvement, accountability and information on how to get involved, and provide resources, incentives and leadership support. In other words, the company has a strong need for the sustainable 'honeybee' leadership approach advocated by Avery and Bergsteiner (2011) identified as involving stakeholders and having social and sharing capacities. Despite comments from survey respondents such as the 'Sustainability tail should not wag the business dog', many respondents identified the possibility of working with clients to engage them in sustainability initiatives on projects, both within the company and within clients companies to not only reduce environmental impact and emissions but also to reduce costs right along business supply chains where appropriate.

It is suggested that such a strategy may be supported if a Green HRM framework was introduced (see Table 15.1) covering all HR policies and procedures from entry to exit point, with the various promotive and preventive HR managers signatures in place there is likely to be greater employee buy in with regard to the implementation of sustainability initiatives. As Renwick et al. (2008) point out, there is a need for Green HRM policies and processes to be implemented throughout an organization's 'entry to exit' points. This would help to address all of the factors found to be lacking in the organization studied at the time of the survey and would also instil the need for sustainability initiatives as 'front of mind'. Based on the findings of this study, employees need to be supported, trained, involved, empowered, recognized and rewarded for sustainability initiatives to become effective. Specifically, Baumgartner and Ebner (2010) identified four categories related to the way in which organizations embed sustainability—introverted (basic compliance with industry standards); extroverted/transformative (focus on external relationships); conservative (internal orientation) and visionary—the latter focuses on sustainability within all business activities. Visionary, sustainable leadership is a clear requirement for any sustainability initiatives to succeed in the company reported here.

15.6 Conclusion

In conclusion, the results show that the survey managed to capture the current level of sustainability initiatives in the company, and to identify the obstacles preventing employees from taking action and improving sustainability performance. The results of this study confirm Doppelt's (2003) and Baumgartner's (2010) findings regarding the importance of leadership support, employee involvement and the provision of sufficient resources (time and budget) as key drivers of project success. Further, Jonas (2010) states the need to define reasonable, transparent rules and processes (as well as commitment to them) when introducing projects, how they relate to corporate strategy. The data also shows that employees need to feel a sense of accountability and be educated with regard to the capabilities and skills required to address environmental sustainability issues. Without accountability for sustainability targets, the day-to-day operation and the 'need to get the job done' will dominate managers' and employees' agendas. Doppelt (2003) argues that sustainability initiatives have to be driven 'top-down' by a company's leadership who are responsible for providing a clear vision and this was largely absent from this organization. The results also show that some employees are improving their 'ecological footprint' at home, demonstrating concern about sustainability and environmental performance in their home environment, but lack the opportunity to get involved in sustainability initiatives at work. This suggests that sustainability initiatives could be driven from the 'bottom-up' if employees are allowed the time and resources and given sufficient autonomy and authority to make the required changes. The question is not necessarily how to create awareness about sustainability, but rather how to harness the energy and passion of employees and allow them to make a difference as per sustainable leadership practices outlined earlier (see Avery and Bergsteiner 2011) and Hargreaves and Fink (2004). As one participant stated in his comments, *there is a lack of clarity as to how to get involved. I have a great deal of interest in and desire to work on Sustainability in projects. But the route to do so is muddled and unclear. Our people are very talented; many of them would have the capabilities to lead a sustainability proposal so management need to develop a career path that includes sustainability*. The data supports the outlined model of organizational characteristics and management aspects as drivers of sustainability initiatives and performance outcomes (Fig. 15.1), as all suggested driver clusters—turbulence, resources, vision and direction, change management, work roles and emotional energy—were found to impact on the outcome variables in terms of the implementation of sustainability initiatives and performance improvements. However, further studies are needed to provide more detail on the differential impact of various sustainability initiatives on aspects of organizational performance across companies and industries and to determine the key drivers of successful sustainability initiatives.

Finally, the data demonstrates that, despite the environmental sustainability being of great concern to employees personally, it has not translated to the same degree into the corporate agenda, which is mainly focused on 'compliance' (Dunphy et al. 2007). As identified earlier, it is proposed that this is because there is an apparent absence of any sustainable leadership and Green HRM initiatives which involve the integration of environmental management (EM) in HRM as per Sharma et al. (1999) which largely depend on the patterns of green decisions and behaviours of HR managers leading to promotive and preventive green signatures (Zoogah 2011). It is suggested that future studies on similar topics might focus on qualitative research which would allow for deeper insights into why and how particular sustainability initiatives are effective (or not). In this case for example, why did senior management introduce sustainability initiatives without any attempt to embed them within company practice/client relationships, reward systems and more.

References

Adams, C. A., & Frost, G. R. (2008). Integrating sustainability reporting into management practices. *Accounting Forum, 32*(4), 288–302.
Australian Government Department of Climate Change. (2008). Carbon pollution reduction scheme: Australia's low pollution future. White Paper. Available at http://www.climatechange.gov.au/whitepaper/report/index.html.
Avery, G. C., & Bergsteiner, H. (2011). Sustainable leadership practices for enhancing business resilience and performance. *Strategy & Leadership, 39*(3), 5–15.
Baumgartner, R. J., & Ebner, D. (2010). Corporate sustainability strategies: Sustainability profiles and maturity levels. *Sustainable Development, 18*(2), 76–89.
Benn, S., & Bolton, D. (2011). *Key concepts in corporate social responsibility*. California: Sage.
Benn, S., & Dunphy, D. C. (Eds.) (2007) *Corporate governance and sustainability: Challenges for theory and practice*. London: Routledge.
Brower, M., & Leon, W. (1999). *The consumer's guide to effective environmental choices: Practical advice from the union of concerned scientists*. New York: Three Rivers Press.
Brundtland, G. H. (1987). *Our common future: The world commission on environment and development*. Oxford: Oxford University Press.
Daily, B., & Huang, S. (2001). Achieving sustainability through attention to human resource factors in environmental management. *International Journal of Operations and Production Management, 21*(12), 1539–1552.
Daly, H. (1996). *Beyond growth: The economics of sustainable development*. Boston: Beacon Press.
Doppelt, B. (2003). *Leading change toward sustainability. A change-management guide for business, government and civil society*. Sheffield: Greenleaf Publishing.
Dunphy, D., Griffiths, A., & Benn, S. (2007). *Organizational change for corporate sustainability* (2nd ed.). New York: Routledge.
Elkington, J. (1998). *Cannibals with forks: The triple bottom line for 21st century business*. Oxford: Capstone.
Enticott, G., & Walker, R. M. (2008). Sustainability, performance and organizational strategy: An empirical analysis of public organizations. *Business Strategy and the Environment, 17*, 79–92.
Epstein, M. J., & Roy, M. J. (2001). Sustainability in action: Identifying and measuring the key performance drivers. *Long Range Planning, 34*(5), 585–604.
Gilley, K. M., Worrell, D. L., Davidson, W. N., III, & El-Jelly, A. (2000). Corporate environmental initiatives and anticipated firm performance: The differential effects of process-driven versus product-driven greening initiatives. *Journal of Management, 26*, 1199–1216.
Hak, T., Moldan, B., & Dahl, A. L. (2007). *Sustainability indicators, SCOPE 67*. London: Island Press.
Hargreaves, A., & Fink, D. (2004). The seven principles of sustainable leadership. *Educational Leadership, 61*(7), 8–13.
Holmberg, J., Lundqvist, U., Robèrt, K.-H., & Wackernagel, M. (1999). The ecological footprint from a systems perspective of sustainability. *International Journal of Sustainable Development and World Ecology, 6*, 17–33.
Holmberg, J., & Robert, K.-H. (2000). Backcasting from non-overlapping sustainability principles—A framework for strategic planning. *International Journal of Sustainable Development and World Ecology, 7*, 291–308.
Jonas, D. (2010). Empowering project portfolio managers: How management involvement impacts project portfolio management performance.*International Journal of Project Management, 28*(8), 818–831.https://doi.org/10.1016/j.ijproman.2010.07.002
Jorgensen, H. H., Owen, L., & Neus, A. (2008). *IBM global making change work*. Somers: IBM Global Business Services.

Judge, W. Q., & Douglas, T. J. (1998). Performance implications of incorporating natural environmental issues into the strategic planning process: An empirical assessment. *Journal of Management Studies, 35,* 241–262.

Judge, W. Q., & Elenkov, D. (2005). Organizational capacity for change and environmental performance: An empirical assessment of bulgarian firms. *Journal of Business Research, 58*(7), 893–901.

Kramar, R. (2014). Beyond strategic human resource management: Is sustainable human resource management the next approach? *The International Journal of Human Resource Management, 25*(8), 1069–1089. https://doi.org/10.1080/09585192.2013.816863

Kramar, R., & Jones, G. (2010). *Sustainability in strategic human resource management.* Prahran, VIC: Tilde University Press.

Orlitzky, M., Schmidt, F. L., & Rynes, S. L. (2003). Corporate social and financial performance: A meta-analysis. *Organization Studies, 24,* 403–441.

Paehlke, R. (2005). Sustainability as a bridging concept. *Conservation Biology, 19,* 36–38.

Parry, W. (2008). Achieving exceptional performance across times of change. Whitepaper, ChangeTrack Research CTRE, Sydney.

Parry, W., Kirsch, C., Carey, P., & Shaw, D. (2013). Empirical development of a model of performance drivers in organisational change projects. *Journal of Change Management, 14*(1), 99–125.

PricewaterhouseCoopers (2009). *Sustainability yearbook.* http://www.pwc.com/extweb/pwcpublications.nsf/docid/A1A21B9F14C2FBF985257552007570E9. Retrieved June 22, 2009.

Pujari, D., Wright, G., & Peattie, K. (2003). Green and competitive. Influences on environmental new product development performance. *Journal of Business Research, 56,* 657–671.

Ramus, C. A. (2002). Encouraging innovative environmental actions: What companies and managers must do. *Journal of World Business, 37,* 151–164.

Renwick, D., Redman, T., & Maguire, S. (2008). Green HRM: A review, process model, and research agenda. *University of Sheffield Management School Discussion Paper, 1,* 1–46.

Renwick, D. W., Redman, T., & Maguire, S. (2013). Green human resource management: A review and research agenda. *International Journal of Management Reviews, 15*(1), 1–14.

Russo, M. V., & Fouts, P. A. (1997). A resource-based perspective on corporate environmental performance and profitability. *Academy of Management Journal, 40*(3), 534–559.

Sauer, C., & Cuthbertson, C. (2003). *The state of IT Project management in the UK 2002–2003.* Oxford: Templeton College.

Sharma, S., & Henriques, I. (2005). Stakeholder influences on sustainability practices in the Canadian forest products industry. *Strategic Management Journal, 26*(2), 159–180.

Sharma, S., Pablo, A, & Vredenburg, H. (1999). Corporate environmental responsiveness strategies: The importance of issue interpretation and organizational context. *Journal of Applied Behavioral Science, 35*(1), 87–108.

Speth, J. G. (2008). *The bridge at the edge of the world: Capitalism, the environment, and crossing from crisis to sustainability.* Devon: Yale University Press.

Weber, O., Koellner, T., Habegger, D., Steffensen, H., & Ohnemus, O. (2005). *The relation between sustainability performance and financial performance of firms.* GOE Report No. 5-2005, GOE, Zurich. www.goe.ch.

Wilkinson, A., Hill, M., & Gollan, P. (2001). The sustainability debate. *International Journal of Operations and Production Management, 21*(12), 1492–1502.

Zoogah, D. B. (2011). The dynamics of Green HRM behaviours: A cognitive social information processing approach. *German Journal of Research in Human Resource Management, 25*(2), 117–139.

Chapter 16
Sustainability in Conformity Assessment: Flexibility of Technical Harmonization

Raimonda Liepiņa, Inga Lapiņa and Jānis Mazais

Abstract The beginnings of the European Union (EU) can be attributed to the desire to promote mutual cooperation and trade in order to support production facilitation. This chapter aims to present recommendations for the improvement of the technical harmonization and conformity assessment system based on the evaluation of the existing approaches. The necessity for assessment of the existing technical harmonization approaches arose in line with the development of manufacturing and technologies, changes in management strategies and development of global value chains (GVC) where different stages of the production process are located across different countries. The research mainly employed qualitative research methods: analysis of regulations and binding documents, logical constructive analysis and comparison, interviews with experts. The authors have established an interrelation between the technical harmonization approaches and are proposing to adopt a new approach—the Technical Harmonization Approach. Through that authors encompass all elements that are essential for product quality assurance and conformity assessment to facilitate product global supply and distribution. In addition, the authors propose to adopt unified requirements for metrology and conformity assessment of products when they are in use within the EU single market. In order to facilitate the application of requirements, the authors have grouped them and propose to separately regulate each of these groups. Through that authors propose development of post sales activities. The development of methodologies of technical harmonization approaches would facilitate the

---

R. Liepiņa · I. Lapiņa (✉) · J. Mazais
Department of Quality Technologies, Institute for Quality Engineering,
Faculty of Engineering Economics and Management, Riga Technical University,
Meža iela 1/1-310, Riga 1048, Latvia
e-mail: Inga.Lapina@rtu.lv

R. Liepiņa
e-mail: Raimonda.Liepina@rtu.lv

J. Mazais
e-mail: Janis.Mazais@rtu.lv

© Springer Nature Singapore Pte Ltd. 2018
J. Connell et al. (eds.), *Global Value Chains, Flexibility and Sustainability*,
Flexible Systems Management, https://doi.org/10.1007/978-981-10-8929-9_16

work of manufacturers and other stakeholders; it would promote manufacturing of qualitative products as well as sustainable development of entrepreneurship. It is suggested that the results of this research can be used by a number of stakeholders: manufacturers, traders, consumers, etc. At the same time, the results can be used as a basis for further improvement of technical harmonization approaches and sustainability of conformity assessment that would facilitate global trade and help manufacturers to participate in GVCs.

Keywords Conformity assessment · Flexible systems management Global value chain · Technical harmonization

16.1 Introduction

As emphasized by Gereffi and Fernandez-Stark (2016), the global value chain (thereafter—GVC) framework focuses on all sequences of value added, from conception to production and end use. They pointed out that GVC also examines standards, regulations, products, processes and markets in specific industries and places, thus providing a holistic view of global industries. Inomata (2017) mentioned that the main objective of GVC is to explore the interplay between value distribution mechanisms and organization of the cross-border production—consumption nexus. Authors would like to point out that this clarifies the link between GVC and technical harmonization. In connection with GVC, Gattorna (2013) came to the conclusion that actually there is no difference between the two terms: supply chain and value chain, therefore the authors will further use these terms interchangeably.

The beginnings of the European Union (thereafter—EU) can be attributed to the desire to promote mutual cooperation and trade. The precondition for the single market was elimination of trade barriers along the supply chain to ensure free movement of products, services, people and capital. The diversity of historical and cultural backgrounds, economic and technological development in each EU member state was the reason for issuing unified regulatory documents (*acquis communautaire*). It is one of the major EU achievements and also an example of elimination of technical barriers and mutual recognition of applicable requirements in the EU and worldwide (Maciejewski 2017).

Alesina et al. (2005) believe that it is possible to ensure the single market by harmonization and mutual acceptance of national provisions. Pelkmans (2006) points out that compliance with unified requirements among the EU member states (horizontal trust) and between the EU and the member states (vertical trust) is provided within the framework of technical harmonization and mutual recognition.

The principle of mutual recognition leads to broad freedom of choice of law within the EU internal market: market participants can volunteer being subjected to the qualification standards of a different member state and can thus operate throughout the EU under the laws of their state of origin, provided they fulfil these standards (Behme 2016).

Mutual recognition is directly related to conformity assessment. As conformity assessment guarantees safety of the product, it is essential to acknowledge its compliance with the established requirements. Mutual recognition is the principle according to which goods lawfully produced in one country cannot be banned from sale on the territory of the other country. Even if they are produced with different technical or quality specifications (Masserlin 2011). That is because countries have to mutually recognize the conformity assessment results issued in either countries. Through that countries ensure that product compliance has been affirmed within the conformity assessment process, and this brings mutual trust and recognition. Thus, the ability of states to influence economic processes is limited and competition between them is fostered. Nicolaides (1998) points out that it is one of the main reasons that have contributed to the development of technical harmonization within the EU.

In the course of time, with the aim to ensure technical harmonization the EU has developed a variety of approaches: *the Old Approach*, *the New Approach*, *the Global Approach*, *the New Legislative Framework* and the *Agreement on Technical Barriers to Trade* (or *TBT Agreement*) were established by the World Trade Organization (thereafter—WTO) at the world level. The main purpose for these approaches was to promote trade among states. In order to ensure product compliance with the requirements and complete trust among the EU member states, the regulations initially covered all products and stated the same requirements for all of them; these regulations were later named *the Old Approach*. Time showed that this approach is not flexible enough, that it does not ensure a dynamic development of the market. As a result, a decision was taken to improve the existing approach and the basic principles of *the New Approach* (Resolution 85/C 136) were approved. However, unfortunately *the New Approach* identifies only essential requirements for product groups in order to protect human health, life or environment. To establish unified principles for conformity assessment (i.e. procedures and affirmation mark—CE marking), a few years later a new technical approach—*the Global Approach* (Resolution 90/C 10) was approved (Decision 93/465/EEC).

Over time product range increased, manufacturers' competence improved and capabilities grew. Therefore, the EU Resolution to improve the technical harmonization issues (Resolution 2003/C 282) was adopted. In 2008, *the New Legislative Framework* was approved in order to facilitate free movement of products, to emphasize the importance of accreditation and to explain the importance of the CE marking. However, its adoption did not resolve such issues as systematization of the technical harmonization approaches or establishing their interrelationships.

Technical harmonization approach is changing over time; consequently, the business environment and supply chain are changing too. This at times may have fairly turbulent and dramatic consequences, creating uncertainties and dynamics of higher order. In order to cope with them, both for survival and growth in a competitive manner, business organizations have to look for innovative strategies and mechanisms (Sushil 2012). One of the strategies how to work in this changing market is flexible systems management (FSM). Upton and Sushil described manufacturing flexibility as ability to change or react with minimum time, effort, cost or performance (Mishra et al. 2014). That is important in the global and competitive world.

At the same time, we can see how significant are common rules as well as freedom and flexibility in product development for manufacturers, and how it is influenced by globalization. That is why for manufacturers the development of technologies and management strategies in connection with GVC are important.

Gereffi et al. (2005) proposed GVCs based on 'global commodity chain' and 'value chain' principles. Yin et al. (2017) believe that GVC is formed within the disintegration and extension of value space, because the collective manufacturing ends in a product. In addition, there is a circular link between GVC and intra-product internal division in manufacturing. Zhou (2013) pointed out that in GVC an enterprise not only interacts with other enterprises in the industry, but also forms a special relation with vertically related upstream and downstream enterprises. Ghannam (2016) was more concrete: GVC is a grouping of business organizations that sell goods and services on the market or the whole multitude of interactions between third persons (i.e. suppliers, manufacturers, distributors and customers). In addition, through that value can be added to material objects. The idea of the value chain is based on the process view of organizations, the idea of seeing a manufacturing or service organization as a system made up of subsystems, each having inputs, transformation of processes and outputs. That very precisely describes technical harmonization where (despite the chosen module) all above-mentioned parties are more or less involved and through that approval of interconnection is given in theories between conformity assessment and GVC.

The chapter aims to present recommendations for the improvement of the technical harmonization. The necessity for assessment of the existing technical harmonization approaches arose in line with the development of manufacturing and technologies, changes in management strategies and development of GVC where different stages of the production process are located across different countries.

The need to improve the technical harmonization approaches evolved with the development of technologies, management strategies, globalization, changing legislation and economy, as well as the fact that not all outstanding issues were resolved by the adoption of *the New Legislative Framework*. A number of stakeholders (manufacturers, traders, consumers, etc.) can use the results of this research. At the same time, they can be used as a basis for further improvement of technical harmonization approaches and sustainability of conformity assessment.

The research mainly employed qualitative research methods: analysis of regulations and binding documents, logical constructive analysis and comparison, interviews with experts. The research is related mostly to the EU market of products in connection with the product conformity assessment issues.

16.2 Evaluation of *the Old Approach*

The basic principle of *the Old Approach* is mandatory, detailed coordination and regulation of technical rules and specifications, i.e. determining them by regulations. This approach fully reflects the quality evolutionary breakdown by Sheps (2009) during the period up to 1950, when it was believed that quality means compliance with certain requirements, including specific standards or instructions. That influences production volumes and promotes supply chain. The authors believe that this theory has raised awareness of product recognition as adequate if it meets certain requirements.

The view that requirements for one kind of products or product groups need to be standardized is used in determining the legislative requirements for the products at the national level. Initially, this was done to facilitate the growth of production volumes. In the course of time, it was discovered that this method could protect national markets from competitors and restrict product imports. It also explains why in the EU single market the need for harmonization of requirements arose—to remove trade barriers that had been established within the framework of the national market. This is also why there efforts to apply unified requirements for products or product groups in all member states. Therefore, it is considered that technical harmonization originated in the harmonization of requirements at national levels and it is identified with *the Old Approach* (Lohbeck 1998).

After the introduction of *the Old Approach*, it was considered that more detailed requirements in the EU would promote a common understanding of the free movement of products and economic development, including development of production and trade. It was necessary to perform coordination of the member states' views more frequently due to the changes and development of technologies and other industrial solutions. The change-making process was long and it was not possible to provide the necessary changes in time. It also threatened the trade as within the framework of very detailed regulatory requirements, it was impossible to use innovative solutions, and that hindered technological development (Andersson et al. 2008; Saam and Sumpter 2008).

Product identification and compliance assessment was made more complicated by the fact that unified marking of products had not been determined. Consequently, the examination of nearly all products was performed, which created a lot of pressure on the customs and market surveillance authorities.

Upon the evaluation of *the Old Approach*, the authors identified the following weaknesses that contributed to the adoption of a new technical harmonization approach:

- detailed regulation of technical specifications and requirements;
- excessive uniformity of products;
- application of mandatory standards;
- different conformity assessment requirements for products;
- particular conformity assessment procedure(s) only can be used;
- up-to-date information on conformity assessment bodies is not available;

- limited development of new products;
- scientific potential and technological progress is not fully used;
- technical barriers created by national regulations.

At present, two issues are topical: (1) mandatory application of standards and (2) unified approach to conformity assessment when the product is being used. The authors believe that these two issues need to be addressed within the EU and it is necessary to reach a common solution for standards application and to develop one EU legal act for conformity assessment requirements when products are put to use.

16.3 Evaluation of *the New Approach*

In 1985, a resolution was adopted on *the New Approach* (Resolution 85/C 136) aiming to follow unified principles for technical harmonization and standardization. The main initiators of the basic idea of *the New Approach* were the EU institutions (Gehring and Kerler 2008). It is based on the following principles (Resolution 85/C 136, EC Guide 2000):

- only the essential requirements for products are to be included in the regulations;
- technical specifications for the products are to be included in the harmonized standards;
- use of harmonized standards and other standards is voluntary;
- the product compliance with the harmonized standards confirms that it meets the essential requirements.

Pelkman (1987) believes that the adoption of *the New Approach* had an especially great potential and role in economic development, as it prevented formation of new trade barriers, development of standardization was encouraged and *the New Approach* was included in ensuring product compliance. Ruževičius (2008) considers that with the development of technical harmonization, the EU has established an effective means for reducing trade barriers, which is further fostered by international cooperation agreements on mutual recognition. The authors believe that because of the growing competition, *the New Approach* has encouraged entrepreneurs to improve their operations and become more accountable to ensure that products comply with specified requirements. At the same time, the authors wish to point out that *the New Approach* has improved the following fundamental issues:

- requirements are determined for product groups, rather than specific products;
- they cover horizontal risks in areas that are not subject to regulation;
- they are based on general ideology of the optimal technical harmonization aiming to abolish national regulations;
- closer cooperation is promoted between state institutions and market participants.

The main prerequisite for the implementation of *the New Approach* is clear regulation of essential requirements and their separation from the technical specifications. The regulations contain only those requirements that protect human health, life and environment, i.e. provide safety. In order to assess the potential risks of the products and determine the unified requirements, the regulated product group needs to be sufficiently homogeneous. In this connection, Playle (2011) pointed out that the range of products covered by *the New Approach* directives is very wide, as evidenced in their context where the term 'product' is attributed to a wide variety of objects (i.e. accessories, assemblies, devices, instruments, etc.).

According to the basic principles of *the New Approach*, detailed technical specifications for products are included in international standards, use of which is voluntary. Manufacturers are free to choose the technical solution, i.e. harmonized standards or validated methods, thus providing compliance with essential requirements (Burrows 2011). When choosing a particular technical solution, the process must be documented; if required or if stated by the regulations, it is necessary to invite the relevant bodies to perform specific conformity assessment procedures (Vaquier et al. 2009).

In Fig. 16.1, the authors depict the differences of standards and other requirements between the regulated and the non-regulated sphere, *the Old Approach* and *the New Approach*.

Thus, along with the development of technical harmonization and the adoption of the New Approach, in more and more spheres manufacturers are given freedom of choice when ensuring the product compliance. At the same time, the competence of the conformity assessment bodies involved has to be high to ensure product conformity assessment, as well as identify non-compliant products.

Playle (2011) points out that during the product design stage manufacturers should consider a number of issues which will determine whether during the production stage it will be possible to fully ensure that products comply with the requirements:

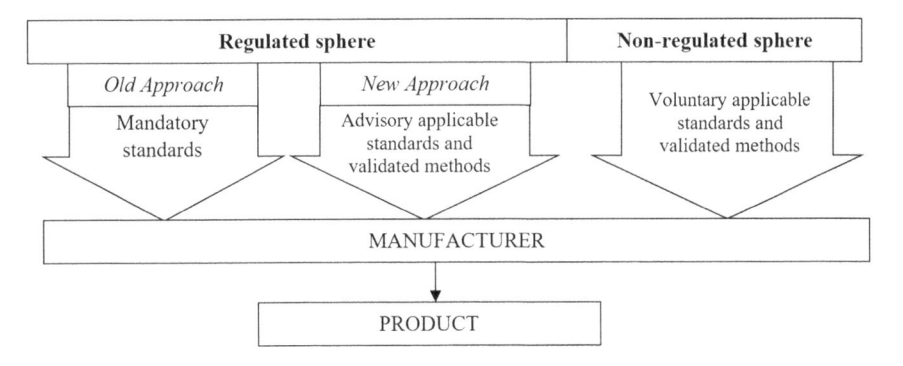

Fig. 16.1 The use of standards, depending on the requirements of regulations (created by the authors)

- what kind of products are planned to be manufactured;
- which market is planned for the product to be placed on;
- whether regulations are set for such kind of products in the particular region;
- whether harmonized standards are set for the product to comply with the essential requirements;
- what reasonable alternatives to the harmonized standards can be chosen;
- which of the possible conformity assessment procedures to choose;
- what documents are required for compliance assessment.

The authors would like to stress that it is possible to find similarities in the ideology of *the New Approach* and FSM. That can be proved by the fact that *the New Approach* created big changes and novelties in the market through changes in legislation. Because of that, manufacturers needed to change their strategies and choose the appropriate way to provide conformity assessment for concrete manufactured products. In addition, the important arguments for manufacturers resulting from these decisions are: how to do it with minimum time, costs, performance and effort. Thus, manufacturers can be more efficient adapting their operations due to different kinds of changes (e.g. technologies, regulatory acts, etc.) and the impact of globalization.

In comparison with *the Old Approach*, *the New Approach* is more flexible, within its framework manufacturers are protected from a variety of product safety risks; the declaration of conformity and CE marking ensure the product compliance with the requirements, and manufacturers and traders are given more freedom to ensure products compliance (Pelkmans 1987; Filiač 2003).

Crenna et al. (2009) pointed out that the requirements for measuring instruments are an example of how regulations for one particular sphere can be improved from *the Old Approach* to *the New Approach*. The requirements in *the New Approach* are more flexible, without strict technical regulations and the production process is not affected. On the basis of the above mentioned, as well as on detailed analysis of the measuring instruments group case, the authors can say that this sphere is one of the successful examples of the development of technical harmonization.

In Fig. 16.2, the authors depict the requirements that are regulated by *the New Approach*, which nowadays is regarded a 'good legislation practice'.

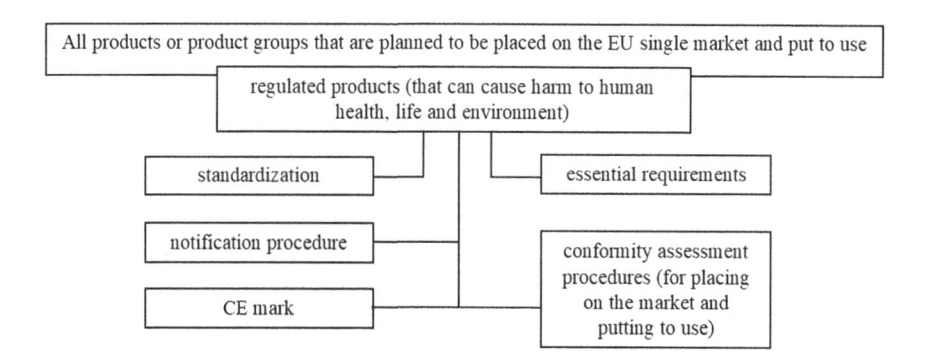

Fig. 16.2 Requirements of *the new approach* (created by the authors)

Thus, with the development of technical harmonization and transfer to *the New Approach*, manufacturers can freely use their technical capabilities and solutions, thus facilitating the emergence of innovations, social benefits, satisfying customer needs and wishes by ensuring that the theoretical aspects are properly applied. Moreover, that reflects the interconnection between technical harmonization and the FSM theory.

16.4 Evaluation of *the Global Approach*

In order to establish unified requirements for conformity assessment, in 1989 a resolution on *the Global Approach* (Resolution 90/C 10) was adopted and a decision was taken about conformity assessment procedures (conformity assessment modules and conformity assessment affirmation mark—CE marking) (Decision 93/465/EEC). The authors wish to point out that *the Global Approach* for product conformity assessment actually complements *the New Approach* and is so integrated into its framework that today the concept of *the New Approach* in most cases refers to the requirements defined in both the above-mentioned approaches.

Therefore, after *the Global Approach* came into force, many existing regulations were revised in order to reduce the number of products that are subject to these norms as well as to develop product requirements. To ensure the reliability of conformity assessment, it is essential that competency of all involved parties in conformity assessment is approved and the transparency of the operations is ensured. After the product is assessed, it is affixed the CE marking as a proof that it complies with the requirements and on the basis of which it can be placed on the market and put to use in the EU (Stephenson 1997; Tricker 2000; Poncibò 2007).

Therefore, many interested parties (manufacturers, test laboratories, distributors, etc.) are involved in conformity assessment process. They all act together with the aim to place on the market and put to use products which are safe. This is clearly linked to the GVC theory, which says that GVC is a grouping of business organizations selling goods and providing services on the market and there is important interaction and relation between all involved parties (Zhou 2013; Ghannam 2016). Tippman (2013) also agrees that a link can be found between conformity assessment and GVC.

For example, GVC theory elements can be found through the activities of the involved parties in CE marking affixing, use and monitoring scheme (see Fig. 16.3).

The aim of all conformity assessment activities is to ensure that only compliant products are placed on the market and put to use. If clear mutual interaction between modules and conformity assessment activities is performed, it will be easier for the manufacturer to make a decision.

Within *the Global Approach*, certain unified policies and systems for conformity assessment have been defined, stressing the significance of accreditation and standardization. The main innovation within *the Global Approach* was the creation

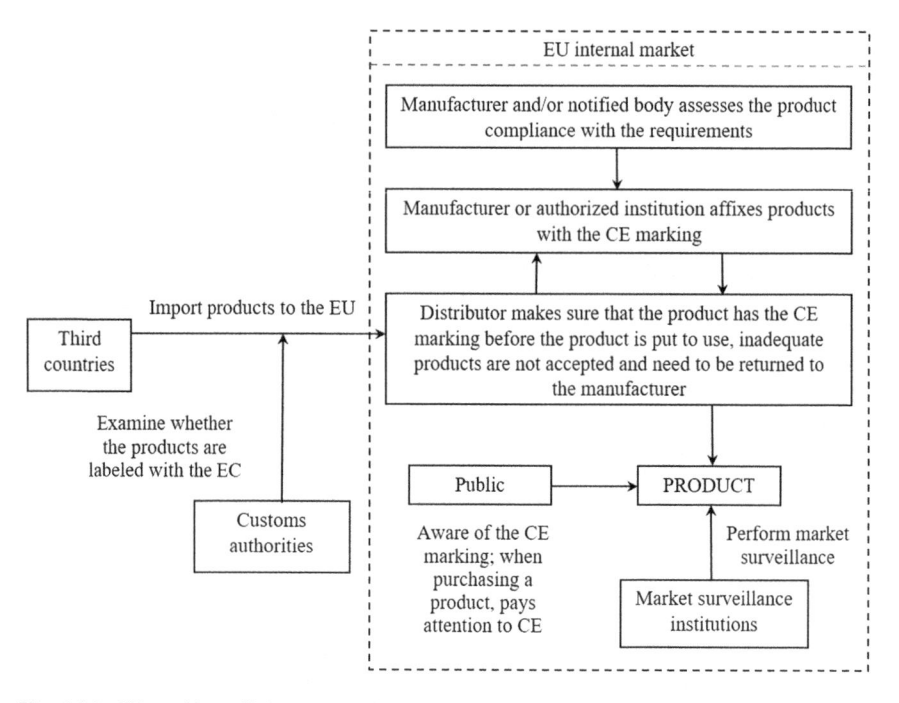

Fig. 16.3 CE marking affixing, use and monitoring scheme (created by the authors)

of unified methodology for conformity assessment procedures (modules). The modules are classified in accordance with the application stages (design and/or production). The modules are structured so that manufacturers, taking into account the product specifics, their technological capabilities, as well as competences and practice in product quality control, could choose the way in which to ensure the product conformity assessment. The requirements regulated by *the Global Approach* are depicted in Fig. 16.4.

Thus, with the development of *the Global Approach* and its integration with *the New Approach*, technical harmonization transferred to a new level, where manufacturers have more freedom and flexibility to choose how to provide product compliance and to ensure that different stakeholders with exact tasks are involved in the concrete process stage. Through that, the authors reveal the interrelation between conformity assessment and the GVC.

16.5 Evaluation of *the New Legislative Framework*

During more than 25 years since *the New Approach* came into force, a number of problems, shortcomings and inconsistencies in technical progress have been identified. Among the most significant are: non-compliant products which are placed on

```
┌─────────────────────────────────────────────────────────────────────┐
│ All products or product groups that are planned to be placed on the │
│      EU single market and put to use and which are used             │
└─────────────────────────────────────────────────────────────────────┘
              ┌──────────────────────────────────────────┐
              │ regulated products (that can cause harm  │
              │      to human health, life and environment)│
              └──────────────────────────────────────────┘
   ┌──────────────────┐                    ┌──────────────────┐
   │  accreditation   │                    │ mutual recognition│
   └──────────────────┘                    └──────────────────┘
   ┌──────────────────┐                    ┌──────────────────┐
   │  standardization │                    │ conformity assessment
   └──────────────────┘                    │ procedures (for placing
   ┌──────────────────┐                    │ on the market and putting
   │     CE mark      │                    │ to use)          │
   └──────────────────┘                    └──────────────────┘
```

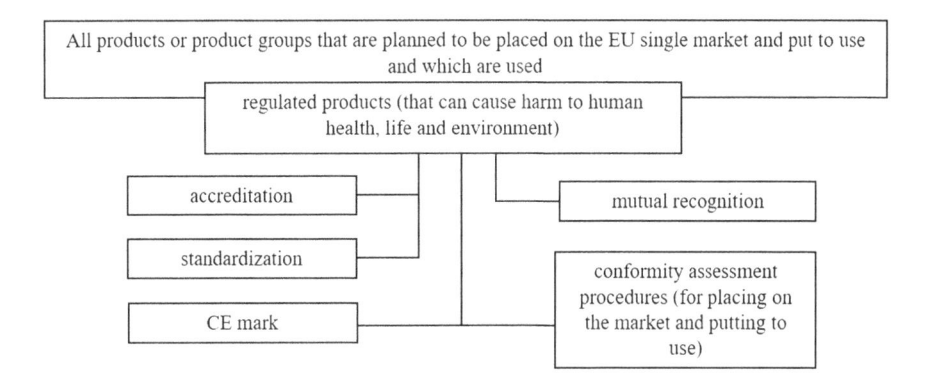

Fig. 16.4 Requirements of *the global approach* (created by the authors)

the market, the notified bodies do not work according to unified requirements, the regulations are interpreted in different ways and there is a certain confusion in their practical application (European Commission 2000).

In order to strengthen the EU single market conditions for products and to promote industrial products entering the market, the main objectives set by EU institutions were:

- to reduce the conditions which could restrict free movement of products within the EU single market by improving the legislative framework;
- to enhance the conditions and requirements for the notification of conformity assessment bodies and to promote the use of accreditation;
- to explain the importance of the CE marking.

Three regulations have been adopted to ensure the principles of *the New Legislative Framework*. Regulation No. 765/2008 and decision No. 768/2008/EC improve the existing requirements in order to promote the operation of the EU single market while emphasizing the significance of accreditation and market surveillance. Regulation No. 764/2008 defines the principles of mutual recognition, thereby protecting the single market from inadequate, life-threatening, safety and environment threatening and non-protective products for consumers.

When evaluating *the New Legislative Framework* in accordance with the objectives set, Zlámalová (2010) concludes that a variety of issues has been improved and believes that this approach edits and complements *the New Approach*. Besides the evaluation carried out by Zlámalová, the authors (Liepina et al. 2013) also analysed the regulations of *the New Legislative Framework* and found out that the following main issues have been improved:

- the duties of the parties involved in conformity assessment have been defined in more detail;
- the number of conformity assessment procedures has been increased;
- the responsibilities of the market surveillance system and institutions have been developed;

- accreditation is set as a prerequisite for mutual recognition of products and the issued conformity assessment results;
- standardization principles will be determined in a separate legal act (regulation).

Based on the evaluation, the authors argue that *the New Legislative Framework* edits and complements both *the New Approach* and *the Global Approach*. That also stresses the link between conformity assessment and GVC. At the same time, with the adoption of the new regulation, the following critical issues have not been addressed: requirements for the competence of conformity assessment bodies and for involvement of subcontractors, updating information on the notified bodies, guidelines on the application of the regulations, etc.

16.6 Development or *the Technical Harmonization Approach*

One of the major problems identified by the authors during the study and from their practical experience is lack of understanding of the existing technical harmonization approaches and their interrelationships, interchangeability and application procedures that can be observed among the involved parties and the society.

It is necessary to ensure unified requirements and a common understanding of their application within the EU single market. In this regard, the authors have developed interrelations of the existing technical harmonization approaches and propose to adopt a new approach encompassing all the elements that are essential to ensure product quality and conformity assessment (see Fig. 16.5).

The authors propose to call this approach the 'Technical Harmonization Approach', given that it will apply to all elements pertaining to product quality

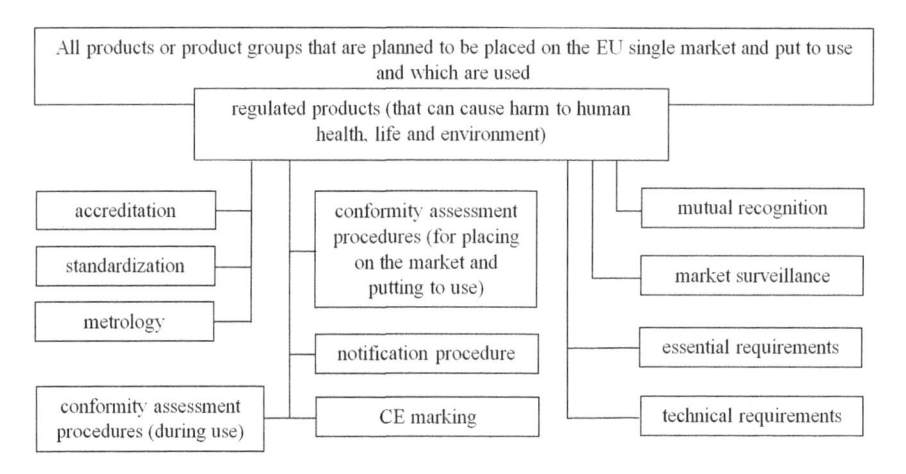

Fig. 16.5 Proposal to adopt *the technical harmonization approach* (created by the authors)

assurance and conformity assessment. The first step would be to adopt this regulation, which would replace the existing technical harmonization approaches and regulate the framework for this approach. Separate regulations would be necessary for individual elements, element groups, products or product groups, thus, when making amendments, it would no longer be necessary to change the overall concept of the approach. At the same time, it would facilitate the awareness of the involved parties and the public of the product conformity assessment process, still holding the linking with GVC.

The authors propose to divide elements into the following groups:

- essential and technical requirements;
- conformity assessment before the product is placed on the market and put to use, CE marking, notification process;
- conformity assessment of the products in use;
- accreditation;
- standardization;
- metrology;
- market surveillance;
- mutual recognition.

Most of the elements are already regulated within the framework of different technical harmonization approaches. Until now, in the EU unified requirements were not set for metrology and conformity assessment for the products in use. Up to now, questions pertaining to metrology were regulated only with respect to conformity assessment of particular measuring instruments; whereas questions pertaining to the conformity assessment of the products in use were regulated at the national level. At present, mainly measuring instruments are subject to subsequent conformity assessment, the frequency of subsequent verification is determined for them as well.

16.7 Conclusion

Along with the formation of the EU single market, technical barriers to trade were removed and technical harmonization was adopted. The range of products offered on the market still grew, they were so numerous and different that it was impossible to adopt unified, detailed requirements for all products, as originally intended by *the Old Approach* (which was established in accordance with the scientific theories about quality management of that time).

In order to ensure a more liberal approach to product compliance and promote industrial growth, *the New Approach* was adopted. For its support, *the Global Approach* was developed. Nowadays, *the New Approach* is used more and more widely in combination with *the Global Approach*, without emphasizing discrepancies between these two approaches. As a result, within 25 years, a number of changes have been made with regard to the requirements and conformity assessment of various products. Consequently, manufacturers' responsibility has increased, as already during the product design stage they must be sufficiently competent to be able to make decisions on which the product's full compliance with the requirements will depend.

In order to improve the existing technical harmonization approaches, *the New Legislative Framework* was adopted. The authors believe that the adopted solutions are general; they explain and slightly complement the existing approaches. Within this framework, the role of accreditation was enhanced, a market surveillance system was developed and mutual recognition was improved. However, *the New Legislative Framework* does not completely resolve all concerns related to the product conformity assessment issues, as evidenced in the survey results.

Due to the fact that there is absence of a logical interrelation and interchangeability between technical harmonization approaches, the authors propose adopting a new approach—*the Technical Harmonization Approach*. This approach includes all the elements that are essential for product quality assurance and conformity assessment. Most of the elements have already been regulated by legislation. In addition, the authors propose to adopt unified requirements for metrology and conformity assessment of products when they are in use within the EU single market. In order to facilitate application of the requirements, the authors have grouped them and propose to separately regulate each of these groups. Adoption of the proposed *Technical Harmonization Approach*, unified metrology and conformity assessment requirements can unburden the work of manufacturers, traders and other involved GVC participants.

References

Alesina, A., Angeloni, I., & Schuknecht, L. (2005). What does the European Union do? *Public Choice, 123*(3–4), 275–319.

Andersson, F., Arvķus, C., Haase, P., & Renman, A. (2008). Measures for enhanced co-operation in the area of technical rules, Part 3. *The contribution of trade to a New EU growth strategy, Ideas for a more Open European Economy.* Kommerskollegium National Board of Trade, Stockholm, Sweden. http://www.kommers.se/upload/Analysarkiv/In%20English/Analyses/LS%20Technicalrules.pdf.

Behme, C. (2016). The principle of mutual recognition in the european internal market with special regard to the cross-border mobility of companies. *European Company & Financial Law Review, 13*(1), 31–54.

Burrows, N. (2011). Harmonisation of technical standards: reculer pour mieux sauter? *The Modern Law Review, 53*(5), 597–603.

Council Decision 93/465/EEC of 22 July 1993 Concerning the modules for the various phases of the conformity assessment procedures and the rules for the affixing and use of the CE conformity marking, which are intended to be used in the technical harmonisation directives. *Official Journal of the European Communities, 30.8.93*(L223), 23–39. http://eur-lex.europa.eu/LexUriServ/LexUriServ.do?uri=OJ:L:1993:220:0023:0039:EN:PDF.

Council Resolution of 10 November 2003 on the Communication of the European Commission 'enhancing the implementation of the new approach directives'. *Official Journal of the European Communities*, 2003/C 282, 3–4. http://eur-lex.europa.eu/LexUriServ/LexUriServ.do?uri=OJ:C:2003:282:0003:0004:EN:PDF.

Council Resolution of 21 December 1989 on a Global approach to Conformity Assessment. *Official Journal of the European Communities*, 16.1. 90/C 10, 1–2. http://eur-lex.europa.eu/LexUriServ/LexUriServ.do?uri=OJ:C:1990:010:0001:0002:EN:PDF.

Council Resolution of 7 May 1985 on a New approach to technical harmonization and standards. *Official Journal of the European Communities*, 4.6. 85/C 136, 1–9. http://eur-lex.europa.eu/LexUriServ/LexUriServ.do?uri=OJ:C:1985:136:0001:0009:EN:PDF.

Crenna, F., Rossi, G. B., & Bovio, L. (2009). Probabilistic measurement evaluation for the implementation of the measuring instrument directive. *Measurement, 42*(10), 1522–1531.

European Commission (EC). (2000). *Guide to the implementation of directives based on the new approach and the global approach*. Luxembourg: Office for Official Publications of the European Communities.

Filiač, V. (2003). Conformity assessment to electrical products in the CR. *Electrical Engineering, Czech Industry, 4*, 10–11.

Gattorna, J. (2013). The influence in customer buying behaviour on product flow patterns between trading countries, and the implications for regulatory policy. In *Global value chains in a changing world* (pp. 201–244). WTO Publications.

Gereffi, G., & Fernandez-Stark, K. (2016). *Global value chain analysis: A primer* (p. 34). Center on Globalization, Governance & Competitiveness, Duke University. http://www.cggc.duke.edu/pdfs/Duke_CGGC_Global_Value_Chain_GVC_Analysis_Primer_2nd_Ed_2016.pdf.

Gereffi, G., Humphrey, J., & Sturgeon, T. (2005). The governance of global value chains. *Review of International Political Economy, 12*(1), 78–104.

Gehring, T., & Kerler, M. (2008). Institutional stimulation of deliberative—Decision-making: division of labour, deliberative legitimacy and technical regulation in the European single market. *Journal of Common Market Studies, 46*(5), 1001–1023.

Ghannam, A. (2016). Business integration unit (BIU) adapted for industrial global value chain on the web. *Journal of Electrical Systems and Information Technology, 3*(1), 127–140.

Inomata, S. (2017). Analytical frameworks for global value chains: An overview. *Global value chain development report 2017 "measuring and analyzing the impact of GVCs on economic development"* (chapter 1, pp. 15–28). International Bank for Reconstruction and Development/The World Bank. https://www.wto.org/english/res_e/booksp_e/gvcs_report_2017.pdf.

Liepiņa, R., Lapiņa, I., & Mazais, J. (2013). Improvement of conformity assessment system: technical harmonization adjustment. In *Proceedings of the 17th World Multi-Conference on Systemics, Cybernetics and Informatics* (Vol. II, pp. 37–42). Orlando, Florida, USA.

Lohbeck, D. (1998). *CE marking handbook*. A practical approach to global safety certification. Chapter 1—Europe's Approach to Total Harmonization. Elsevier Inc.

Maciejewski, M. (2017). Free movement of goods. *Fact sheets on the European Union—2017* (pp. 1–5). Available at: http://www.europarl.europa.eu/ftu/pdf/en/FTU_3.1.2.pdf.

Masserlin, P. (2011). The European Union single market in goods: Between mutual recognition and harmonisation. *Australian Journal of International Affairs, 65*(4), 410–435.

Mishra, R., Pundir, A. K., & Ganapathy, L. (2014). Manufacturing flexibility research: A review of literature and agenda for future research. *Global Journal of Flexible Systems Management, 15*(2), 101–112.

Nicolaides, P. (1998). The role of member states as rule-makers in the European Union. *Intereconomics, 33*(1), 3–10.

Pelkmans, J. (1987). The new approach to technical harmonization and standardization. *Journal of Common Market Studies, 25*(3), 249–269.

Pelkmans, J. (2006). European industrial policy. *International Handbook on Industrial Policy*, 45–78.

Playle, M. (2011). CE marking—The essential requirements. In C. Dale & T. Anderson (Eds.), *Advances in systems safety* (pp. 251–271). London: Springer.

Poncibò, C. (2007). Private certification schemes as consumer protection: A viable supplement to regulation in Europe? *International Journal of Consumer Studies, 31*(6), 656–661.

Ruževičius, J. (2008). The study of quality certification system of Lithuania. *Engineering Economics, 2*(57), 78–84.

Saam, N., & Sumpter, D. (2008). EU institutional reforms. How do member states reach a decision? *Journal of Policy Modeling, 30*(1), 71–86.

Sheps, I. (2009). From product quality to organization quality. In *Proceedings of Fifth International Working Conference "Total Quality Management—Advanced and Intelligent Approaches"* (pp. 41–46). Belgrade.

Stephenson, S. M. (1997). Standards, conformity assessment and developing countries. *World Bank Research Working Paper No. 1826*.

Sushil. (2012). Multiple perspectives of flexible systems management. *Global Journal of Flexible Systems Management, 13*(1), 1–2.

Tippman, C. (2013). *The national quality infrastructure, policy brief "the innovation policy platform"* (pp. 1–12). https://innovationpolicyplatform.org/sites/default/files/rdf_imported_documents/TheNationalQualityInfrastructure.pdf.

Tricker, R. (2000). *CE conformity marking and new approach directives*. Oxford: Butterworth-Heinemann Linacre House.

Vaquier, C., Legrand, D., & Caldani, C. (2009). Qualification Opérationnelle du Systèmein Formatique d'un Depot de Sanget de ses Échanges Dedonnées. *Transfusion Clinique et Biologique, 16*(2), 245–252.

Yin, X., Dong, C., & Liu, C. (2017). Global value chain restructuring in the trade of knocked down products. *Transactions of FAMENA, 41*(1), 91–98.

Zhou, R. (2013). Research on vertical structure evolution of global value chain & enterprise innovation. In *2013 International Conference on Management Science and Engineering 20th Annual Conference Proceedings Management Science and Engineering (ICMSE)* (pp. 1848–1853).

Zlámalová, J. (2010). Chosen influences of "revision of new approach". *World Academy of Science, Engineering and Technology*, 291–296.

Chapter 17
Evaluation of Market Surveillance Implementation and Sustainability

Svetlana Mjakuškina and Inga Lapiņa

Abstract The establishment of global value chains requires changes in the approach to market surveillance. Intermediate inputs have become an important part of the world trade, particularly as they are increasingly being sourced through imports rather than domestic production. The nature of internal markets combined with the effects of the global supply chain makes it increasingly necessary to adopt a truly coordinated approach to market surveillance. Market surveillance practices among the European Union Member States and worldwide differ by each country. Within the European Union it is the responsibility of each individual Member State, which has different resources, priorities and legislative framework, to develop and sustain their internal market surveillance. Different countries around the world develop their own standardization arrangements and start to produce more products that only conform to their own safety standards. The aim of this chapter is to analyse approaches to market surveillance through different product groups, in order to evaluate the differences between the sectors and countries.

Keywords Globalization · Global supply chain · Global value chain
Market surveillance · Product safety · Sustainability

S. Mjakuškina · I. Lapiņa (✉)
Department of Quality Technologies, Institute for Quality Engineering,
Faculty of Engineering Economics and Management, Riga Technical University,
Riga, Latvia
e-mail: inga.lapina@rtu.lv

S. Mjakuškina
e-mail: svetlana.mjakuskina@rtu.lv

S. Mjakuškina
Products and Services Surveillance Department, Consumer Rights Protection Centre,
Riga, Latvia

© Springer Nature Singapore Pte Ltd. 2018
J. Connell et al. (eds.), *Global Value Chains, Flexibility and Sustainability*,
Flexible Systems Management, https://doi.org/10.1007/978-981-10-8929-9_17

17.1 Introduction

Global trade and product manufacturing in the modern economy is characterized by two interconnected processes—fragmentation of the manufacturing process across different geographies (global supply chain) and greater global interdependency between the countries known as Globalization. The fragmentation of the manufacturing process means that each element of the production is performed by a separate actor located in a different geographic area. This leads to a greater interdependency between the countries involved in the manufacturing process. This is a very unique environment that has become possible with technological and legal advancements that the world experienced in the past decades. It brings some additional unique challenges for the market surveillance. No country is immune to these global characteristics though each country has its unique challenges, due to its unique economic and legal environment. To better understand the influences the globalization and global supply chain have on product market surveillance, this study will look at the European Union's path and experience in more details as a case study of this topic. An internal single market developed by the European Union that ensures free circulation of people, money, services and products within the European Community is one of the main achievements of the European Union. The legal basis is determined in Articles 26, 28–37 of the Treaty on European Union and the Treaty on the Functioning of the European Union. The New Approach and the European Standardization place a significant role in free product circulation and it is the key element of the created system. The European Union Directives, the so-called 'New Approach Directives' define essential requirements related to the health, safety and environmental issues. Majority of sectors are covered by the 'New Approach Directives', which means common requirements and also methods for conformity assessment procedures to evaluate and ensure the compliance of the products. The manufacturer is responsible for the product compliance with the essential requirements. The manufacturer may use the harmonized European Standards to reach the compliance of the products with the applicable essential requirements. The use of the harmonized European standards is voluntary but at the same time, the use of the standards published in the Official Journal of the European Union provides the presumption of conformity to the essential requirements set out in the applicable product regulations as far as particular risks are covered by this standard. Only those products that meet the essential requirements can be placed on the market. The regulation clearly determines that when manufacturers place a product on the market they should ensure that the product has been designed and manufactured in accordance with the essential requirements set out in the applicable legislations that cover the particular product. The manufacturer shall declare the compliance of the products with the applicable legislation by drawing the declaration of compliance. The base of the system is the trust that the manufacturer will only place those products on the market that have gone through the appropriate conformity assessment procedure and are compliant. The importer will ensure that the product manufacturer has carried out the appropriate conformity assessment procedure. The existing system determines clear rules and removes any technical barriers, so economic operators can benefit from the free circulation of goods. The free circulation of goods increases the competition and as a result, manufacturers face the challenge of cutting down the cost while ensuring they meet the consumer expectations.

The Regulation (EC) No. 765/2008 of the European Parliament and of the Council of 9 July 2008 establishes an overall framework of rules and principles in relation to market surveillance within the European Union. As defined in the Regulation No. 765/2008, market surveillance is the activities carried out and measures taken by public authorities to ensure that products comply with the requirements set out in the relevant Community harmonization legislation and do not endanger health, safety or any other aspects of public interest protection. Surveillance as defined in the EN ISO/IEC 17000:2004 'Conformity assessment—Vocabulary and general principles' means systematic iteration of conformity assessment activities as a basis for maintaining the validity of the statement of conformity. The statement of conformity in the European Union means that only compliant products can be made available on the European Union market.

Market surveillance plays a significant role not only in the protection of consumer interests but also in ensuring fair competition among economic operators (Product Safety Forum of Europe (PROSAFE) 2013). In the European Union, market surveillance for non-food products is the responsibility of each Member State. It means that each market surveillance authority acts within its jurisdiction, taking into account the available resources and the determined priorities. The aim of this chapter is to analyse approaches to market surveillance through different product groups, in order to evaluate the differences between the sectors and countries.

17.2 Influence of the Globalization Processes

Globalization has changed the business structure and introduced the concept of the global supply chain (Meixell and Gargeya 2005). This global framework reduces the cost of production and leads to a higher degree of specialization, where companies are performing a task in the production chain that becomes their base competence. The performance of this particular task is allocated to a specific company in the supply chain. This process is known as outsourcing.

The supply chain covers all stages of the manufacturing process, from raw material allocation to the product delivery to the end user. The ultimate goal is to deliver maximum value to the consumer with the least possible costs (Ibrahim et al. 2015).

As a result of a higher degree of the fragmentation of the manufacturing process where each company is responsible only for a specific step in the process, it becomes harder to have a full control over the quality of the product. Therefore, a greater number of products have a higher degree of risk of safety compliance violations at one of the steps in the supply chain (Ruiz-Torres and Mahmoodi

2008). In order to survive in the frame of the demand of the customer changes and the complexities in the product, it is significant for companies to ensure flexibility in the supply chain. The quality of the information flow plays the main role in improving the flexibility of supply chain (Singh and Sharma 2014).

The establishment of global value chains (hereafter—GVC) requires changes in the approach to market surveillance. Intermediate inputs have become an important part of the world trade, particularly as they are increasingly being sourced through imports rather than domestic production. Intermediate inputs now represent more than half of the products imported by the Organization for Economic Co-operation and Development (hereafter—OECD) economies and close to three-fourths of the imports of the large developing economies, such as China and Brazil (Ali and Dadush 2011).

The border control of products entering the market is one of the elements of market surveillance. The increasing amount of imported products requires effective allocation of market surveillance resources. The border control of products has to be effective in identifying non-compliant products that may pose health and safety or environmental risks, and it also must be efficient with a quick product turnover to make sure that it does not delay the product delivery. A delay in the process creates obstacles for local businesses and may negatively affect the trade as a whole. GVC trade is particularly affected by trade barriers: when products and services cross borders multiple times, both as imports and exports, trade costs are compounded. This is especially problematic for the firms in Low-Income Developing Countries and for Small and Medium Enterprises, which are less able to absorb these costs (OECD and the World Bank Group 2015).

The regulators understand the need for a time-sensitive process to ensure quick movement of products that is reflected in some of the regulations currently in place. For example, according to Article 28 of Regulation (EC) No. 765/2008 a product the release of which has been suspended by the authorities in charge of external border controls pursuant shall be released if, within the 3 working days of suspension of release, those authorities have not been notified of any actions taken by the market surveillance authorities.

Inefficient regulatory requirements can also create obstacles and restrain international trade. For example, it has been identified that technical regulations on agricultural trade significantly delay trade in some subsectors, but at the same time, well-designed regulations and conformity assessment procedures can facilitate trade (van Tongeren et al. 2009, 2010). Standards can also facilitate trade if they can provide information to potential suppliers and overcome problems of informational asymmetry that would otherwise stifle exports (Disdier et al. 2008).

The effects of the globalization process are not limited to the business and its structure but also influence regulation and surveillance practices. The globalization process creates a significant challenge for the market surveillance authorities to ensure effective surveillance implementation. Market surveillance not only achieves a certain level of safety on the market but also maintains fair market practices.

17.3 Market Surveillance Implementation

Market surveillance systems exist in most countries worldwide. The number of the European Union Member States has increased over time and reached its current level of 28 countries. The total population of the European Union in 2016 was 510,284,430 (Official website of the European Union 2016a). Since 2005, more than 20,000 measures have been taken against unsafe products found within the European Union European Commission Rapid Alert System (hereafter—RAPEX) (RAPEX 2017). As of 31 December 2016, the OECD Global portal on product recalls had 15,693 records on non-food product recalls (OECD 2017). The number of product recalls per country of jurisdiction is summarized in Fig. 17.1. The analysis of data on unsafe products found in countries with high or low population rate showed that in the countries with a higher population a lower number of unsafe products were found. There is a need to further analyse this data to identify the causes of this correlation.

In the European Union, market surveillance for non-food products is the responsibility of each Member State. The analysis of the available data on the market surveillance authorities by sector identified that in small countries like Malta or Latvia market surveillance is more centralized. One authority ensures the control of almost all non-food products. At the same time in countries like the United Kingdom or Germany, control is more decentralized, for example 20 authorities ensure the control of electrical appliances in Germany (see Table 17.1). The RAPEX notifications as well as the OECD global portal on product recalls showed that the most notified product categories are: toys, electrical appliances, motor vehicles, clothing, textiles and fashion items, child articles.

The study of the RAPEX notifications submitted by Germany, France, Italy, the Netherlands, Slovenia, Latvia and Malta for different product groups was performed. The analysis of the market surveillance sample data indicates a possible correlation between the decentralization of the surveillance authorities and the

Fig. 17.1 Number of product recalls per country of jurisdiction and population. *Source* Official website of the European Union (2016d) Living in the EU and European Commission Rapid Alert System (RAPEX)

Table 17.1 Summary of RAPEX notifications by country and product group

Country	Population	Amount of notification on dangerous products in RAPEX (2005–2016)	Toys — Number of market surveillance authorities	Toys — Amount of notification on dangerous toys (2005–2016)	Toys — Amount of notifications per market surveillance authority	Electrical equipment — Number of market surveillance authorities	Electrical equipment — Amount of notification on dangerous electrical equipment (2005–2016)	Electrical equipment — Amount of notifications per market surveillance authority
Germany	82,175,684	2320	17	366	22	20	178	9
France	66,759,950	1136	2	332	166	3	158	53
Italy	60,665,551	480	3	131	44	6	32	5
Netherlands	16,979,120	610	1	175	175	3	42	14
Slovenia	2,064,188	236	1	97	97	2	25	13
Latvia	1,968,957	225	1	101	101	1	13	13
Malta	434,403	181	1	25	25	1	37	37

Sources 1 Official website of the European Union (2016d) Living in the EU. 2 European Commission Rapid Alert System (RAPEX) and 3 Official website of the European Commission (2016b) List of national market surveillance authorities by sector number of detected dangerous products that pose a risk to public health and safety. It is advised to further investigate this possible trend through a deeper analysis.

In 89% of the cases, the country of origin of non-compliant toys is outside the European Union, (see Fig. 17.2). The same situation is seen in relation to notified unsafe electrical appliances. The country of origin of unsafe electrical appliances in 84% of the cases is outside the European Union.

The country of origin of 73% of non-compliant toys and 65% of non-compliant electrical appliances is China. The data clearly identifies the need to focus on border control of products. Taking into account the existing system within the European Union when market surveillance is the responsibility of the Member States, the prioritization of border control of products faces the same challenges. Each Member State in cooperation with the customs authority may determine its own priorities for controls. It is not limited to the identification of the selected product group, but also to such criteria as—minimal amount of imported products, performed inspection—administrative checks, physical checks or testing. The absence of common criteria for border control of products can make the placement of non-compliant products on the market possible.

Overall, the current approach to market surveillance is based on product approach, the market surveillance authorities make random checks or control based on particular criteria for the product compliance. This approach gives an opportunity to evaluate the compliance of the particular product and, in case of any deviation, take corrective measures. According to the authors, such approach does not guarantee process effectiveness within the business to ensure the compliance of the products made available on the market. In the existing environment of limited resources, the control of the processes that the economic operator uses can help better ensure the alignment with the requirements. According to the authors, this will give a greater influence on the compliance of products made available on the market by the particular economical operator.

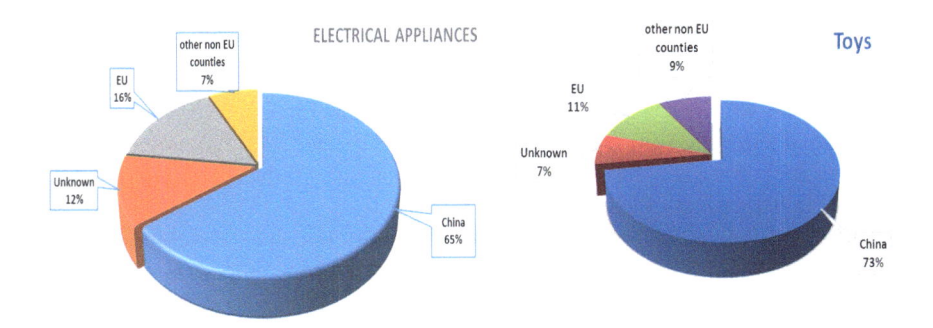

Fig. 17.2 Countries of origin of electrical appliances and toys in the RAPEX system. *Source* European Commission Rapid Alert System (RAPEX)

Efficient and effective market surveillance is the cornerstone of a successful consumer product safety policy in the EU (Meglena Kuneva, European Commissioner for Consumers).

17.4 Best Practices in Market Surveillance

Different authors have identified possible reasons influencing the compliance of products in various sectors. Erroneous test results, uncertainty in the applicable requirements and their interpretation; unclear responsibilities; equal understanding of safety issues and practices; suitable strategies for tackling differing requirements in several markets; local modification of the products and the awareness of these modifications are determined as reasons of possible non-compliances (Liepiņa and Korabļova 2014; Vasara and Kivistö-Rahnasto 2015).

As a result of the scientific articles analysis, multiple factors influencing the safety compliance of products have been identified: globalization, economy, behaviour, environment, information, manufacturing, new technology and process management (Baram 2007; Midler 2007; Coulibaly et al. 2008; Tang 2008; Rausand and Utne 2009; Berman and Swani 2010; Pyke and Tang 2010; Horaa et al. 2011; Maruchek et al. 2011; Xiulia et al. 2012; Fiegenwald et al. 2013; Walkington et al. 2013; Liepiņa and Korabļova 2014; Wogalter et al. 2014; Mrugalska and Tytyk 2015; Vasara and Kivistö-Rahnasto 2015; Mauborgne et al. 2016).

Additional factors were identified through the scientific articles analysis results validation by the focus group of six experts responsible for the market surveillance of non-food products. The role of the market surveillance and its effectiveness are identified as one of the key elements that influence the compliance of the product. The globalization process and the nature of the European Union market require a coordinated market surveillance approach.

There are various documents written by different authors and organizations that summarize best practices in the field of non-food market surveillance. The following are some of the examples available in the field:

- A Guide to Good Practice developed by the International Organization for Standardisation;
- The Best Practices Techniques, developed by the Product Safety Forum for Europe (hereafter—PROSAFE);
- The Update on the Market Surveillance Model Initiative, developed by the United Nations Economic Commission for Europe (hereafter—UNECE) Working Party on Regulatory Cooperation and Standardization Policies.

The purpose of these documents, taking into account the recognized differences among countries, is to harmonize the approaches to ensure an efficient and effective market surveillance process.

Fig. 17.3 Common criteria of the best practice techniques (created by the authors)

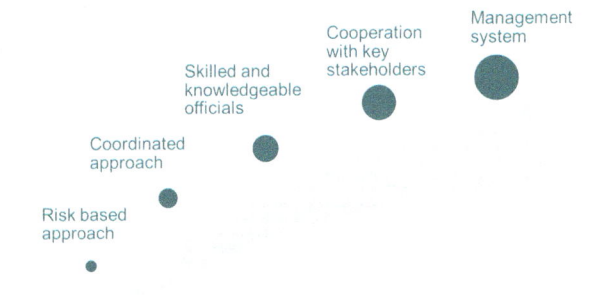

The analysis of the existing best practice techniques has identified the following common criteria (see Fig. 17.3).

- A risk-based approach to establish priorities and to allocate the available resources exactly where they are needed. A combination of a great number of products on the market and a lack of required resources place a significant importance on a strategically targeted approach to resource allocation to ensure greater efficiency. Effective and proportional corrective actions—products that are deemed dangerous to the public health and safety or provide any other risks to consumer interests should be withdrawn or recalled from the market. Such activities should be effective and proportional.
- A coordinated approach to the enforcement of corrective actions across jurisdictions. In the frame of globalization, it is crucial to have an effective exchange of information among the market surveillance authorities not only on domestic, regional but also international market surveillance.
- Skilled and knowledgeable market surveillance officials for the proper performance of the determined tasks.
- Cooperation with the key stakeholders. A greater awareness of rules and regulations by the consumers leads to a mechanism of market self-control as the consumers are demanding or requesting products to be in alignment with the key regulations. This approach will lead to a supply of products that are in conformance with the safety requirements as these are the products that consumers demand.
- A management system that allows evaluating the results and making necessary changes within the required timelines.
- A regulatory framework that ensures that the market surveillance authorities have the required powers to perform inspections. For example, during the International Product Safety Week 2016 that was launched in Brussels, it was mentioned that not all market surveillance authorities have the capacity to fully perform the required activities in relation to the products made available on the e-shops.

The global nature of business creates a significant challenge for the market surveillance authorities, which are limited by their jurisdictions, to trace the required information about each step of the manufacturing process. This leads us to the research completed by Hendrikx et al. (2016), which demonstrated that a greater budget does not mean a better market surveillance system. Therefore, it is not the budget but the effectiveness of the surveillance processes that leads to a better market surveillance system (Hendrikx et al. 2016).

The effectiveness depends on the following number of factors:

1. The quality and accuracy of information available on a particular topic such as data on injuries caused by non-food products and non-compliances found elsewhere which could be used for priority setting.
2. Resource availability such as human and financial resources, taking into account that the market surveillance authorities are outsourcing product testing to laboratories outside their own jurisdictions.
3. A communication and coordination mechanism among market surveillance authorities as well as other parties involved, such as notified bodies, conformity assessment bodies, customs authorities and media.
4. Another key element of effectiveness is the availability of enforcement procedures. Market surveillance without enforcement measures becomes an information gathering activity that does not change the behaviour in the market. (Wainwright 2014).

17.5 Conclusion

There are different approaches to market surveillance within each European Union Member State enforced internally and the situation is even more variable if we look outside the European Union. The environment of the open market and the free circulation of products that exist within the European Union require a more coordinated market surveillance approach, with common priorities and resources. There is a need to focus more on border control of products. The effective system for such controls should be created. The authors think that there is a need to evaluate the possibility of creating conformity assessment criteria on the basis of integrated management systems that could help economic operators, in particular importers, to evaluate the compliances of the imported products.

The growth of e-commerce and the development of new supply chains and remote storage facilities, often outside the jurisdiction of the European Union, will also require changes to the current market surveillance framework. The location of the manufacturer can also have an impact as products can be produced for markets other than the European Union, and countries can be producing more complex products, or using new technologies for the first time and it takes time to solve all the initial problems. In the framework of Global Value Chains and limited resources, there is a need for an effective model to improve the efficiency of the approach to market surveillance, and the switch from a product-based approach to the process-based one can be the right solution in this environment.

References

Ali, S., & Dadush, U. (2011). The rise of trade in intermediates: Policy implications. *International Economic Bulletin, 10*. Carnegie Endowment for International Peace, Retrieved from http://carnegieendowment.org/2011/02/10/rise-of-trade-inintermediates-policy-implications/458.

Baram, M. (2007). Liability and its influence on designing for product and process safety. *Safety Science, 45*(1), 11–30.

Berman, B., & Swani, K. (2010). Managing product safety of imported Chinese goods. *Business Horizons, 53*(1), 39–48.

Coulibaly, A., Houssin, R., & Mutel, B. (2008). Maintainability and safety indicators at design stage for mechanical products. *Computers in Industry, 59*(5), 438–449.

Disdier, A. C., Fontagne, L., & Mimouni, M. (2008). The impact of regulations on agricultural trade: Evidence from the SPS and TBT Agreements, *0063 bn'? 006CZm*.

European Commission Rapid Alert System (RAPEX) (2017). Retrieved from http://ec.europa.eu/consumers/consumers_safety/safety_products/rapex/alerts/main/?event=main.search.

Fiegenwald, V., Bassetto, S., & Tollenaere, M. (2013). Controlling non-conformities propagation in manufacturing. *International Journal of Production Research, 52*(14), 4118–4131.

Hendrikx, I., Tuneski, N., & Jovanoski, B. D. (2016). Dynamic simulations of market surveillance actions. In *2016 IEEE symposium on product compliance engineering (ISPCE)*, Anaheim, CA, pp. 1–6. https://doi.org/10.1109/ispce.2016.7492846.

Horaa, M., Bapuji, H., & Roth, A. V. (2011). Safety hazard and time to recall: The role of recall strategy, product defect type, and supply chain player in the U.S. toy industry. *Journal of Operational Management, 29*(7), 766–777.

Ibrahim, H. W., Zailani, S., & Tan, K. C. (2015). A content analysis of global supply chain research. *An International Journal, 22*(7), 1429–1462.

International Organization for Standardization (ISO) (2012). A guide to good practice principles and practices in product regulation and market surveillance. Retrieved from http://www.iso.org/iso/casco_guide.pdf.

Liepiņa, R., & Korabļova, L. (2014). Market surveillance of toys: Situation assessment and improvement. In *19th International scientific conference: Economics management 2014*, ICEM 2014.

Maruchek, A., Greis, N., Mena, C., & Cai, L. (2011). Product safety and security in the global supply chain: Issues challenges and research opportunities. *Journal of Operational Management, 29*(7), 707–720.

Mauborgne, P., Deniaud, S., Levrat, E., Bonjour, E., Micaëlli, J.-P., & Loise, D. (2016). Operational and system hazard analysis in a safe systems requirement engineering process—Application to automotive industry. *Safety Science, 87*(August), 256–268.

Meixell, M. J., & Gargeya, V. B. (2005). Global supply chain design: A literature review and critique. *Transportation Research Part E, 41*(6), 531–550.

Midler, P. (2007). Quality fad: China's great business challenge. Retrieved from http://knowledge.wharton.upenn.edu/article.cfm?articleid=1776.

Mrugalska, B., & Tytyk, E. (2015). Quality control methods for product reliability and safety. *Procedia Manufacturing, 3*(1), 2730–2737.

Official Website of the European Commission (2016a). Eurostat. Retrieved from http://ec.europa.eu/eurostat/tgm/table.do?tab=table&init=1&language=en&pcode=tps00001&plugin=1.

Official Website of the European Commission (2016b). List of National Market Surveillance Authorities by sector. Retrieved from http://ec.europa.eu/DocsRoom/documents/20322/attachments/1/translations/.

Official Website of the European Commission (2016c). List of National Market Surveillance Authorities by EU Country. Retrieved from http://ec.europa.eu/DocsRoom/documents/20321/attachments/1/translations/.

Official Website of the European Union (2016d). Living in the EU. Retrieved from https://europa.eu/european-union/about-eu/figures/living_en.

Organization for Economic Co-operation and Development (OECD) and the World Bank Group (2015). Policy options in trade and complementary areas for GVC integration by small and medium enterprises and low-income developing counties. Retrieved from https://www.oecd.org/trade/OECD-WBG-g20-gvc-report-2015.pdf.

Product Safety Forum of Europe (Prosafe) (2013). Best practices techniques in market surveillance. Retrieved from http://www.prosafe.org/index.php?option=com_zoo&task=item&item_id=1490&Itemid=270.

Pyke, D., & Tang, C. S. (2010). How to mitigate product safety risks proactively? Process, Challenges and Opportunities. *International Journal of Logistics Research and Application: A Leading Journal of Supply Chain Management, 13*(4), 243–256.

Rausand, M., & Utne, I. B. (2009). Product safety—Principles and practices in a life cycle perspective. *Safety Science, 47*(7), 939–947.

Regulation of 7 July 2008 No. 765/2008 of the European Parliament and of the Council setting out the requirements for accreditation and market surveillance relating to the marketing of product and repealing Regulation (EEC) No. 339/93. Retrieved from http://eur-lex.europa.eu/legal-content/EN/TXT/?uri=CELEX:32008R0765.

Ruiz-Torres, A. J., & Mahmoodi, F. (2008). Outsourcing decision in manufacturing supply chains considering production failure and operating costs. *An International Journal Integrated Supply Management, 4*(2), 141–158.

Singh, R. K., & Sharma, P. B. (2014). Development of framework for analyzing flexibility in supply chain. In M. K. Nandakumar et al. (Eds.), *Organisational flexibility and competitiveness, flexible system management.* India: Springer. https://doi.org/10.1007/987-81-322-1668-1_19.

Statistics Canada (2016). Retrieved from http://www.statcan.gc.ca/tables-tableaux/sum-som/l01/cst01/demo02a-eng.htm.

Tang, C. S. (2008). Making products safe: Process and challenges. *International Commerce Review, 8*(1), 48–55.

The Organization for Economic Co-operation and Development (OECD) Global Portal on Product Recalls. Retrieved from http://globalrecalls.oecd.org/.

van Tongeren, F., Beghin, J., & Marette, S. (2009). A cost-benefit framework for the assessment of non-tariff measures in agro-food trade. In *OECD Food, Agriculture, and Fisheries Working Paper 21,* OECD Publishing, Paris.

van Tongeren, F., Disdier, A. C., Ilicic-Komorowska, J., Marette, S., & von Lampe, M. (2010). Case studies of costs and benefits of non-tariff measures: Cheese, Shrimp, and Flowers. In: *OECD Food, Agriculture, and Fisheries Working Paper 28,* OECD Publishing, Paris.

Vasara, J., & Kivistö-Rahnasto, J. (2015). A qualitative examination of safety-related compliance challenges for global manufacturing. *Theoretical Issues in Ergonomics Science, 16*(4), 429–446.

Wainwright, N. (2014). Ten years of joint cross-border EMC market surveillance. But are products any more compliant? In *Proceeding of the 2014 international symposium on electromagnetic compatibility (EMC Europa 2014),* Gothenburg, Sweden, Sept 1–4, 2014.

Walkington, J., Sugavanam, S., & Nunns, S. R. (2013). One approach to functional safety assurance and safety lifecycle compliance. In *8th IET international system safety conference incorporating the cyber security conference 2013.*

Wogalter, M. S., Laughery, K. R., Vredenburgh, A. G., Deppa, S. W., Lueder, R., & Zackowitz, I. B. (2014). Child injury: Forensic human factors points to the need for better product designs and warnings. In *Proceeding of the Human Factors and Ergonomics Society 58th annual meeting*.

Working Party of Regulation Cooperation and Standardization Policies (2009). Market surveillance update on the market surveillance initiative draft guide to the use of the general market surveillance procedure. Retrieved from https://www.unece.org/fileadmin/DAM/trade/wp6/documents/2009/wp6_09_GMS_012E.pdf.

Xiulia, L., Baozhia, C., Yinglib, B., & Baohong, Z. (2012). Study on effect of product liability to inherent safety. *Procedia Engineering, 45,* 271–275.

Chapter 18
A Glimpse of Sustainable Electronics Manufacturing for India: A Study Using PEST-SWOT Analysis

Manoj Kumar Singh, Harish Kumar, M. P. Gupta and J. Madaan

Abstract The new business models, new technology, and innovations are the key pillars of organizational sustainability and profitability in any sector. Increasing industrialization and high competition among the firms create challenges to grow potentially and sustain it. The "best of technological solutions" and "enactments of new laws" are the key driving factors for sustainability in high-technology manufacturing industries in any country. The growth of electronics manufacturing industries (EMI) is very crucial for India and the government policies influencing the sector need proper interrogation for economic growth. This study explores the key factors to drive sustainability in EMI sector in India through the Political, Economic, Social and Technological (PEST) and Strength, Weakness, Opportunities, and Threat (SWOT) analysis. The findings suggest some internal and external factors which would be necessary for the growth of electronics manufacturing sector in a sustainable manner and to contribute effectively to Make in India campaign toward the nation building.

Keywords Economic growth · Electronics manufacturing industries (EMI)
Sustainability · SWOT analysis

M. K. Singh (✉) · H. Kumar · M. P. Gupta · J. Madaan
Department of Management Studies, Indian Institute of Technology Delhi,
New Delhi, India
e-mail: manojksiet@gmail.com

H. Kumar
e-mail: harishkr08@gmail.com

M. P. Gupta
e-mail: mpgupta@dms.iitd.ac.in

J. Madaan
e-mail: jmadaaniitd@gmail.com

© Springer Nature Singapore Pte Ltd. 2018
J. Connell et al. (eds.), *Global Value Chains, Flexibility and Sustainability*,
Flexible Systems Management, https://doi.org/10.1007/978-981-10-8929-9_18

18.1 Introduction

The manufacturing sector of India is facing serious challenges and is way behind world-class practices (Dangayach and Deshmukh 2003; Arnold et al. 2016). The sector is facing stiff competition due to imports and multinational companies. The manufacturing industries' growth rates are not highly persistent across time, which is in distinction with the evidence from developed countries (Mathew 2017). The competitors are equipped with the latest technology and have developed the capabilities of bringing new products in responsive manner and time frame (Chandra Pankaj 1998). The high-technology sectors like electronics manufacturing industries are also facing similar issues and challenges. In order to overcome the issues and challenges, adjustments in policies are required to gain sustainability and competitiveness.

The electronics industry of the country in initial phase was primarily dominated by the government or government undertakings or subsidiaries. Post implementation of the economic reforms of 1991, the country started the journey on capitalized line (Thakur et al. 2012). The reforms led to ease in foreign investment norms, allowing 100% FDI in almost all sectors, reduction in tariff structure, goods trade liberalization, etc.

The ecosystem created by the government has given impetus to the entrepreneurship and flexibility in government functioning. The flexibility imbibed is required for growth and sustainability of the industry (Sushil 2000; Momaya et al. 2017). The electronics manufacturing sector is influenced by other sectors, like automobile, information communication tools, etc., at the same time. The EMI has the potential for creating employment opportunities for semi-skilled and skilled manpower (Singh et al. 2016). Simultaneously, the EMI has a direct impact on the socioeconomic development of the country. The user-friendly electronics goods equipped with ICT resources can be used in e-learning, telehealth, and e-governance initiatives in both rural and urban areas (Gupta et al. 2004; Kumar et al. 2016), but the indigenous growth of electronics goods is at a nascent stage of development in the country.

18.2 Literature Review

The electronics manufacturing sectors are the fastest growing sector in the country. The government's recent policy announced in 2012 targeted a turnover of $400 Billion by 2020. On ease of doing business front, the initiatives taken are allowing 100% FDI through automatic route, capital subsidy, and availability of development assistance. In India, the electronics industry is classified into six segments namely consumer electronics (having huge market), industrial electronics, computers, components, communication and broadcasting. Presently, the manufacturing of electronics goods is around 1.31% of the global production, whereas in neighboring country China, the figure has increased from 17% in 2004 to 29.2% in 2012. With this current rate of production in our country, the demand and supply gap is estimated to reach $1200 Billion by 2020.

The consumption of Electronic Hardware in 2014–15 was $63.6 Billion, whereas imports accounted for 58% of the total consumption (NITI Aayog 2016). In India, most of the electronics products are available through imports only to complete the demand. Supply chain and reverse supply chain challenges are also significant and these challenges need to be addressed effectively to enhance the performance of EMI sector in India (Madaan and Wadhwa 2007; Tyagi et al. 2015). The demand for electronics goods is seen due to advancement of Information Communication Technology (ICT) infrastructure, increase in per capita income, consumer awareness, other government initiatives, high usage and availability of Internet including broadband connections and mobile phones and availability of high-end technology products at low cost.

The challenges faced by the country in hardware manufacturing are due to various reasons like the high cost of power available to industries, scarcity of finance, inadequate infrastructure, poor supply chain issues, etc. The latest or incumbent technology of EMI is replacing the existing technology and becoming a part of the system. The same is forcing organizations to migrate to the new technology platform in less time (Gupta and Jana 2003; Kume and Fujiwara 2016). Indian EMI are facing supply chain, infrastructure, and regulatory issues which are debilitating their competitiveness (Kaur et al. 2017). The major causes of increase in production cost are mainly high cost of power, finance, logistics, and raw material. Thereby, higher value addition increases the product costs. Thus, it is essential to recognize the need of EMI as a priority sector and facilitate the growth and sustainable development.

18.3 Methodology

The sustainability discussed in the research chapter has been taken from the perspective of manufacturing industry. Sustainability cannot be applied in a homogenous manner for all sectors of the economy. The context of sustainability is viewed and discussed in four domains namely political, economic, social, and technological. Industry deals with the context of external and internal factors. The external factors include outside stakeholders, operating business environment which are also analyzed by using a macro-environmental tool such as PEST. The internal context of the industry refers to its internal stakeholders, government roles and policies, consumer perspectives, capabilities, etc. (Pojasek 2013). The internal context is analyzed using the SWOT analyses. Both internal and external contexts in view of EMI are necessary in order to understand the challenges faced to attain the sustainability. The study applies PEST and SWOT analysis to assess the external and internal factors for EMI sector in India.

18.3.1 PEST Analysis

The PEST is an important tool and used before SWOT analysis. The PEST factors usually help in identifying the SWOT factors. PEST helps in assessing the external environment and emphasizes on factors such as market conditions, competitors, or business. The technique is used as a marketing tool, business assessment, and decision-making technique, whereas SWOT assess the internal factors for a business or a proposition (Ha and Coghill 2008). PEST tool helps in solving the unclear and complex problem in clear format using four perceptions that can help in improve decision-making processes. A PEST study can throw up light on vital problems, which one might miss otherwise (Peng and Nunes 2007). The PEST analysis is used in Table 18.1 to highlight important issues and concern of electronics manufacturing industries.

Table 18.1 PEST analysis of electronics manufacturing industries

Political	Economic
• Environmental issues and resource consumptions • Prevailing and upcoming legislations • International legislation like WTO • National and international regulatory bodies • Government policies on manufacturing sector • Trading policies • Domestic market lobbying/international pressure groups • Wars and conflicts • Foreign policy • Recent government initiative "Make in India" for manufacturing industries	• Economic growth of country • Growth of different sectors in the country • GDP of the country • Overseas economies and trends • Capital funding, grants, and initiatives • Tax structure • Seasonality/natural calamities • Trade and market cycles • Industry-specific factors • Interest and exchange rates' effect on the sector • International trade/monetary issues/rating agencies
Social	Technology
• Purchasing power • Living standards • Demographics • Consumer attitudes and opinions • Laws in existence • Brand power, company, technology image • Major events/festival • Buying access and trends • Marketing, advertising, and publicity • Ethical issues	• Research and development funding • Competing technology advances • Technology dependence • Replacement technology/solutions • Manufacturing capacity • Information and communication technology • E-commerce technology • Technology policy • Innovations/patents • Intellectual property rights issues

18.3.2 SWOT Analysis

The SWOT analysis has used the acronyms Strengths, Weaknesses, Opportunities and Threats (Piercy and Giles 1989; Kearns 1992). The SWOT helps in providing a clear framework for the business plan, and reviewing direction and strategy of an organization (Lee et al. 2000). Therefore, SWOT analysis is utilized to address the following basic questions for electronics industries:

- What is the strength of an EMI in the prevailing atmosphere?
- What are the opportunities available in EMI for the investors and entrepreneurs for doing business?
- What are the weaknesses of an EMI in the prevailing business conditions?
- What are the threats to the investors or the entrepreneurs in EMI for doing business?

18.4 Findings and Discussion

PEST analysis has been performed to understand the political, economic, social, and technological factors, which affect the EMI sector externally (Table 18.1).

The SWOT analysis was performed for EMI sector after PEST analysis for assessing the Strengths, Weakness, Opportunities and Threats. The SWOT analysis (Table 18.2) explores the various factors for business and industrial improvements.

The PEST factors are compared with the SWOT factors. Table 18.3 analyses the external factors with the internal factors for EMI sector. This provides an in-depth analysis of the current situation of EMI sector in India.

The PEST tool explores the political, economic, social, and technological dimensions of the country. The focus of the country on manufacturing sector including the high-technology sector makes a way out for the sustainability of the EMI. Simultaneously, Make in India initiatives of the government have given the impetus to the investors and entrepreneurs. Make in India initiatives could help in driving the latest technology and investments in the country if implemented seriously, which may enhance the technological capability of the country. Recently announced new electronics policy focuses on creating a talent pool in the field of electronics, from design to testing and manufacturing. The government will simultaneously boost the research and development in electronics by creating a better human resource in the electronics industry. The investors including the FDIs are being encouraged and motivated by incentives such as benefits in tax, discounts on infrastructure and machinery expenditure, and ease in procedural hurdles. India's rising per capita income and improvements in living standards have created a huge demand for high-technology goods which further makes India a huge lucrative market, so that both investors and consumers are mutually benefited.

By doing the SWOT analysis, several factors relevant to EMI were identified and the conclusion drawn from the applied methodology is that the rising figure of foreign investments, raising per capita income, huge market demand, and low-cost

Table 18.2 SWOT analysis of electronics manufacturing industries

Strengths	Weaknesses
• Availability of cheap labor • Availability of skilled and technically qualified manpower • Huge market potential • Matured electronics component industry • Better political environment • Rising income • High capability in software skills • Growing foreign investment • Ease of doing business • Recently taken initiatives like Make in India, Digital India, Skill India, etc.	• Poor IPR management and piracy • Poor supply chain coordination • Weak infrastructure • Focus on small components' manufacturing • Focus on assembling of components • Poor investment in R&D • Nonavailability of land • Poor coordination between central and regional governments • Low level of motivation for entrepreneurs • Failure to establish the "Brand Name" • Digital inequalities
Opportunities	Threats
• Huge market opportunities • Better investment opportunities (investment incentives, tax holidays) • Increased contract manufacturing • Export benefits/incentives • Stable political environment • Rapid growth in mobile subscriber penetration • Encouragement of domestic manufacturing • New policies and reforms to encourage more investment into the sector • India emerging as a center for chip design services	• Dependence on imported goods, raw material, and key components • Low level of technological innovations • Poor technology forecasting • WTO agreements • Free trade agreements with countries (ASEAN) • Power shortage in country • Competition from countries like China, Taiwan, and South Korea • Rising infrastructure costs • Currency fluctuations • Global economic slowdown • Low prices of electronics goods

accessibility of manpower are the main driving factors for EMI in India. At the same time the factors giving threat and weakness need to be addressed effectively, then only the objectives of sustainability of EMI can be implemented.

The literature supports the functioning of "clusters" of EMI connected vertically and horizontally. Supplier and manufacturing industries gain substantial advantages in terms of coordination within clusters, as they produce inputs that are widely used and are important to innovation or upgradation. The basic-operating norm on which clusters are established is "Collaborating while competing", providing a supportive ecosystem.

The agreements of WTO and free trade agreements raise the global competition in zero duty regimes. The cluster concept offers manufacturing-friendly ecosystem and competitive environment for the domestic industry. The cluster increases the productivity, innovation, customization, joint ventures initiatives, economies of scale, and the environmental safety standards and reduces the unproductive and input raw material costs in the industry segment (Dhir and Sushil 2017). It is simultaneously observed that the customers get the advantage of technology and

18 A Glimpse of Sustainable Electronics Manufacturing for India …

Table 18.3 Summary of PEST and SWOT analysis of EMI in India

SWOT/PEST	Strength (S)	Weakness (W)	Opportunities (O)	Threats (T)
Political aspect (P)	• National and international regulatory bodies • Make in India campaign for manufacturing promotion • New manufacturing policy, 2011 • New electronics policy, 2012	• Strict labor laws • Land issues • Weak relation between state and central government. • Different priorities of state and central government • Government commitment for capital return • Wider gaps in policy making and implementing agency • Poor resource consumption	• Foreign direct investment through automatic route • Time-bound framework for project approval/ implementation	• Restriction from opponent parties • Cheap manufacturing in foreign country • Internal treaties (WTO agreements) • War and conflict • Domestic market lobbying/ international pressure groups
Economic aspect (E)	• Rising income of citizens • Better economic environment • Low inflation • Location advantage • Incentives for investment in manufacturing • Huge domestic demand • Market and trade cycles	• Low investments in infrastructure • Inverted duty structure on in-house produced goods • Difficult exit mechanisms • Poor supply chain coordination of components • Poor ecosystem for business • Raw material availability	• Boosting Special economic zones • Lower interest rate loan for manufacturers/ entrepreneurs • More share in GDP contribution • Schemes like M-SIPS should be extended up to 2020 • Cluster formation	• Overseas economies and trends • Legal issues • Raising imports of goods • Depreciation in Indian rupees • Domestic vendors not inspired (e.g., Karbonn or Micromax) by government schemes • International monetary issues
Social aspect (S)	• Cheap labor • Huge market potential • Different demographics conditions	• Unskilled labor • Low labor mobility • Regulations of working conditions	• Training programs for labors • Employment opportunities for youth • Effective planning system	• Low-level e-waste public perception • Laws affecting social issues

(continued)

Table 18.3 (continued)

SWOT/PEST	Strength (S)	Weakness (W)	Opportunities (O)	Threats (T)
Technological aspect (T)	• Technological absorption • Raising no. of technological agreements	• Dependent on technological know-how of high-end products • Low expenditure on R&D	• Consumer opinion for new product/service design • Technology image • Potential for technological innovations • Sustainable investment in green technologies	• Foreign superior technology • High-end technological innovations • Digital inequalities

information at an optimized cost. A set of standard indicators (Table 18.4) have been chosen to map the growth and targets of EMI, which lead to the sustainable development of manufacturing industries.

Further, some suggestions have been drawn based on Tables 18.3 and 18.4 in order to attain the sustainability of EMI sector in India (Fig. 18.1).

Indian EMI sector could be sustainable in terms of the political environment, if government processes are transparent, government policies are innovative, the role of state and central government are clearly defined, wisely consumption of available resources and some flexible labor laws enhance the ease of doing business.

In terms of the economic environment for the growth of EMI sector, India should be efficient in quality infrastructure, develop special economic zones, use renewable energy source, mobilizing the funds, effective waste management, and producing quality product at low cost with high manufacturing productivity. EMI sector may also be improved via formation of industrial clusters, effective trade cycle, and growth of various sectors which consume the electronics products.

Social aspects of EMI sector could be improved by focusing on customers' needs, predicting market potential, opportunities for employment, and quality of life. Social and ethical values are also having a significant impact on the growth of electronics industries. The organizations should also be focusing on cutting the pollution level in their manufacturing cycles.

EMI competitiveness and quality of products/services could be enhanced by using world-class high- end technology, which also improves the technological capability of the organizations. Industries must focus on recycling of electronics waste. Innovative and new products can attract more customers for a longer period of time. Hence, increase the market capability of the organizations.

Table 18.4 Indicators for sustainable development from the electronics manufacturing perspectives

Indicators for EMI sector
• Competitiveness proofing (competitiveness proofing is a reinforced analysis of the impacts of new policy proposals)
• Focus on research and innovations of electronics products and manufacturing
• Recycle of electronics waste for the conservation of material
• Collaborative research taken up by the firms
• Customer centric
• Operational excellence
• Technological capability
• Human resource management
• Financial management (capability to mobilize funds)
• Mergers and acquisitions
• Deliver the quality goods at low cost
• Performance of manufacturing industry
• Usage of nonconventional sources of energy by industries

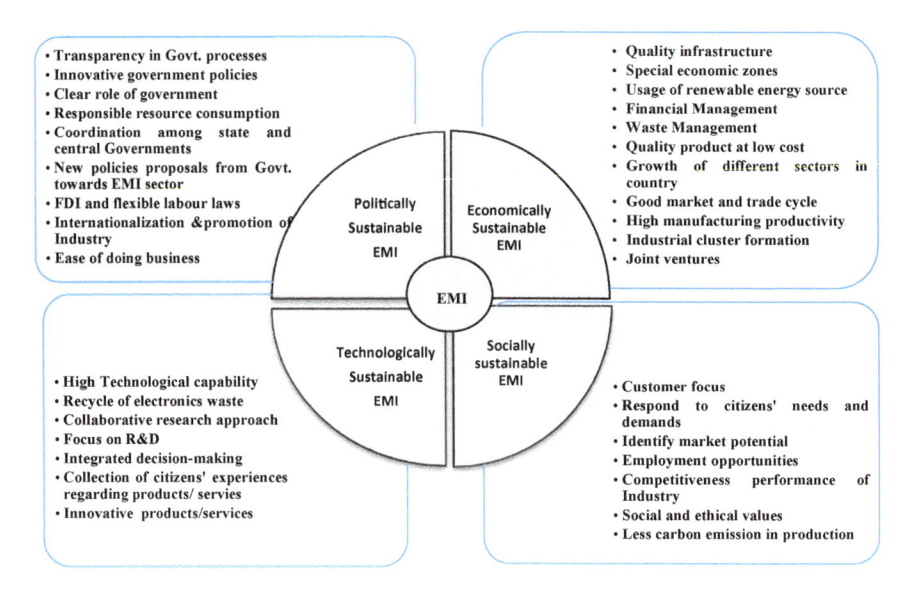

Fig. 18.1 Conceptual framework for the sustainable growth and development for EMI sector

18.5 Conclusions and Recommendations

The sustainability is a crucial issue in a manufacturing organization. The study identifies the position of EMI in the perspective of its growth and investment through PEST and SWOT analysis. Sustainability in EMI sector could be mainly addressed by improving government policies and coordination, FDI, better economic environment, product design according to market demand, regulating working conditions, and using advanced technological solutions for manufacturing.

Apart from these, the sector's weakness can be removed by taking strong decisions on land, labor, and good relation between center and states governments. The gaps in policies and uncertainty in policies implementations are hindering the competitiveness of the EMI sector. Some of the initiatives have been taken through the "Make in India" campaign for developing better environment, joint ventures, and strengthening the manufacturing industries. The decision on FDI and the timeline of the projects can enhance the sustainability of the electronics industries associated with threats like WTO agreements and cheaper manufacturing offered from neighboring countries.

References

Arnold, J. M., Javorcik, B., Lipscomb, M., & Mattoo, A. (2016). Services reform and manufacturing performance: Evidence from India. *The Economic Journal, 126*(590), 1–39.

Chandra Pankaj, T. S. (1998). Competitiveness of Indian manufacturing. *Vikalpa, 12*(3), 25–36.

Dangayach, G. S., & Deshmukh, S. G. (2003). Evidence of manufacturing strategies in Indian industry: A survey. *International Journal of Production Economics, 83*(3), 279–298.

Dhir, S., & Sushil, (2017). Flexibility in modification and termination of cross-border joint ventures. *Global Journal of Flexible Systems Management, 18*(2), 139–151.

Gupta, M., & Jana, D. (2003). E-government evaluation: A framework and case study. *Government Information Quarterly, 20*(4), 365–387.

Gupta, M. P., Kumar, P., & Bhattacharya, J. (2004). *Government online: Opportunities and challenges*. New Delhi: Tata McGraw-Hill.

Ha, H., & Coghill, K. (2008). E-government in Singapore—A swot and pest analysis. *Asia-Pacific Social Science Review, 6*(2), 103–130.

http://www.makeinindia.com/. Retrieved August 31, 2016.

Kaur, S. P., Kumar, J., & Kumar, R. (2017). The relationship between flexibility of manufacturing system components, competitiveness of SMEs and business performance: A study of manufacturing SMEs in Northern India. *Global Journal of Flexible Systems Management, 18*(2), 123–137.

Kearns, K. P. (1992). From comparative advantage to damage control: Clarifying strategic issues using SWOT analysis. *Nonprofit Management & Leadership, 3*(1), 3–22.

Kumar, H., Singh, M. K., & Gupta, M. P. (2016, September) Smart governance for smart cities: A conceptual framework from social media practices. In *Conference on e-Business, e-Services and e-Society* (pp. 628–634). Springer International Publishing.

Kume, K., & Fujiwara, T. (2016). Production flexibility of real options in daily supply Chain. *Global Journal of Flexible Systems Management, 17*(3), 249–264.

Lee, S. F., Lo, K. K., Leung, R. F., & Sai On Ko, A. (2000). Strategy formulation framework for vocational education: Integrating SWOT analysis, balanced scorecard, QFD methodology and MBNQA education criteria. *Managerial Auditing Journal, 15*(8), 407–423.

Madaan, J., & Wadhwa, S. (2007). Flexible process planning approaches for sustainable decisions in reverse logistics system. *Global Journal of Flexible Systems Management, 8*(4), 1–8.

Mathew, N. (2017). Drivers of firm growth: Micro-evidence from Indian manufacturing. *Journal of Evolutionary Economics, 27*(3), 585–611.

Momaya, K. S., Bhat, S., & Lalwani, L. (2017). Institutional growth and industrial competitiveness: Exploring the role of strategic flexibility taking the case of select institutes in India. *Global Journal of Flexible Systems Management, 18*(2), 111–122.

NITI Aayog, Government of India. (2016, May). *Make in India strategy for electronic products*.

Peng, G. C. A., & Nunes, M. B. (2007) Using PEST analysis as a tool for refining and focusing contexts for information systems research. In *6th European Conference on Research Methodology for Business and Management Studies*, ECRM 2007, July 9th–10th, 2007, Lisbon, Portugal. Academics Conference International (pp. 229–236).

Piercy, N., & Giles, W. (1989). Making SWOT analysis work. *Journal of Marketing Intelligence & Planning, 7*(5/6), 5–7.

Pojasek, R. B. (2013). Organizations and their contexts: Where risk management meets sustainability performance. *Environmental Quality Management, 22*(3), 81–93.

Singh, M. K., Kumar, H., Gupta, M. P., & Madaan, J. (2016, September). The social media cone: Towards achieving the manufacturing competitiveness goals. In *Conference on e-Business, e-Services and e-Society* (pp. 53–58). Springer International Publishing.

Sushil, S. (2000). Concept of systemic flexibility. *Global Journal of Flexible Systems Management, 1*(1), 77–88.

Thakur, B., Gupta, R., & Singh, R. (2012). Changing face of India's industrial policies: A look. *International Journal of Scientific and Research Publication, 2*(12), 1–7.

Tyagi, M., Kumar, P., & Kumar, D. (2015). Assessment of critical enablers for flexible supply chain performance measurement system using fuzzy DEMATEL approach. *Global Journal of Flexible Systems Management, 16*(2), 115–132.

Chapter 19
Selection of Sustainable Suppliers

Pravin Kumar and Rajesh Kumar Singh

Abstract Due to the growing importance of environment and sustainability in global business, organizations are trying their best to make their production systems sustainable. Today, the focus is not only on individual production systems, but also on sustainability issues in the supply chain. In the supply chain network, organizations are forced to streamline their purchasing activities in order to be competitive in the global market. To manage the purchasing activities proficiently, the selection process of sustainable suppliers has become very important. Initially, the cost was one of the important factors for supplier evaluation, but due to increasing competition and globalization of the business activities, the cost of a product has already been standardized in the market and other factors such as quality, flexibility, reliability, geographical location, market share, sustainability, etc., have become more prominent in supplier evaluation. Presently, the market is highly volatile due to uncertainty in demand, short product life cycle, increasing awareness of customers regarding product quality, cost, technology, etc. In this situation, the role of a supplier in supply chain becomes crucial to meet the market uncertainty in terms of volume and variety. The buyers expect that suppliers should be sustainable in terms of cost, quality, flexibility, and green operations. In this chapter, an approach to select sustainable suppliers has been illustrated. The performances of suppliers are evaluated using fuzzy TOPSIS (Technique for Order Preference by Similarity to Ideal Solution). TOPSIS is an outranking method in which decision-making units are rated against the criteria and evaluated by finding closeness to the ideal solution.

P. Kumar (✉)
Department of Mechanical Engineering, Delhi Technological University,
Delhi 110042, India
e-mail: pravin.papers@gmail.com

R. K. Singh
Operations Management Area, Management Development Institute (MDI),
Gurgaon 122007, Haryana, India
e-mail: rksdce@yahoo.com

This chapter may help managers to incorporate multiple decision makers in the decision-making process. In addition to this, the linguistic vagueness of the decision makers can be captured in terms of the inputs.

Keywords Flexibility · Fuzzy sets · Green operations · Multi-criteria decision-making · Supplier selection · TOPSIS

19.1 Introduction

According to Elkington (1998), sustainability is the triple bottom line theory of combining environmental, social, and economic aspects into the organizational decision-making by utilizing the resources of today without damaging the needs of future generations. With the decline of the natural environment, e.g., declining raw material resources, excess waste sites, and growing levels of pollution, the significance of sustainable supply chain management (SSCM) has increased (Srivastava 2007; Singh et al. 2016; Chhabra et al. 2017). Ahi and Searcy (2013) defined sustainable supply chain management as including various aspects of social, economic, and environmental sustainability into supply chain management. Sustainable supply chain management (SSCM) can be also defined as integrating environmental thinking into supply chain management processes, including product design, material sourcing and selection, manufacturing processes, delivery of the final product to the consumers, as well as the end-of-life management of the product after its useful life.

Shen et al. (2013) and Govindan et al. (2013a, b) observed that suppliers are the main link for achieving social, environmental, and economic gains and executing sustainable supply chain initiatives. Thus, for a sustainability-focused supply chain, sustainable supplier selection (SSS) is a crucial strategic choice in the management (Amindoust et al. 2012), and needs to be analyzed systematically for execution of sustainability in the supply chains (Grimm et al. 2016). In the present context, supplier selection process has become more complex and dynamic due to the imposition of the policy related to pollution control and environmental management. Wolf and Seuring (2010) reported the awareness of consideration of environmental factor as a major criterion for supplier selection, considering some cases from the industry. Weber et al. (1991) reviewed and classified 74 related articles for the criteria and supplier selection processes which have appeared since 1966. Kumar et al. (2008, 2011) and Singh et al. (2010) have also worked on the supplier selection, considering the optimization of the total value of purchase as one of the objectives in quota allocation problem. The strategic or long-term partnership with the supplier has become a general trend in the modern business. Therefore, to maintain a long-term relationship and meet the competition in the market, a buyer is required to develop its suppliers technically and financially (Pal et al. 2013).

A number of criteria and methods have already been tested in the past research for an effective supplier selection. In spite of a lot of work available in this area, the supplier selection problem has been an area of interest for researchers and practitioners. In this chapter, some of the common criteria/attributes have been considered for evaluation of suppliers' performance and a rank has been produced. The rating of suppliers with respect to the criteria is based on fuzzy sets. Fuzzy logic has been used here to translate the linguistic inputs of the decision makers into numeric or quantitative values. The rest of the chapter has been arranged as follows: Sect. 19.2 reviews the past work done on supplier selection; Sect. 19.3 demonstrates the methodology used for supplier selection; Sect. 19.4 represents the case illustration; and Sect. 19.5 draws the conclusions.

19.2 Literature Review

The organization's operations are evaluated by the principles of Environmental Management Systems (EMS), which describe policies, procedures, and audit protocols to enhance the environmental performance. Under strict environmental regulations, the International Organization for Standardization (ISO) 14000 series driven by stakeholders, community or regulators is one of the most recognized EMS (Nawrocka et al. 2009). These standards were prepared to develop an extensive method for standardizing and managing the main environmental tools like that of life-cycle assessment (ISO 2010; Prajogo et al. 2012). All supply chain members are affected indirectly to select more environmental-friendly practices by ISO 14001. According to Nawrocka et al. (2009), Azevedo et al. (2011), Eltayeb et al. (2011), Xu et al. (2013), and Kumar et al. (2017a, b), systematic approach based on ISO 14001 reduces negative environmental effects of organizations, decreases resource consumption and waste, and contributes to quality improvement.

The positive effects of green practices are described by the green performance of the supplier on the organization's natural environment. According to Eltayeb et al. (2011) and Zhu and Sarkis (2004), reduction in liquid/solid wastes, emissions, energy utilization, hazardous and toxic materials, and improvement in employee and community health are main factors for analyzing green performance. Enhancement of organization image and community relations, environment-related plans and actions are also included in management performance measures (Lin 2013). It is observed that green practices positively affect performance (Zhu and Sarkis 2004; Montabon et al. 2007).

In literature, different researchers have addressed the various features of green and sustainability-related supplier decisions. Walton et al. (1998) determined green strategy in the supply chain of five furniture companies. They observed that most of the times the companies used ecological criterion for designing any supply chain network. Hsu and Hu (2009) in their supplier selection process suggested speculative substance management to lessen environmental degradation. Based on performance, a model that assesses the factors to select a green supplier was proposed (Lee et al. 2009). Shaw et al. (2012) have analyzed a model for supplier selection decisions linked to carbon emissions. The performance of the supplier related to carbon management issues was analyzed by a model proposed by Hsu et al. (2013). The two most influencing criteria in supplier selection were "carbon information" and "training related to carbon management". Shen et al. (2013) have considered nine green supplier criteria with respect to their environmental performance. To evaluate green supplier development programs, a two-step (performance criteria and green criteria) supplier evaluation framework was proposed (Akman 2015). Bai and Sarkis (2014) proposed a model based on sustainability factors to analyze supplier selection decisions. Amindoust et al. (2012) captured three criteria and eight sub-criteria in their ranking model for evaluating the supplier selection in a sustainable supply chain context. Govindan et al. (2013a, b) proposed a model where organizations can implement sustainability by recognizing and ranking opportunities in their supply chain activities. Grimm et al. (2014) have observed that the involvement of strategic business partners has a positive result to manage sub-suppliers' compliance with corporate sustainability standards (SCCSS).

From 2000 to 2008, the basis for the supplier evaluation and selection were reviewed through the literature (Ho et al. 2010). It was observed that the most accepted criterion was quality, followed by delivery, price/cost, manufacturing capability, service, management, technology, research and development, finance, flexibility, reputation, relationship, risk, and safety and environment (Ho et al. 2010; Kumar et al. 2013). Currently, sustainable supplier selection models presume that development is not explicitly given the sustainability capabilities. For improving sustainability capabilities, investments in suppliers may be necessary. In the development of their sustainability capabilities, the level of training, equipment, organizational, or knowledge sharing may differ for all the suppliers. According to Genovese et al. (2013), Govindan et al. (2013b), sustainability integration into supplier selection is still in the nascent stage, therefore a framework for sustainable suppliers' election is needed. It can be beneficial to both practitioners and researchers. There has been significant discussion related to supplier selection studies for improving the supplier capabilities with regard to enhancing their environmental performance (Govindan et al. 2013a; Kumar et al. 2014; Jia et al. 2015). Different aspects in sustainable supplier selection may be price, lead-time, quality, speed, delivery performance, reliability, greenhouse effect, reusability, CO_2 emission, carbon footprinting, etc.

Sustainable supplier selection is a multi-criteria decision-making problem and is integrated with all the purchasing and demand fulfillment decisions. Ting and Cho (2008) used an integrated method of AHP and MOLP for supplier selection considering various quantitative and qualitative attributes. Kayakutulu and Buyukozkan (2011) analyzed the performance factors for logistics-related activities in a value chain. Product postponement is a strategy to provide flexibility in the production of variants of products as per requirement of the markets. Saghiri and Hill (2014) have reported the impact of supplier relationships on product postponement strategy. For best-class logistics network, the delivery time reduction is the real element while the flexibility in service, accuracy in order fulfillment, and on-time delivery are the prerequisites (Bottani and Rizzi 2006; Sushil 2014; Mangla et al. 2014). Framework for flexibility in supply chain was proposed by Singh and

Sharma (2014). It was found by Mason-Jones and Towill (1998) that most companies were working with relatively same machines, technology, and expertise. To establish world-class enterprise, it is most important to have the time compression strategies. According to Kumar and Singh (2012), the delivery of the right products on a timely basis and accurately to the customer is the main function of the supplier. The need of flexibility in supply chain operations was emphasized by Sharma et al. (2010). Agility is an important parameter of the performance of a manufacturing company and agility cannot be achieved without integration of suppliers in the design and manufacturing activities. Kumar et al. (2017a, b) determined the agility index of an automobile company using graph theory and interpretive structural modeling approach. Kumar et al. (2011) have already summarized the various criteria for supplier selection in the research work, including Abratt (1986), Billesbach et al. (1991), Dickson (1996), and Chan and Kumar (2007).

For sustainable supply chain partnership, selecting suppliers is a complex process (Sarkis and Dhavale 2015). To measure the technical, environmental, and eco-efficiency standards of suppliers, a model was proposed by Mahdiloo et al. (2015). Su et al. (2016) concluded that the recycle/reuse/reduce options are the top criterion for supplier selection to improve sustainable supply chain management (SSCM). A research framework to determine the ability of sub-suppliers to attain compliance with sustainability standards was proposed by Grimm et al. (2016). They analyzed that from a quantitative study perspective, it is very difficult to measure sub-suppliers compliance with the main business organization's corporate sustainability standards.

Among three dimensions—social, economic, and environmental, environmental dimension achieved maximum priority in the study by Luthra et al. (2017). A supplier selection mechanism was proposed based on product transportation distance by Yu et al. (2016). In product transportation distance, total transportation distance covered from the assembly of raw materials to the designing of the final product during the lifetime of a product is recorded. The researchers analyzed that during supplier selection, both the commercial and environmental dimensions had an effective incentive mechanism in the supply chain network of transportation to reduce CO_2 emissions. Trapp and Sarkis (2016) proposed an optimization model for simultaneous supplier selection and development within environmental sustainability reference using binary integer programming.

To improve the environmental performance, the policy maker should sometimes subsidize suppliers (Xie 2016). For all three "pillars" of sustainability, i.e., energy efficiency (environment), consumer surplus (society), and the profits of organizations (economy), there does not exist a single best cooperative strategy. By making parameter adjustments like enhancing price, lowering the supplier's share of instinct demand potential and lowering the manufacturer's fixed cost, the energy efficiency can be improved. For sustainable supply chain management, Song et al. (2017) proposed a framework for supplier selection. Based on a systematic review of sustainable supplier selection criteria a pair-wise comparison method, DEMATEL, and rough set theory have been proposed. This method analyzed the critical criteria affecting the performance of sustainable supplier selection. For obtaining optimal cluster of sustainable suppliers the precision of DE (Differential Evolution) and MODE (Multi-Objective Differential Evolution) were obtained by Jauhthe integrated approach of fuzzyar and Pant (2017).

The performance of the supplier is a key element in a company's success or failure. To attain the goals of low cost, consistent high quality, flexibility and quick response, companies have increasingly considered better vendor-selection approaches. The overall goal of selection is to identify high-potential suppliers and their optimum quota allocations (Singh et al. 2010). An effective and appropriate vendor selection method is, therefore, very crucial to the competitiveness of companies (Singh et al. 2008). In this chapter, economic and environmental sustainability have been considered as the supplier selection criteria.

19.3 Research Methodology

A number of research methodologies have been reported in the literature related to supplier selection. Bevilacqua et al. (2006) and Kumar et al. (2011) proposed and illustrated a decision model for supplier selection based on Total Quality Management (TQM) tool such as QFD and fuzzy logic. Among the other approaches, Qureshi et al. (2009) used graph theoretic approach and matrix method under fuzzy environment for a selection of logistics service providers. Jain et al. (2009) summarized the criteria and strategic supplier selection process and reviewed a number of research papers. Hasan et al. (2008) used Analytic Network Process (ANP) and Data Envelopment Analysis (DEA) for supplier selection in an agile manufacturing environment. Rajan et al. (2007) presented a multi-phase decision-making model to evaluate and select a set of vendors for a specified set of products with respect to product prioritization and customer expectations. Wu et al. (2009) emphasized the supplier selection with bundling problem using ANP and MIP (Mixed Integer Programming). Kumar and Singh (2012) used the integrated approach of fuzzy AHP and TOPSIS for 3PL selection in a supply chain. Thus, a number of mathematical tools have been applied for such types of the multi-criteria decision-making problems. In this chapter, three decision makers have been involved for a rating of the suppliers. They rated the suppliers on the linguistic scale and it has been further converted into a quantitative scale for the mathematical analysis. A fuzzy TOPSIS is used to rank the suppliers. Technological service flexibility dimensions were evaluated by Kumar et al. (2017a, b) of Internet Malls.

After the review of sustainable supplier selection criteria, only broad criteria have been included in this chapter. The importance of these criteria with the support of few industrial buyers is rated on the linguistic scale (further converted into the fuzzy scale). On the fuzzy scale with the help of the buyers with respect to all criteria, the shortlisted suppliers are again rated based on their performance. The following subsection discusses the calculation of the final ratings of the suppliers using fuzzy TOPSIS.

19.3.1 Fuzzy Sets

Definition 1 Let X be a universe set. The fuzzy set $\tilde{A}$ is defined by a membership function $\mu_{\tilde{A}}(x) = [0, 1]$, where $\mu_{\tilde{A}}(x)$, $\forall x \in X$, indicates the degree of membership of $\tilde{A}$ to X.

Definition 2 A triangular fuzzy number $\tilde{A}$ is defined as (a^l, a^y, a^u), $a^l \leq a^y \leq a^u$. The membership function $\mu_{\tilde{A}}(x)$ is defined by

$$\mu_{\tilde{A}}(x) = \begin{cases} 0, & x \leq a^l \\ \frac{x-a^l}{a^y-a^l}, & a^l < x < a^y \\ \frac{a^u-x}{a^u-a^y}, & a^y < x < a^u \\ 0, & x \geq a^u. \end{cases} \qquad (19.1)$$

Definition 3 The distance between two fuzzy numbers (Chen 2000; Li and Yang 2004) especially in Electre method can be represented by

$$d(\tilde{A}, \tilde{B}) = \sqrt{\frac{\sum_{k=1}^{3}(A_k - B_k)^2}{3}}. \qquad (19.2)$$

19.3.2 Fuzzy TOPSIS

A number of variants of TOPSIS method have been in use for the decision-making process. In this chapter, the concept of decision-making with the help of fuzzy TOSPSIS has been taken from the research work of Chen (2000). From the given area of research and based on the expert's opinion in the recent past, Fuzzy TOPSIS has been a popular research tool. Having fuzzy values ensures to take realistic values (Kumar and Dash 2017).

Step 1: Preparation of fuzzy decision matrix: To prepare a fuzzy decision matrix of "m" alternatives and "n" attributes, fuzzy importance of the attributes are determined at first. The decision makers are given different weightages on the basis of their experience and level in organization hierarchy, e.g., the first, second, and third decision makers among the three are assigned with the weights 40, 35, and 25% respectively. After deciding the weights for the decision makers, the fuzzy importance of attributes is decided by a weighted average of the ratings of attributes by the decision makers using following formula:

$$\tilde{w}_j = \frac{1}{K}\left(\sum_{k=1}^{3} \tilde{w}_{jk}\right), \qquad (19.3)$$

where $k = 1, 2, \ldots K$ is the number of decision makers, $j = 1, 2, \ldots n$ is the number of attributes, and $\tilde{W}_{jk}$ is the importance of jth attributes assigned by kth decision makers.

After deciding the importance of the attributes, various alternatives are rated against each attribute by all the K decision makers and the final fuzzy rating of alternatives is determined by weighted average using following formula:

$$\tilde{x}_{ij} = \frac{1}{K}\left(\sum_{k=1}^{3} \tilde{x}_{ijk}\right), \tag{19.4}$$

where $k = 1, 2, \ldots K$ is the number of decision makers, $i = 1, 2, \ldots m$ is the number of alternatives, $j = 1, 2, \ldots n$ is the number of attributes, and $\tilde{x}_{ijk}$ is the rating of ith alternative against the jth attributes by kth decision maker.

The decision matrix can be represented as

$$\tilde{U} = \begin{array}{c} \\ \\ \\ \\ \end{array} \begin{matrix} \tilde{W}_1 & \tilde{W}_2 & \ldots & \tilde{W}_n \end{matrix} \\ \begin{bmatrix} \tilde{x}_{11} & \tilde{x}_{12} & \ldots & \tilde{x}_{1n} \\ \tilde{x}_{21} & \tilde{x}_{22} & \ldots & \tilde{x}_{2n} \\ . & . & \ldots & . \\ \tilde{x}_{m1} & \tilde{x}_{m2} & \ldots & \tilde{x}_{mn} \end{bmatrix}. \tag{19.5}$$

Step 2: Preparation of normalized decision matrix: A linear-scale normalization is applied to ensure that all values in the elements in the decision matrix have homogeneous and comparable units. Moreover, this transformation guarantees that every triangular fuzzy number belongs to [0, 1], which reduces the complexity of the mathematical operations. The normalized fuzzy decision matrix is shown below

$$\tilde{R} = [\tilde{r}_{ij}]_{m \times n} \tag{19.6}$$

$$\tilde{r}_{ij} = \left(r_{ij}^l, r_{ij}^\gamma, r_{ij}^u\right) = \left(\frac{x_{ij}^l}{c_j^*}, \frac{x_{ij}^\gamma}{c_j^*}, \frac{x_{ij}^u}{c_j^*}\right)$$
$$c_j^* = \max_i(x_{ij}^u), \ j \in B, \tag{19.7}$$

where B is the set of benefit attributes, $i = 1, 2 \ldots, m$ and $j = 1, 2, \ldots, n$.

$$\tilde{r}_{ij} = \left(r_{ij}^l, r_{ij}^\gamma, r_{ij}^u\right) = \left(\frac{a_j^-}{x_{ij}^u}, \frac{a_j^-}{x_{ij}^\gamma}, \frac{a_j^-}{x_{ij}^l}\right)$$
$$a_j^- = \min_i(x_{ij}^l), \ j \in C, \tag{19.8}$$

where C is the set of cost attributes, $i = 1, 2 \ldots, m$ and $j = 1, 2, \ldots, n$.

Step 3: Compute the weighted normalized matrix: Multiply the standard rating of the alternatives with the importance of corresponding attributes to compute the weighted normalized matrix using the following formula:

$$\tilde{v}_{ij} = (\tilde{r}_{ij}) \times (\tilde{w}_j) = \left(r_{ij}^l, r_{ij}^y, r_{ij}^u\right) \times \left(w_j^l, w_j^y, w_j^u\right). \quad (19.9)$$

Step 4: Positive and negative ideal solutions and closeness to ideal solution: Chen (2000) extended the TOPSIS method to the fuzzy group multi-attribute decision-making under fuzzy environments. The distances and closeness coefficient used.

$$d(x_i, x^+) = \sum_{j=1}^{n} d(\tilde{v}_{ij}, \tilde{a}_j^+) = \sum_{j=1}^{n} \sqrt{\frac{\left(1-v_{ij}^l\right)^2 + \left(1-v_{ij}^y\right)^2 + \left(1-v_{ij}^u\right)^2}{3}},$$

$$d(x_i, x^-) = \sum_{j=1}^{n} d(\tilde{v}_{ij}, \tilde{a}_j^-) = \sum_{j=1}^{n} \sqrt{\frac{\left(v_{ij}^l\right)^2 + \left(v_{ij}^y\right)^2 + \left(v_{ij}^u\right)^2}{3}},$$

and

$$C(x_i) = \frac{d(x_i, x^-)}{d(x_i, x^+) + d(x_i, x^-)}, \quad (19.10)$$

where x^+ and x^- are the fuzzy ideal solution and the fuzzy negative ideal solution, whose weighted normalized fuzzy vectors are $\tilde{a}_j^+ = (1, 1, 1, 1, 1, 1)^T$ and $\tilde{a}_j^- = (0, 0, 0, 0, 0, 0)^T$, respectively. $C(x_i)$ is closeness to the ideal solution.

19.4 Case Illustration

In this research, an automobile manufacturing company was consulted for performance evaluation and selection of auto component suppliers. Three decision makers at the managerial level were involved in the rating of suppliers. These decision makers are concerned with purchasing of auto components and supplier relationship management. The weightage of their individual decision is given as per their level of responsibilities in the company. The main criteria chosen for the supplier evaluation are cost, quality, flexibility services, market share, and green performance. Cost covers all the costs such as transportation cost, material cost, manufacturing cost, etc. Quality is related to the quality of product and services including certification and awards received by the supplier. Flexibility is related to the ability to change the order size, design of product, order time, and delivery time as per requirement of the buyer. Services are concerned with the variety of services provided by the supplier such as logistics, warehousing facility, post sales services, etc. Market share of the supplier shows its reputation in the market. Green performance is concerned with the effort applied by the supplier for cleaner and green production. Multiple dimensions such as green product design and development, processes, materials which are related to recyclable and reusable, carbon emissions, energy consumption, etc., are included in the green performance.

A linguistic scale is used to find the importance of the criteria. The triangular fuzzy number (TFN) is used to convert the linguistic scale into the quantitative scale as shown in Table 19.1.

Similarly, a linguistic scale and fuzzy scales are used to rate the suppliers with respect to all the benefit criteria as shown in Table 19.2.

A different scale is used to rate the supplier with respect to the cost criteria as shown in Table 19.3.

A weighted average of the rating of importance of criteria is calculated as shown in Table 19.4.

Table 19.1 Linguistic and fuzzy scales used for the importance of the criteria

Linguistics and fuzzy importance weight of criteria	
Very very low (VVL)	(1, 1, 3)
Low (L)	(1, 3, 5)
Medium (M)	(3, 5, 7)
High (H)	(5, 7, 9)
Very high (VH)	(7, 9, 9)

Table 19.2 Linguistic and fuzzy scales used for the rating of the suppliers w.r.t. benefit criteria

Linguistics and fuzzy rating scale for alternatives	
Poor (P)	(1, 1, 3)
Satisfactory (S)	(1, 3, 5)
Good (G)	(3, 5, 7)
Very good (VG)	(5, 7, 9)
Excellent (EX)	(7, 9, 9)

Table 19.3 Linguistic and fuzzy scales used for the rating of the suppliers w.r.t. cost criteria

Linguistics and fuzzy rating scale for alternatives	
Very low (VL)	(1, 1, 3)
Low (W)	(1, 3, 5)
Medium (M)	(3, 5, 7)
High (H)	(5, 7, 9)
Very high (VH)	(7, 9, 9)

19 Selection of Sustainable Suppliers

Table 19.4 Weighted average of importance rating of criteria

Criteria	Linguistic importance rating of criteria			Fuzzy rating
	D1 (0.4)	D2 (0.35)	D3 (0.25)	
C1 (cost)	H	H	VH	(1.83, 2.5, 3)
C2 (quality)	VH	VH	H	(2.17, 2.83, 3)
C3 (flexibility)	VH	H	VH	(2.1, 2.61, 3)
C4 (services)	H	H	VH	(1.83, 2.5, 3)
C5 (market share)	H	M	H	(1.43, 2.1, 2.76)
C6 (green performance)	M	H	M	(1.23, 1.9, 2.56)

After deciding the fuzzy weightage of the criteria, the rating of the suppliers by all the three decision makers was recorded as shown in Table 19.5.

With the help of Eq. (19.4) and Table 19.5, a decision matrix is prepared as shown in Table 19.6.

Now, normalization is required to bring the entire measurement on one scale, i.e., 0–1. Normalization is done using Eqs. (19.6)–(19.8) and a normalized decision matrix is produced as shown in Table 19.7.

Now weights of all the criteria are multiplied with the corresponding ratings of the suppliers (Eq. 19.9) in the normalized decision matrix as shown in Table 19.8.

Table 19.5 Rating of suppliers w.r.t. various criteria

Criteria	Decision makers	A1	A2	A3	A4	A5
C1	D1	H	M	H	H	M
	D2	H	M	H	H	M
	D3	H	H	H	H	M
C2	D1	S	P	G	S	S
	D2	S	S	VG	S	S
	D3	G	S	G	P	S
C3	D1	P	P	S	VG	G
	D2	P	S	S	G	S
	D3	S	S	S	G	S
C4	D1	G	G	S	G	G
	D2	S	G	S	G	G
	D3	G	G	P	G	VG
C5	D1	G	VG	VG	G	G
	D2	G	G	VG	G	VG
	D3	G	VG	VG	S	G
C6	D1	S	G	S	G	S
	D2	S	S	P	VG	S
	D3	P	P	S	VG	G

Table 19.6 Decision matrix

Criteria	A1	A2	A3	A4	A5
C1	(1.67, 2.33, 3)	(1.16, 1.83, 2.5)	(1.67, 2.33, 3)	(1.67, 2.33, 3)	(1.0, 1.67, 2.33)
C2	(0.5, 1.16, 2.67)	(0.33, 0.73, 1.4)	(1.23, 1.9, 2.56)	(0.33, 0.83, 1.5)	(0.33, 1, 1.67)
C3	(0.33, 0.5, 1.16)	(0.33, 0.73, 1.4)	(0.33, 1.0, 1.67)	(1.26, 1.93, 2.6)	(0.6, 1.26, 1.93)
C4	(0.76, 1.43, 2.1)	(1.0, 1.67, 2.33)	(0.33, 0.83, 1.5)	(1.0, 1.67, 2.33)	(1.16, 1.83, 2.5)
C5	(1.0, 1.67, 2.33)	(1.43, 2.1, 2.76)	(1.67, 2.33, 3)	(0.83, 1.5, 2.16)	(1.23, 1.9, 2.56)
C6	(0.33, 0.83, 1.5)	(0.6, 1.1, 1.76)	(0.33, 0.76, 1.43)	(1.4, 2.06, 2.73)	(0.5, 1.16, 2.67)

$a_1 = 1, c_2^* = 2.67, c_3^* = 2.6, c_4^* = 2.5, c_5^* = 3, c_6^* = 2.73$

Table 19.7 Normalized decision matrix

Criteria	A1	A2	A3	A4	A5
C1	(0.33, 0.43, 0.6)	(0.4, 0.54, 0.86)	(0.33, 0.43, 0.6)	(0.3, 0.43, 0.6)	(0.43, 0.6, 1.0)
C2	(0.19, 0.43, 1.0)	(0.12, 0.27, 0.52)	(0.46, 0.71, 0.99)	(0.13, 0.31, 0.56)	(0.12, 0.37, 0.62)
C3	(0.13, 0.19, 0.43)	(0.13, 0.28, 0.54)	(0.13, 0.38, 0.64)	(0.48, 0.74, 1.0)	(0.23, 0.48, 0.74)
C4	(0.3, 0.57, 0.84)	(0.4, 0.67, 0.93)	(0.13, 0.33, 0.6)	(0.4, 0.67, 0.93)	(0.46, 0.73, 1.0)
C5	(0.33, 0.56, 0.78)	(0.48, 0.7, 0.92)	(0.56, 0.78, 1.0)	(0.28, 0.5, 0.72)	(0.41, 0.63, 0.85)
C6	(0.12, 0.3, 0.55)	(0.22, 0.4, 0.64)	(0.12, 0.28, 0.52)	(0.51, 0.75, 1.0)	(0.18, 0.42, 0.98)

Finally, the distances of the alternatives, i.e., suppliers are measured from the negative and positive ideal solutions using Eq. (19.10). Finally, the closeness to the ideal solution is calculated using Eq. (19.10) as shown in Table 19.9.

Thus, the rank of suppliers is decided on the basis of the closeness to the ideal solution $C(A_j)$. The value very close to one is superior in the performance. Hence, the rank of the supplier is given below as

A4 > A2 > A3 > A1 > A5

The most efficient supplier is A4 since it is closest to the ideal solution, i.e., 1, then A2 has the second rank, A3 has the third rank, A1 has the fourth rank, and A5 has the fifth rank. Using the fuzzy TOPSIS we can rank the suppliers based on their performance.

Table 19.8 Weighted normalized matrix

Criteria	A1	A2	A3	A4	A5
C1	(0.6, 1.1, 1.8)	(0.73, 1.35, 2.58)	(0.6, 1.1, 1.8)	(0.6, 1.1, 1.8)	(0.78, 1.5, 3)
C2	(0.41, 1.21, 3)	(0.26, 0.76, 1.56)	(1.0, 2.0, 3.0)	(0.26, 0.84, 1.68)	(0.26, 1.04, 1.86)
C3	(0.27, 0.49, 1.29)	(0.27, 0.73, 1.62)	(0.27, 1.0, 1.92)	(1.0, 1.93, 3)	(0.48, 1.25, 2.22)
C4	(0.55, 1.42, 2.52)	(0.73, 1.67, 2.79)	(0.23, 0.82, 1.8)	(0.73, 1.67, 2.79)	(0.84, 1.82, 3)
C5	(0.47, 1.17, 2.15)	(0.68, 1.47, 2.53)	(0.8, 1.63, 2.76)	(0.4, 1.05, 1.98)	(0.58, 1.32, 2.34)
C6	(0.14, 0.57, 1.4)	(0.27, 0.76, 1.63)	(0.14, 0.53, 1.33)	(0.63, 1.42, 2.56)	(0.22, 0.8, 2.5)

Table 19.9 Closeness to the ideal solution

	A1	A2	A3	A4	A5
$d(A_j, A^-)$	7.976004	8.492303	8.573633	9.441831953	9.915194
$d(A_j, A^+)$	4.555993	4.705679	4.820588	5.137727623	5.697466
$C(A_j)$	0.636451	0.643455	0.640099	0.647607488	0.635074

19.5 Conclusion

For survival of the business in global markets, organizations are trying to make whole value chain sustainable in terms of social, economical and environmental factors. Majorly problems happen due to inbound part of the supply chain. Therefore, to improve the effectiveness of inbound supply chains, selection of suppliers based on sustainability measures is very important. In this chapter, some of the shortlisted auto component suppliers are ranked on the basis of sustainability measures. Different measures considered for ranking of sustainable suppliers are cost, quality, flexibility, services, market share, and green performance.

Green performance consists of multiple dimensions such as green process and product design, selection of green raw materials, carbon emissions and energy consumptions, etc. The uniqueness of this approach is to incorporate the vagueness in decision-making which can be represented in the form of a linguistic scale. The linguistic scale is not a crisp scale which can be easily converted into the quantitative scale. Thus, in this case, fuzzy sets are very helpful. TOPSIS is used to find the order preference of the suppliers and fuzzy extended TOPSIS is able to incorporate the vagueness in decision-making. This integrated tool may help the managers to find the preference order of alternatives, not only in the case of supplier selection but also in many other cases in which more than one alternative are available, like project selection, facility location, the hiring of people, selection of sources of energy, market selection, etc. The acceptability of the methodology is very high because it may be integrated with AHP (Analytical Hierarchy Process), QFD (Quality Function Deployment), ANP (Analytic Network Process), etc. This approach can be applied to other similar situations such as selection of location, processes, technologies, etc., as the future scope of the study. This study may be further expanded after considering more sustainability factors for supplier selection. These factors may also be prioritized on the basis of their importance for sustainability.

Acknowledgements The authors would like to thank editors of the book and reviewers for their valuable comments to improve quality and content of this chapter.

References

Abratt, R. (1986). Industrial buying in high-tech markets. *Industrial Marketing Management, 15*(4), 293–298.

Ahi, P., & Searcy, C. (2013). A comparative literature analysis of definitions for green and sustainable supply chain management. *Journal of Cleaner Production, 52*(August), 329–341.

Akman, G. (2015). Evaluating suppliers to include green supplier development programs via fuzzy C-means and VIKOR methods. *Computer and Industrial Engineering, 86*(August), 69–82.

Amindoust, A., Ahmed, S., Saghafinia, A., & Bahreininejad, A. (2012). Sustainable supplier selection: A ranking model based on fuzzy inference system. *Applied Soft Computing, 12*(6), 1668–1677.

Azevedo, S. G., Carvalho, H., & Machado, V. C. (2011). The influence of green practices on supply chain performance: A case study approach. *Transportation Research Part E, 47*(6), 850–871.

Bai, C. A., & Sarkis, J. (2014). Determining and applying sustainable supplier key performance indicators. *Supply Chain Management: An International Journal, 19*(3), 275–291.

Bevilacqua, M., Ciarapica, F. E., & Giacechetta, G. (2006). A fuzzy-QFD approach to supplier selection. *Journal Purchasing and Supply Management, 12*(1), 14–27.

Billesbach, T. J., Harrison, A., & Croom-Morgan, S. (1991). Supplier performance measures and practices in JIT companies in the US and the UK. *International Journal of Purchasing and Material Management, 27*(4), 24–28.

Bottani, E., & Rizzi, A. (2006). A fuzzy TOPSIS methodology to support outsourcing of logistics services. *Supply Chain Management: An International Journal, 11*(4), 294–308.

Chan, F. T. S., & Kumar, N. (2007). Global supplier development considering risk factors using fuzzy extended AHP-based approach. *Omega: International Journal of Management Science, 35*(4), 417–431.

Chen, C. T. (2000). Extensions of the TOPSIS for group decision-making under fuzzy environment. *Fuzzy Sets and Systems, 114*(1), 1–9.

Chhabra, D., Garg, S. K., & Singh, R. K. (2017). Analyzing alternatives for green logistics in an Indian automotive organization: A case study. *Journal of Cleaner Production, 167*(November), 962–969. https://doi.org/10.1016/j.jclepro.2017.02.158.

Dickson, G. W. (1996). An analysis of vendor selection systems and decisions. *Journal of Purchasing, 2*(1), 5–17.

Elkington, J. (1998). Partnerships from cannibals with forks: The triple bottom line of 21st-century business. *Environmental Quality Management, 8*(1), 37–51.

Eltayeb, T. K., Zailani, S., & Ramayah, T. (2011). Green supply chain initiatives among certified companies in Malaysia and environmental sustainability: Investigating the outcomes. *Resources, Conservation and Recycling, 55*(5), 495–506.

Genovese, A., Lenny Koh, S. C., Bruno, G., & Esposito, E. (2013). Greener supplier selection: State of the art and some empirical evidence. *International Journal of Production Research, 51*(10), 2868–2886.

Govindan, K., Khodaverdi, R., & Jafarian, A. (2013a). A fuzzy multi criteria approach for measuring sustainability performance of a supplier based on triple bottom line approach. *Journal of Cleaner Production, 47*(May), 345–354. https://doi.org/10.1016/j.jclepro.2012.04.014.

Govindan, K., Rajendran, S., Sarkis, J., & Murugesan, P. (2013b). Multi criteria decision making approaches for green supplier evaluation and selection: A literature review. *Journal of Cleaner Production, 98*(July), 66–83. https://doi.org/10.1016/j.jclepro.2013.06.046.

Grimm, J. H., Hofstetter, J. S., & Sarkis, J. (2014). Critical factors for sub-supplier management: A sustainable food supply chains perspective. *International Journal of Production Economics, 152*(June), 159–173. https://doi.org/10.1016/j.ijpe.2013.12.011.

Grimm, J. H., Hofstetter, J. S., & Sarkis, J. (2016). Exploring sub-suppliers' compliance with corporate sustainability standards. *Journal of Cleaner Production, 112*(Part 3), 1971–1984. https://doi.org/10.1016/j.jclepro.2014.11.036.

Hasan, A. M., Shankar, R., & Sarkis, J. (2008). Supplier selection in an agile manufacturing environment using data envelopment analysis and analytical network process. *International Journal of Logistics Systems and Management, 4*(5), 523–550.

Ho, W., Xu, X. W., & Dey, P. K. (2010). Multi-criteria decision making approaches for supplier evaluation and selection: A literature review. *European Journal of Operational Research, 202*(1), 16–24.

Hsu, C. W., & Hu, A. H. (2009). Applying hazardous substance management to supplier selection using analytic network process. *Journal of Cleaner Production, 17*(2), 255–264.

Hsu, C. W., Kuo, T. C., Chen, S. H., & Hu, A. H. (2013). Using DEMATEL to develop a carbon management model of supplier selection in green supply chain management. *Journal of Cleaner Production, 56*(October), 164–172. https://doi.org/10.1016/j.jclepro.2011.09.012.

ISO Survey. (2010). http://www.iso.org/iso/iso-survey2010.pdf.

Jain, V., Benyoucef, L., & Deshmukh, S. G. (2009). Strategic supplier selection: Some emerging issues and challenges. *International Journal of Logistics Systems and Management, 5*(1/2), 61–88.

Jauhar, S. K., & Pant, M. (2017). Integrating DEA with DE and MODE for sustainable supplier selection. *Journal of Computational Science, 21*(July), 299–306. https://doi.org/10.1016/j.jocs.2017.02.011.

Jia, P., Govindan, K., Choi, T. M., & Rajendran, S. (2015). Supplier selection problems in fashion business operations with sustainability considerations. *Sustainability, 7*(2), 1603–1619.

Kayakutulu, G., & Buyukozkan, G. (2011). Assessing performance factors for a 3PL in a value chain. *International Journal of Production Economics, 131*(2), 441–452.

Kumar, A., & Dash, M. K. (2017). Using fuzzy Delphi and generalized fuzzy TOPSIS to evaluate technological service flexibility dimensions of internet malls. *Global Journal of Flexible Systems Management, 18*(2), 153–161.

Kumar, D. T., Palaniappan, M., Kannan, D., & Shankar, K. M. (2014). Analyzing the CSR issues behind the supplier selection process using ISM approach. *Resources, Conservation and Recycling, 92*(November), 268–278. https://doi.org/10.1016/j.resconrec.2014.02.005.

Kumar, P., Shankar, R., & Yadav, S. S. (2008). An integrated approach of analytic hierarchy process and fuzzy linear programming for supplier selection. *International Journal of Operational Research, 3*(6), 614–631.

Kumar, P., Shankar, R., & Yadav, S. S. (2011). Global Supplier Selection and Order Allocation using FQFD and MOLP. *International Journal of Logistics Systems and Management, 9*(1), 43–68.

Kumar, P., & Singh, R. K. (2012). A fuzzy AHP and TOPSIS methodology to evaluate 3PL in a supply chain. *Journal of Modelling in Management, 7*(3), 287–303.

Kumar, P., Singh, R. K., & Kumar, R. (2017a). An integrated framework of interpretive structural modeling and graph theory matrix approach to fix the agility index of an automobile manufacturing organization. *International Journal of Systems Assurance Engineering and Management, 8*(1), 342–352. https://doi.org/10.1007/s13198-015-0350-x.

Kumar, R., Singh, R. K., & Shankar, R. (2013). Study on coordination issues for flexibility in supply chain of SMEs: A case study. *Global Journal of Flexible Systems Management, 14*(2), 81–92.

Kumar, P., Singh, R. K., & Vaish, A. (2017b). Suppliers' green performance evaluation using fuzzy extended ELECTRE approach. *Clean Technologies and Environmental Policy, 19*(3), 809–821. https://doi.org/10.1007/s10098-016-1268-y.

Lee, A. H., Kang, H. Y., Hsu, C. F., & Hung, H. C. (2009). A green supplier selection model for high-tech industry. *Expert Systems with Applications, 36*(4), 7917–7927.

Li, D.-F., & Yang, J.-B. (2004). Fuzzy linear programming technique for multi-attribute group decision making in fuzzy environments. *Information Sciences, 158*(January), 263–275. https://doi.org/10.1016/j.ins.2003.08.007.

Lin, R. J. (2013). Using fuzzy DEMATEL to evaluate the green supply chain management practices. *Journal of Cleaner Production, 40*(February), 32–39. https://doi.org/10.1016/j.jclepro.2011.06.010.

Luthra, S., Govindan, K., Kannan, D., Mangla, S. K., & Garg, C. P. (2017). An integrated framework for sustainable supplier selection and evaluation in supply chains. *Journal of Cleaner Production, 140*(Part 3), 1686–1698. https://doi.org/10.1016/j.jclepro.2016.09.078.

Mahdiloo, M., Saen, R. F., & Lee, K. H. (2015). Technical, environmental and ecoefficiency measurement for supplier selection: An extension and application of data envelopment analysis. *International Journal of Production Economics, 168*(October), 279–289. https://doi.org/10.1016/j.ijpe.2015.07.010.

Mangla, S. K., Kumar, P., & Barua, M. K. (2014). Flexible decision approach for analysing performance of sustainable supply chains under risks/uncertainty. *Global Journal of Flexible Systems Management, 15*(2), 113–130.

Mason-Jones, R., & Towill, D. (1998). Time compression in supply chain: Information management is the vital ingredients. *Logistics Information Management, 11*(2), 93–104.

Montabon, F., Sroufe, R., & Narasimhan, R. (2007). An examination of corporate reporting, environmental management practices and firm performance. *Journal of Operations Management, 25*(5), 998–1014.

Nawrocka, D., Brorson, T., & Lindhqvist, T. (2009). ISO 14001 in environmental supply chain practices. *Journal of Cleaner Production, 17*(16), 1435–1443.

Pal, O., Gupta, A. K., & Garg, R. K. (2013). Supplier selection criteria and methods in supply chains: A review. *International Journal of Social, Behavioral, Educational, Economic and Management Engineering, 7*(10), 1395–1401.

Prajogo, D., Tang, A. K. Y., & Lai, K. (2012). Do firms get what they want from ISO 14001 Adoption? An Australian perspective. *Journal of Cleaner Production, 33*(September), 117–126. https://doi.org/10.1016/j.jclepro.2012.04.019.

Qureshi, M. N., Kumar, P., & Kumar, D. (2009). Selection of logistics services provider (LSP) under fuzzy environment: A graph-theoretic and matrix approach. *International Journal of Logistics Systems and Management, 5*(5), 551–573.

Rajan, A. J., Rao, K. S., & Ganesh, K. (2007). VEPCE: Decision-making model for vendor evaluation with respect to product prioritization and customer expectation. *International Journal of Logistics Systems and Management, 3*(1), 34–55.

Saghiri, S., & Hill, A. (2014). Supplier relationship impacts on postponement strategies. *International Journal of Production Research, 52*(7), 2134–2153.

Sarkis, J., & Dhavale, D. G. (2015). Supplier selection for sustainable operations: A triple bottom-line approach using a bayesian framework. *International Journal of Production Economics, 166*(August), 177–191. https://doi.org/10.1016/j.ijpe.2014.11.007.

Sharma, M. K., Sushil, & Jain, P. K. (2010). Revisiting flexibility in organizations: Exploring its impact on performance. *Global Journal of Flexible Systems Management, 11*(3), 51–68.

Shaw, K., Shankar, R., Yadav, S. S., & Thakur, L. S. (2012). Supplier selection using fuzzy AHP and fuzzy multi-objective linear programming for developing low carbon supply chain. *Expert Systems with Applications, 39*(9), 8182–8192.

Shen, L., Olfat, L., Govindan, K., Khodaverdi, R., & Diabat, A. (2013). A fuzzy multi criteria approach for evaluating green supplier's performance in green supply chain with linguistic preferences. *Resources, Conservation and Recycling, 74*(May), 170–179. https://doi.org/10.1016/j.resconrec.2012.09.006.

Singh, R. K., Garg, S. K., & Deshmukh, S. G. (2008). Challenges and strategies for competitiveness of SMEs: A case study. *International Journal for Services and Operations Management, 4*(20), 181–200.

Singh, R. K., Kumar, P., & Gupta, V. (2010). Fuzzy statistical approach for vendor selection in supply chain. *International Journal of Logistics Systems and Management, 7*(3), 286–301.

Singh, R. K., Rastogi, S., & Aggarwal, M. (2016). Analyzing the factors for implementation of green supply chain management. *Competitiveness Review, 26*(3), 246–264.

Singh, R. K., & Sharma, P. B. (2014). Development of framework for analyzing flexibility in supply chain. In *Organizational flexibility and competitiveness, flexible systems management* (pp. 273–283). New Delhi: Springer.

Song, W., Xu, Z., & Liu, H. C. (2017). Developing sustainable supplier selection criteria for solar air-conditioner manufacturer: An integrated approach. *Renewable and Sustainable Energy Reviews, 79*(November), 1461–1471. https://doi.org/10.1016/j.rser.2017.05.081.

Srivastava, S. K. (2007). Green supply-chain management: A state-of-the-art literature review. *International Journal of Management Reviews, 9*(1), 53–80.

Su, C. M., Horng, D. J., Tseng, M. L., Chiu, A. S., Wu, K. J., & Chen, H. P. (2016). Improving sustainable supply chain management using a novel hierarchical grey-DEMATEL approach. *Journal of Cleaner Production, 134*(Part-B), 469–481.

Sushil, (2014). The concept of a flexible enterprise. In Sushil & E. A. Stohr (Eds.), *The flexible enterprise, flexible systems management* (pp. 3–26). New Delhi: Springer.

Ting, S.-C., & Cho, D. I. (2008). An integrated approach for supplier selection and purchasing decisions. *Supply Chain Management: An International Journal, 13*(2), 116–127.

Trapp, A. C., & Sarkis, J. (2016). Identifying robust portfolios of suppliers: A sustainability selection and development perspective. *Journal of Cleaner Production, 112*(Part 3), 2088–2100. https://doi.org/10.1016/j.jclepro.2014.09.062.

Walton, S. V., Handfield, R. B., & Melnyk, S. A. (1998). The green supply chain: Integrating suppliers into environmental management processes. *Journal of Supply Chain Management, 34*(2), 2–11.

Weber, C. A., Current, J. R., & Benton, W. C. (1991). Vendor selection criteria and methods. *European Journal of Operational Research, 50*(1), 2–18.

Wolf, C., & Seuring, S. (2010). Environmental impacts as buying criteria for third party logistical services. *International Journal of Physical Distribution & Logistics Management, 40*(1/2), 84–102.

Wu, W.-Y., Sukoco, B. M., Li, C.-Y., & Chen, S. H. (2009). An integrated multi-objective decision making process for supplier selection with bundling problem. *Expert Systems with Applications, 36*(2), 2327–2337.

Xie, G. (2016). Cooperative strategies for sustainability in a decentralized supply chain with competing suppliers. *Journal of Cleaner Production, 113*(February), 807–821. https://doi.org/10.1016/j.jclepro.2015.11.013.

Xu, L., Mathiyazhagan, K., Govindan, K., Haq, A. N., Ramachandran, N. V., & Ashokkumar, A. (2013). Multiple comparative studies of green supply chain management: Pressures analysis. *Resources, Conservation and Recycling, 78*(September), 26–35. https://doi.org/10.1016/j.resconrec.2013.05.005.

Yu, F., Xue, L., Sun, C., & Zhang, C. (2016). Product transportation distance based supplier selection in sustainable supply chain network. *Journal of Cleaner Production, 137*(November), 29–39. https://doi.org/10.1016/j.jclepro.2016.07.046.

Zhu, Q., & Sarkis, J. (2004). Relationships between operational practices and performance among early adopters of green supply chain management practices in Chinese manufacturing enterprises. *Journal of Operations Management, 22*(3), 265–289.

Chapter 20
Flexible Waste Management Practices in Service Sector: A Case Study

Aarti Singh and Sushil

Abstract Dynamics of global environment can be achieved in service sector by managing waste in the service sector organizations. This chapter highlights the role of waste management in service sector organizations, specifically in the hotel industry. In this chapter, waste management in the hotel industry has been analyzed through a case study, wherein Situation–Actor–Process and Learning–Action–Performance (SAP–LAP), SAP–LAP linkages, Total Interpretive Structural Modelling (TISM) and Flowing Stream Strategy (FSS) have been used to conduct the waste management case study in a hotel. In SAP framework, situation includes the present scenario of waste management practice followed in the hotel. Actors are the participants that affect the situation, and on the basis of SAP–LAP, analysis has been performed. TISM is used for identifying the driving and dependent factors in the hotel waste management. The final outcome of TISM model has been analyzed through FSS and SAP–LAP linkages framework. The outcome of chapter provides the roadmap of waste management scenario in the hotel, which explains the waste management strategies in term of FSS elements, i.e. raise, maintain and reduce.

Keywords FSS · SAP–LAP · SAP–LAP linkages · Service sector
TISM · Waste management

20.1 Introduction

In service sector organizations, waste management is an important criterion, which makes the organizations sustainable. Various waste management processes have been adopted to regulate the waste generation in an organization. Reduce, Reuse,

---

A. Singh (✉) · Sushil
Department of Management Studies, Indian Institute of Technology Delhi,
Vishwakarma Bhawan, Shaheed Jeet Singh Marg, New Delhi 110016, India
e-mail: singhaartij@gmail.com

Sushil
e-mail: sushil@dms.iitd.ac.in; profsushil@gmail.com

Recycle and Recover are the main processes used for managing waste in organizations, which are also known as the 4 R's of waste management. These waste management processes have been regulated by implementing new tools and adopting new technologies for managing waste in the service sector organizations (Lee 2001; Zotos et al. 2009). In this chapter, the hotel industry has been chosen as the service sector organization for analyzing waste management processes. As hotel industry is the best service sector which contributes to the economy of the nation by providing its services to tourists, at the same time it also generates different types of waste (Shanklin et al. 1991). The hotel industry also affects the environment by consuming a high amount of energy, food, water and other resources. This huge consumption of resources generates energy waste, food waste, water and gaseous effluents (Erdogan and Baris 2007). Such extensive category of waste can be managed by appropriate planning, processing and policing (APAT 2002; Trung and Kumar 2005; Mensah 2006). In India, there is a systematic chain of hotels which promote tourism by providing facilities to their customers without compromising their waste management and sustainability (Lee 2001). Hence, in this chapter, waste management in the hotel industry has been analyzed through a case study, where a five-star sustainable hotel has been chosen for studying waste management practices in the hotel. A fictitious name, Indian Hotel Limited (IHL) has been given to the hotel because of confidentiality issues. However, the data used here is original.

The objectives of this chapter are as follows:

- To analyze the hotel in term of waste management through mixed method analysis, where the verified waste management factors were analyzed by TISM followed by FSS partially.
- To develop a SAP–LAP framework in the case hotel.
- To analyze various linkages between SAP–LAP elements.

20.2 Waste Management in Hotels

Hotels being the essential part of the tourism industry, consume a large amount of durable and non-durable goods for providing food, services and hospitality to the customers (Bohdanowicz and Martinac 2007). During the consumption of resources, hotels generate waste which affects the surrounding environment. This indicates that waste management is a necessary process of hotel management. It has also been revealed by various researchers that hotels adopt waste management practices for maintaining sustainability and to protect the environment (Kumar 2005; Mensah 2006). Thus, hotels have well-defined waste management and sustainability policies. However, strict norms and continuous follow-up practices are required to manage waste and protect the adjacent environment. These environmental protection and waste management practices solely depend on the hotel's top management (Dewhurst and Thomas 2003; Bohdanowicz 2005; Le et al. 2006; Radwan et al. 2012). The waste management practices in the form of solid waste management technologies and energy audits affect the economy of hotels. Accordingly, operating and installation costs are a major decision-making factor of waste management practices in hotels (Akis 2001; Arbulú et al. 2015). Here, waste management in the hotel industry has also been studied regarding the environmental impact. The waste has been divided into three categories—energy waste, effluent discharge and solid waste, for calculating the environmental impact of the hotel on its surroundings. The literature also indicates that there is no generic model of waste management in the hotel industry (Bohdanowicz and Martinac 2007; Erdogan and Baris 2007). In this chapter, the waste management factors identified through content analysis (see: Singh and Sushil 2017) have been verified in IHL, which is a premium LEED (Leadership in Energy and Environmental Design) Platinum-certified hotel and known for its waste management and sustainable practices. The conceptual framework of waste management in the hotel has been developed and analyzed through partial FSS, SAP–LAP framework and SAP–LAP linkages framework.

20.3 Methodology

Mixed method methodology has been used for conducting the case study (Dubey et al. 2015). In this methodology, SAP–LAP framework is used for defining the factors and TISM is used for finding the hierarchical relationship among the waste management factors. The TISM outcome is verified through FSS and SAP–LAP linkages framework.

20.3.1 SAP–LAP Framework

The SAP–LAP framework has been developed by Sushil (2000a, b, 2001, 2009). This framework is used to understand the situation and to find the learning issues in an organization. This framework is a combination of two frameworks, namely SAP and LAP frameworks. In SAP framework, the situation is defined through actor and process, where the actor is the main contributor to treat with the situation. However, LAP framework is used to study learning, action and performance as shown in Fig. 20.1. This framework has been used in many researches for analyzing different management issues (Sushil 2001; Palanisamy 2001, 2012; Husain et al. 2002; Kak and Sushil 2002; Gupta 2003; Thakkar et al. 2008; Charan 2012; John and Ramesh 2012; Mahajan et al. 2013; Nasim and Sushil 2014; Rizk 2014; Yadav and Sushil 2014).

In this chapter, verified waste management factors have been categorized into SAP–LAP elements of the framework as shown in Table 20.1 (see: Singh and Sushil 2017). Here, some factors are used for defining the situation of waste management in the hotel. The waste management factors which influence waste management strategies, planning and execution are used for defining actor element

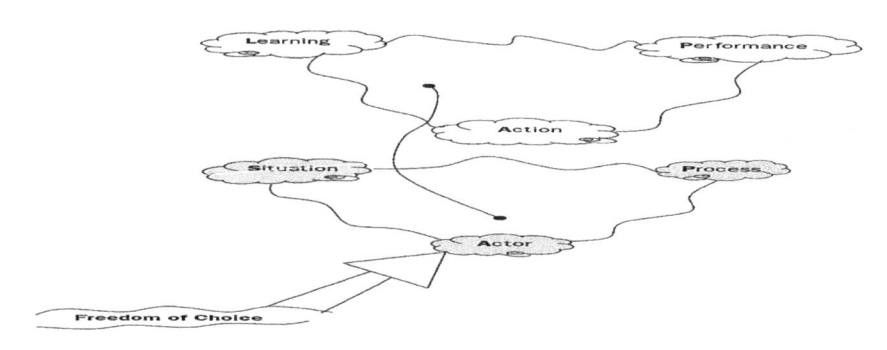

Fig. 20.1 SAP–LAP framework. *Adopted* Sushil (2000a, b)

of the SAP–LAP framework. The process element is defined through the waste management factors, which affect waste management process followed in the hotel. The SAP framework has been concluded into Learning, Actions and Performance, i.e. LAP framework. In LAP framework, performance element has been chosen from waste management factors which affect the waste management performance in the hotel. It leads to learning and action used for upgrading waste management in the hotel.

Table 20.1 Defining waste management factors in IHL hotel as SAP–LAP

	Situation	
S1	Wastivity reduction	Sushil (1980, 1990), Sushil and Vrat (1989), Sharma et al. (1994), Vrat (2014), Sushil (2015)
S2	Environment pollution	Sakai et al. (1996), El-Fadel et al. (1997), Song et al. (2015)
	Actor	
A1	Governmental directives	Saxena et al. (1992), Manga et al. (2008), EPA (2015), ESS (2015)
	Processes	
P1	Waste management technologies	Yager et al. (1997), Usui et al. (2001), Hicks and Yager (2006), CEA (2011), Shetty (2011)
	Research and development	Yuan and Shen (2011), Ion and Gheorghe (2014)
	Learning	
L	Awareness	Millam and Pizam (1995), Clarck and Squire (1998), Barr (2007)
	Action	
AC	Execution of waste management norms	Manga et al. (2008), Zu et al. (2008), Shekdar (2009), Srivastava and Sushil (2013)
	Performance	
PF	Economic investment	Emery et al. (2007), Shekdar (2009), Costa et al. (2010)

Source Singh and Sushil (2017)

20.3.2 TISM Development

TISM is an interpretive expansion of ISM methodology (Sushil 2012a, 2017a). It is used to discover the hierarchical relationship among the factors (Nasim 2011; Prasad and Suri 2011; Wasuja et al. 2012; Srivastava and Sushil 2013; Mangla et al. 2014; Khatwani et al. 2015). 'What', 'how' and 'why' relationships among the factors have been defined by TISM, which are further used to develop a conceptual framework (Whetten 1989; Sushil 2012a).

In this chapter, TISM is used to develop the hierarchical relationship among the waste management factors in the hotel. The outcome of TISM has been used to find the raise, maintain and reduce elements of FSS among the waste management factors. The final TISM model of waste management for IHL hotel provides linkages among the waste management factors in the hotel and categorizes them as dependent and driving factors.

20.3.3 Flowing Stream Strategy

Flowing Stream Strategy (FSS) is defined as 'strategic management of change which can be better leveraged with a clear understanding of continuity of the organization' (Sushil 2005, 2012b). The FSS has been defined with continuous and change forces, which must be balanced in the organization. The FSS framework has been used partially for defining flexibility in IHL hotel case study. The raise, maintain and reduce elements are used for defining flexibility in the hotel (Yadav 2014).

20.3.4 SAP–LAP Linkages Framework

SAP–LAP linkages frame was developed by Sushil (2009). It is a generic framework used to find the interrelationship between SAP–LAP elements (Sushil 2017b). The steps used in SAP–LAP linkages framework are as follows:

Step 1 Develop SAP–LAP framework
Step 2 Define SAP–LAP elements in the case organization
Step 3 Develop scales and assess the elements in the framework of assessment matrices.
Step 4 Develop binary and interpretive self-interaction matrices for the elements
Step 5 Develop cross-interaction matrices
Step 6 Interpret the relationships

The waste management situation has been analyzed in the case organization by using SAP–LAP linkages framework, which consists of these six steps. Three types of matrices have been used to define the SAP–LAP linkages framework, namely 'assessment matrix, self-interaction matrix, and cross-interaction matrix'. Assessment has been done on the basis of score and assessment matrix is used to assess element of the framework. However, self-interaction and cross-interaction matrices are made on the basis of respondent output in terms of 0 and 1. The SAP–LAP Linkages framework has been used in this chapter to analyze waste management in IHL hotel.

20.4 Background of the Case Company

IHL hotel (fictitious name) has been selected as a case organization in the service sector. Initially, the identified waste management factors have been verified in the hotel, which enriched the strength of factors. Further, the waste management process has been illustrated by using mixed method methodology in the hotel (Eisenhardt 1989; Dubey et al. 2015).

IHL hotel is a sustainable hotel from a well-known hotel series in India. It originated from conglomerate series of the enterprise. This conglomerate initially started as cigarette manufacturer, which further diversified itself into the hotel industry, paper and pulp manufacturing, and food industry. This diversification regenerated itself into a renowned hotel series. The first hotel which introduced the conglomerate organization in the hospitality industry was established in Chennai in 1975. Presently, there is more than 100 chain of hotels in 70 destinations across India. Some premium hotels of this conglomerate extension are LEED® Platinum-certified because of their sustainability and waste management practices. They also expanded themselves with a premium brand of palaces, forts, havelis and resorts which are known for their brand and luxury in India. These joint ventures promote their quality and business. Indian Hotel Limited comes under the series of luxury hotels, which is a LEED Platinum-certified hotel and provides branded accommodation, branded cuisines and Go Green concepts to the customers (ITC 2012, 2013, 2014).

20.5 Illustration of the Case Organization in Terms of Waste Management

The hotel industry has been chosen as the service sector industry for the purpose of the case study, because the hotel provides services to their customers and at the same time manages its waste and sustainability. The case has been explained below by the following three steps:

Step I Identify and Categorize waste management factors as situation–actor–process–learning–action–performance in the case company.

Step II Develop the hierarchical relationship among the waste management factors in the case organization and analyze it through partial FSS.

Step III Identify strategic actions for managing waste in the case organization and align them with strategic direction by using SAP–LAP linkages framework.

These steps of case analyses in IHL hotel waste management are extended below.

20.5.1 Identify and Categorize Waste Management Factors

The waste management factors of the organization identified from the literature survey have been verified and validated by using content analysis technique (for detail see: Singh and Sushil 2017). The waste management factors have been defined in terms of SAP–LAP framework. The sharply defined waste management factors for IHL hotel are shown in Table 20.1.

20.5.2 Develop the Hierarchical Relationship Among the Waste Management Factors

Total interpretive structural modelling is used as a tool for tracking the hierarchical relationship between the elements. It has been used in various management problems to develop the hierarchical path between the factors (Sushil 2012a). This is a mixed methodology, which is used to map the dependent and driving factors in the hierarchical relationship between the elements (Whetten 1989; Sushil 2012a). TISM was conducted over IHL hotel, where experts from hotel dealing with waste management were chosen for conducting the study. Verified waste management factors have been used for mapping hierarchical relationship among the waste management factors. The hierarchical relationship between the waste management factors (designated as WF) has been checked as suggested by Sushil (2016) and the details are shown in Appendix; the final TISM model for IHL hotel is shown in Fig. 20.2. TISM digraph shows that governmental directives are the driving factors, which play a vital role in managing wastivity and environmental pollution in the hotel. Wastivity and environmental pollution are the dependent factors, which were affected by all other factors in a hierarchical manner for managing waste. On the basis of TISM, strategic direction of waste management factors has been plotted in the form of strategic direction diagram shown in Fig. 20.3. The strategic actions on the basis of the strategic diagram are shown in Table 20.2.

308   A. Singh and Sushil

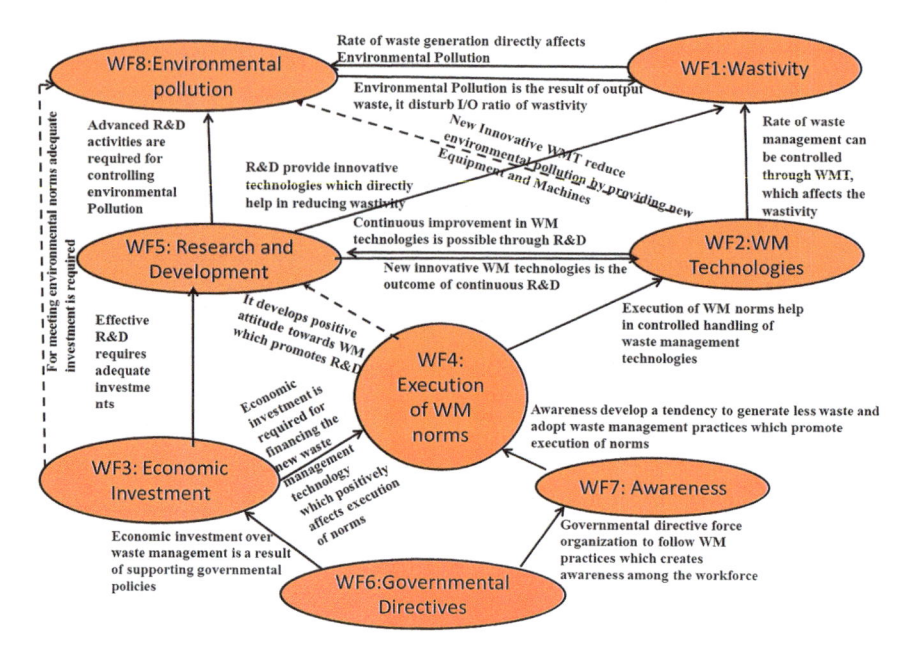

Fig. 20.2 TISM for waste management in the IHL Hotel

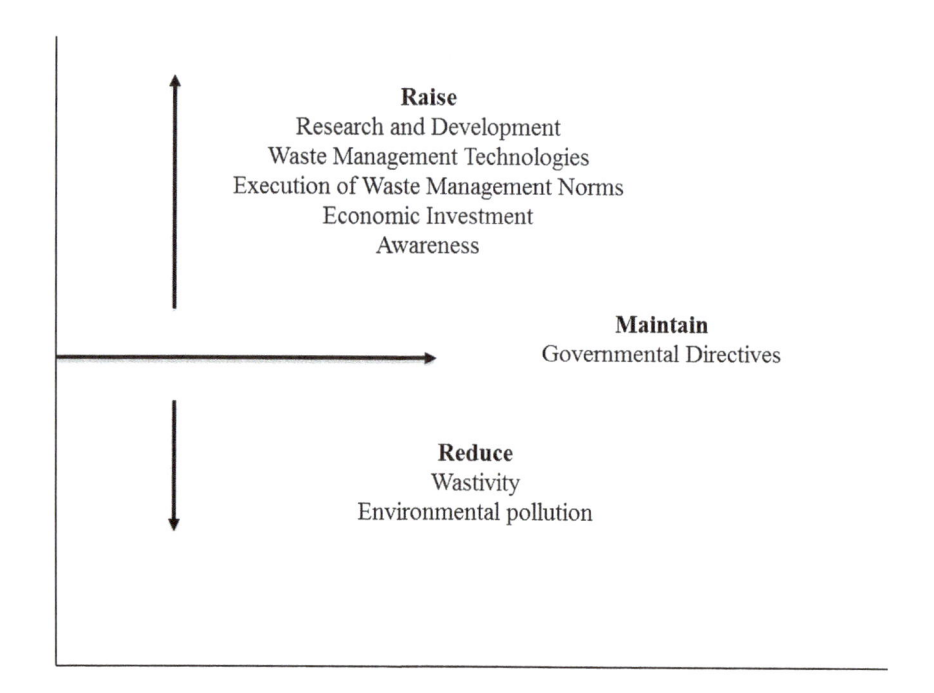

Fig. 20.3 Strategic direction of waste management for managing waste in the IHL hotel

Table 20.2 Strategic actions for waste management in the IHL hotel

Strategic actions	Strategic direction		
	Raise	Maintain	Reduce
Eco educational games Eco educational toolkit Welcome environment Energy saving Water management Educational toolkit for environment Using renewable energy Green banqueting	Research and development Waste management technologies Execution of waste management Norms Economic investment Awareness	Governmental directives	Wastivity Environmental pollution

20.5.3 Using SAP–LAP Linkages Framework

The verified waste management factors have been categorized in SAP–LAP form as shown in Table 20.1. The SAP–LAP linkages framework has been used for assessing waste management factors in the Indian Hotel Limited. SAP–LAP linkages framework has been divided into the following steps:

Step 1 Develop SAP–LAP framework.
Step 2 Define SAP–LAP elements in the case organization.
Step 3 Develop scales and assess the elements in the framework of assessment matrix.
Step 4 Develop binary and interpretive self-interaction matrices for the elements.
Step 5 Develop cross-interaction matrix.

Thus, SAP–LAP framework in the organization has been defined in Table 20.1. Assessment matrix for the framework has been defined in Table 20.3.

Table 20.3 Assessment matrix in IHL hotel (Based on the five-point Likert scale)

	Elements	Assessment of state
	Situation	
S1	Wastivity reduction	3
S2	Environment pollution	5
	Actor	
A1	Governmental directives	5
	Processes	
P1	Waste management technologies	4
P2	Research and development	5

20.5.3.1 Assessment Matrix

The assessment matrix is the qualitative and quantitative representation of the situation. The framework elements have been measured on a five-point Likert scale. In this study, situation, actor and process elements of the framework have been measured in Indian Hotel Limited on the five-point Likert scale, which ranges from 'strongly disagree' (1) to 'strongly agree' (5). Assessment matrix of Indian Hotel Limited has been shown in Table 20.3.

20.5.3.2 Self-interaction Matrix

The self-interaction matrix helps to predict the relationship between various elements of the framework. The design considers both, binary matrix and interpretative matrix; these matrices have been used for defining the interrelationship between various elements of the framework. The binary matrix has been defined with 0 and 1, where 1 indicates the positive relationship between the elements, and 0 indicates no relationship between the elements. The self-interaction matrices are shown, in Table 20.4.

Discussion: The important waste management factors, identified from the literature and verified by the experts (see: Singh and Sushil 2017), are selected for conducting the SAP–LAP linkages. These factors are selected as important elements of the situation, actor and process framework. The situation, actor and process elements are verified in the context of waste management in Indian Hotel Limited. The self-interaction matrix of wastivity and environmental pollution represents situation elements. Wastivity represents 'the ratio of the waste to input'. Hence, wastivity has been used to define waste in the hotel. Wastivity situation is designated as S1.

Situation 1 (S1): Waste management in the IHL hotel can be done by reducing the ratio of waste to input (Wastivity).

Accordingly, environmental pollution represents the second situation element of waste management in the IHL hotel and this situation is designated as S2.

Table 20.4 Self-interaction matrices between various elements of framework

Self-interaction matrix for situation elements	
S1	S2
	1
	Wastivity directly affects the rate of waste generation and environmental pollution is the outcome of waste generation
Self-interaction matrix for processes elements	
	P2
P1	Continuous improvement in waste management technologies is possible through R&D

Situation 2 (S2): Waste management in the Indian Hotel Limited can be done by controlling environmental pollution because of the hotel.

The outcome of self-interaction matrix shows that both environmental pollution and wastivity are related and directly proportional to each other.

The process elements in the hotel are waste management technologies and research and development (R&D). It has been identified in the case that these are the main processes, which affect waste management situation in the hotel. Waste management technologies element is represented by P1. Research and development element is represented by P2. The self-interaction matrix of process elements shows that these two processes are directly proportional to each other and affect the waste management of the hotel in almost similar ways.

20.5.3.3 Cross-interaction Matrix

Cross-interaction matrix is used to plot the relationship between different elements of the SAP–LAP framework. It is used for finding the relation between situation and actor, actor and process, process and learning, learning and action, and action and performance. Cross-interaction matrix is a combination of binary matrix and interpretation matrix. The results of the binary matrix are represented as 0 and 1; where, if an element *a* affects element *b*, then it is represented by 1, and if an element *a* does not affect element *b*, then it is represented by 0. The cross-interaction matrices are shown in Table 20.5.

Discussion: The cross-interaction matrix of situation and actor shows that situation elements, i.e. wastivity and environmental pollution are affected by the actor element. It also represents that governmental directive is a dominating element, and plays a vital role in managing waste of the hotel. The second cross-interaction matrix between actor and process elements shows that governmental directive is a dominating actor and it affects both the process elements. The cross-interaction matrix for process and learning shows that both processes, i.e. waste management technologies and research and development are regulated by the government. Their development and government policies result in awareness for managing waste in the hotel. Fourth cross-interaction matrix about learning (awareness) and action (execution of waste management norms) concludes that learning element (awareness) is essential for the execution of waste management norms in the hotel. The last cross-interaction matrix between action and performance, i.e. between execution and economic investment, shows that execution is an action element and economic investment is the performance element. It indicates that economic investment is needed for execution of norms about waste management in the hotel.

Table 20.5 Cross-interaction matrices between various elements of framework

Cross-interaction matrix for situation and actor elements

	Situation 1	Situation 2
Actor	1	1
	Governmental directives forcefully implement different governmental policies and norms which control wastivity	Environmental pollution can be controlled by implementing waste management notification

Cross-interaction matrix for actor and process elements

	Process 1	Process 2
Actor	1	1
	Government provides incentives for promoting new innovative technologies for managing waste	Government provides fund for development of research and development

Cross-interaction matrix for process and learning elements

	Process 1	Process 2
Learning	1	1
	Government acts as the driver for managing waste in the organization. It regulates as well as initiates waste management by directing laws, forming new policies and funding for research and development which promotes innovative technologies. Thus, government acts as an awaking agent which creates awareness in the organization for managing waste	

Cross-interaction matrix for learning and action elements

	Learning
Action	1
	Awareness creates knowledge which affects and generates a positive attitude toward waste management; this results in the execution of waste management norms and policies

Cross-interaction matrix for action and performance elements

	Action
Performance	1
	Economic investment provides a medium which helps in execution of norms for managing waste

20.6 Discussion

In this chapter, IHL hotel has been chosen to analyze through mixed method methodology. In mixed method methodology SAP–LAP, SAP–LAP linkages and TISM are used to study waste management in the hotel. TISM methodology has been used to identify the raise, maintain and reduce factors in the hotel. Then, these factors have been cross-verified by using SAP–LAP linkages framework. The strategies used for managing waste in the hotel have been analyzed in term of raise, maintain and reduce. The TISM model of waste management in IHL hotel is slightly different from the generic waste management model; it shows that governmental directive is the driving factor which drives economic investment and awareness to the execution of waste management norms in the hotel. Thus, this chapter shows that in IHL hotel, economic investment and awareness are equally important for executing waste management norms.

The hotel's waste management strategies are analyzed on the basis of raise, maintain and reduce elements; which helps to maintain continuity and change in the hotel as shown in Table 20.2. The TISM model and partially defined FSS elements are further verified by using SAP–LAP linkages framework. The SAP–LAP linkages framework also indicates that government is an important actor and governmental directive drives the waste management process in the hotel. Hence, it is proved that governmental directive is the main driving force for managing waste in the organization. Wastivity and environmental pollution are dependent factors which were affected by other hierarchical factors for managing waste in the hotel. The implication of this research is to provide a waste management model for the service sector; it also provides a basic idea about the waste management hierarchy in the service sector. This framework has been used to develop a better waste managing policy in hotel industriey.

20.7 Conclusion

SAP–LAP, TISM, partial flowing stream strategy, and SAP–LAP linkages frameworks have been used to analyze waste management practices in the hotel. Verified waste management factors which were distributed according to SAP–LAP framework are used for portraying TISM framework. The TISM framework has been used to discover waste management hierarchy, dependent and driving factors in the hotel. This methodology provides raise, maintain and reduce elements (partial FSS elements) of waste management. The SAP–LAP linkages framework has also been verified the TISM results. The results conclude that governmental directive plays a vital role in the waste management of the hotel. Governmental directives act as an environmental activist who drives the hotel to invest in waste management and creates awareness about managing waste. The strategies of hotels are changed for a continuous waste management practice in the hotel.

Appendix

See Tables 20.6, 20.7 and 20.8.

Table 20.6 Reachability matrix

Dimensions code	WF1	WF2	WF3	WF4	WF5	WF6	WF7	WF8
WF1	1	0	0	0	0	0	0	1
WF2	0	1	0	0	1	0	0	1
WF3	1	1	1	1	1	0	1	0
WF4	1	1	0	1	0	0	0	1
WF5	1	1	0	0	1	0	0	1
WF6	1	1	1	1	1	1	1	1
WF7	1	0	1	1	0	0	1	1
WF8	1	0	0	0	0	0	0	1

Table 20.7 Transitive reachability matrix

Dimensions code	WF1	WF2	WF3	WF4	WF5	WF6	WF7	WF8
WF1	1	0	0	0	0	0	0	1
WF2	1[a]	1	0	0	1	0	0	1
WF3	1	1	1	1	1	0	1	1[a]
WF4	1	1	0	1	1[a]	0	0	1
WF5	1	1	0	0	1	0	0	1
WF6	1	1	1	1	1	1	1	1
WF7	1	1[a]	1	1	1[a]	0	1	1
WF8	1	0	0	0	0	0	0	1

[a]Transitive relationships

Table 20.8 Different waste management factors classified into different levels

Dimensions code	Strategic waste management factor	Level
WF1	Wastivity	1
WF2	Waste management technologies	2
WF3	Economic investment	4
WF4	Execution of waste management norms	3
WF5	Research and development	2
WF6	Governmental directives	5
WF7	Awareness	4
WF8	Environment pollution	1

References

Akis, S. (2001). Sürdürülebilir turizm: bir alan araştırmasının sonuçları (Sustainable tourism: Results of a field research). *Anatolia Turizm Araştırmaları Dergisi, 12*(1), 17–25.

APAT. (2002). Italian National Agency for the Protection of the Environment and for Technical Services (APAT), Tourist Accommodation EU eco-label Award Scheme. Final report, Retrieved on July 15, 2006.

Arbulú, I., Lozano, J., & Rey-Maquieira, J. (2015). Tourism and solid waste generation in Europe: A panel data assessment of the Environmental Kuznets Curve. *Waste Management, 46* (December), 628–636.

Barr, S. (2007). Factors influencing environmental attitudes and behaviors a U.K. case study of household waste management. *Environment and Behavior, 39*(4), 435–473.

Bohdanowicz, P. (2005). European hoteliers' environmental attitudes greening the business. *Cornell Hotel and Restaurant Administration Quarterly, 46*(2), 188–204.

Bohdanowicz, P., & Martinac, I. (2007). Determinants and benchmarking of resource consumption in hotels—case study of hilton international and scandic in Europe. *Energy and Buildings, 39* (1), 82–95.

CEA Report. (2011). Fly ash generation at coal/lignite based thermal power stations and its utilization in the country for the year 2010–11. Available at http://www.cea.nic.in/reports/articles/thermal/fly_ash_final.pdf. Retrieved on Aug 19, 2014.

Charan, P. (2012). Supply chain performance issues in an automobile company: A SAP-LAP analysis. *Measuring Business Excellence, 16*(1), 67–86.

Costa, I., Massard, G., & Agarwal, A. (2010). Waste management policies for industrial symbiosis development: Case studies in European countries. *Journal of Cleaner Production, 18*(8), 815–822.

Clark, R. E., & Squire, L. R. (1998). Classical conditioning and brain systems: The role of awareness. *Science, 280*(5360), 77–81.

Dewhurst, H., & Thomas, R. (2003). Encouraging sustainable business practices in a non-regulatory environment: A case study of small tourism firms in a UK National Park. *Journal of Sustainable Tourism, 11*, 383–403.

Dubey, R., Gunasekaran, A., Papadopoulos, T., & Childe, S. J. (2015). Green supply chain management enablers: Mixed methods research. *Sustainable Production and Consumption, 4*, 72–88.

Eisenhardt, K. M. (1989). Building theories from case study research. *Academy of Management Review, 14*(4), 532–550.

El-Fadel, M., Findikakis, A. N., & Leckie, J. O. (1997). Environmental impacts of solid waste landfilling. *Journal of Environmental Management, 50*(1), 1–25.

Emery, A., Davies, A., Griffiths, A., & Williams, K. (2007). Environmental and economic modelling: A case study of municipal solid waste management scenarios in Wales. *Resources, Conservation and Recycling, 49*(3), 244–263.

EPA. (2015). Environmental Protection Act, 1986. Available at http://www.indiastat.com/environmentandpollution/11/frequentlyaskedquestionsfaqs/13409/stats.aspx. Retrieved on March 10, 2016.

Erdogan, N., & Baris, E. (2007). Environmental protection programs and conservation practices of hotels in Ankara, Turkey. *Tourism Management, 28*(2), 604–614.

ESS. (2015). Sector-wise number of industries inspected under environmental surveillance squad (ESS) in India (2011–2012 to 2014–2015-up to January, 2015). Available at http://www.indiastat.com/table/environmentandpollution/11/pollutingindustries/216/850033/data.aspx. Retrieved on March 10, 2016.

Gupta, A. B. (2003). Managing of manufacturing flexibility in a piston ring manufacturing plant-a case study. *Global Journal of Flexible Systems Management, 4*(1 & 2), 49–56.

Hicks, J., & Yager, J. (2006). Airborne crystalline silica concentrations at coal-fired power plants associated with coal fly ash. *Journal of Occupational and Environmental Hygiene, 3*(8), 448–455.

Husain, Z., Sushil, & Pathak, R. D. (2002) A technology management perspective on collaborations in the Indian automobile industry: A case study. *Journal of Engineering and Technology Management, 19,* 167–201.

ITC. (2012). Annual sustainability report. Available at, http://www.itcportal.com/sustainability/sustainability-report-2012/sustainability-report-2012.pdf. Retrieved on June 20, 2016.

ITC. (2013). Annual sustainability report. Available at, http://www.itcportal.com/sustainability/sustainability-report-2012/sustainability-report-2012.pdf. Retrived on June 21, 2016.

ITC. (2014). Annual sustainability report. Available at, http://www.itcportal.com/sustainability/sustainability-report-2014/sustainability-report-2014.pdf. Retrieved on June 20, 2016.

Ion, I., & Gheorghe, F. F. (2014). The innovator role of technologies in waste management towards the sustainable development. *Procedia Economics and Finance, 8,* 420–428.

John, L., & Ramesh, A. (2012). Humanitarian supply chain management in India: A SAP-LAP framework. *Journal of Advances in Management Research, 9*(2), 217–235.

Kak, A., & Sushil. (2002). Strategy based on core competence and flexibility: Learning issues for four Indian organizations. *Global Journal of Flexible Systems Management, 3*(2&3), 55–70.

Khatwani, G., Singh, S. P., Trivedi, A., & Chauhan, A. (2015). Fuzzy-TISM: A fuzzy extension of TISM for group decision making. *Global Journal of Flexible Systems Management, 16*(1), 97–112.

Kumar, S. (2005). Resource use and waste management in Vietnam hotel industry. *Journal of Cleaner Production, 13*(2), 109–116.

Lee, K. F. (2001). Sustainable tourism destinations: The importance of cleaner production. *Journal of Cleaner Production, 9*(4), 313–323.

Le, Y., Hollenhorst, S., Harris, C., McLaughlin, W., & Shook, S. (2006). Environmental management: A study of Vietnamese hotels. *Annals of Tourism Research, 33*(2), 545–567.

Manga, V. E., Forton, O. T., & Read, A. D. (2008). Waste management in cameroon: A new policy perspective? *Resources, Conservation and Recycling, 52*(4), 592–600.

Mangla, S. K., Kumar, P., and Barua, M. K. (2014). Flexible decision approach for analyzing performance of sustainable supply chains under risks/uncertainty. *Global Journal of Flexible Systems Management, 15*(2), 113–130.

Mahajan, R., Garg, S., & Sharma, P. B. (2013). Frozen corn manufacturing and its supply chain: Case study using SAP–LAP approach. *Global Journal of Flexible Systems Management, 14*(3), 167–177.

Mensah, I. (2006). Environmental management practices among hotels in the greater Accra region. *International Journal of Hospitality Management, 25*(3), 414–431.

Milman, A., & Pizam, A. (1995). The role of awareness and familiarity with a destination: The central Florida case. *Journal of Travel Research, 33*(3), 21–27.

Nasim, S. (2011). Total interpretive structural modeling of continuity and change forces in e-government. *Journal of Enterprise Transformation, 1*(2), 147–168.

Nasim, S., & Sushil. (2014). Flexible strategy framework for managing continuity and change in e-government. In Sushil & E. A. Stohr (Eds.), *The flexible enterprise. Flexible systems management.* New Delhi: Springer, 47–66.

Palanisamy, R. (2001). Evolving internet business model for electronic commerce using flexible systems methodology. *Global Journal of Flexible Systems Management, 2*(3), 1–12.

Palanisamy, R. (2012). Building information systems flexibility in SAP–LAP framework: A case study evidence from SME sector. *Global Journal of Flexible Systems Management, 13*(1), 57–74.

Prasad, U. C., & Suri, R. K. (2011). Modelling of continuity and change forces in private higher technical education using total interpretive structural modelling. *Global Journal of Flexible Systems Management, 12*(3&4), 31–40.

Rizk, M. (2014) Rapid deployment approach through flexible system design: Breakthrough in technology innovation and process optimization for eClinical trials. In: Sushil & E. A. Stohr (Eds.), *The flexible enterprise, Flexible systems management* (pp. 257–272). New Delhi: Springer.

Radwan, H. R., Jones, E., & Minoli, D. (2012). Solid waste management in small hotels: A comparison of green and non-green small hotels in Wales. *Journal of Sustainable Tourism, 20* (4), 533–550.

Sakai, S., Sawell, S. E., Chandler, A. J., Eighmy, T. T., Kosson, D., Vehlow, J., et al. (1996). World trends in municipal solid waste management. *Waste Management, 16*(5–6), 341–350.

Saxena, J. P., Sushil, & Vrat, P. (1992). Scenario building: A critical study of energy conservation in the Indian Cement Industry. *Technological Forecasting and Social Change, 41*(2), 121–146.

Shanklin, C. W., Petrillose, M. J., & Pettay, A. (1991). Solid waste management practices in selected hotel chains and individual properties. *Journal of Hospitality & Tourism Research, 15* (1), 59–74.

Sharma, H. D., Sushil., & Gupta, A. D. (1994). Entropy, quality and wastivity: A unified view of system performance. *Kybernetes, 23*(8), 47–54.

Shekdar, A. V. (2009). Sustainable solid waste management: An integrated approach for Asian Countries. *Waste Management, 29*(4), 1438–1448.

Shetty, M. S. (2011). *Concrete technology: Theory and practice*. New Delhi, India: S. Chand & Company Pvt. Ltd.

Singh, A., & Sushil. (2017). Developing a conceptual framework of waste management in the organizational context. *Management of Environmental Quality, 28*(6), 786–806.

Song, M., Wang, S., & Cen, L. (2015). Comprehensive efficiency evaluation of coal enterprises from production and pollution treatment process. *Journal of Cleaner Production, 104* (October), 374–379.

Srivastava, A. K., & Sushil. (2013). Modelling strategic performance factors for effective strategy execution. *International Journal of Productivity and Performance Management, 62*(6), 554–582.

Sushil. (1980). *Systems approach to waste management in India*. Unpublished M. Tech Dissertation, IIT Delhi.

Sushil, & Vrat, P. (1989). Waste management policy analysis and growth monitoring: An integrated approach to perspective planning. *International Journal of Systems Science, 20*(6), 907–926.

Sushil. (1990). Waste management: A systems perspective. *Industrial Management & Data Systems, 90*(5), 1–67.

Sushil. (2000a). Situation-actor-process options: Mapping and enhancing flexibility. *Systems Research and Behavioral Science, 17*(3), 301–309.

Sushil. (2000b). SAP-LAP models for inquiry. *Management Decision, 38*(5), 347–353.

Sushil. (2001). SAP-LAP framework. *Global Journal of Flexible Systems Management, 2*(1), 51–55.

Sushil. (2005). A flexible strategy framework for managing continuity and change. *International Journal of Global Business and Competitiveness, 1*(1), 22–32.

Sushil. (2009). SAP-LAP linkages-a generic interpretive framework for analyzing managerial contexts. *Global Journal of Flexible Systems Management, 10*(2), 11–20.

Sushil (2012a). Interpreting the interpretive structural model. *Global Journal of Flexible Systems Management,13*(2), 87–106.

Sushil. (2012b). Making flowing stream strategy work. *Global Journal of Flexible Systems Management, 13*(1), 25–40.

Sushil. (2015). Managing wastivity for sustainability. *Global Journal of Flexible Systems Management, 16*(1), 1–2.

Sushil. (2016). How to check of total interpretive structural models? *Annals of Operations Research*, 1–15. https://doi.org/10.1007/s10479-016-2312-3.

Sushil. (2017a). Modified ISM/TISM process with simultaneous transitivity checks for reducing direct pair comparisons. *Global Journal of Flexible Systems Management, 18*(4), 331–351.

Sushil. (2017b). Theory building using SAP-LAP linkages: An application in the context of disaster management. *Annals of Operations Research.* https://doi.org/10.1007/s10479-017-2425-3.

Thakkar, J., Kanda, A., & Deshmukh, S. G. (2008). Interpretive structural modeling (ISM) of IT-enablers for indian manufacturing SMEs. *Information Management & Computer Security, 16*(2), 113–136.

Trung, D. N., & Kumar, S. (2005). Resource use and waste management in Vietnam hotel industry. *Journal of Cleaner Production, 13*(2), 109–116.

Usui, H., Li, L., & Suzuki, H. (2001). Rheology and pipeline transportation of dense fly ash-water slurry. *Korea-Australia Rheology Journal, 13*(1), 47–54.

Vrat, P. (2014). *Materials, management: An integrated systems approach.* New Delhi: Springer.

Wasuja, S., Sagar, M., & Sushil, A. (2012). Cognitive bias in salespersons in specialty drug selling of pharmaceutical industry. *International Journal of Pharmaceutical and Healthcare Marketing, 6*(4), 310–335.

Whetten, D. A. (1989). What constitutes a theoretical contribution? *Academy of Management Review, 14*(4), 490–495.

Yager, W. J., Hicks, J. B., & Fabianova, E. (1997). Airborne arsenic and urinary excretion of arsenic metabolites during boiler cleaning operations in a slovak coal-fired power plant. *Environmental Health Perspectives, 105*(8), 836–842.

Yadav, N. (2014). Flexibility aspects in performance management system: An illustration of flexible strategy game-card. *Global Journal of Flexible Systems Management, 15*(3), 181–189.

Yuan, H., & Shen, L. (2011). Trend of the research on construction and demolition waste management. *Waste Management, 31*(4), 670–679.

Yadav, N., & Sushil. (2014). Theoretical roots of flexible strategy game-card: An evolving strategic performance management framework. In Sushil & E. A. Stohr (Eds.), *The flexible enterprise, Flexible systems management* (pp. 99–109). New Delhi: Springer.

Zotos, G., Karagiannidis, A., Zampetoglou, S., Malamakis, A., Antonopoulos, I. S., Kontogianni, S., et al. (2009). Developing a holistic strategy for integrated waste management within municipal planning: Challenges, policies, solutions and perspectives for hellenic municipalities in the zero-waste, low-cost direction. *Waste Management, 29*(5), 1686–1692.

Zu, X., Fredendall, L. D., & Douglas, T. J. (2008). The evolving theory of quality management: The role of six sigma. *Journal of Operations Management, 26*(5), 630–650.

Chapter 21
Shifts Between Technology Push and Market Pull Strategies for Sustainable Development in Manufacturing Industries

A. P. S. Sethi, I. P. S. Ahuja and Anuj Singla

Abstract The research on Technology Push (TP) and Market Pull (MP) or Demand Pull (DP) is prevailing for many years. Earlier studies revealed the significance of letting MP shape the development of technology, but this frequently leads to incremental innovation and would be primarily unfavorable to nationwide competitiveness, taking the focus away from primitive research, the utilization of which is responsible for economic progress. TP-oriented manufacturing enterprises are established to commercialize an explicit or an emerging technology. This type of orientation generally comprises a resource-based "probe and learn" methodology to enter into market but now in this hypercompetitive market, a profitable industry balances its technological target with valuable management strategies. The purpose of this research chapter is to have an insight of shifts between TP and MP strategies in manufacturing enterprises for sustainable development. A research has been planned to develop a conceptual framework to explore shifts between TP and DP strategies for sustainable development in manufacturing enterprises and the research proposal is presented in this chapter. The chapter reveals the various attributes that govern the shift of TP strategy to MP strategy and vice versa in an organization with the ultimate goal of sustainable development. As per the complexity of context and the fact that such studies can be performed primarily by closely treading and

---

A. P. S. Sethi (✉)
Department of Mechanical Engineering, Baba Banda Singh Bahadur Engineering College, Fatehgarh Sahib 140407, Punjab, India
e-mail: sethiaps@gmail.com

I. P. S. Ahuja · A. Singla
Department of Mechanical Engineering, Punjabi University, Patiala 147002, Punjab, India
e-mail: ahujaips@yahoo.co.in

A. Singla
e-mail: anujsingla86@gmail.com

analyzing the techniques adopted by various organizations, it was considered appropriate to carry out the study of shifts between TP and MP strategies for sustainable development in manufacturing industries.

Keywords Market Pull · Shifts · Sustainable development · Technology Push

21.1 Introduction

The agitator for change is technology. Change and advancement are intrinsic parts of management of technological field. Industry develops by transferring technology from one firm to the other and across the nations. Technology is not neutral. It includes and reflects value systems and its transfer. Technology is significant in changing and destroying values of the products. It may stimulate the equality of revenue or may decline it. It is inferred that technology not only affects society, but society also sets limits on the choice and development of technology.

The concept of TP and MP was initiated by Schon (1967) as basic dynamic practices subsequent to the development of a new technology. Two thoughts, specifically TP and DP were proposed. TP supports the thought that innovation is stimulated by science and activates technology, whereas, DP proposes that client needs are vital simulators of technology acceptance. It was inferred that the major role is played by Demand Pull, so the needs for innovation should be given careful consideration than technical ability (Chau and Tam 2000).

According to Drury and Farhoomand (1999), TP and DP are basic and diverse designs of improvement and diffusion of technical improvements. On one hand, TP needs an adopter to accord with the technology, and on the flipside, DP needs the technology to fit the accommodator. It has been observed that, internal levels are more crucial from the Demand Pull than from the Technology Push point of view and the most elevated level happens when the driving force for the appropriation began from internal DP. Abbasi et al. (2017) discussed the findings of research conducted between 2013 and 2016, based on the promotion of technology layout for the Creative Industries. The roadmap presented in their work was built based on input from communities of creative and Information and Communication Technologies (ICT) during the validation phases of the research. Therefore, the study is directed toward the development of latest technologies and related business models and expertise, and provides guidance for making strategies in this regard. Kocak et al. (2017) reported that dedicated technology orientation leads to radical innovation, while responsive market regulation actively affects incremental innovation.

The welfare of a community is affected by the manner in which its economy handles its duties, utilizes its resources and attains its targets favorably. On one side, growth means a rise in per capita income, while on the flipside development has other objectives also, like, raising the economic condition of the poor, rise in employment, better implementation of resources, and encourage social equality (Salih 2003).

Certainly, numerous definitions of sustainability are suggested over the time. According to World Commission on Environment and Development, *sustainable development is a process of development in which the exploitation of capital, the introduction of innovative advancements, and institutional transformation are made steady eventually according to the existing demand.* Sustainable progress and social security can only be accomplished if humans are able to make overall employments and better living conditions for human ethical quality. TP and DP globally, along with industrial revolution, lead to competitive sustainable manufacturing. It is important to underline that world nations show different levels of development, from economic growth to economic development and beyond. Sustainable development is rising as a world-wide decisive perception to correlate economical, social, and environmental challenges as shown in Fig. 21.1. The transformation of industry must be supported by the system. Figure 21.2, in turn, should become more robust and sustainable (Jovane et al. 2008).

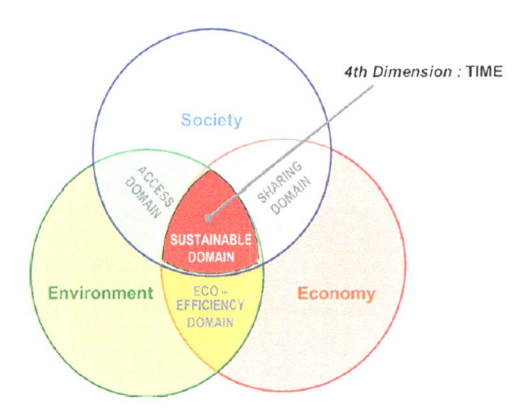

Fig. 21.1 Fundamentals of sustainable development (Jovane et al. 2008)

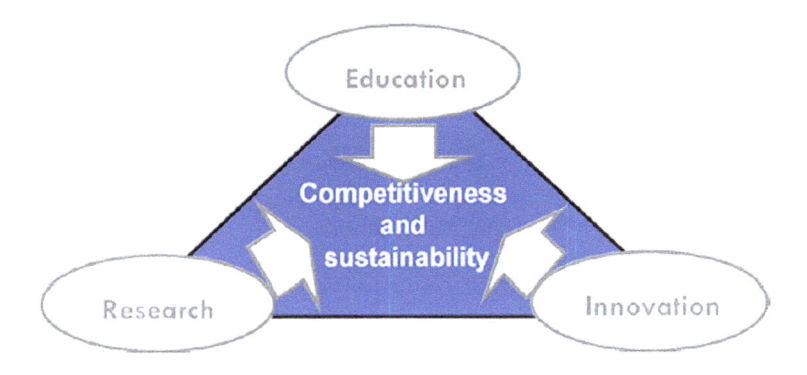

Fig. 21.2 The knowledge triangle (Jovane et al. 2008)

The manufacturing industry is looking for a neutral set of indicators to measure sustainability of products and processes. A few complications have been faced by industries in terms of accepting correlated terminologies and choosing particular indicators for various conditions of sustainability (Joung et al. 2012).

21.2 Technology Push

TP strategy corresponds to an ideology related to products, "if we build it, they will adopt it", whereas DP places different requisites.

Subsequent analysis of latest technology is pivotal for a sustainable and prosperous future. However, contiguous changes in the global markets impose challenges for long-term policy and strategy making (Saritas et al. 2017). As per the notion of Chidamber and Kon (1994), the business sector recommends that companies advance in the light of market needs, while the technical advocates assert that change in technology is the critical manager of the development. All in all, exact explorations on technological advancement are uncertain in regard to TP-DP argument. Howells (1997) suggested that only firms can perform the innovative activity. As the technology-market coordinating procedure is crucial to innovation, comparison among use, need and intended use has been made to get more exactness. Table 21.1 shows research on TP strategies by different researchers. Relevant issues, aspects, and implications are portrayed in Table 21.1.

Table 21.1 Technology push strategy

Author(s) (Year)	Strategic issues	Aspects/objectives	Implications/results
Chidamber and Kon (1994)	• Variance among TP and DP • Companies policy • National policy	• To review the interaction between strategy, R&D, and marketing groups of firms as determinants	• The TP-DP research depends strongly on the research methodology attributes that regulate innovation success and the level of analysis
Howells (1997)	• Technologically determinist	• To attract the significance of 'technologically determinist' label	• Needs and use enable an actual discussion on the connection among technology and demand in innovation procedure
Drury and Farhoomand (1999)	• Catalyst for acceptance of information technology	• To investigate effects of latest technology	• The arrival of new technologies motivates industries to update their database
Chau and Tam (2000)	• Finances involved in accepting new technology	• Higher profits than costs	Proposed benefits are: • Flexible environment unreserved by patents • More options for hardware • Utilizing IT assets more efficiently

(continued)

Table 21.1 (continued)

Author(s) (Year)	Strategic issues	Aspects/objectives	Implications/results
Schmoch (2007)	• Factual study related to cycles of technology	• Examination of a larger set of technologies	• The exposure of new fundamental ideas which prompts significant technological exercises with extensive market plans
Nemet (2009)	• Part of technology in monetary success • Representing the process of innovation	• To check whether innovation is affected by demand or by development in technology	• TP acknowledged few implications of innovation process
Varadarajan et al. (2010)	• Interactive technology	• Defining the methodologies • To prescribe alterations in retailer's policies	Interactive technologies: • May have a direct and indirect impact on retailer's policies • Allow small enterprises to strongly face large premier firms
Horbach et al. (2012)	• Determinants of eco-innovation in general • Organizational innovations	• To find different environmental field determinants • To target eco-innovations carried out by industries	• The current control is significant only for air, water, soil, and noise emissions, not for recycling and energy consumption
Stefano et al. (2012)	• Strategy • Innovation • Entrepreneurship studies	• To verify the relevance of technology as an origin of innovation and analyzing the part of demand	• Majority of technological innovations have their source in science but still need a market to be commercialized substantially
Peters et al. (2012)	• Domestic TP strategy • Foreign TP policy	• To analyze the influence of TP policies on innovative output	• Higher the domestic and foreign TP strategy funding in a technological area, significant will be a nation's innovative potency
Lubik et al. (2013)	• TP start-ups	• To examine the influence of TP to industry transformation	• TP start-ups often change to a MP arrangement due to new associates or transition in management preferences

21.3 Demand Pull

Demand Pull (market need) is a recognized need that stimulates innovation using research and development. Industries manufacture the required products, do its marketing, and fulfill the demand of its consumers. In addition to this, Demand Pull inflation is likely to emerge when total demand overtakes total supply in an economy. This is broadly perceived as too much money chasing too few goods. Parker (1997) focused on new and emerging technologies, each accentuating demonstration and deployment with varying degrees. One thread tying them together is the importance of Demand Pull. It was inferred that DP is a significant departure in technology development and deployment. Seyoum (2004) stated that the level of demand for high-technology products in a nation is a strong forecaster of export execution and other variables like customer satisfaction. A proper clarification of this relation will assist industries to formulate proper strategies for encouraging overall growth and sustainable development. According to Sastry (2011), business being the most significant sector is the main strength of a market. Moreover, the industries impact the economy and employment, and the sustainable development favors business as well as society at large. As a result numerous national companies have become global and strongly contended with established multinational players in the market.

Today's manufacturing scenario is illustrated by accelerated changes in the market and enhanced competitive strategies. Majority of the companies are using similar manufacturing techniques, therefore the struggle is not only based on manufacturing approach, but how strongly a firm governs technology apropos its consumers (Singla et al. 2017). Yadav (2012) stated that trade is an essential benchmark among different aspects of globalization. It incorporates ever-changing plans of the industries, which are more extensive as compared to the previous formats. With the passage of time, several emerging economies have influenced the demand for products in the global arena and proved to be the contemporary drivers of development. Table 21.2 portrays analysis on DP by different researchers and it depicts relevant strategic points; aspects; and implications of DP strategy.

Table 21.2 Demand Pull strategy

Author(s) (Year)	Strategic issues	Aspects/objectives	Implications/results
Chidamber and Kon (1994)	• Operator of industrial innovation	• To investigate foundation of market demand as drivers of innovation	• Most of the conflict among DP and TP forces is due to various research plans
Howells (1997)	• Origin of Innovation	• Investigation of determinants of industrial innovation	• The significance of demand over TP is not validated
Drury and Farhoomand (1999)	• DP—an origin of motivation	• Examination internal, external and financial advantages of DP	• The benefits acquired are affected by management issues
Chau and Tam (2000)	• Organizational size and cost of migration	• To analyze the effect of adoption decision for open systems	• Companies will not accept new technologies in the absence of an identified demand

(continued)

Table 21.2 (continued)

Author(s) (Year)	Strategic issues	Aspects/objectives	Implications/results
Schmoch (2007)	• Cyclical developments	• A close investigation of basic mechanisms	Analysis leads to the discovery of regular cycles of technology: • Science/Technology Push • Market Pull
Nemet (2009)	• Fluctuations in market conditions	• To explain the negative response of innovations to the strong MP practices	• Active concurrence on a single dominant approach • Rejecting R&D funding
Varadarajan et al. (2010)	• Retailing strategy	• To study how a retailer competes in the market	The integral measures of retailing policy contain: • Professional model • Customer oriented retailing plan • Retailing blend
Horbach et al. (2012)	Sources of eco-innovations: • Firm-specific factors • Technology • Market • Regulation	• To introduce the concept of customer benefits	• No substantial force for eco-innovation from demand side is available as eco-friendly devices are very costly
Stefano et al. (2012)	• Demand as an origin of innovation • A contrast among internal and external causes of innovations.	• To recognize market characteristics which influence the execution of innovation	• Innovations which originates from an actual DP strategy still need technological proficiencies to be developed effectively
Peters et al. (2012)	• Domestic and foreign market strategy	• To analyze how the locus of strategies effects DP policies on innovative output	• Larger the domestic and foreign DP market created by policies, significant will be a nation's innovative output
Lubik et al. (2013)	• Strategic transition in industrial start-ups	• To examine how MP is relevant to start-ups	• Most of the start-ups opening with MP orientation shifts to TP orientation

21.4 Sustainable Development

Sustainable development has been defined by various perspectives; however, the most commonly cited definition is from *Our Common Future*: Sustainable development is an advancement which addresses the current needs without negotiating the capacity of next generations to satisfy their own requirements (Brundtland 1987). The secret of an industry's sustainable development lies in performing well at every step of the value chain (Kak and Sushil 2002). Sustainable development wishes to look at the world as an entity that connects time and space. There are four equally critical essential measurements to evaluate sustainable development (Holden et al. 2014):

- Ensuring long-term ecological sustainability.
- Fulfilling fundamental requirements.
- Encouraging intra-generational equity.
- Encouraging inter-generational equity.

These dimensions are *fundamental objective values and not subjective individual preferences*. Thus, they are not negotiable.

Primary Dimension 1: Ensuring long-term ecological sustainability
The word sustainability came from ecological science. It expresses the conditions that should be available for the biological system to manage itself over the long haul.

Primary Dimension 2: Fulfilling fundamental human needs
Fulfilling essential human needs is the main part of sustainable development. Indeed, the idea of need is implanted in the meaning of sustainable development. Thus, fulfilling essential human needs and guaranteeing long haul biological manageability constitute vital preconditions for sustainable development.

Primary Dimensions 3 and 4: Encouraging inter- and intra-generational equity
The basic necessity to conserve the earth's biological systems has led several authors to infer that the idea of sustainable development should be understood as pertaining exclusively to physical sustainability. However, the Brundtland Report rejects such a conclusion. It expresses that even physical sustainability cannot be ensured unless development policies pay attention to such considerations as changes in access to assets and in the distribution of costs. Furthermore, it guarantees that social equity among generations should consistently be continued to equity within each generation. Thus, social equity as an integral part of sustainable development has two measurements, time and space. From this point of view, sustainable development has results for equity within and between generations both globally and nationally (Table 21.3).

Table 21.3 Parameters of sustainable development

S. No.	Parameters	To measure these parameters
1	Economic	Keeping up a sustainable population Keeping up efficiency and benefit of the environment and natural resources
2	Ecological	Embracing ecological administration force in policy and decision-making Securing the environment and conserving natural assets
3	Technological	Advancing appropriate management of wastes and residuals Embracing environment-friendly technologies
4	Political	Empowering the people Retaining peace and order
5	Sociocultural	Encouraging resource access and upholding property rights Encouraging environmental awareness, imparting environment morality and supporting environment management decision
6	Institutional	Enhancing institutional ability to govern sustainable development

21.5 Shifts Between Technology Push and Market Pull Strategies

As per TP-DP practitioners, and industrial managers, the field of TP-DP is continuously growing. The interactions among TP-DP strategies depend on industrial life cycles and status of local market (Choi 2017).

It is very surprising to learn from the literature that not much has been written about TP and DP strategies in manufacturing industries in the less-developed countries (as compared to developed countries) in general and India in particular. After the liberalization of Indian economy and globalization of trade, commerce, and industry, being initiated in 1991, there had been a continuously increasing competition in Indian manufacturing industry. Indian technology researchers have started penning down the things but only in a very limited domain. There have been sufficient cases of technology management available in the literature but these do not give any insights on transition in TP and DP strategies and the subsequent experiences in achieving sustainable development in the manufacturing industry. There has been a lot of research done on adoption of technology, but the research regarding the linkages between Technology Push and Demand Pull strategies, and sustainable development is missing. So a research has been planned to develop a conceptual framework to explore shifts between TP and DP strategies for sustainable development in manufacturing enterprises and the research proposal has been presented in this chapter.

As traditional manufacturing is gradually outsourced to lower cost areas, strategy makers seek leadership in emerging firms by motivating innovative industries to follow competitiveness. Developing companies are those where a technology prevails but a new technology suppresses the current value chain to fulfill customer demands. Therefore, this field exhibits a proof of both TP and MP strategies. There is a need to understand MP and TP orientations in manufacturing industries, explicitly investigating how and why these orientations shifts.

Each MP-oriented company has its basic product concept from the chances its management anticipated in the market. To advertise the concept, firm attains essential technology by developing it or by purchasing it. A reaction of the market is then procured in the development stage of product and is sold in the market if industry acquired the idea. As and when the product is spread in market and customer feedback is received, enterprises shift their concentration to their technology for evident grounds. Industries wish to enhance their prime technology to boost competitiveness, amend the product better fit into the market and provide desired complementary innovations. The transfer of technology focus depicts that these companies have started to compete for their technologies with other market requirements (Freeman 1982). Their technical know-how motivates them to check for the further development of existing technology despite knowing that this requires a substantial modification of policies towards improving the technology. In some of the developed companies, the two strategies have shown the signs of coexistence.

TP-oriented companies possess unique technologies where an end user and value chain to the customers has not been secured. A company, trying to advertise a novel technology, may see potential benefits over comparable ones (Schumpeter 1928). Majority of the TP-oriented companies start with a new technology with no market demand in view and they focus entirely on developing that technology. Some experimental marketing often takes place and the industry tends to remain inward until something initiates a transition. A developing technology has numerous applications in different markets. In this context, industries have restricted market know-how and rely on past knowledge. The external forces may tend to cause the firms to start accepting market-oriented practices. The initial transition against MP strategy may be due to the recognition of actual versus assumed customer demands or a radical transformation in management. The market may motivate firms to manufacture new products that are sustained by its current technology. It appears that these companies mainly concentrate on technological advancement until some catalyst, generally external, demands a transition.

As per the extensive literature review and discussions with TP-DP practitioners, the following questions have been developed. The response of various organizations will be collected through a questionnaire survey after its proper content validation.

- How shall you utilize your new product innovation capabilities?
- What will be your strategy if strong R&D capability is available in your company?
- What will be your approach if your company starts enhancing its corporate strategies?
- Which strategy does your company follow when export orientation is on a rise?

- What will be your strategy to utilize new knowledge accumulated by your company?
- What strategy does your company follow when the level of competition starts increasing?
- What will be your strategy if the demand for products increases?
- What will be your strategy if there is a decrease in your product's market share?
- What strategy does your company follow if the government norms have to be stringently followed?
- How shall you utilize your large existing manufacturing infrastructure?
- The labor unions support your company in?
- What strategy does your company follow if it finds some unsatisfied needs of customers?
- What will be your strategy if there is a fall in profit margins of your company?
- Which strategy you will opt if the life of old technology starts declining?
- Which strategy you will opt to enhance your business performance?
- What will be your strategy if the productivity of your company starts decreasing?
- What approach does your company pursue if the customer satisfaction is not up to the mark?

The response to these questions shall be multiple options where the respondent will tick the preferred options (may be more than one to each question). Flexible System Methodology will be used as a tool to help evolve the problem in a Situation, Actor and Process (S-A-P) interplay. Empirical studies yield rich data for statistical analysis that will be used for drawing relevant inferences. Further, some case studies will provide deep insight into the problem by giving a real picture of the industrial situation. Synthesis of the learning issues of both empirical studies and case studies will help evolve a management process by using qualitative methods like Option Field/Profile Methodology (OFM/OPM), Analytic Hierarchy Process (AHP), and Fuzzy Set Theory (FST). An implementation plan shall be suggested to manage the industrial situation.

21.6 Conclusion

Certainly, a literature review on various industries exhibit that, ideally, firms should balance TP and MP strategies inside their policies (Nemet 2009; Mowery and Rosenberg 1979), whereas in less-developed economies, manufacturing industries usually lack in resources to concentrate on both instantly. TP-oriented firms generally shift to MP strategy because of new partners and shifts in decision maker's preferences, normally due to financier pressure or monetary constraints imposed by longer starting times. On the flipside, most of the companies starting with a MP strategy shift toward a TP orientation because early market experiences necessitate the improvement in operations to raise output or to fulfill a demand for technologically sound products. The results of the present research shall help companies in successful transition or shift between, and later balance, these strategies; and managing manufacturing, outsourcing, and scaling-up decisions.

References

Abbasi, M., Vassilopoulou, P., & Stergioulas, L. (2017). Technology roadmap for the creative industries. *Creative Industries Journal, 10*(1), 40–58.

Brundtland (1987). *Our common future, world commission on environment and development.* Oxford: Oxford University Press.

Chau, P. Y. K., & Tam, K. Y. (2000). Organizational adoption of open systems: A 'technology-push, need-pull' perspective. *Journal of Information & Management, 37*(5), 229–239.

Chidamber, S. R., & Kon, H. B. (1994). A research retrospective of innovation inception and success: The technology-push demand-pull question. *International Journal of Technology Management, 9*(1), 1–27.

Choi, H. (2017). Technology-push and demand-pull factors in emerging sectors: Evidence from the electric vehicle market. *Industry and Innovation*, 1–20. https://doi.org/10.1080/13662716.2017.1346502.

Drury, D. H., & Farhoomand, A. (1999). Information technology push/pull reactions. *Journal of Systems and Software, 47*(1), 3–10.

Freeman, C. (1982). *The economics of industrial innovation.* Cambridge, MA: MIT Press.

Holden, E., Linnerud, K., & Banister, D. (2014). Sustainable development: Our common future revisited. *Journal of Global Environmental Change, 26*(May), 130–139.

Horbach, J., Rammer, C., & Rennings, K. (2012). Determinants of eco innovations by type of environmental impact: The role of regulatory push/pull, technology push and market pull. *Journal of Ecological Economics, 78*(June), 112–122.

Howells, J. (1997). Rethinking the market-technology relationship for innovation. *Journal of Research Policy, 25*(8), 1209–1219.

Joung, C. H., Carrell, J., Sarkar, P., & Feng, S. C. (2012). Categorization of indicators for sustainable manufacturing. *Ecological Indicators, 24*(January), 148–157.

Jovane, F., Yoshikawa, H., Alting, L., Boër, C. R., Westkamper, E., Williams, D., et al. (2008). The incoming global technological and industrial revolution towards competitive sustainable manufacturing. *CIRP Annals-Manufacturing Technology, 57*(2), 641–659.

Kak, A., & Sushil (2002). Sustainable competitive advantage with core competence: A review. *Global Journal of Flexible Systems Management, 3*(4), 23–38.

Kocak, A., Carsrud, A., & Oflazoglu, S. (2017). Market, entrepreneurial, and technology orientations: Impact on innovation and firm performance. *Management Decision, 55*(2), 248–270.

Lubik, S., Lim, S., Platts, K., & Minshall, T. (2013). Market-pull and technology-push in manufacturing start-ups in emerging industries. *Journal of Manufacturing Technology Management, 24*(1), 10–27.

Mowery, D., & Rosenberg, N. (1979). The influence of market demand upon innovation: A critical review of some recent empirical studies. *Research Policy, 8*(1), 102–153.

Nemet, G. F. (2009). Demand-Pull, technology-push, and government led incentives for non incremental technical change. *Journal of Research Policy, 38*(5), 700–709.

Parker, S. (1997). Closing comments: Market pull versus technology push. *Energy Engineering, 94*(6), 73–76.

Peters, M., Schneider, M., Griesshaber, T., & Hoffmann, H. V. (2012). The impact of technology push and demand-pull policies on technical change: Does the locus of policies matter? *Journal of Research Policy, 41*(8), 1296–1308.

Salih, T. M. (2003). Sustainable economic development and the environment. *International Journal of Social Economics, 30*(1/2), 153–162.

Saritas, O., Dranev, Y., & Chulok, A. (2017). A dynamic and adaptive scenario approach for formulating science and technology policy. *Foresight, 19*(5), 473–490.

Sastry, T. (2011). Exploring the role of business in society. *Journal of IIMB Management Review, 23*(4), 246–256.

Schmoch, U. (2007). Double-boom cycles and the comeback of science-push and market-pull. *Journal of Research Policy, 36*(7), 1000–1015.

Schon, D. (1967). *Technology and social change*. New York: Delacorte.

Schumpeter, J. (1928). The instability of capitalism. *The Economic Journal, 38*(151), 361–386.

Seyoum, B. (2004). The role of factor conditions in high-technology exports: An empirical examination. *The Journal of High Technology Management Research, 15*(1), 145–162.

Singla, A., Ahuja, I. P. S., & Sethi, A. P. S. (2017). The effects of demand pull strategies on sustainable development in manufacturing industries. *International Journal of Innovations in Engineering and Technology, 8*(2), 27–34.

Stefano, G. D., Gambardella, A., & Verona, G. (2012). Technology push and demand pull perspectives in innovation studies: Current findings and future research directions. *Journal of Research Policy, 41*(8), 1283–1295.

Varadarajan, R., Srinivasan, R., Vadakkepatt, G. G., Yadav, M. S., Pavlou, P. A., Krishnamurthy, S., et al. (2010). Interactive technologies and retailing strategy: A review, conceptual framework and future research directions. *Journal of Interactive Marketing, 24*(2), 96–110.

Yadav, P. (2012). India's changing trade pattern in the process of globalization. *Procedia of Social and Behavioral Sciences, 37,* 157–166. https://doi.org/10.1016/j.sbspro.2012.03.283.

Index

A
Abnormal returns, 47–49, 52, 54, 57, 59
Accounting information, 49
Acquisitions, 47–50, 279
Actor related gaps, 200
Adaptability, 40, 44, 65, 119, 120, 123, 131, 205
After sales service, 3, 4, 8
After sales service flexibility, 3, 5, 8
AGMARKNET, 187–191, 194–203
Agricultural e-trading system, 188, 202
Agricultural marketing, 188–192, 194, 197, 199, 202, 203
Agricultural marketing reforms, 188
Agricultural produce marketing committee, 188
Aligned direction, 230
Alignment, 9, 34, 65, 145–148, 150, 153, 155, 263, 265
Alternative power supply, 177
Altshuller's matrix, 37
Amalgamation, 48, 50, 52, 58
American option, 164, 166–170
Analytical Hierarchy Process (AHP), 12, 173, 177, 178, 180, 182, 286, 288, 296, 329
Anthropology, 64, 70, 71
Anti-trafficking statutes, 72
Apple, 10
Application of Inventive principles, 37
Asia-Pacific, 223
Assessment matrix, 306, 309, 310
Attraction benefits, 226
Aurospharma company, 83
Automation, 40, 133

Autonomy, 94, 98, 99, 101, 216, 230, 237
Average Abnormal Returns (AARs), 54
Awareness building, 181–183
Awareness creation, 177

B
BCG, 10
Behavioral flexibility, 205–211, 214–218
Behavioral flexibility training, 217
Behavioural node archetypes, 124, 126
Bermudan options, 164–167, 169, 170
Best practices techniques, 264
Big data analytics capabilities, 9
Boundary trigger, 162
Built-in nested plasticity, 125
Business models, 16, 271, 320
Business strategy, 9, 145–148, 150, 152–155

C
Capital seeking, 79, 82, 83
Carbon information, 286
Career growth, 143, 210
Center for Monitoring Indian Economy (CMIE), 52, 53
Change management, 176, 228, 237
China, 33, 89–91, 260, 263, 273, 276
Client relationships, 223, 237
Cloud computing, 9
Club goods, 17, 21, 24–26
Cluster actors, 18, 22
Clustered firms, 28
Cluster management, 17, 24–26, 28
Cluster management activities, 15, 17, 21, 24–27

Cluster managers, 15, 17, 18, 20, 21, 25–28
Cluster performance, 19
Cluster-specific knowledge, 20
CMIE database, 52
Commitment, 44, 136, 143, 217, 218, 223, 230, 233, 235, 236, 277
Commodity transactions, 188–191, 193, 196, 202
Communication, 21, 44, 80, 90, 93, 98, 141, 142, 233, 235, 266, 272, 273, 320
Compaq, 10
Compatible system, 177
Compensation and Employee Welfare, 136
Competition, 6, 18–21, 33, 35, 48, 67, 78, 92, 140, 243, 246, 259, 271, 272, 276, 283, 284, 327, 329
Competitive resources, 21
Conformity assessment, 241–254, 258–260, 266
Conformity assessment criteria, 266
Consolidation, 33, 47, 48, 50, 52, 58, 59
Contextual relationship, 96, 151
Continuity forces, 145, 146, 148–150, 153, 155
Contract law, 70
Control and liability, 64, 70, 71
Core competencies, 149, 150, 152–155
Corporate/company law, 27, 47, 48, 53, 67–70, 72, 73, 139, 141, 223, 225, 227, 236, 237, 286, 287, 328
Corporate social responsibility, 227
Correlation, 66, 166, 168–170, 182, 227, 261
Creative element, 123–128, 131
Credibility, 93, 98
Credit availability, 34
Critical continuity forces, 145, 146, 148, 150, 152, 153, 155
Cross-functional teams, 10
Cross-interaction matrices, 305, 306
Cumulative abnormal return, 54, 57
Cumulative Average Abnormal Return (CAAR), 54, 57
Current customer base, 149, 150, 152, 153
Customer-centric market, 7
Customer requirements, 6, 11, 182
Customer value, 3
Customized services, 8, 11, 12

D
Data Envelopment Analysis (DEA), 288
Defence Public Sector Undertakings (DPSU), 143
Degeneracy, 119, 123, 130
Dell, 7
Demand pull strategy, 324
Design-change flexibility, 7
Design changes, 6
Destroy Value, 320
Developing country, 173, 174, 176, 183
Differentiation, 21, 24, 28, 67, 68, 120, 235
Digital India, 190, 276
Digraph, 97, 152, 307
Direct marketing model, 7
Direct marketing through e-commerce, 7, 11, 12
Directorate of Marketing and Inspection, 188
Drivers of sustainability initiatives, 223, 225, 237
Due diligence, 72
Dynamic pricing, 8, 11, 12

E
EBIT, 163, 164
Economically Sustainable, 295
Economic growth, 34, 271, 274, 321
Effective change management, 176, 177, 181–184
E-governance, 188, 191, 197, 272
Electronic hardware, 273
Electronic National Agriculture Market (eNAM), 187–197, 202, 203
Electronics manufacturing industries, 271, 272, 274, 276
Electronics products, 36, 39–44, 273, 279
Electronic trading portal, 192
Emerging markets, 77–79, 83, 84, 90
Emotional energy, 228, 230, 237
Employee attitudes, 231, 232
Employee trust, 218
Enterprise resource planning, 5
Entrepreneurship, 35, 40, 44, 242, 272, 323
Environmental management, 224, 237, 284
Environmental management systems, 285
Environmental sustainability, 223, 227, 230, 231, 233, 235–237, 284, 287, 288
Ethics, 142, 218
European Union (EU), 72, 90, 241–246, 249, 251–254, 257–259, 261–264, 266
Event-induced variance, 47, 57, 59
Event study, 49, 52, 54
Exchange rate risk, 5
Excludability, 21, 24, 25
Existing culture, 149, 150, 152, 153
Existing physical infrastructure, 148–150, 152, 155
Existing process and services, 150, 152
Expat resources, 94

Index 335

Expertise in existing technology, 149, 150, 152, 153, 155
External expansion, 47, 48

F
Factors responsible for resistance, 174, 176–178
Family business groups, 50
Firm infrastructure, 3, 9
Flexibility, 4–10, 12, 40, 42, 63–66, 70, 71, 73, 74, 122, 149, 153, 154, 162, 205–209, 211, 214, 217, 218, 250, 260, 272, 283, 286–288, 291, 293, 295, 305
Flexibility and chain integration, 63, 64, 70
Flexibility in international investments, 5
Flexibility Initiatives, 3–5, 7–12
Flexibility in organization's structure, 149, 150, 152
Flexibility in product development, 244
Flexibility in project selection, 5
Flexible adaptation, 119
Flexible benchmarking, 133
Flexible compensation, 9, 10
Flexible decisions, 163
Flexible HR System, 207, 208, 210, 211, 214, 216–218
Flexible production systems, 5
Flexible Systems Management (FSM), 244
Flexible waste management, 301
Flexi-time/Flexi-place, 9
Flowing Stream Strategy (FSS), 301–303, 305, 307, 313
Ford, 10
Forecasting sales, 165
Foreign direct investment, 89, 90, 277
Free Cash Flow (FCF), 163
Freedom of choice, 207, 242
Fuzzy sets, 285, 295
Fuzzy TOPSIS, 283, 288, 289, 294

G
Gap analysis, 189, 197, 200
General problem facing, 20
Global approach, 243, 249–253
Global IJVs, 77, 83, 84
Global International Joint Ventures, 77
Globalization, 33, 34, 89, 90, 248, 258–260, 264, 265, 283, 324, 327
Globalization processes, 259
Global supply chain, 257–259
Global Value Chain (GVC), 33, 40, 42, 63, 67, 242
Governmental agencies, 44
Government policy, 177

Grand challenge, 40
Green employer branding, 226
Green HRM, 223–226, 236, 237
Green inductions, 226
Green job descriptions, 226
Green operations, 283
Green performance, 285, 291–293, 295
GSign Test, 54

H
Health care service, 173, 174, 180
Health information systems, 173–176, 180, 182, 183
Health service industry, 174
Health service organizations, 174, 175, 180
Hierarchical relationship, 96, 145, 146, 150, 303, 305, 307
High-profile disclosures, 68
Honda, 7, 8
HQ involvement, 95, 98, 99, 101
HQ Strategy (HS), 92, 95, 99
HR practices, 9, 10, 208, 211
HR processes, 226
Human resource flexibility, 3, 9
Human Resource Management (HRM), 3, 9, 217, 218, 224, 279

I
ICT infrastructure development, 176, 177
ICT projects, 176, 177
IHL hotel, 305–310, 312, 313
Imparting ICT training, 177
Imparting training, 181–183
Implementation cost, 180
Implementation of sustainability initiatives, 228, 235–237
Inbound logistics, 3, 5–7
India, 10, 33–36, 38, 40, 42–45, 47, 50, 59, 78, 80–82, 84, 89–91, 95, 96, 101, 134, 139, 140, 175, 187, 188, 190–192, 202, 203, 205, 271–277, 279, 280, 302, 306, 327
Indian mergers, 50
Industry-related resources, 22
Informal institutions, 19
Information and Communication Technology (ICT), 8, 174, 188, 190, 274
Information networks, 19
Infrastructure creation, 34
Innovation, 7, 10, 18, 21, 33, 35, 38, 44, 65, 77, 78, 80, 83, 84, 89–92, 94, 100, 102, 142, 149, 217, 218, 228, 249, 276, 319, 320, 322–325, 328
Innovation capacities, 20

Innovation value chain, 89, 90, 102
Innovative inventory management, 119–121, 128, 130
Institutional resources, 18, 19, 21, 23, 27
Integrate information systems, 173
Integration, 39, 63, 67, 68, 70, 71, 74, 148, 173, 187, 189, 202, 203, 224, 237, 250, 286, 287
Interaction matrix, 11, 97, 306, 309–312
Internal expansion, 47
International Joint Ventures (IJVs), 77–84
International organization for standardisation, 264
Interpretation, 96, 97, 151, 152, 166, 264, 311
Interpretive logic, 96, 151, 153, 155
Interpretive Ranking Process (IRP), 3–5, 11, 12
Interruption in utility supply, 180, 183
Inventory management, 120, 123–126, 128, 131
Inventory profile, 126
Investing in access to high speed internet, 177
Investing in hardware and software, 177
Investing in ICT infrastructure, 181
Investment expense, 162, 164
Involvement of lead customers, 10

J
Japan, 50, 162
Japanese multinational enterprises, 16
Judicial case law, 73

K
Key challenges, 193
Key network characteristics, 122
Knowledge dynamic capability, 93
Knowledge triangle, 321
KPMG, 10

L
Labor flexibility, 7
Lack of awareness about the benefits of HIS, 180, 183
Lack of IT knowledge and training, 175, 180, 182, 183
Lack of telecommunication infrastructure, 175, 180, 182, 183
Law, 63, 64, 68–73, 242
Laws and regulations, 19
Leadership, 28, 68, 93, 98, 101, 138, 141, 142, 223, 224, 228–231, 233–237, 303, 327
Leadership development, 135, 141
Learning, 24, 77–79, 82–84, 131, 140, 141, 187, 189, 197, 202, 224, 228, 272, 301, 303, 304, 306, 311, 312, 329

Learning flexibility, 9
Legacy database, 150, 152, 153
Legal liability, xi
Legal procedures for mergers, 50
Level partition, 97, 151
Local embeddedness, 92, 100
Local market, 92, 100, 101, 327
Local resources, 18, 28, 93, 100
Locational resources, 15–22, 24–28
Logistics flexibility, 3, 5, 7

M
Machine flexibility, 7
Mahindra, 10
Maintenance cost, 180, 183
Manpower planning, 141, 142
Manufacturing flexibility, 5, 7, 244
Manufacturing industries, 271, 272, 274, 276, 280, 320, 327–329
Market fluctuations, 6, 64, 71
Marketing and sales, 3, 4, 8
Marketing and sales flexibility, 3, 5
Marketing reforms, 188
Market pull, 7, 319, 325
Market seeking, 79, 82, 83
Market surveillance, 245, 251, 253, 254, 257–267
Market surveillance implementation, 261
Market surveillance systems, 261
Maruti Suzuki, 8
McKinsey, 10
Median Abnormal Returns (MARs), 54
Merger announcements, 55, 56
Mergers, 47–50, 52, 54, 58, 59, 279
Merger through absorption, 48, 50, 52, 58
Micro, Small and Medium Enterprises (MSME), 33
Microsoft Excel, 162
Mitigation strategies, 177, 182, 184
Modification and upgradation of information systems, 5
Monitoring scheme, 249, 250
Monte Carlo simulation, 161, 166, 170
MSME competitiveness, 33
MSME ecosystem, 35, 38–40, 42, 43, 45
MSME sector, 33–35, 39, 41, 45
Multi-criteria decision making, 286
Multi-criteria ranking, 5, 10–12
Multidimensional real options, 5
Multi National Enterprise (MNE), 16, 89, 90

N
National e-Governance Plan (NeGP), 190
Network science, 119, 131

Index 337

Network skeleton, 123, 124, 126
New approach, 27, 241, 243, 246–254, 258
New Legislative Framework, 243, 244, 251, 252, 254
Node-level plasticity, 125, 127
Non-compliant applicants not recruited, 226
Norwest energy, 81, 83

O

Old approach, 243, 245, 247, 248, 253
Operating environments, 65
Operations, 3, 4, 7, 40, 48, 50, 58, 59, 82, 121, 122, 148, 188, 224, 225, 227, 230, 233, 246, 248, 249, 285, 287, 290, 329
Operations flexibility, 3, 5
Optimization, 127, 147, 163, 284, 287
Oracle Crystal Ball, 162
Order tracking, 7, 11, 12
Organizational characteristics, 229, 231, 232, 237
Organizational citizenship behavior, 218
Organizational flexibility, 44
Organizational performance, 9, 146, 209, 223, 225, 227–229, 235, 237
Organizational productivity, 207, 208, 217
Organizational role stress, 205, 206, 209–211, 215–217
Organizational sustainability, 207, 229, 271
Outbound logistics, 3, 5, 7
Outbound logistics flexibility, 3
Outsourcing procurement, 10
Outward Foreign Direct Investment (OFDI), 77, 78, 80, 83, 84

P

Pay and benefits flexibility, 9
Performance appraisal flexibility, 9
Performance improvements, 229, 235, 237
Performance Management System, 138, 139
PEST analysis, 274, 275
Physical contradictions, 37
Place of work flexibility, 9
Plasticity–rigidity cycle, 122
Pooled interdependence, 80, 82
Precision-Weighted Cumulative Average Abnormal Return (PWCAAR), 54, 57
Pricing flexibility, 8
Private as well as public funding, 27
Private goods, 24–26, 28
Probability distribution, 167, 168, 170
Problem modeling, 37
Procedural mechanism, 69
Process related gaps, 187
Procurement, 4, 10, 24, 169, 230, 233
Procurement flexibility, 3, 9, 10
Product and service offerings, 68
Product flexibility, 8
Productivity growth, 20
Product-mix flexibility, 5
Product safety, 248, 259, 264, 265
Product upgradation and switching, 8, 11, 12
Professional services company, 223, 225, 230
Promotion flexibility, 8
Proposition, 4, 5, 11, 26, 27, 79, 80, 83, 225, 274
Psychometric properties, 205, 211
Public goods, 24–26
Public policy, 17, 20, 26, 27
Punctuated equilibrium, 121

Q

QFD resistance, 177
Quality and reliability, 41, 42
Quality management, 67, 138, 253

R

RAPEX System, 263
R&D investment, 93, 98, 99, 101
R&D subsidiary innovation, 89
Reachability matrix, 97, 151, 152
Realizing opportunities for sustainability, 229
Real Options Approach (ROA), 161, 162
Reciprocal interdependence, 80
Recruiting IT skilled people, 177, 181
Recruitment and attracting talent, 136
Recruitment of green aware employees, 226
Re-engineering, 133, 203
Regional clusters, 16, 17, 25
Regional resources, 18, 21, 22
Regulatory framework, 265
Research question, 17
Resilience, 119
Resistance factors, 173–175, 177–184
Resource-oriented understanding, 18
Resources, 15–23, 25–28, 34, 59, 64, 66, 78–82, 92, 93, 95, 98, 99, 101, 120, 124, 126, 127, 129, 133, 142, 147, 149, 163, 175, 200, 203, 209, 217, 224, 227–231, 234–237, 257, 259, 260, 263, 265, 266, 272, 284, 302, 320, 327, 329

Resource seeking, 79, 81–83
Restricted-access resources, 19, 22, 23, 25–28
Retention, 135, 141
Reward systems, 223, 226, 237
Robots, 7
Robustness, 42, 119, 131
Role overload stress, 209
Routing flexibility, 7
Russian pharmaceutical industry, 82

S
Sales, 8, 24, 68, 142, 161–166, 170, 292
SAP–LAP framework, 189, 303–305, 309, 311, 313
SAP–LAP linkages, 301, 303, 305, 306, 309, 310, 312, 313
Seasonal Autoregressive Integrated Moving Average (SARIMA), 161–166, 168, 170
Self-determination, 93
Self-interaction matrix, 306, 310, 311
Self-sufficiency, 42, 44
Semiconductor design industry, 90, 95, 101
Semiconductor, subsidiaries, 90, 91, 96, 100, 102
Separation strategies, 37
Sequential interdependence, 80, 81
Service sector, 153, 301, 302, 306, 313
Short-run performance, 59
Short-term performance, 59
Situation-Actor-Process-Learning-Action-Performance (SAP-LAP), 197, 301, 305, 309, 312, 313
Situation related gaps, 198
Skill development, 34
Slack, 93, 98
Small and Medium Enterprises (SMEs), 20, 27
Socially sustainable, 295
Soft drink manufacturing, 162, 166
Solutions, 33, 35–37, 41–45, 119, 121–124, 146, 178, 245, 249, 254, 271, 274, 280, 291, 294
Specialist support services, 19
Spin-offs, 47
Stability landscape, 120–122, 126, 128–131
Stakeholders, 34, 44, 150, 173, 187–191, 197, 199, 203, 224, 225, 228, 231, 236, 242, 244, 250, 265, 273, 285
Star network, 120, 130
Stepwise regression analysis, 233
Stock exchange, 52, 53
Strategic alliances, 16, 190, 199
Strategic asset seeking, 79, 81, 83
Strategic direction, 307–309
Strategic electronics components, 44

Strategies for addressing resistance, 176
Strategy, 4, 16, 20, 27, 35, 58, 67, 82, 90, 92, 97, 98, 100, 102, 145–148, 153, 155, 178, 179, 182, 183, 236, 275, 285–287, 313, 319, 322–325, 327–329
Strategy alignment, 154
Subsidiary innovation, 90–92, 95, 101, 102
Subsidiary innovation factors, 91, 92, 102
Subsidiary mandate, 94, 98, 99, 101
Subsidiary traits, 90, 92, 95, 97, 100–102
Substantiation, 37
Succession planning, 135, 137, 141
Suggestion scheme, 139, 140
Supplier selection, 10, 284–288, 295, 296
Supply chain flexibility, 6, 66
Supply chain network, 120, 130, 285, 287
Supply chains, 4, 20, 63–68, 70–74, 236, 266, 284, 295
Survey, 94, 95, 101, 153, 184, 210, 223, 225, 227, 229, 230, 233, 234, 236, 254, 307, 328
Sustainability, 223–225, 227–237, 242, 244, 271–273, 275, 276, 279, 280, 283–287, 295, 296, 302, 306, 321, 322, 326
Sustainability leadership, 230
Sustainability reporting, 227
Sustainability strategy, 225, 228
Sustainable development, 224, 227, 242, 273, 279, 319–321, 324, 326, 327
Sustainable electronics manufacturing, x
Sustainable leadership, 223, 224, 228, 236, 237
Sustainable suppliers, 283, 286, 288, 295
Sustainable supplier selection, 284, 286–288
Sustainable supply chain management, 284, 287
SWOT analysis, 273–277, 280
Symmetrical weak-linkedness, 128, 130
Systematisation and flexibility, vii
Systemic integration, vii, 63, 64
Systemic resources, 19, 22, 25–27

T
Talent management, 133–137, 139, 142
Target problem, 36, 37
Tax rate, 164
Teamwork, 93, 98, 142
Technical contradiction, 37, 43
Technical harmonization, 241, 244
Technological excellence, 175
Technologically sustainable, 280
Technological transfer, 67
Technology development, 3, 9, 10, 324
Technology flexibility, 3
Technology push, 319, 320, 325

Index

Technology push strategy, 322
Technology strategy, 145–148, 150, 152–155
Technology transfer, 77–80, 83, 84
Test statistics, 55
Theory of inventive problem solving, 33, 34
Time flexibility, 9
TISM-IRP, 5
TISM-ST model, 101, 108
Topological phase transition, 119, 120, 131
TOPSIS, 283, 288, 289, 291, 295
Total Interpretive Structural Modelling (TISM), 5, 11, 12, 84, 89, 91, 96–102, 145, 146, 150, 152, 153, 155, 301–303, 305, 307, 308, 312, 313
Total quality management, 288
Toyota, 7
Traceability statutes, 72
Training and development, 137, 141, 226
Transitivity check, 97, 151, 152
Transnational trade, 67
Trimming, 37
Triple Bottom Line (TBL), 224
TRIZ, 33–37, 39, 41–45
TRIZ contradiction matrix, 41, 43
TRIZ matrix, 39, 41, 42
TRIZ methodology, 33, 36, 39, 41, 42, 45
Tunisian India Fertilizers (TIFERT), 82, 83
Turbulence, 230, 237

U

Ubiquities, 22
Uncertain demand, 162, 163, 170, 171
United Nations, 72, 189, 264
USA, 50, 175

V

Valuation, 3–6, 11, 12, 165
Valuation of operating flexibility, 5
Value-adding activities, 3, 4, 18, 20
Value-adding potential, 16
Value Adding Web, 18
Value addition criteria, 11, 12
Value chain, 3–6, 8, 9, 91, 242, 244, 286, 295, 326–328
Value chain activities, 11, 12
Value chain analysis, 4, 66, 67
Value creation potential, 17, 21, 22, 25, 28
Valuing financial flexibility, 4
Variable capacity of supply chain, 6, 11, 12
Variable manufacturing capacity, 7
Viable networks, 119, 120, 130, 131
Volkswagen, 7, 68
Volume flexibility, 7, 162
Vulnerability, 147

W

Waste management, 39, 279, 301–313
Waste management practices, 302, 303, 306, 313
WHAT-HOW relationship matrix, 177, 178
Work place flexibility, 9
Work roles, 228, 230, 237
World Bank, 67, 260
World Trade Organisation (WTO), 44, 67, 243, 274, 276, 277, 280
Worldwide value chains, 16